Tibetan Buddhists in the Making of Modern China

Tibetan Buddhists in the Making of Modern China

Gray Tuttle

 COLUMBIA UNIVERSITY PRESS   NEW YORK

COLUMBIA UNIVERSITY PRESS
Publishers Since 1893
New York   Chichester, West Sussex
Copyright © 2005 Gray Tuttle

Library of Congress Cataloging-in-Publication Data
Tuttle, Gray.
Tibetan Buddhists in the making of modern China /
Gray Tuttle.
p.   cm.
Includes bibliographical references and index.
ISBN 978-0-231-13447-7
1. Tibet (China)—History—1951–
2. Buddhism—China—Tibet—Politic aspects.
I. Title: Tibetan Buddhists in the making of modern
China. II. Title.
DS786.T866   2004
951'.505—dc22   2004050213

Columbia University Press books are printed on
permanent and durable acid-free paper.

Printed in the United States of America
Designed by Audrey Smith

Dedicated to my grandmother
Lillian Kirby Tuttle (1912–2002)
AND *to the people of Amdo and Wutaishan*

Our country is the leader of the nations of Asia; this is already commonly acknowledged throughout the world. Internally, the regions of Mongolia, Tibet, Qinghai and Kham, and externally, the regions of Indo-Burma, Thailand and Indonesia—these nations are all united really by having Buddhism as their center. . . . [If] we don't respect Buddhism, who will respect us?

—*Dai Jitao, describing the proper place of Buddhism in Nationalist China*

Contents

Illustrations

Acknowledgments

THIS BOOK is the outcome of more than a decade of interaction with people and places, texts and ideas. I want first to thank the people of Amdo and Wutaishan, in the aggregate, as I hesitate to name individuals until I know how this work will be received in certain circles. One exception is my Tibetan friend, whom I will call A bo, who critically assisted me in my research abroad and was generally a wonderful companion over two summers of travels and travails. For introducing me to these places and people, Raoul Birnbaum and Paul Nietupski have my eternal gratitude. Without the support of my grandmother, Lillian K. Tuttle, who traveled with me to Tibet and China in 1991, this project might never have been conceived.

Without the training and guidance of my advisers, the dissertation that served as the first draft of this book would likewise never have been completed. I am very grateful for all the assistance and inspiration I have received from William Kirby, Leonard van der Kuijp, Philip Kuhn, and Nicola Di Cosmo. My master's work with Professor Di Cosmo as well as course work with Professors Kuhn and van der Kuijp shaped my knowledge of the historical background of Chinese and Tibetan relations, which was critical for understanding the modern period. From Professor van der Kuijp's support for my ever expanding topic and pleasant lakeside afternoons spent combing over drafts I have learned a model of mentoring that I hope to be able to emulate. Professor Kirby's seminar on Republican-period China helped to reshape my thesis, and throughout the writing process he provided an ideal audience for presenting this research on the role of Tibetan Buddhists in the context of modern Chinese history, all the while giving me excellent and challenging suggestions to improve my organization and presentation. Professor Kuhn's insights and broad perspective on the place of my work in Asian history were vital in helping me step back from the details and recast my research for a broader audience.

A host of other scholars have contributed to my thoughts and presentation of the present book. For their response to early work on this project, I appreciate the valuable critiques of Robert Sharf, Janet Gyatso, Kurtis Schaeffer, Natalie Gummer, and Sucheta Mazumdar. I am also most grateful for the stimulating conversations and advice of Robert Gimello, Robert Weller, Prasenjit Duara, Evelyn Rawski, Nicola Di Cosmo, and Mark Elliot.

For keeping me up to date with the latest sources, I extend my gratitude first to Gene Smith of the Tibetan Buddhist Resource Center. Elliot Sperling, Liu Kuo-wei, James Bosson, and Lawrence Epstein also provided me with or pointed me toward critical rare sources. I thank the staff of the Harvard Yenching Library, past and present, for marshaling and managing their vast and rich resources for the benefit of us all. Thomas Ford, of Harvard University's Houghton Library, was of great assistance in making William W. Rockhill's materials available. In China the Tibetologists Wang Yao and Luo Rencang shared their vast knowledge of Chinese scholarship on Tibetan Buddhism in Republican China. My thanks also go out to a host of Chinese historians who allowed me to interview them on this sometimes sensitive topic: Chen Qingying, Deng Ruiling, Huang Xianming, Yang Ming, Ren Xinjian, Chen Bing, Liu Liquan, and Li Shaoming. Similarly I extend my thanks to the Tibetans who shared their stories about their own teachers' lives: Chos dpal rgya mtsho, Grags pa rgya mtsho, and Mi nyag Mgon po.

My first Tibetan teachers, *Sku ngo* Thupten Tsephel Taikhang, the late *A mdo dge bshes* Thub bstan rgya mtsho, and Ladakhi *dge bshes* Blo bzang tshe rten were invaluable for their assistance in understanding the context of people and events in modern Tibet. Thanks also, for everything, to Joshua and Diana Cutler of the Tibetan Buddhist Learning Center in New Jersey, my home away from home. For logistical assistance in Beijing, I thank the directors and staff of the China Tibetology Center, especially Li Guoqing. For help with gaining access to Chinese archival materials, Long Darui's introductions as well as those of Du Yongbin proved invaluable.

For financial assistance I relied on the Graduate Student Council, Harvard University's Asia Center, a Foreign Language and Area Studies Fellowship, and, most important, a dissertation completion fellowship from the Whiting Foundation and the Sidney R. Knafel Fellowship of the Weatherhead Center for International Affairs at Harvard University.

I wish to thank my editor, Anne Routon, first for being willing to read an unrevised dissertation and then for shepherding it through the process of review and revision. In the later stages of revision, Matthew Kapstein played an important role in making critical suggestions to improve the manuscript, for which I am especially grateful. Raoul Birnbaum, Karl Gerth, Peter Hansen, Diana Cutler, Elliot Sperling, Lauran Hartley, and Robert Barnett also offered additional suggestions as to how I could clarify and refine my presentation of specific aspects of the work. Rita Bernhard was a pleasure to work with in the copyediting stage, making many improvements in phrasing and style, and played a crucial role in my decision to use a phonetic version of Tibetan. Many thanks too to Leslie Kriesel for overseeing the editorial work in its final stages. In the end, I have realized that there is probably no end to the corrections and additions I could make, but I present the work as it is and take responsibility for the flaws that remain.

To my parents, June and Stanton Tuttle, I owe a debt that I can never hope to repay. I thank them especially for their support through all my years of education in increasingly esoteric topics. I greatly admire the strength and calmness of my brother Bradley, who overcame a life-threatening bout with cancer in 2000 thanks to the brilliance and kindness of Dr. Peter Black and the excellent staff of Brigham and Women's Hospital. I appreciate his companionship and shared love of the natural world, my chief distraction from my work.

On this note, I am also grateful to the place where I live, Petapawag and Squannassit, otherwise known as Groton and Pepperell, for the wilderness solitude that was so conducive to the writing of this book. Thanks to our dogs, Nubi, Chip, and Fern—who dragged me away from the computer or translating when I had been at it too long—I have only had to get reading glasses and not lost my sight entirely in this process. For keeping my focus on the relevant, for seeing me through the throes of multiple drafts, for incisive editing, for keeping the home fires burning during my long absences for research, and for her constant companionship, I thank my beloved partner Michelle Lerner.

Note on Transliteration

TO RENDER the Tibetan names and terms recognizable by nonspecialists, I have employed the University of Virginia Tibetan and Himalayan Digital Library's Simplified Phonetic Transcription of Standard Tibetan (THDL Simplified Phonetics) created by David Germano and Nicolas Tournadre. The reasons for using such a system have been aptly described by its creators on the THDL Web site: "While multiple systems are currently used for transliterating Tibetan words with the Roman alphabet in ways that precisely render the Tibetan spelling, one system has emerged as a de facto international standard: the Wylie system. However, no such standard has emerged for the *phonetic* rendering of Tibetan, and in fact there is no single phonetic system in widespread use." I should note that this system is based on the Central Tibetan dialect of Tibetan (spoken by less than half the Tibetan population). Many of the people described in this book were from areas in which very different dialects of Tibetan were spoken, and I was tempted to use these local pronunciations. In the interest of standardization, I have decided to use this new system in the hope that it will become the standard in the field. I have made only a few exceptions, which are noted below. I thank Steven Weinberger for checking my list for the correct usage of the transcription system. Appendix 2 provides readers with the correct Tibetan spellings rendered according to the Wylie system, introduced by Turrel Wylie as "A Standard System of Tibetan Transcription" in the *Harvard Journal of Asiatic Studies* 22 (1959).

However, I did not use this system to modify proper names in the bibliographic information (author, title, place of publication) as these references are only useful to those who read Tibetan. I also did not alter the Tibetan terms or phrases given in parentheses to clarify what I am translating into English, again because this information is only of use to Tibetologists who would want to know the Tibetan of the term or phrase in question. Finally, in the numerous instances when I am citing other scholarly sources, which use Wylie or other transliteration systems, the original spelling has been preserved.

Of my four exceptions to the THDL Simplified Phonetics system, two will surprise few people. For Tibet's two best-known lamas I have chosen to use the easily recognizable spellings: "Panchen Lama" and "Dalai Lama." For two other lamas, who originally hailed from the Monguor regions on the borders of Tibet and China, I have chosen to render their titles in ways that preserve the local pronunciation, historically derived from Chinese terms. Thus the Tibetan "Thu'u bkwan" is rendered "Tukwan" to reflect the Chinese "tuguan" (meaning "local official"), while Tibetan "Lcang skya" is rendered "Changja" to reflect the Chinese "Zhangjia" (meaning "Zhang family").

With regard to Chinese romanization, I have preserved the dialectic variations so well known in the West, for example, Sun Yat-sen and Chiang Kai-shek. Otherwise I use the pinyin system of romanization. Although this system is not easy to pronounce correctly without linguistic training, as anyone who teaches Chinese history to undergraduates will know, it has the advantage of being the standard in the field. For conversion of pinyin to the Wade-Giles system, which is more easily pronounced by nonspecialists, see *The Chicago Manual of Style,* 15th ed. (Chicago: University of Chicago Press, 2003), 426–427 (Table 10.2).

Tibetan Buddhists in the Making of Modern China

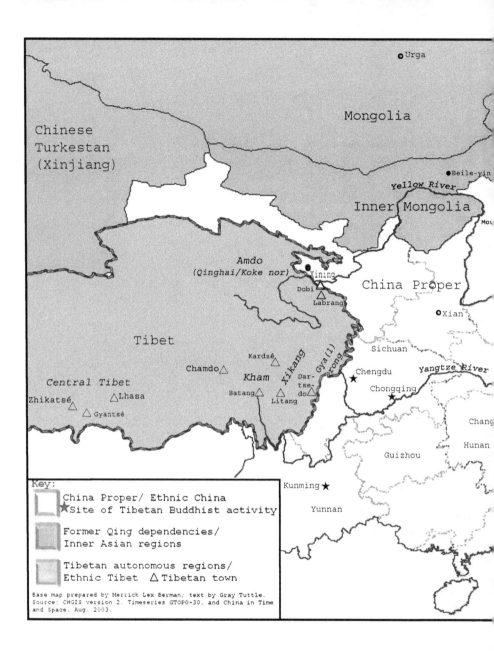

Key:

China Proper/ Ethnic China
★Site of Tibetan Buddhist activity

Former Qing dependencies/
Inner Asian regions

Tibetan autonomous regions/
Ethnic Tibet △Tibetan town

Base map prepared by Merrick Lex Berman; text by Gray Tuttle.
Source: CHGIS version 2. Timeseries GTOPO-30, and China in Time
and Space. Aug. 2003.

Tibet and Tibetan Buddhist Activity in China

The base map was prepared by Merrick Lex Berman. The source of the national and provincial boundaries are based on the digitalized maps of PRC representations of the Qing empire in 1820 drawn from the China Historical Geographical Information System (CHGIS) version 2, Timeseries GTOPO-30, August 2003. Please note that this representation includes territory disputed by the Tibetan government-in-exile and the India government (territory on the northwest and northeastern frontiers of India). The boundaries for the Tibetan cultural world (and autono-mous political units under the PRC) are drawn from the county boundaries in 1990 contained in the CHGIS version 2, China in Time and Space, August 2003.

Introduction

WHEN YOU LOOK at a map of China, there is Tibet. But how did Tibet become part of China? Why is Tibet still part of China? For anyone who looks closely at this issue, it is not obvious that Tibet would have become a part of modern China or even that it will remain a part of China. Although the answers to the questions above are complicated, the critical event that decided how Tibet would become a part of modern China is clear. Yet much of the cultural history before and since this critical event have remained unexplored. In the spring of 1951 the People's Liberation Army of the recently declared People's Republic of China was camped in eastern Tibet, and the fourteenth Dalai Lama had retreated to the Indian border. At stake was the fate of the Tibetan nation and the shape of the Chinese state, that is, the resolution of almost forty years of conflicting perceptions of the status of Tibet. If the Tibetans would concede that Tibet was a part of China, this would mark a major triumph for the Communist state in achieving a task at which the Nationalist Chinese had failed for more than two decades. The Tibetan negotiators sent to Beijing, no doubt under duress, signed a diplomatic agreement that acceded to most of China's demands, ending Tibet's decades of independence and centuries of self-rule, albeit with promises of continued autonomy and the preservation of Tibetan religious and social traditions. The United States, keen to undermine the Communist regime at the start of the Cold War, promised aid and recognition to the young Dalai Lama if he would come out against the agreement.[1]

The Tibetan leadership certainly had knowledge of how Buddhism and national autonomy had fared under the Communists in the Kalmyck and Buriat parts of Russia and in Mongolia; nevertheless, Tibetan noble and monastic elites advised the young Dalai Lama to rebuff the offer from the United States and return to Tibet to work with the Chinese. The residents of the three major monasteries surrounding Lhasa, in some sense constituting much of whatever Tibetan "public opinion" existed in pre-Communist Tibet, had seen ample evidence that China was Buddhist. In the 1930s and 1940s Tibetan lamas who had lived in China could communicate their welcome in China, while Chinese monks and lay Buddhist envoys helped to shape the Lhasa community's view of the Chinese. Thus the Chinese Communists benefited from the Republic's propaganda efforts in this regard. If we forget this context, focusing only on the handful of Tibetan elite who had traveled abroad to meet with Europeans and Americans, we lose much of the history of this period. Ignorance of the cultural contacts that I detail in this book has made it difficult to understand how the noble and monastic elite, and the monastic population in general, decided how to respond to the Chinese threat and associated offer of reconciliation. As there were no newspapers or other regular means for most Tibetans to learn about the outside world, the general population in Tibet would, at best, only have had a vague idea of what communism meant. In any case, even among those knowledgeable about the outside world, there was no real debate about the agreement once it was presented to the Dalai Lama and the Tibetan National Assembly. The Seventeen-Point Agreement, the only of its kind as the Chinese Communist government asserted its control of the former Qing empire's dependencies, seems to have reassured the Tibetan elites that their privileges and religious culture could be maintained in Tibet.[2] The Chinese government, first the Nationalists and later the Communists, succeeded in convincing at least some Tibetans that they were not the enemies of Tibetan religion and culture that they would prove to be in the 1960s and 1970s. Chinese demonstrations of religious and cultural respect for Tibet—initiated by a Chinese public, embraced by Chinese politicians, and communicated to Tibetans by Tibetan and Chinese adherents of Tibetan Buddhism—made a deep impression on Tibetans.[3] So how did the Chinese government come up with such a plan, so atypical for a secular state in the process of nation building?

The history of Inner Asian relations with China was critical in developing this approach. Tibetan Buddhists (in Tibetan and Mongolian regions) inhabited roughly one-half the territory over which the Qing dynasty (1644–1911) ruled, albeit in different ways. Even today, one-quarter of the territory of the People's Republic of China is designated autonomous Tibetan regions, prefectures, or counties. Although in demographic terms the population of these portions of Asia has scarcely seemed significant compared to that of the Chinese, the territory they inhabit was and is seen as vital to Chinese security and resource interests.[4] Moreover, despite their small population, the religious traditions of Tibetan Buddhists have been a potent cultural force in Asian history, with which the rulers of China have had to reckon since the rise of the Mongol empire in the thirteenth century to this day.

In the present work I analyze one aspect—the effort to include Tibet as part of the new China—of how the dynastic Qing empire (1644–1911) became the modern Chinese nation-state. In so doing I offer insights into the impact of modern ideas of nationalism, race, and religion on social organization in Asia. The transition from the traditions of a dynastic empire to a modern nation-state was neither instantaneous nor a complete transformation. The territory of East Asia's largest empire, the Qing dynasty, has largely been preserved in the nation-state of the People's Republic of China. However, in the case of Tibet, the rhetoric of nationalism and racial unity proved largely powerless to effect this transition. Instead, religion served as the crucial link between the social organization of the dynastic empire and that of the nation-state. Adherents of Tibetan Buddhism, both Chinese and Tibetan, actively engaged with Chinese politicians in an effort to protect and advance their religious interests within the new state formation.

I examine Tibet's inclusion as part of contemporary China in order to demonstrate the crucial role Buddhists played in China's transition from a dynastic empire to a nation-state. I contrast the social organization of the East Asian imperial framework with the modern nations that now occupy the former territory of the Qing empire. As Benedict Anderson has argued in *Imagined Communities*, the primary modes of social organization prior to the existence of nation-states were the dynastic realm and the religious community. The dynastic realm was linked to a dynasty, a family, and not to an ethnic group or nation. The religious community was not territorial but instead was held together by sacred language and practices.[5] In East and Inner Asia the Qing dynasty was the overarching political entity that linked four principal religious communities: the Confucian communities of East Asia (now China Proper, Korea, and Vietnam); the Chinese Buddhist community of China Proper; the Muslim communities of East and Central Asia (now parts of Ningxia, Qinghai, Gansu, and Yunnan provinces, as well as Xinjiang and areas in Kazakhstan, etc.); and the Tibetan Buddhist communities of Inner Asia (now parts of Inner Mongolia, Gansu, Qinghai, and Sichuan provinces, Mongolia, and even parts of Russia from Siberia to the Volga River). Although the Qing dynastic family was composed largely of ethnic Manchus, with some Mongol intermarriage, the Qing empire was not identified with a single ethnic group or nation.

In the final decades of the Qing empire efforts were made to adapt to the modern ideas being introduced from Europe, but none of the new ideas of social organization could quickly or completely replace some two millennia of relations based on dynastic and religious communities. This book explores the influence of the introduction of the modern ideas of nationalism, race, and religion on the relations between Chinese and Tibetans. I argue that neither nationalism nor racial unity could simply take the place of the dynastic and religious communities. The dynastic community truly failed to adapt to the modern period, as evidenced in the weak remnants of the Qing dynasty marched out by the Japanese as the puppet government of Manchuria in 1930s. The religious community, on the other hand, was able to adapt effectively to modern circumstances. When the rhetoric of nationalist and racial unity failed to hold together the territory of the former Qing empire, Chinese and Tibetan Buddhists joined forces to promote their religion within the new context of the nation-state. In the end, the presence of the Buddhist religious community was essential to bridge the gap between the imperial Qing dynasty and the modern Chinese nation-state.

For this to occur, "Buddhism" first had to become a world religion. Only after Chinese and Tibetan "Buddhisms" had become subsets of a universal religion could the state employ this rubric to try to create an imagined community that could link Tibetans with at least some Chinese. In describing the process by which Tibetan Buddhism became part of Buddhism writ large, my research is linked to the study of the globalization of religions that followed the Chicago Parliament of World Religions in 1893 and the modern uses of religion by state actors. The story I tell illustrates the transition from the diverse East Asian traditions, which were not considered part of the same religion, to an understanding of Buddhism as a single religion. What is now called "Tibetan Buddhism" was called Lamaism (*Lama jiao*) by Chinese well into the 1930s.[6] Similarly, some Tibetans in twentieth-century China merely transliterated the Chinese Buddhist term for their religion (Ch. *Fo jiao* became Tib. *Bu ja'o*). Although we now translate this as "Chinese Buddhism," the Tibetans did not. In essence, in the early twentieth century Tibetans did not typically express a shared concept of "Buddhism" that could be understood as a common base for ethnic "variants." Starting in the 1920s and progressing into the 1940s, many Chinese and some Tibetans came to view these separate traditions as part of the larger entity, Buddhism. The Communists in China have taken this idea even further, by making Tibetan and Chinese (Han) Buddhist traditions merely ethnic varieties of "China's Buddhism" (*Zhongguo Fojiao*). Over this half-century Tibetan Buddhism went from being an alien religion to merely a shared part of a national tradition in the eyes of some Chinese.

The inclusion of religion within a nationalist framework links this work to a growing body of literature by historians, political scientists, anthropologists, and scholars of religious studies who are investigating the intersection between the nation and religion.[7] My research also explores this nexus and adds significantly to the evidence that religion cannot merely be associated with "tradition" that is ultimately displaced by "modernity" in the form of the nation. Contrary to this view, my findings demonstrate that, in the context of the modern nation-state, both state actors and members of religious institutions readily adopted and adapted religious traditions in order to advance their respective interests. In the case of Tibet, some lamas seeking to regain territory and autonomy lost to the Dalai Lama's government aided the Chinese Republican efforts to claim Tibet as part of China. The intersection and negotiation of these interests often led to unintended consequences. Just as the state can "use" religion for its ends, such as to divide or unite an ethnic group, religious institutions can also "use" the state to accomplish certain goals, such as the maintenance of prestige or property.[8] In this volume I explore the historic context that allowed political and religious actors in early twentieth-century Asia to negotiate their interests and examine the outcome and effects of these negotiations on Chinese and Tibetan relations.

Countering Nationalist Historiography

Surprisingly, this is the first book-length study in English devoted to the history of modern Chinese and Tibetan relations that relies extensively on both Chinese and Tibetan language material. This is largely owing to the nationalist urges that have prompted the writing of most of the existing studies. The seminal work of Heather Stoddard, soon to be available in an English translation, is a shining example of an exception to this general rule.[9] The works of Ya Hanzhang and Danzhu Angben (Don grub dbang 'bum) documenting the lives of the successive Dalai and Panchen Lamas are also exceptional in their use of both Chinese and Tibetan materials, although they are extreme examples of the nationalist trend typical in Sino-Tibetan historiography.[10] The French scholar Fabienne Jagou used many of the same sources employed by Ya and Danzhu Angben to examine the life of the ninth Panchen Lama (Lozang Tupten Chökyi Nyima, 1883–1937)[11] from a less nationalistic perspective.[12]

The balance of the other research on modern Sino-Tibetan relations fails to examine both Chinese and Tibetan language materials together. Some scholars, such as Warren Smith (*Tibetan Nation*) and Tom Grunfeld (*The Making of Modern Tibet*), do not consider the primary sources of either of these languages. Recently some Tibetologists have explored much of the Tibetan language material on this subject, most notably Melvyn Goldstein (*A History of Modern Tibet, 1913–1951: The Demise of the Lamaist State*) and Tsering Shakya (*The Dragon in the Land of Snows: A History of Modern Tibet Since 1947*). Both scholars also had access to some officially approved but extremely problematic memoirs (some originally written in Tibetan and some originally written in Chinese but available in Tibetan translations).[13] Aside from this collection of memoirs, the number of printed Tibetan language sources on early twentieth-century Tibetan history is surprisingly small.[14] Unfortunately, scholars in the West have generally failed to make use of the copious Chinese language materials for this period. It seems

that, until the present generation, those who were interested in Tibet rarely studied Chinese, and of those who did, none chose to make this period of history
their specialty, again with the exception of Heather Stoddard. Scholars of modern Chinese history have likewise generally shied away from the challenges of
learning Inner Asian languages, although this, too, is changing.

My own interest in the topic of Sino-Tibetan relations grew out of an awareness that neither Chinese nor Tibetan versions of modern history are sufficient if
studied alone. My experience in the field (1991, 1993, 1997, 1999) on the Sino-
Tibetan borderlands (mostly Amdo/Sichuan-Qinghai) and some areas of China
Proper inhabited by groups of Tibetans (Mount Wutai, Chengdu, Beijing) led me
to conclude that there had been and continued to be a lively, though complicated, cultural exchange between Chinese and Tibetans that had gone unexplored. Since then my research has confirmed that this exchange continues to be
crucial in negotiating relations between Chinese and Tibetans. Until quite
recently Holmes Welch's *Buddhist Revival in China* (1968) and Shi Dongchu's
Zhongguo Fojiao jindai shi (*History of Modern Chinese Buddhism*) (1974) comprised
the only book-length research that had taken much notice of these cultural and
educational interactions. Shi Dongchu was a disciple of Taixu (1890–1947), the
monk famed for "reviving" Chinese Buddhism, and so his account has emphasized some aspects of modern Chinese Buddhist history that reflect the perspective of this particular lineage. Other recent scholars researching the role of Tibetan
Buddhism in China include Mei Jingshun of Taiwan and several European scholars—including Françoise Wang-Toutain, Ester Bianchi, and Monica Esposito.
With the exception of Mei, these researchers have focused more on the religious
aspects of Sino-Tibetan exchanges than on their political repercussions.[15]

The necessary condition for broadening and extending this previous scholarship has been the gradual revival of Tibetan Buddhism in China since the end of
the Cultural Revolution. With this revival and the relative freedom of the
Chinese presses, Buddhists throughout the country wrote and printed local histories and biographies that were not explicitly devoted to the agenda of the
Communist Party, although that agenda could never be directly challenged.
While researching the life of Sherap Gyatso, a Tibetan monk who had a central
role in mediating between China and Tibet in both the Republican and
Communist eras, I discovered a host of recently published biographies, memoirs,
and reprints concerned with Tibetan Buddhism in the Republican period.
Mostly the work of Chinese monks who had embraced Tibetan Buddhism in the
second quarter of the twentieth century, these synoptic accounts allowed me to
reconstruct enough of the story to know where to look for additional sources.

Central among these other sources are Republican-period Buddhist publications, such as *Haichaoyin* (*Voice of the Ocean's Tide;* a reference to Buddha's teach-

ings), started by the reformist monk Taixu, (Haichaoyin) reported and commented on the development of Tibetan Buddhism among the Chinese as well as the government's interest in this new phenomenon.[16] Taixu's collected works are also filled with references to the place of Tibetan Buddhism in China. Other Republican-era Buddhist memorial volumes, dedicated to Tibetan Buddhist teachers or the rituals they performed in China, gave me insight into the social context of the period. The principal archival sources for this work are drawn from the Chongqing city archive, which holds the voluminous records of the Sino-Tibetan Buddhist Institute (Han Zang jiaoli yuan) that operated outside the city from 1932 to 1949. The collected writings of the Chinese Nationalist Party (Guomindang) politician Dai Jitao also reveal the level of involvement of top Chinese politicians with Tibetan Buddhists in China. Recent interest in the topic in China and Taiwan also has led to certain advances in our knowledge of the intermediaries between China and Tibet in the modern period.

Tibetan sources that touch on this topic are more difficult to come by, in part because of government censorship of materials that might damage the "national interests" of either China or the Tibetan government-in-exile. Although apparently censored by the Tibetan government-in-exile,[17] Thupten Sangay's *Rgya nag tu Bod kyi sku tshab don gcod skabs dang gnyis tshugs stangs skor gyi lo rgyus thabs bral zur lam* (*Experiences of a Former Tibetan Representative in China, 1930–1939*) frankly discussed the political roles of official Tibetan representatives residing in Republican China. The biographies and collected writings of the Panchen Lama, Lozang Tupten Chökyi Nyima, and Sherap Gyatso were also crucial in assessing the extent to which these prominent Tibetans accepted Chinese political rhetoric about Tibet.

Transitions: Making National, Going Global

Although certain links exist between the modern nation-state of China and the dynastic empires that preceded this recent creation, it was by no means a foregone conclusion that the new "China" would include the Inner Asian domains of the Manchu Qing empire. As John King Fairbank argued in *Trade and Diplomacy on the China Coast: The Opening of the Treaty Ports, 1842–1854*:

> The vast areas of outer Mongolia, Tibet, and Turkestan where the Manchu power was later established became subject not to China but to the dynasty— a fact which was to provide the logical basis for their defection from the Chinese Republic at the time of the revolution of 1911. Inner Asia until then was not under China but under the Manchus.[18]

Evelyn Rawski, in the conclusion to *The Last Emperors*, articulated this problem in the context of the modern Chinese nation-state: "The breakaway movements of the post-1911 period are testimony to the fact that we cannot simply equate the Qing empire with a nation-state called China."[19] No Chinese civil official had ever been appointed as the leading imperial representative to Tibet; this had been the purview of the Qing military elite, almost exclusively Manchus and Mongols.[20] Nor had Chinese ideology or political systems ever penetrated Tibet. Confucianism, civil service exams, the writing system, and other trappings of Chinese civilization that had spread elsewhere in East Asia were never introduced in Tibet. In addition, in the early twentieth century the modern Chinese nation's predominantly secular ideology severed even the weak link of a shared interest in the religious underpinnings of state authority.

In this historical context, what is most surprising is that the Chinese cared at all that Tibet be included as part of the Chinese nation-state. This concern for Tibetan territory among the Chinese (as opposed to the Mongols or Manchus of earlier dynasties) was a modern novelty and required a long educational campaign on the part of certain nationalist Chinese. The principal challenge for Chinese nationalists bent on retaining all the territory of the Qing empire was to discover a viable connection between the Tibetans and the Chinese to replace the Manchu emperor's role of overseer and protector of a religious polity. Whereas the Qing dynasty had adopted the rhetoric of patron and priest relations that had been current during the Mongol Yuan empire's domination of East Asia, during the early Republican period, the Chinese initially declined to embrace this model. Instead, they attempted to use modern racial and nationalist strategies to include Tibet within the new nation. Yet this strategy failed the Chinese, especially in this time of military weakness. Manchuria fell to Japanese aggression, as did Inner Mongolia; Outer Mongolia and, at times, Chinese Turkestan fell under the sway of the Russians; and Tibet was dominated by the British. Against these imperialist forces, the Chinese had neither effective military capabilities nor very persuasive ideologies.

Aside from the first and the last few years of the Chinese Republic, the Tibetans had little to be concerned about in the rhetoric of Chinese nationalists. Too weak to assert control of Tibet by force for most of the Republican period, Chinese leaders did not threaten Tibet but instead tried to gently woo Tibet into choosing to join the modern Chinese nation-state. The idea that other races (or nations) would *willingly* join the new Chinese state was a critical part of Sun Yatsen's legacy. Ultimately the Republican insistence that Tibet become a part of China by choice, and not through force, has been neglected in Asian studies.[21] But ignoring almost three decades of persuasive rhetoric on the part of the Chinese limits our ability to understand why the Tibetans made some of the choices they did. Without a Chinese military threat, why should the Tibetans have risked the disruptions and transformation that would have been entailed by the militarization of their society? Given the vacillating British support for Tibetan autonomy (which vanished completely with India's independence), why should the Tibetans have given up hope of peaceful relations with China?

I argue that the Chinese advocated discourses of racial and national unity in an attempt to incorporate Tibet but that these failed completely. Instead, Buddhist culture became the glue that could reconnect parts of the Qing empire that had disintegrated under the secularly conceived Chinese Republic. The modern conception of Buddhism as a world religion allowed a handful of Buddhists—both Chinese and Tibetan—to join forces in an effort to remain relevant within the modern nation-state.

How and why did some Buddhists embrace this role? When revolution brought the Qing empire to an end in 1911, the Dalai Lama took control of affairs in Tibet—repatriating Chinese forces there by sea (via India) and tightening administrative control. The Chinese Republic was at a loss as to how to deal with this independent Tibet. Then, in 1924, the Panchen Lama fled Tibet for a life in exile in China. He felt himself the victim of the Dalai Lama's efforts to build a centralized Tibetan nation-state. When he arrived in China, the officials there welcomed him but initially made no attempt to "use" him to solve the problem of Tibet's independence. The Panchen Lama spent his time teaching Buddhism to Mongol and Chinese Buddhists, which helped popularize Tibetan Buddhism in China.

Meanwhile, the new Chinese Republic tried two secular strategies in an effort to include Tibetans in the new nation. The first approach was to use a racial discourse known as the "Five Races Harmoniously Joined" (*Wuzu gonghe*) to suggest to the Tibetans and other major "races" that their interests would be included in the new China. From 1912 to 1927, this idea was represented by a national flag, which had five colored stripes of equal size to represent the equality of the races (1912–1927). This idea was also enshrined in one of the names for the new country, the "Republic of the Five Races" (*Wuzu gongheguo*). However, even Tibetans sympathetic to the Republican regime quickly recognized not only that the new nation was dominated by the Chinese but also that the Chinese had no ability to control the other peoples (or "races"), such as the Muslims, who militarily threatened Tibetans in Qinghai and Gansu. The rhetoric of racial equality was doubly proved hollow by the political domination of Chinese interests in the Republic and the military domination of Muslim or Chinese warlords on the Tibetan borderlands.

With the failure of this racial rhetoric and the rise of the Nationalist Party (Guomindang) to national dominance in 1927, the government advocated the nationalist rhetoric of Sun Yat-sen's *Three Principles of the People* as an alternative prescription for the modernization of Tibet; that is, Sun's strategy of encouraging nationalism was taught, and embraced, by some modern Tibetans on their own terms. At this time, while the Panchen Lama was gradually developing a closer relationship with Chinese politicians, several Tibetans in his entourage were hopeful that Sun's model of nationalist liberation could be applied to Tibetan regions. They did not read Sun as someone who recommended assimilation of the frontier races into the Chinese race. Instead, they recognized Sun's definition of shared racial characteristics (blood, livelihood, language, religion, and customs) among the Tibetans and applied Sun's nationalist thought to their Tibetan nationalist ends. They sought to secure Tibetan autonomy with the assistance of the Chinese, much as the Mongolians had benefited from Soviet assistance in the 1920s. Although Sun would not have condoned complete independence of these territories, it is clear from his writings that he believed that any nation must "evolve naturally and not come about through the use of military conquest (*tianran jihua er cheng de, bu shi yong wuli zhengfu de lai de*)."[22] Dai Jitao also indicated that the Chinese government would not tolerate the oppression of any nation by another.[23] Yet the Chinese failed to support the Tibetans who valued Sun's nationalist tactics. Nascent autonomy movements in eastern Tibet (1930s) and Tibet proper (1940s) quickly faded without China's support. All the while, the Panchen Lama continued to teach Buddhism, now to Chinese politicians—even holding rituals in government buildings.

After nearly two decades of racial and nationalist rhetoric, Chinese politicians finally recognized their failure to attract Tibetans to their cause and started to look for new solutions to what they called the "Tibet problem." This renewed effort provided just the avenue that Buddhists in China had been seeking to address their own concerns. Before considering what the Buddhists had to offer the modern nation, it is important to understand why the Buddhists were willing to help the government in the first place. Secular forces in the various Republican governments had constantly confiscated or threatened to appropriate the substantial landholdings of Buddhist institutions. In response, some Buddhists formed modern religious schools inspired by Western missionary educational institutions. At the same time, ethnically Mongol Tibetan Buddhists also lost the imperial support that had secured their livelihood since the seventeenth century. They turned for support to the Chinese laity, to whom they revealed their rich store of Buddhist esoterica. The joining of these disparate elements—formerly segregated under Qing rule—led to the creation of a pan-Asian understanding of Buddhism among Chinese Buddhists, who eventually embraced the religion formerly known as "Lamaism" (*Lama jiao*) as just another aspect of Buddhism (*Fojiao*).

Until the mid-1920s Chinese Buddhists were largely dependent on non-Chinese (Mongolian, Tibetan, Japanese) for access to esoteric Buddhist salvific techniques. To solve this problem, in 1925 a handful of pioneering Chinese monks set off to study abroad (*liuxue*) in Tibet at the feet of lamas for the first time in history. They faced immense challenges—linguistic (no Chinese-Tibetan dictionary existed), environmental (many became sick or died from Tibetan living conditions such as poor diet and high altitude), political (Tibetan officials thought that they were spies), and financial (they depended on unsteady funding from Buddhist laymen). Very few monks stayed long enough to master the Tibetan language and Buddhist teachings. The two who returned from Lhasa after almost a decade were key figures in bringing Tibetan Buddhism to the Chinese. Their experiences, although the result of their own initiative, later served to provide valuable knowledge about Tibet to Chinese politicians. Many of these monks became involved with the institutions that tried to close the gap between the imagination and the realization of Tibet as part of the modern Chinese nation.

Also in the mid-1920s certain Tibetan lamas were driven into exile in China by the Dalai Lama's effort to consolidate a modern Tibetan national administration. No Chinese politician in the early Republican period chose to support these lamas in their efforts to return to Tibet, so the lamas were initially forced to rely on teaching Tibetan Buddhism to Chinese and Mongolians for their support. In fact, this is the aspect the Tibetan government-in-exile emphasized when one scholar asked about these lamas who lived in China.[24] The political and social turmoil of the period also drew the Chinese people—and eventually the Chinese government—to seek the "protection of the country" (*huguo*) in Tibetan Buddhist rituals. The tremendous popular support for Tibetan Buddhist teachers and practices by Chinese Buddhists was probably the most important factor in the incorporation of Tibet into the modern Chinese imagination of the nation. For example, in 1931, and again in 1934, the Panchen Lama held Kālacakra tantra rituals with well over ten thousand Chinese in attendance each time. These events attracted people from all walks of life, from former presidents of the Republic to common laypersons.

In this context, Tibetan Buddhists in China assumed political roles and the Chinese government started to support the religion. For those Buddhists who believed that their religion still had something to offer the Chinese people, Buddhist solutions for the "Tibetan problem" became an important opportunity to establish this. Later, after the Nationalist Party was settled in its control of China, the Chinese government actively attempted to use Buddhism to incorporate Tibet in the modern Chinese nation-state. The strongest advocate for the central role of Buddhism in uniting the modern Chinese nation was the

Nationalist Party leader Dai Jitao. Dai had been Sun Yat-sen's secretary and one of the principal proponents of Sun's ideology after Sun's death. But Dai had observed early on the failure of Sun's rhetoric to truly unite the foreign exchange students who came to China from surrounding nations. Although Sun's nationalist ideas were attractive to many of these students, Chinese resistance to actually encouraging a practical application of these strategies was discouraging to them. Dai was well aware that Sun's ideology was not attracting interest among the ruling Tibetan elite.

At this time China's leaders were still bound by Sun's insistence that China's other races/nations willingly join the Republic, without coercion. In 1932 provincial militarists sought Nationalist government support for a forceful termination of Tibet's independence. Responding to this suggestion, Dai Jitao instead developed a new strategy that brought exiled lamas into the Nationalist government, with assurances of respect for Buddhism. From all the signs, Dai was a sincere Buddhist who tried to link Buddhist and political ideas to benefit the Chinese state. Rather than repeating the same tired language of the "unity of the five races" and Sun's *Three Principles of the People,* Dai argued that Buddhism was the cornerstone not just of Sino-Tibetan relations but of relations throughout all of Asia—from Indonesia to Mongolia, from Tibet to Japan. Regarding Tibet, he grounded this rhetoric in practical efforts to repair the damaged relations between the Panchen Lama, in exile in China, and the Dalai Lama. He devoted much time and attention to interactions with borderland Tibetans and to Tibetan Buddhist ritual activities in China. Building on two decades of popular religious interaction between Chinese and Tibetans, in 1933 Dai forcefully argued that religion was the one uniting feature shared by China's peoples. In a national radio broadcast he particularly emphasized the importance of Tibetan religion shortly before the Panchen Lama set off on his return to Tibet. This rhetoric had a significant impact on the Chinese imagination of unity with Tibet for the next decade, suggesting that this now shared religion could bridge the gap between the estranged peoples.

The government also gained the support of prominent Tibetans in exile, who hoped that the Chinese government would restore them to their positions of power once the Central Tibetan administration was under Chinese control. In order to appeal to such Tibetans, the Nationalist government was forced to demonstrate its sincerity by respecting Buddhist institutions in China Proper.[25] For this reason, the government quickly gained the support of Chinese monks, such as Master Taixu, who hoped to link Buddhist assistance in resolving the problem of Tibetan independence with government support for Buddhism. The record demonstrates that his hopes were fulfilled. Each time effective measures were passed by the Chinese government to protect Buddhist property, Tibetan Buddhists were directly involved in the process. Furthermore, Taixu found his first government support for developing Buddhist education in the province of Sichuan, which bordered Tibetan regions. He willingly embraced the milder aspects of the colonialist rhetoric of his sponsor but also spoke frankly of his hopes that autonomy and religious freedom would prevail in Tibet.

Starting in 1937 the Nationalist government vigorously embraced schools devoted to modern Tibetan Buddhist education. Earlier government-sponsored schools seemed to have produced few useful intermediaries, probably because of the lack of well-trained teachers and educational materials. The most formal of the new schools shared features with modern American area-studies programs: an intensive focus on language training, an attempt to develop students' knowledge of Tibetan religion, geography, and history, as well as the production of language and history textbooks and a bilingual dictionary. Efforts were also made to encourage an exchange of students with Tibet, but only a handful of teachers came from Tibet to China. Students were often sent to Tibet, sometimes even before they graduated. Other efforts to promote educational exchange included Nationalist support for modern Tibetan monastic schools in the borderlands between China and Tibet.

The final effort to peacefully unite with Tibet was based on a concerted effort to inform the Tibetans—the noble and monastic leadership as well as the monastic population in Lhasa and on the borders—that the Chinese government was supportive of Tibetan Buddhism. This strategy was an outgrowth of cultural exchanges between Tibetans and Chinese, who had realized that ethnicity and nationality, although not enough to hold the peoples together, also did not create an insurmountable barrier to realizing their shared interests. The first positive diplomatic effort in this direction was made in 1934. Upon the death of the thirteenth Dalai Lama, the Panchen Lama was named a commissioner of the Chinese state with responsibility for propaganda on the western frontier. At the same time the Chinese envoy Huang Musong was sent to Tibet with four hundred thousand silver dollars to make religious offerings. Having participated in Tibetan Buddhist rituals in China, he was aware of the central importance of religion to the Tibetans. He followed Buddhist protocol by prostrating himself at the principal religious shrines and distributing cash to twenty thousand monks in Lhasa. He also gave assurances to the Tibetan government that China would respect and support Tibetan Buddhism and preserve the political system that maintained the monasteries if the Tibetan government would acknowledge that Tibet was a part of China. In 1944, when the Chinese were desperate for Tibetan permission for overland transport following the Japanese capture of the Burma Road, they again sent a Buddhist as envoy to Tibet.

Even when the Communists took control of China in 1949 they continued the strategies initiated by the Nationalist government. Buddhist monks, both

Tibetan and Chinese, were crucial advisers and translators for the Communists. When the presence of the Chinese army on their borders forced the Tibetan government to surrender their independence, the Tibetans stipulated that the Chinese representative was to be a Buddhist. The Communists were respectful of the religion for years, until they achieved a strong presence in Tibet. In fact, Tibetan Buddhists continued to play an important role in Asian diplomacy into the late 1950s. Both ethnic Tibetan and Chinese Tibetan Buddhist monks were given prominent positions in official Buddhist organizations and new government educational institutions. Sherap Gyatso even served as an envoy to Southeast Asian countries with Buddhist populations (Nepal, Burma, Thailand, Sri Lanka, and India). The leading Chinese monks who had embraced Tibetan Buddhism continued to lead traditional and modern Buddhist schools within Communist China. Yet when the Communists tried to force reforms on the Tibetan people in the 1950s, they encountered stiff resistance. Once their religion and culture were threatened the Tibetans sought to revolt, with backing from the American Office of Strategic Services (OSS) (and later the Central Intelligence Agency [CIA]) at the height of the Cold War. Chinese government support for Tibetan Buddhism dramatically retracted in the following years and finally turned to suppression under the Cultural Revolution.

Still, since the close of the Cultural Revolution, Tibetan Buddhists have demonstrated that their religion is not dead. The avowedly atheistic Chinese Communist government continues to find that it must support Tibetan Buddhists and their institutions in order to maintain control of Tibet. Thus the Communist Party still recognizes children as new incarnations of lamas, rebuilds temples, and is sponsoring the authoritative new edition of the Tibetan Buddhist canon. In these respects the modern Chinese nation-state has embraced many of the strategies of the former empire in its efforts to maintain Tibet as part of a new "China."

1. Imperial Traditions

WHEN CONSIDERING relations between China and Tibet, one central fact about Tibet must never be forgotten: Buddhist institutions were and still are the bedrock of the Tibetan cultural world. With a few brief exceptions, from 1642 to 1951 power in Tibet was concentrated in the hands of the dominant monastic institutions and a few lay aristocratic families based in and around Lhasa.[1] Whenever Tibetan Buddhist institutions have been threatened, the Tibetan elites have responded defensively; whenever they have been supported, the Tibetan elites have cooperated. In general, studies of modern Tibet have focused too exclusively on political issues that surround "Tibetan independence." Seeking to explain why or how Tibet lost its independence, or never had it in the first place, historians, anthropologists, Tibetan sympathizers, and Chinese apologists have all failed to pay proper attention to the larger aspects of modern Asian history. By this I refer especially to the global forces of nationalism and imperialist commercial interests, with their overarching respective concerns for territory and "free" trade. These forces challenged Tibetan Buddhist culture, in which territorial and trade considerations had always been of secondary importance to the support of the religion. I discuss the impact of these global forces in more detail in the next chapter, but first I must describe the imperial traditions that operated in East and Inner Asia in the previous centuries.

These traditions, established over centuries of imperial rule, created links between imperial elites and the religious community of Tibetan Buddhists. Of course, the presence of these links did not mean that Tibet somehow became one with the empire. Instead, these imperial connections allowed imperial rule to rest lightly on top of the Tibetan cultural and political world. The elite imperial connections were easily severed in the context of modern nationalism, which favored instead the demotic cultural connections between the Tibetan elite and commoners. The work of sociologist Anthony Smith is useful in analyzing why Tibetan Buddhists' interaction with the Mongol and Manchu impe-

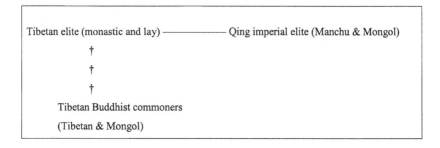

Figure 1.1 Lateral Axis and Vertical Axis of Communities

rial elites functioned so effectively for more than two centuries and then broke
down so quickly under the pressures of global modernization. Smith describes
a typology of historic ethnic communities, which consists of two patterns, a lateral and a vertical one. The lateral community was "usually composed of some
aristocrats and a higher clergy, though it might from time to time include
bureaucrats. . . . It is termed lateral because it was at once socially confined to
the upper strata while being geographically spread out to form often close links
with the upper echelons of neighboring [ethnic groups]."[2] This describes the
Buddhist leaders of Tibet very well, for their power was linked both to the local
Gelukpa Tibetan Buddhist order that had achieved hegemony in the seventeenth century and the neighboring political overseer of this tradition from the
eighteenth century, the Manchu dynastic court. At the same time the vertical
axis of ethnic (and religious) community linked the Tibetan ethnic elites to the
other members of the Tibetan Buddhist cultural world, including the Mongols.

On the vertical axis, "ethnic culture tended to be diffused to other social
strata and classes. Social divisions were not underpinned by cultural differences:
rather, a distinctive historical culture helped unite different classes around a common heritage and traditions."[3] As is clear from Figure 1.1, there is no role for
the Chinese ethnic group in this relationship.

As long as the interests of the ethnic elite in Tibet were served by cooperating with the neighboring ethnic elite of the Manchu Qing empire, these ethnically different elite groups formed a stable, mutually supportive community that
dominated the vertically integrated Tibetan Buddhist cultural world. However,
with the rise of Chinese nationalism and efforts at modernizing the Qing
empire along the lines of a European nation-state, the lateral relations were
weakened and the vertical identification became stronger. As Smith has
explained, lateral relations were generally characterized by accommodation, not
central control.[4] During most of the Qing dynasty's reign, the Tibetan and

Manchu elites were able to cooperate because neither made an effort to spread its culture or political system where such was not welcome. For example, the civil service examination system was unknown in Tibet, and reincarnation was certainly not an acceptable way to transfer power in China. The Tibetan elites accepted a sufficient amount of bureaucratic supervision to satisfy the Qing imperial rulers, and in turn the Qing imperial rulers accepted and supported Tibetan Buddhism sufficiently to convince the Tibetans of their genuine support and interest. However, the Qing imperial institutions deliberately rested very lightly on Tibet. Likewise Tibetans made no attempt to force Tibetan Buddhist institutions on the rest of the Qing empire (as had happened to a degree in the Yuan period).

The Qing empire had become involved with Tibet merely in order to head off potential challenges to the dynasty and instability on the frontiers. Thus Tibet remained a state with its own system of administration, tax collection, and social relations that were quite distinct from those of the Chinese provinces of the Qing empire. Its relations with the Qing empire were handled by the Manchu institutions of the Imperial Household (Neiwufu) and the Court for Managing the Frontiers (Lifanyuan).[5] These Qing imperial relations were built on centuries of previous imperial traditions. What, then, was the historical context for this relationship between the Qing empire and the Tibetan state?

Traditions Linking Tibetan Buddhists and Dynastic Rulers

Patronage Tradition

Ever since the Mongol successors of Genghis Khan's Asia-wide campaign became patrons of Tibetan Buddhism, this religion has been linked with prominent rulers in Asia. The origins of some Tibetan Buddhists' orientation toward patrons from outside Tibetan regions dates back to the time of the Western Xia state (1038–1227). Lamas from a branch of the Kagyüpa school became spiritual preceptors to the ethnically Tangut rulers of the Western Xia state and were still serving in this role when Chinggis Khan (d. 1227) eliminated the state and the family to whom the Tibetan Buddhists had been ministering.[6] The relationship between Pakpa Lama Lodrö Gyentsen (1235–1280) and Khubilai Khan (r. 1260–1294) and the institutions that grew out of it created a close bond between China and Tibet, and between the religious and political functions of Tibetan lamas in the service of the state.

Certain elements of this "contract" remained prominent in Sino-Tibetan relations into the twentieth century, although there was rarely direct continuity. These instances represent an enduring tradition rather than an unbroken one. In his *Tibetan Nationalism: The Role of Patronage in the Accomplishment of a National Identity,* Christiaan Klieger described this Tibetan tradition as follows: "Tibetan culture provides a mechanism whereby forces and personnel from the 'outside' can be utilized . . . to economically and ideologically support the perceived continuation of Tibetan cultural patterns."[7] In the East Asian context, important features of this mechanism include the teacher-student (and parallel donee-donor) relationship between a Tibetan hierarch and an emperor (whether of Mongol, Chinese, or Manchu ethnicity), the support of Tibetan Buddhist monasteries by members of the imperial elites of China, and the conferral of imperial titles upon Tibetan religious rulers by China's leaders. All these features were adopted by the Chinese Republican leadership, as they had been by the three preceding dynasties. The source of these traditions lay in the Tibetan Buddhist culture, which had a well-developed ideology concerning the proper relations between religion and politics.

The Inseparability of Religion and Politics

Far from a conception of the separation of church and state, the Tibetan idea of the inextricable connection between religion and politics (*chos srid zung 'brel*) is that these are not two opposing fields of activity that are meant to be kept separate.[8] The linking of the two arenas is seen as perfectly appropriate in Tibet. As the current Dalai Lama stated in his autobiography, "religion and politics do mix," and "I find no contradiction at all between politics and religion."[9] The support of Buddhism by the ruling families of Tibet was first established during the Tibetan imperial period in the eighth century. Under Mongol rule, prominent lamas and families associated with particular schools of Tibetan Buddhism were granted the right to govern not just monastic estates but entire polities. The emperors who were the sponsors and military support for these Tibetan leaders lived far away, leaving the day-to-day governance of Tibet in the hands of the local Tibetan leaders of religious schools and the powerful corporate estates that grew up around them.

However, unlike in imperial Tibet, where only a single family had the authority to govern, the divided patronage of the Mongol imperial family allowed for competing centers of power, with different Tibetan schools gaining support from different Mongol rulers. In the period of Mongol rule of Tibet this competition was played out between the ruling Sakyapa and different branches of the Kagyüpa and involved various Mongol armies being brought into Tibet to settle local differences. As long as the Sakyapa families were able to rely on the support of the Mongol emperors, they remained the rulers of Tibet. However, with the weakening of the Mongol Yuan dynasty, the Sakyapa school lost real power to a branch of the Kagyüpa school. The leaders of both schools had contact with Ming rulers from whom they received substantial patronage and prestige. In this way a tradition of competition for patronage from non-Tibetan patrons was firmly established by the end of the Ming.[10]

The school that was to earn the support of the Qing dynasty also followed this tradition. In the seventeenth century the relatively young tradition based on the teachings of Tsongkhapa Lozang Drakpa (1357–1419), now known as the Gelukpa school, was seriously threatened by the rulers of Central Tibet, who were largely aligned with the Karmapa branch of the Kagyüpa school.[11] Whether taking a lesson from the period of Mongol domination or merely responding to another rise in Mongol power to the north, the Gelukpa school sought and obtained the support of the Mongols. Like the Sakyapa and the Kagyüpa before them, in the face of the suppression of their tradition and the elimination or crippling of its Tibetan patrons, the Gelukpa leadership asked the Mongols to come and fight for their tradition. Their combined forces were extraordinarily successful, permanently eliminating Kagyüpa control of Tibet. However, even though the Mongol leader ritually offered these conquered territories to the fifth Dalai Lama, Ngakwang Lozang Gyatso (1617–1682), he retained the status of king of Tibet for himself and his descendants. When the last of these Mongol kings of Tibet was killed early in the eighteenth century, the Manchu emperor of China became prominent in the assignment, or at least recognition, of authority in Tibet.

Under the influence of the Qing dynasty, the Dalai Lama's nominal leadership of Tibet continued in name with various restrictions, including the creation of a short-lived Tibetan monarchal institution. From the middle of the eighteenth century imperial representatives (Manchu, *amban*) were sent to oversee affairs in Tibet, in cooperation with the Dalai Lama. In reality, however, Gelukpa prelates largely served as the actual rulers of Tibet, in the capacity of regents for a series of young Dalai Lamas who died before, or shortly after, they reached maturity.[12] Only the thirteenth Dalai Lama, Tupten Gyatso (1876–1933), was able to elevate this institution to what is commonly perceived today as the model for Tibetan leadership: a truly unified secular and religious head of state. His innovation was to consolidate in his hands all the secular power that had so often been associated in principle, but not in practice, with religious leadership. The place of the Dalai Lama in Tibetan society has been studied extensively, but at present we know little about the successive generations of Tibetan Buddhists who represented the Dalai Lama at the Qing court.

Tibetan Buddhist Intermediaries at the Qing Court

The prominent presence of Tibetan Buddhists at court demonstrates the centrality of the patronage tradition in managing Qing-Tibetan relations. While the role of the Qing *ambans* as imperial representatives in Tibet is well known,

Tibetan Buddhist envoys and appointees at the imperial court and Mount Wutai have scarcely received scholarly attention. From the Shunzhi period (1644–1661) until well into the Chinese Republic (1912–1949), the principal representatives of Tibet in China Proper were the head lamas of Mount Wutai and, from the eighteenth century, Beijing's Yonghegong (now popularly know as the Lama Temple). The Buddhist sacred mountain of Mount Wutai served as a refuge from the capital's heat for Tibetan Buddhists at the court from the thirteenth to the twentieth century, while Yonghegong, a former Qing imperial palace, became a Gelukpa college under the Qianlong emperor.[13] The appointment of Tibetan Buddhists as leaders of Mount Wutai grew out of the fifth Dalai Lama's visit to the Qing capital in 1653. Over the next three centuries the various Dalai Lamas appointed dozens of lamas to lead the Chinese and foreign monastic communities at Mount Wutai. Whether Mongol or Tibetan, these lamas had generally spent long years at the cultural center of the Tibetan Buddhist world, Lhasa. Under the Qianlong emperor, Yonghegong became the imperial center for training Mongol, Manchu, and, at least initially, Chinese monks at the court in the Gelukpa school of Tibetan Buddhist doctrine and practice.[14] The abbot and head teachers of this imperial monastery were drawn from Tibetan Buddhists sent from Tibet.

As a counterbalance to the Lhasa-appointed monks, the Qing court supported various other Tibetan Buddhists, most notably the Changja (Mong. Jangjia, Tib. Lcang skya, Ch. Zhangjia) reincarnation series.[15] The various incarnations of the Changja incarnation series rarely trained extensively in central Tibet; instead, they resided at court-granted monastic estates in Beijing, Gansu, Jehol, Inner Mongolia, and on Mount Wutai. From these locations they extended their influence principally to Mongols and Monguors. Nevertheless, unlike the Qing *ambans* resident in Tibet, the Changja Qutughtus were still considered "insiders" to the Tibetan Buddhist world. The early incarnations were recognized as important lamas in Tibet and were able to mediate delicate situations on behalf of the Qing court. Their connections were especially appreciated during the eighteenth century, when the Qing emperors were trying to stabilize the Tibetan government.

With the decline in importance of the Changja incarnation series and the settling of affairs in Tibet, by the nineteenth century the Qing court had routinized the appointment of Tibetan envoys under the direction of the Court for Managing the Frontiers. However, these envoys also continued to have a special relationship directly with the imperial family, which was handled by the Imperial Household Department. Although most of the later figures are shrouded in obscurity, new developments in the twentieth century would elevate the Tibetan envoys at Beijing and Mount Wutai to a central role in bridging the Sino-Tibetan estrangement. The importance of these monastic officials was highlighted in the early years of the Chinese Republic when they became the only real diplomatic link between China and Tibet. *envoys @ Beijing, Mt Wutai*

The substantial presence of Tibetan Buddhists in Beijing and associated imperial sites has become well known through the work of several scholars of Qing history, including Chia Ning, Evelyn Rawski, and Susan Naquin. Chia Ning's research on the Court for Managing the Frontiers reveals that by the end of the dynasty, there were more than 100 high-ranking lamas in Beijing. In the Qianlong reign period more than 1,200 Tibetan Buddhist monks were registered with the Court for Managing the Frontiers.[16] Yet these numbers do not count all the Tibetan Buddhists at the capital. The *Record of Imperial Household Ceremonies* indicates that 2,000 lamas were employed by the dynastic household to recite scriptures in 1780.[17] Evelyn Rawski, in *The Last Emperors,* demonstrated that this was not merely a passing trend, as she noted that 1,516 Tibetan Buddhist monks were still employed by the court in the same way in 1854, three-quarters of a century later.[18] Susan Naquin estimated that there may have been between 4,000 and 5,000 Tibetan Buddhist monks in Beijing during the Qianlong emperor's reign.[19] However, it is a mistake to conclude that, on the basis of these numbers, the ethnic Tibetan presence was large in Beijing.

Although many Tibetan Buddhists lived in and around the Qing capital in Beijing, relatively few of these were actually ethnic Tibetans. In fact, judging from the dynastic records, Mount Wutai's Pusading (from the seventeenth century) and Beijing's Yonghegong (from the eighteenth century) are the only imperial sites that housed Tibetan lamas regularly according to statute, and their numbers were small.[20] The reason for the dearth of ethnic Tibetan monks at imperial sites is hinted at in the Court for Managing the Frontiers sub-statutes dealing with lamas: illness and an inability to acclimate to local conditions is repeatedly associated specifically with lamas coming from Tibet. The Tibetan envoys who represented the Dalai and Panchen Lamas at the court, the lama leaders of Mount Wutai, and the Yonghegong instructor lamas were each mentioned in relation to precedents set for handling a return to Tibet after illness set in or when they were unable to adjust to local conditions.[21] The sixth Panchen Lama, Penden Yeshé (1738–1780) died as a result of contracting smallpox at the capital, and other lamas took heed of this danger. In the twentieth century the Chinese who made their way to Tibet would experience many of the same hardships. Differences in climate, diseases, and diet were significant impediments to communication between China and Tibet as late as the first half of the twentieth century.

The role of Tibetan-appointed lamas as intermediaries between Tibet and the Qing court developed from the fifth Dalai Lama's visit to Beijing in 1653. Nearly a decade prior to the Manchus taking Beijing, ethnic Mongol Tibetan Buddhists brokered the first plans for arranging a meeting between the Shunzhi emperor and the Dalai Lama.[22] After 1653 the Dalai Lama was linked to the Qing court through representatives sent from Tibet to the capital and to Mount Wutai. The specifics of arrangements made at Mount Wutai in the 1650s are recorded in detail only on stele at the mountain or in gazetteers devoted to the sacred site. These developments were probably set in place by the Shunzhi emperor's 1657 order to establish "positions for four *jasagh* lamas at the capital and chief lamas (*shouling lama*) at Shengjing (Mukden), Guihuacheng (Hohhot), etc."[23] This plan, which apparently grew out of the Dalai Lama's visit to court, would eventually be articulated into a complex system of imperial lama appointments in the capital and associated sites. Furthermore, later regulations make it clear that one of the capital's *jasagh* lamas and the leading lama of Mount Wutai were bound by statute to be drawn from a pool of lamas sent from Tibet.[24]

The records of the leading lamas of Mount Wutai provide the fullest picture of these new appointments in the early Qing dynasty. The relations between these monks and the Dalai Lama were so intimate that one Chinese scholar has described the main temples of the mountain as being "directly under the jurisdiction of the Dalai Lama."[25] In 1659 Ngakwang Lozang (Ch. Awang laozang, 1601–1687) was given charge of Mount Wutai's foreign and Chinese lamas (*zongli Wutaishan Fan-Han lama*). This man was a lama of high standing among the Tibetans and had studied with the fifth Dalai Lama, who—according to his memorial stupa—predicted his appointment to the post.[26] In 1661 he wrote the preface to the first Mount Wutai gazetteer issued in the Qing period.[27] That same year he also requested that a Köke nor Mongol prepare the first Mongolian version of a gazetteer.[28] He was succeeded in this post in 1668 by Lozang Tenpel (Ch. Laozang danbei, 1632–1684), a Mongol who had lived at the mountain for years after traveling to the countries (*guo*) of Tibet and Mongolia, no doubt for religious training.[29]

Throughout the Kangxi emperor's reign the appointees to this position of leadership on Mount Wutai enjoyed unprecedented recognition and favors. In 1683 Ngakwang Lozang was given an honorific title. That same year the Kangxi emperor came to the mountain twice to arrange for prayers on behalf of the dynasty. Shortly after these visits Lozang Tenpel was able to secure imperial permission and support to re-tile the roof of Pusading, the main temple at the mountain. The new roof was to be constructed of the imperial yellow-gold ceramic tiles reserved for use on imperial palaces and other elite homes.[30] Thereafter Pusading was also known as an imperial touring-palace (*xinggong*) in honor of the occasional visits the Qing emperors made to the site. The third generation head lama of Mount Wutai, Lozang Tenpa (Ch. Laozang danba), was a disciple of his predecessor. In 1698 he was granted a letter patent, a silver seal, and the title *Qingxiu chanshi*. These imperial gifts gave legal confirmation of his position as *jasagh dalama* in control of Mount Wutai's foreign and Chinese monks (*tidu Wutaishan Fan-Han zhasake dalama*). In 1704 a new *jasagh* lama named Tendzin Gyatso (Ch. Dingzeng jianzuo) was designated. During his tenure the Kangxi emperor and his son, the future Yongzheng emperor, came to Mount Wutai to set up regular long-life prayers at the mountain on the full and new moon of each month.[31]

With the direct involvement of Qing authorities in the affairs of Central Tibet in the eighteenth century, the *jasagh* lamas at Mount Wutai practically cease to be mentioned in the records. In general, vacancies for the position of the Mount Wutai *jasagh* lama were to be filled by a *khenpo* (Ch. *kanbu*) sent from Tibet to the capital. Once in this position, the Mount Wutai *jasagh* lama appointed the other monastic officials at the mountain.[32] A temple inscription from 1768 mentions that the Dalai Lama ordered the *jasagh* lama to repair one of the Mount Wutai temples in 1734. This inscription was carried out under the authority of the imperially designated *jasagh dalama* (*Jinming zhasake dalama*) Gali chenpian'er. This was almost certainly the same man who was mentioned in the 1755 gazetteer as Mount Wutai's imperially designated seal-wielding *jasagh* lama (*Jinming Wutaishan zhangyin zhasake lama*), Gali chenpin.[33] Other specific references to the succeeding generations of *jasagh* lamas are difficult to come by until the mid-twentieth century when these lamas were again to prove essential in communications between China and Tibet.

Once the Qing government extended its power into Tibetan regions in Qinghai and Central Tibet in the eighteenth century, an entirely new group of lamas born on the borderlands between the two countries served as intermediaries between the court and Tibet. The second Changja Qutughtu (Rölpé Dorjé, 1717–1786) was to serve as the Qianlong emperor's trusted envoy to Tibet as early as 1734–35. Having succeeded in providing good service to the emperor, the Changja Qutughtu became established as the most important lama at the capital for the duration of his life. He was instrumental in founding Yonghegong as a monastic training college for Mongol, Manchu, and Chinese monks in 1744. Like the imperial palace-temple at Mount Wutai, Yonghegong combined an imperial palace (in this case, the former residence of the Yongzheng emperor) with a Tibetan Buddhist monastery. From its founding and into the Republican period, the successive Dalai Lamas or their regents sent learned lamas from Tibet to run the monastery and teach its lamas as well as the dynastic family. These Tibetan appointees oversaw the Mongol monks of the imperial Yonghegong monastery and served as one of Beijing's four *jasagh* lamas.[34] In this post the leading lama was accompanied by a lower-ranking monk-official from the Dalai Lama's secretariat office and a translator. These Lhasa-appointed monk-officials served the imperial family as preceptors in Tibetan language and Buddhist teachings.[35] The Forbidden City's Zhongzhengdian, with its Sutra Recitation office, was another imperially sponsored temple that became a crucial center for the dynasty's relations with Tibetan Buddhists. Completely outside the control or oversight of Chinese officials and court, this temple was free to patronize lamas at the capital and manufacture Buddhist paraphernalia as gifts for lamas throughout the empire. This "nucleus of Tibetan Buddhist activities at court," as Rawski called it, was under the jurisdiction of the Imperial Household Department, not the Court for Managing the Frontiers.[36]

The Imperial Household's relations with Tibetan Buddhists at the court demonstrate that the Court for Managing the Frontiers was a useful administrative mechanism, but not the only agency for dealing with Tibetan Buddhists. As Naquin described the situation, "Lamas, monasteries, and the affairs of Central Asia were the business of the throne, not the regular bureaucracy."[37] The Imperial Household played an especially important role in handling religious and financial, as opposed to administrative, lama affairs. The *Record of Imperial Household Ceremonies* (*Neiwufu chudian cheng'an*) indicates that recitations held at Yonghegong and Zhongzhengdian were funded through another of the Imperial City's Tibetan Buddhist temples, Hongrensi.[38] The leaders and staff of both Yonghegong and Zhongzhengdian were rewarded directly by the imperial palace, in addition to their regular stipends from the Court for Managing the Frontiers, as recorded in the *Imperially Commissioned Current Palace Regulations*. Susan Naquin noted that it was unusual that Yonghegong "was supervised jointly by the Imperial Household and the Lifanyuan."[39] The imperial court was quite willing to use unusual arrangements to work with the Tibetans. For example, the Xining *amban* (under the Imperial Household), the Boards of War and Works, and provincial officials were also responsible for handling different aspects of the Tibetan relations with the court.[40]

Thus, contrary to Chia Ning's assessment that the "Li-fan Yuan organized religious affairs in these [Tibetan Buddhist] temples and provided the connection between the lamas and the Ch'ing court,"[41] the Court for Managing the Frontiers (*Lifanyuan*) was clearly not the only government body that handled relations with Tibet and its Buddhist envoys.[42] Instead, it was merely one of a number of existing mechanisms for dealing with outsiders. The Court for Managing the Frontiers also handled relations with Russia until the mid-nineteenth century. Originally created to deal with the Mongols, the court devoted most of its statutory regulations (fifty-five *juan* out of sixty-eight) to that end. This may explain why William Mayers and G.M.H. Playfair translated Lifanyuan as the Mongol Superintendency when they described the Qing administration in 1897.[43] In contrast, a mere five *juan* of statutes governing Lama affairs (*Lama shili*) were appended to these basic regulations, and many of these were also directed specifically at Mongol lamas. Only two *juan* discussed the system of communication with Tibet (*Xizang tongzhi*), which was followed by a single *juan* dealing with Russian statutes.[44] Given this weak link to the Court for Managing the Frontiers, Russia was the first to fall out of the orbit of the court when international diplomacy forced the Qing court to create the Foreign Affairs Office (Zongli yamen).

Tibet, in a similarly tenuous position vis-à-vis the weakening empire, was very nearly separated from the imperial domains by the Russian intrigues in 1902 and the British invasion of 1904.[45] The 1906 transformation of the Lifanyuan into the Lifanbu (most frequently called the Colonial Office, because of its use of colonialist strategies) allowed the empire to hold on to Tibet for a few more years. However, with the demise of the Qing empire, the rapid succession of bureaucracies that replaced the Lifanbu were all equally ineffective at keeping up relations with Tibet.[46] Although these bureaucracies registered Tibetan Buddhist lamas and staff in and around the capital for at least a few years, Central Tibet maintained an aloof de facto independence.[47] Whatever links the Imperial Household managed to preserve with Tibetan lamas after the abdication of the emperor, they were terminated by the 1924 "revision" of the Articles for Favorable Treatment. The revised articles drove the dynastic family out of the imperial city and drastically reduced their annual subsidy, ensuring that they could no longer support Tibetan Buddhists who had served the dynasty.[48]

Nevertheless, the Tibetan government continued to appoint officials to these traditional positions, and they were to play a significant role in linking the Chinese Nationalist government with the Tibetan government after 1927. As I discuss in chapter 3, the traditions established in the first century of Manchu rule in China continued to influence twentieth-century politics. When the Qing dynasty ruled China, initially the emperor handled relations with Tibet directly. Later, imperial government organs such as the Imperial Household and the Court for Managing the Frontiers facilitated them. Yet the bureaucratic routines set in place could never fully replace the personal relationship between Tibetan envoys and the rulers of China. For this reason, the centrality of Tibetan lamas as envoys to the Qing court endured even after the dynasty abdicated rule of China.

Traditions That Divided Tibet from China Proper

Unlike the contentious debates encountered in the historical treatments of Tibet's political or legal status, the history of cultural relations between China and Tibet is relatively uncomplicated: especially compared to the cultural her-

itage shared among East Asian countries, there was little shared culture between
the Chinese and Tibetans until after 1959. A great divide of traditions, stereotypes, and legal precedents separated Chinese and Tibetan Buddhists from viewing each other as co-religionists. A language and knowledge barrier, which the
Qing government only trained certain individuals to overcome, helped keep
Chinese and Tibetans ignorant of each other's culture. Finally, the efforts of the
Qing government to protect borderland peoples from the incursion of Chinese
traders and settlers were most effective when combined with Central Tibet's forbidding geography. Few Chinese settled in Tibet prior to the 1950s, and few of
those who did ever returned home to China to share what they had learned.
This combination of religious, linguistic, governmental, and geographic barriers
between China and Tibet resulted in a great cultural divide that would only partially be bridged in the late twentieth century.

Differing Religious Traditions

Although Republican and even Communist sources on Sino-Tibetan relations tend to emphasize a shared Buddhist heritage, they usually neglect to mention substantive exchanges prior to the 1920s. They also fail to explain why
Chinese Buddhism failed to establish institutional roots in Tibet or why it is that
Tibetan Buddhism became known in China as "the teaching of the lamas" (*lama
jiao*) and, as such, was disparaged as a degenerate distortion of Buddhism. In
describing some of the differences between these religious traditions, I will focus
on the general features that distinguish Chinese and Tibetan Buddhist traditions
from each other. Although this gap in knowledge about the religious exchanges
between China and Tibet is starting to be addressed by scholars of Buddhism
today, early twentieth-century knowledge of these exchanges was limited to the
handful of prominent lamas that appeared at the Mongol Yuan, Chinese Ming,
and Manchu Qing courts.[49] Far from altering the course of Chinese or Tibetan
Buddhist traditions, the prominence accorded to these lamas tended to so offend
Chinese sensibility that divisions between Chinese and Tibetan Buddhists, at
least in orthodox settings, were strengthened. There were certainly exceptions to
this general rule, but I present the matter in its simplest terms here because this
is how most Chinese and Tibetan Buddhists seem to have understood the distinctions between their religious traditions in early twentieth-century China.
The work of Holmes Welch and even John Blofeld reflects much of this popular understanding of the divisions between these forms of Buddhism.[50] Like
these two pioneer researchers of modern Asian Buddhism, I do not insist so
much on the validity of these distinctions as I acknowledge that they seemed to
shape the mindset of many Buddhists in Asia at the time.

In the early twentieth century, modern Chinese Buddhists like Taixu used a tripartite division to describe Buddhist doctrinal differences. Taixu believed that there were three classes of Buddhism in the world, and he wanted all three to be included in a reformed Chinese Buddhism. In this respect, China was well represented only in terms of the Mahayana tradition. In particular, he and his students saw Chan and Pure Land practices as the most prominent to shape Chinese Buddhism in the modern period. He made an effort to bring elements of the Theravada tradition into China through an exchange of teachers and students between Ceylon (Sri Lanka) and China.[51] As for the Tantrayana tradition, some of Taixu's students went to Japan to study the esoteric traditions that had been transmitted there from China in the Tang, but mostly they felt that the esoteric vehicle (*micheng*) was truly preserved only in Tibet.[52] Taixu and his students were exceptional in their interest in merging all three of these traditions, but they clearly saw the Tibetan tradition as esoteric and different from their own.

In general, the leaders of these separate traditions did not value the teachings and practices of the others. In Tibet, at least in the orthodox strain of the Gelukpa school, the memory of one eighth-century Chinese Buddhist teacher (merely called *hwa-shang*, from Ch. *hesheng*, monk) still served as the straw man centuries later for exemplifying the inefficacy of the (purported) lack of respect for textual studies and conceptual thought in Chan practice.[53] Similarly, many Chinese developed a particularly strong aversion to Tibetan Buddhist esoteric practices after Mongol rule in the Yuan dynasty. The fall of the Yuan empire was frequently associated with the dissolute Buddhist practices that were rumored to have taken place at the court.[54] The elaborate Tibetan Buddhist meditations, practices, and their associated mandalas and mantras—generally conveyed in private to advanced Buddhist practitioners—were adopted by the Mongols in the Yuan and Qing periods, as well as by certain Chinese (during the Ming) and Manchu emperors. These practices were viewed with contempt by most Chinese officials and literati.[55] For example, when the Ming dynasty's Zhengde emperor tried to invite a Tibetan incarnation to court, his top advisers protested that "this religion [was] 'wildly heterodox and unorthodox'" (*xiewang bu jing*).[56] In fact, the Ming dynasty was the first to create legal boundaries between Chinese and Tibetan beliefs. In her study of Peking, Naquin informs us that "by law, no Chinese (*Hanren*) was permitted to become a Tibetan Buddhist monk." This barrier weakened over time, but it was not widely overcome until the mid-twentieth century.[57] Although "the early Ming prohibition against Chinese (*Hanren*) who studied Tibetan Buddhism seems to have been rescinded, and imperial attempts to keep lamas housed in the large monasteries and prevent unseemly contact with lay people may not have been very successful," we still have no detailed information on Chinese, especially lay Chinese, studying Tibetan Buddhism until the Republican period.[58]

Monastic Chinese interest in Tibetan Buddhist teachings is hinted at in key imperial sites in the Qing dynasty, but real cultural exchange appears limited. For example, three hundred Chinese monks (Tib. *Rgya ban ri khrod pa*, Ch. *Han seng qingxiu zhe*) came from Mount Wutai to Beijing to meet with the Dalai Lama in 1653.[59] Also during the Qing period some of the Tibetan Buddhist leadership in and around Beijing were ethnic Chinese (*Han*) monk officials. These included one of Beijing's four leading lamas and part of the staff of Yonghegong. These Chinese monk-officials were explicitly associated with managerial, and not teaching, duties, as was the case with Mongol appointees.[60] Thus, from the Yuan to the Qing, the religious exchange between China and Tibet was characterized by the religious culture of Tibet extending in a limited way into Chinese regions in response to patronage by Mongol, the occasional Chinese, and Manchu emperors.

Documented cultural exchange between Qing China and Tibet outside the scope of religious teachings was extremely limited. Luciano Petech discussed the nature of influence between these two cultures in his *China and Tibet in the Early Eighteenth Century*. He dismissed any real literary influence between China and Tibet. In his analysis, aside from a fair number of words borrowed from the Chinese language, the only areas of rather limited influence from China were on the state dress and the Chinese cooking adopted by the Tibetan nobility. He concluded that the most profound influence Chinese culture had on the culture of Tibet was in the field of painting and, to a lesser degree, architecture. These arts were applied almost exclusively to religious purposes in Tibet; thus the effect of Manchu and Mongol patronage may explain the relatively larger role in transforming these arts. As for Tibetan cultural influence on China, Tibetan temple architecture as well as Buddhist images and scriptures certainly had a high-profile appearance in and around the court and all along the northern borderlands. Aside from these relatively minor details, no real cultural interaction between the Chinese and Tibetans up to the end of the Qing period has yet been the focus of sustained scholarly research.[61]

Qing Knowledge of Tibet

One must examine the nature of Qing knowledge and experience in Tibet to understand why modern China could not initially maintain the relations with Tibet that had endured for the previous centuries. Qing techniques for dealing with Inner Asians such as Tibetan Buddhists often excluded Chinese people entirely. Rawski has noted that "Manchu officials were required to communicate in Manchu and documents relating to the imperial lineage, banner affairs, and Inner Asian military matters were often written only in Manchu."[62] In the case of Tibet, early communications were only partially committed to writing, with a portion to be transmitted orally.[63] This may have changed after 1657, when the Qing court established the Tibetan School (*Tanggute guanxue*) in order to train Mongols to do the clerical and translation work of the Court for Managing the Frontiers.[64] Tibetan language training, like the number of registered lamas in the capital, seems to have reached its peak in the eighteenth century.[65] The almost exclusive appointment of Mongols and Manchus to positions of leadership with the Court for Managing the Frontiers and as *amban*s in Tibet left the Chinese largely ignorant of the nature of Qing-Tibetan relations, at least until the late Qing period.[66]

The only accounts of Chinese who knew the Tibetan language date from the last decades of Qing rule. The most detailed account left by a Chinese who lived in Tibet in the Qing period was the biography of Zhen Canzhi (1893–?), who served as a translator in the Lhasa *amban*'s office. His father had been chief secretary to the *amban,* so Zhen's work provides unique insights into the lives of long-term Chinese residents in Tibet.[67] Zhen remarked that "in order to understand a foreign nation you must speak the language of its subjects and study their history and religion." However, very few Chinese accomplished this goal in the Qing or even early Republican period. Moreover, Zhen's knowledge was lost to the Chinese government, because he was employed by Christian missionaries in Sikkim when he left Tibet.[68] Zhang Yintang, the first Chinese civil official to serve in Tibet, also wrote an account of his time in Tibet (1906–1910).[69] Another exceptional figure was the Lhasa-born Tibetan Muslim, Liu Manqing.[70] She served as a semi-official Republican envoy to Tibet. The very fact that the Chinese government employed a woman, quite exceptional in the 1930s, for a diplomatic role indicates just how uncommon such intermediaries were. The literary record of these rare intermediaries was not to become widely available until long after Qing rule ended in Tibet.

Michel Foucault, in his book *Power/Knowledge,* made the case that in modern times, "it is impossible to govern a State without knowing its population."[71] Although he was discussing the exercise of power in modern Europe, the association of knowledge of a people with the power to control a population was also applied in the European colonial experience. Such was not the case with the Qing exercise of power in Tibet.[72] In fact, there was an incredible scarcity of information on Tibet produced by or accessible to Chinese in the late nineteenth and early twentieth centuries. Given Foucault's model, it is no wonder that the Chinese lost control of Tibet with the fall of the Qing.

The first two centuries of Qing influence in Tibet produced only a handful of works that dealt with Tibet, whether as part of encyclopedic surveys or as works specifically dedicated to Tibet. An excellent study of what was available to a well-informed scholar of China and Tibet in the late nineteenth century illustrates the paucity of Chinese language resources on Tibet. William Woodville Rockhill, American minister to China and explorer of Tibet, explained that, in preparation for translating a "Topographical Description of Tibet" (*Wei-Zang tu zhi*), he went through "all the procurable publications on the subject" while in Beijing for four years. He further elaborated that in supplementing his translation he employed "all Chinese works published down to the present day [ca. 1891]." These sources, amassed over a century and a half of Qing dominion over Tibet, amount to six texts dedicated solely to Tibet and seven more general works that treat Tibetan topics within their purview (whether administrative, historical, or geographical). No doubt a comparison with the British sources on Indian topics (in the period contemporaneous with the Qing presence in Tibet) would reveal a startling contrast to this paucity. Despite Tibet having been part of the Qing empire for so long, the scarcity of Chinese language information available on Tibet was very comparable to that which D. R. Howland found for Japan in the same period, as detailed in his *Borders of Chinese Civilization*.[73] This was because Tibet, like Japan, had largely remained beyond the cultural borders of China.

Moreover, Rockhill, a political figure with a substantial budget and a collector for the Library of Congress, was ideally positioned to gain access to all publicly available resources on Tibet. He could afford to purchase multivolume sets of Chinese sources such as the dynastic histories of the Tang and Ming periods or the Qing dynastic gazetteer (*Da Qing yi tong zhi* in five hundred volumes) that were certainly not readily available to most Chinese. Rockhill credited these sources for providing "rich materials for a better knowledge of Tibet . . . [compared to] the rather meager notes and often hearsay information furnished by European and Indian explorers."[74] How little could he have expected the great change in Western knowledge of Tibet that coincided with the British invasion of Tibet in 1904, shortly after he wrote those words. The sum total of works produced in 150 years of Qing dominion in Tibet was quickly surpassed by the scholarly knowledge about Tibet generated by European and Indian scholars in the final decade of the nineteenth century and the first decades of the twentieth century.

Furthermore, the scope of even the best Qing resources on Tibet was extremely narrow. For the most part they were of military or trade value only, listing travel routes and local products. No readily accessible dictionary or Chinese language grammar existed for learning the Tibetan language. No work gave more than passing notice to the history or religion of Tibet. In sum, these materials reveal the truly limited nature of Qing knowledge about Tibet, which might be compared to knowing about the trade routes and products of medieval

Europe without knowing Latin or much about Catholicism. Yet the Chinese government-sponsored acquisition of further knowledge about Tibet (as a goal of the Chinese government) would not arise until after the Nationalist Party (*Guomindang*) controlled China.

Multiethnic Imperial Tradition

The final imperial tradition that influenced modern Sino-Tibetan relations was the multiethnic composition of many of the empires based in China over the centuries. Typically this tradition is viewed as foreshadowing a modern discourse of multiethnic unity. However, this imperial tradition was more often associated with enforcing divisions and disparities between groups of people. The link between imperial tradition and modern discourse is most often made with regard to the Qing empire. The empire, especially as it was constituted under the Qianlong emperor, is often loosely associated with the Chinese Republican rhetoric of the "*wuzu gonghe.*" This term is variously translated as the "Republic of Five Races" or the "Five Races Harmoniously Joined." The discrepancy between translations shows that the concept could be understood both as a political system, in which five races were joined in a single state structure, or as a racial ideal, in which case the "harmonious" links took priority over any particular conception of state structure. The source of the idea of the *wuzu gonghe* is almost invariably traced to the Qianlong reign of the Qing dynasty. However, despite the apparent correspondence in the multiethnic conceptions of the state in the imperial and Republican periods, they could scarcely be more different. The case of the Republican state is detailed in the next chapter. Here I concentrate on the Qing.

The Qing emperors sought submission of the frontier elites (Manchu tribal leaders, Mongol clergy and nobility, Tibetan clergy and nobility, and Muslim *begs*) and went to great lengths to segregate these groups from their Chinese officials and subjects. The Willow Palisade, separating Manchuria from China Proper, is just the best known, if least successful, of the protective measures put in place to limit Chinese migration into Inner Asia. Statutes forbidding intermarriage between Chinese and Inner Asians (particularly Manchus and Mongols) constituted another mechanism for enforcing cultural boundaries.[75] I suspect that these barriers were erected to avoid the complications that had plagued other "conquest" dynasties—the "weakening" of the Liao and Jin elites through intermarriage and acculturation, the ethnic tensions that grew up between Mongols and Chinese during the Yuan, and the resentment against Tibetan Buddhists so prominent at the end of the Yuan and into the Ming dynasty.

But what benefit did the Qing emperors reap from these efforts? Pamela Crossley has argued in her *Translucent Mirror* that five constituencies (Manchu, Mongol, Chinese, Tibetan, and Turkistani) were most frequently designated as central to the Qing dynasty in monumental inscriptions at key imperial sites such as Beijing and Jehol. The value of these constituencies was that each represented a powerful and distinct cultural tradition (a civilization) that held sway over a large number of diverse peoples. That a group possessed a written language was not sufficient cause for inclusion; for example, the Yi had a script which was not elevated to the position of these central five.[76] Instead, as Crossley noted, history was a crucial aspect in determining the value of a constituency. Of central importance was the power of a particular culture to influence history.[77] The Manchus had the dynastic claim to power, but they had only recently entered into the making of history in Asia. Thus they sought legitimacy from a variety of historically potent cultural legacies. They laid claim to the Chinese conception of the mandate of Heaven and utilized the Confucian rituals associated with ruling China. Just as essential to their claim to legitimacy was the legacy of the Mongol empire, which was joined to the Manchu dynasty by marriage, as well as by tokens of power (the Yuan jade seal, a Yuan Buddhist image housed in the Mahakala complex in Mukden and later Beijing). Tibetan Buddhist culture also possessed the potential for providing legitimacy for rivals to the Qing dynasty.[78] Redirecting this legitimacy toward the Manjugosha (Manchu) emperor was, as Farquhar described, an essential aspect of Qing rulership.[79] The Turkestani culture of Central Asia was not such a crucial aspect of Qing rule but nevertheless represented an alternate civilization that could not be ruled on the basis of Confucian ideals. Each of these five groups had certain cultural elements that had the power to extend legitimacy both within its own region and often beyond its ethnic territory.

The Qing dynasty tried to garner the support of each of these groups. The early Manchu successes had brought many Mongols and Chinese willingly under their sway. But for more than a century after the dynasty settled in China, the Manchu claim to the Mongol imperial legacy was contested by the Zungars in the west. Tibetan Buddhist culture was shared by Mongols and Zungars, and was used to legitimize rival claimants to Qing Inner Asia dominion (witness Ligdan Khan and Galdan). Islam was a critical factor in linking the Muslim subjects of the Qing empire to the Central Asian city-states to the west. For much of the Qing empire, the Confucian model of rulership might suffice, but these cultural regions required special treatment. Whereas the Miao, Yi, and dozens of other distinct peoples had no comparable indigenous systems to compete with being governed by the powerful Qing dynasty, Tibetans and Mongols had alternate expectations of legitimacy that could threaten, or be incorporated into, the

Qing dynastic system. This factor was central to the dynasty's special treatment of these two groups.

Essential to maintaining the legitimacy these cultural groups could assign to the Qing dynasty was a preservation of the distinctiveness of each culture. For this reason, the idea that Qing rulers "unified" these groups must be understood as James Millward described it: the relations were organized vertically between the dynasty and its separate constituent elements.[80] In no sense were these five groups merged as a unified group. The Qing interest in maintaining these cultural divisions became almost reflexive by the end of the dynasty, even if it had no practical ideological value at that time. For example, as late as 1902, when the Manchu leadership was considering turning over control of Tibet to the Russians, they included clauses in the drafted agreement that would have barred Christian missionaries from Tibet and protected Tibetan temples and sacred sites from destruction.[81]

Whether they bound Tibetan and dynastic elites together or separated Tibetans from the Chinese, imperial traditions were potent forces in managing relations between the Tibetan elites and the ruling dynasties of China. Religious patronage, Tibetan conceptions of the union of religion and politics, and religious envoys between China and Tibet remained central to managing Sino-Tibetan relations in the postimperial period. On the other hand, the traditional barriers between Chinese and Tibetans would take the better part of a century to overcome. The global conceptions of nationalism, race, and religion that were central to the Chinese efforts to dismantle the cultural divide between China and Tibet are discussed in the following two chapters.

2. Global Forces in Asia (1870s–1910s)

RUSSIAN AND BRITISH commercial interests and Chinese nationalist and racial ideologies (the result of the encounter with European and Japanese imperial power) ultimately resulted in a shift in the relations between the elites of the Qing empire and the Tibetan Buddhist cultural world. The Russians and British were also engaged in nationalistic intrigues, but financial exploitation was their primary interest in Tibet. By the same token, the Chinese had commercial interests in Tibet; however, Chinese nationalists were most concerned with preserving what they perceived as the territorial integrity of a beleaguered Chinese nation. Anthony Smith has suggested that "the two trajectories of the rise of capital and the emergence of the nation are better kept apart," yet he recognized that "there is indeed a close parallel in the periodization of the rise of both the nation and of capital to world hegemony, and it is not an accidental one."[1] This chapter attends to the clear link between the rise of Western imperial and commercial plans for Tibet and the deployment of nationalist ideology to try to reconfigure Tibet's relations with China Proper. I also consider the introduction of racial ideology to China and the impact this modern discourse had on Chinese perceptions of their relations with Tibetans.

Russian designs on Tibet drew the British to Lhasa, and the 1904 British invasion drove Tibet into the global arena of contested nation-states. The British claimed the threat of Russian influence in Tibet and the enforcement of previous treaties as the principal justifications for their invasion. However, the leader of the British "mission" described the real motive as the means to secure long-desired free trade between British India and Tibet. This invasion resulted in a major shift in the relations of the Tibetans with their nominal overlord, the Qing empire. Chinese officials, especially those appointed to Tibet and Sichuan, were quick to respond to the British threat and were determined to bring Tibet firmly under the control of China. In the process of accomplishing this goal, these ethnic Chinese tried to impose cultural and political reforms on the Tibetans. The appointment of such nationalist Chinese officials ruptured the delicate relationship that the Manchu and Mongol representatives of the Qing empire had maintained with the Tibetan Buddhist elite for almost two centuries. The result, de facto Tibetan independence, could hardly have been more distant from the goals of the Chinese but served the interests of the British well enough. Later, Republican government officials may have been convinced by their own national and racial discourse of the unity of the Republic of the Five Races (*Wuzu Gongheguo*). However, the de facto independence of Central Tibet clearly demonstrated that such ideas had no currency in Tibet. During the turbulent years of the Chinese Republic the Chinese could do little but exploit every internal problem of the nascent Tibetan nation-state to challenge the independence they had helped provoke.

Western Imperialist Commercial Interests in Tibet

The status quo of Qing frontiers was threatened when the British became involved with Tibet, the most loosely ruled of the Qing empire's satellite dependencies. The negotiations with Tibetans began as early as the late eighteenth century, with diplomatic relations between the representatives of the British East India Company and the Panchen Lama. When this initial contact occurred, the Manchu and Mongol representatives of the Qing empire and the ruling Tibetans in Lhasa closed ranks to maintain an Asian interstate system that was beneficial to the elites of both states. The result was that European envoys, and even most travelers, were kept out of Lhasa for more than one hundred years.

This initial contact deserves some attention, as it set the precedent for the British interest in Tibet. First, it should be noted that the contact was the result of British involvement in the military affairs—and thereby interstate relations—of Asia. In 1772 the British East India Company, then controlling Bengal, came to the aid of the neighboring state of Cooch Bihar in resisting the aggression of Bhutanese forces. The Bhutanese, in turn, enlisted the diplomatic intercession of the sixth Panchen Lama, Penden Yeshé (1738–1780). This gave the British their first opportunity for direct communication with Tibetans, which they determined should result in "a general treaty of amity and commerce between Bengal and Tibet."[2] At this point the British knew very little about Tibet and treated the Panchen Lama as more of an authority than his position actually merited. In fact, they thought of Tibet and Bhutan as a single polity, and although they had their sights set on commerce with the political center of Tibet (Lhasa, in the province of Ü), they hoped to secure an agreement merely by dealing with a powerful prelate in the neighboring province of Tsang. The British East India agent was instructed as follows:

The design of your mission is to open equal communication of trade between the inhabitants of Bhutan [Tibet] and Bengal. . . .You will take with you samples, for a trial of such articles of commerce as may be sent from this country. . . . And will diligently inform yourself of the manufactures, productions, goods, introduced by the intercourse with other countries, which are to be procured in Bhutan.[3]

British military power in this case had brought them into contact with a powerful Tibetan, but the Lhasa authorities could not be prevailed upon to open "free commercial communication" with people south of the Himalayas. In fact, the two southern powers—the British in Bengal and the Gurkhas of Nepal—seem to have been linked in the minds of the Lhasa authorities and the Qing overseers there. The Gurkha invasions of Tibet in the following decades confirmed the worst fears of the Lhasa and Beijing elites and led to a firm closure of the southern border to any possibility of unhindered trade with the British.[4]

Unpleasant as this was to the British, this limitation did not indicate a strictly isolationist policy for Tibet. In fact, Tibetans were trading with people in all directions. A 10 percent duty was levied on all goods entering Tibet, whether from China, Nepal, Bhutan, or British India.[5] Kashmiri, Nepalese, Mongolian, Muslim Hui, and Chinese traders were welcome in Central Tibet, while Tibetans traded goods directly with the Bhutanese, Ladakhis, and other culturally Tibetan peoples on the southern side of the Himalayas.[6] The British were well aware of these facts and wanted to establish themselves on an equal basis within this system of Asian interstate commerce.

What the British did not understand was that the Tibetan Buddhist elites also profited greatly from a tea-trade monopoly with China, from the direct patronage of the Qing court, and from rich donations made by Tibetan monasteries located in regions more directly controlled by the Qing empire. In effect, the Tibetans really only declined to become involved in what appeared to them to be small and inconsequential trade, through Sikkim, with a very problematic people. Opening trade with the British would have occasioned a challenge to an Asian interstate system that was functioning well. Moreover, every region to which Tibetan traders regularly traveled could be considered Buddhist, whereas India was perceived to have fallen to the Muslims long before. Certainly Tibetans were willing enough to deal with Muslims when they came to Tibet, so religion could not have been the sole limiting factor. The Tibetans instead pleaded that the Qing emperor would be displeased with the trade and that the weather in India was too hot for Tibetan traders. In the end, it seems that the Lhasa elites just saw too little incentive in open commerce with the British.[7] In fact, through the good services of the Bhutanese,

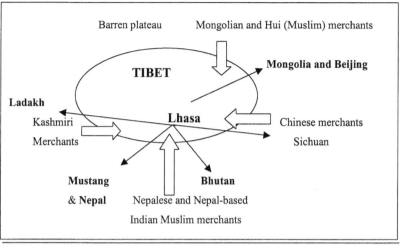

Key:

———————→ indicates direction of Tibetan trade with bordering regions

⟹ indicates direction of foreign trade with Tibet

Figure 2.1 Commercial Relations Between Tibet and Its Neighbors

the Tibetans could get all they wished of the products of Bengal without having to deal directly with the British.[8]

Negotiating with China to Get to Tibet

The focus on trade had been natural for the British East India Company, yet this commercial model of interstate relations was also maintained by the British government when it started to govern India directly in 1859. The British had let the matter of trade with Tibet rest for almost a century until 1873, when the growing tea trade in British India was seeking new markets. The strict embargo on tea to Tibet pained the British, as they had been made aware almost a century before that individual Tibetan traders often dealt in annual tea trading valued up to £30,000.[9] By the 1890s the tea trade with Sichuan alone was worth more than £148,000 and moved some ten million pounds of tea into Tibet every year.[10] In addition, industrial Britain was seeking new markets and new supplies of raw materials: "besides tea, the Bengal Government thought that Manchester and Birmingham goods and Indian indigo would find a market in Tibet, and that we should receive in return much wool, sheep, cattle, walnuts, *etc from Tibet*

Tibetan clothes, and other commodities."[11] In *Tibet and the British Raj*, Alex McKay explained that the British government at home and in India had come "under the pressure from powerful trading lobbies waiting to open Tibet to free trade."[12] Though the British government did not always act as quickly as these lobbies would have liked, it generally did accept the task of advancing trade opportunities.

In the interest of overcoming the resistance that had kept the British out of Tibet for the past century—a resistance that had consistently been explained as occasioned by a desire not to offend the Qing emperor—the British secured the Chefu convention with the Qing government in 1876. This convention, entered into for the explicit purpose of protecting and aiding British exploratory missions to Tibet, proved to be completely useless. The Qing authorities encountered resistance from the Tibetans when they tried to exact the corvée transport labor even for their own *ambans*.[13] They could provide no such services for the British nor even grant them access to Tibet, though they were surely happy not to cooperate with the British plans for expanding their commerce into Tibet.

The British refused to ignore or forget the potential market of Tibet's "three million tea drinkers" and used international boundary disputes to try to exact the desired trade privileges. When Tibetan soldiers crossed an unmanned border some eighteen miles into the British protectorate of Sikkim in 1886, the British cited this Tibetan "aggression" as the cause for a renewed effort at settling affairs with Tibet. Agreements signed with the Qing court in 1890 and 1893 were directed at settling these border and trade relations with Tibet. Despite the fact that the excuse for negotiating the treaties was the resolution of territorial issues, the British were satisfied as soon as they secured trade privileges. As long as "the returns of trade between British territory and Tibet showed a marked increase," the British were willing to dismiss any contestation of the borders.[14] Trade clearly came before territorial concerns for the British. Thus, for nearly a quarter of a century, the British in India were content to see rising market returns.[15] The issues of deciding the exact borders, of direct communication with the Tibetans, and of access to the government in Lhasa were of insufficient importance to demand military attention from the British.

The Tibetans Seek Alternatives

For more than a century, then, the Lhasa-based Buddhist leaders of Tibet had used the excuse of Qing overlordship to keep out the threat of the British. However, as the Qing empire was weakened by internal revolts and external pressures, this screen was failing to guard the Tibetans from the incursions of the British. The Qing government had three times (1876, 1890, and 1893) signed away the rights of Tibet to protect itself from British interests. As the British found, the Tibetan elites were nevertheless successful in protecting their own interests, no doubt with the tacit support of the Qing court. However, when the possibility of a new patron was presented through the intermediary of the (Russian) Buriat Mongolian monk Dorjiev (1854–1938), the thirteenth Dalai Lama, Tupten Gyatso (1876–1933), expressed a cautious interest. Numerous Buriat and Kalmyck Buddhists from Russia entered Tibet as pilgrims and students (and sometimes spies as the British suspected), especially in the late nineteenth and early twentieth centuries.[16] The Tibetan monastic leaders, far from being isolated from world politics, were making an effort to negotiate their relations with the modern powers that were encroaching from all directions.

In fact, the first signs of Tibetan nationalism are associated with the year 1895, when the thirteenth Dalai Lama came to majority and the Qing empire was defeated in a war with Japan. One account held that the thirteenth Dalai Lama was the first Dalai Lama to reach maturity in a century and a half because the Tibetan "national party [was] incensed at the continual interference of China in the government of the country," and thus this "party" supported the Dalai Lama becoming a real leader for Tibetan interests.[17] In discussions with the Dalai Lama's representative at the Sikkim border, a British officer concluded that the 1895 Tibetan transgression of the Sikkim border "symbolized a spirit of Tibetan nationalism." Apparently the Tibetans no longer felt "bound by a treaty which had been negotiated on their behalf by Britain and China."[18] From this point on the Dalai Lama started to ignore the Qing representative in Tibet. In 1895–96 the Dalai Lama founded an arsenal in Lhasa that made modern rifles in order to equip a Tibetan national army.[19] Still, no drastic measures to eliminate the Qing influence from Tibet were made for almost two decades. Similar developments were taking place in Korea, where the Japanese were the neighboring, and nascent, empire seeking to wrest Korea's independence from the Qing empire, through treaties. Like the Koreans, the Tibetans tried to play two empires off against each other to their own advantage.[20] The Qing imperial relations with Tibet served as a convenient excuse for avoiding diplomatic relations with the British. But as power slipped from the Qing empire, the Tibetans considered their options.

The Tibetan elites became divided into factions based on which power they thought held the most promise for advancing their interests. Some advocated maintaining relations with the Qing empire, as Tibetans viewed the Qing as a Buddhist dynasty; some saw establishing regular relations with British India as the best option for advancing Tibetan interests in the modern world; and others felt that the Russian empire offered the best of both worlds: the protection of a modern European empire that ruled over a significant Tibetan Buddhist population.[21] The Dalai Lama's most knowledgeable adviser on European affairs was none other than Dorjiev, who, in 1898, had returned to Tibet from France (via British India) in order to consult with the Dalai Lama. The lama was convinced by Dorjiev to seek Russian support for Tibet. When Dorjiev returned from his 1900 meeting with Tsar Nicholas II, the Dalai Lama apparently said that, "Tibet had found its patron, more [strong] and more reliable than China."[22] These amicable relations were to continue for some years, and a literature grew up in Tibetan and Russian that linked Russia and its imperial family with the messianic Tibetan concept of the mythical kingdom of Shambhala.[23]

Dorjiev's ideas included a pan-Mongolism that was attractive to both the Russians and the Tibetans. In this scenario the Russians would support Tibetan Buddhism for the same reason the Manchus had in the early years of the Qing dynasty: being the principal patron of the Dalai Lama would confer the allegiance of the Mongol adherents of Tibetan Buddhism on that patron. Thus, just as Tibet was losing the protection of the Qing empire, Dorjiev convinced the Dalai Lama that there was a new protector for Tibetan Buddhist interests. The tsar promised aid to the Tibetans, which was interpreted as a promise of protection against British incursions.[24]

When pressed by the British about their relations with the Tibetans, the Russians were quick to explain that Dorjiev's mission was "of the same character as those sent by the Pope to the faithful in foreign lands." This dismissive comment was paired with the statement that Dorjiev merely "came occasionally to Russia with the object . . . of making money collections for his [Gelukpa] Order from the numerous Buddhists in the Russian Empire."[25] The collections of such funds were of real significance to Lhasa Tibetans. Through the donations of the Russian faithful, the central monasteries of Tibet had far more to gain than they did from British trade.[26] The religious economy of Tibet was no small matter, as a rich artistic and literary culture and tens of thousands of monks depended upon the donations of the faithful. Sir Francis Younghusband, the military leader of Britain's 1904 invasion of Tibet, at least displayed an astute awareness of the importance of Dorjiev's mission to Russia, whatever its official character. He saw that the Russian interest emulated that of the early Qing empire and was fully cognizant of the fact that religion and politics were clearly united in the Tibetan view.[27]

The British Invasion: Trade Privileges at Last

British fears were calmed by Russian assurances until 1902, when the Russian government tried to negotiate political and commercial rights in Tibet in exchange for aid to the Qing empire on other fronts.[28] The British had learned

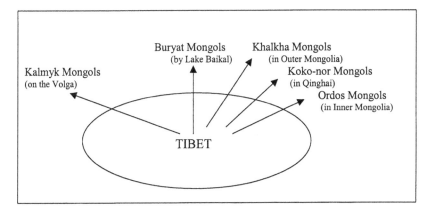

Figure 2.2 Tibetan Buddhist (Gelukpa) Influence on the Mongols

of and feared Russian trade interests in Tibet as early as the 1780s but were content as long as they could maintain an equal footing with the Russians in Tibet.[29] By the end of the nineteenth century British, Russian, and even French missionaries, officials, explorers, and Chambers of Commerce representatives were all eagerly investigating the possibilities for exploiting Tibet's resources and trade opportunities. The French were considering extending their control of Indo-China north through Yunnan and into eastern Tibet. For the Russians and British, relations with Tibet were linked to the Great Game.[30] The Russians had launched numerous explorations from the north.[31] The British in India, concerned about Russian influence in Tibet, sent the spies into Tibet who inspired Rudyard Kipling's *Kim*. Once Lord Curzon was viceroy in India (1899), the British no longer confined themselves to clandestine moves to counter Russia getting the upper hand in Tibet. From 1899 to 1904 the British in India decided that only direct dealings with the Dalai Lama could secure their interests, because "if the Chinese ever had authority in Tibet, they certainly have none now."[32] Yet the British were unable to open communication directly with the Dalai Lama, while the Russians had the insider Dorjiev working for them.

To this advantage, the Russians added direct negotiations with the Manchus over the status of Tibet. By 1902 the Russian minister in Peking suggested that the Qing government grant Tibet independence. Again, the similarity to Korean circumstances was remarkable, as the same approach had been taken by the Japanese when negotiating the Treaty of Shimonoseki in 1895, which forced the Qing to acknowledge that Korea was independent.[33] Versions of the potential treaty between the Russian and Qing empires reveal the efforts of the Russo-

Chinese Bank to "conduct a geological survey of Tibet." The details of invest-
ments and profit sharing on Russian mines in Tibet, including a provision "not
to tax the import into Tibet of mining machinery and equipment," demonstrate
the imperial commercial interests that motivated Russian efforts.[34] The British
used this possibility of Russian access to Tibet as the *causa belli* for their own
invasion of Tibet.

The British admitted that there was no real possibility of the Russians ever
posing any threat to British India. Moreover, the Russian hopes for concluding
a treaty with the Qing died with the Manchu negotiator Ronglu in 1903.[35] Yet
the Great Game was on in Central Asia, and the power of rhetoric gave the
British Government of India the ammunition it needed on the home front. By
stirring up fear of Russian plots, the British in India finally had some leverage
for exacting the substantive trade privileges they had sought for years. Having
alerted the Russians of the impending "mission" to Tibet and informed the
Chinese and Tibetans "that the mission was of an exclusively commercial character," the British invaded Tibet in 1903.[36] The response of the Chinese and
Tibetans was no different than had been observed for the previous century and
a half: delay tactics, refusal to communicate, and placing blame on each other.
The Tibetan government snubbed the Chinese, apparently certain of Russian
assistance. By 1904 the Tibetans were disappointed by the failure of Russian aid
to appear. But the Russians were engaged with the Japanese in Manchuria and
were threatened by revolution at home. Dorjiev and his associates offered the
only "Russian" contribution to Tibet's war effort. Dorjiev himself took charge
of a new Tibetan mint, while one of his protégés set up an Indian rifle factory.[37]
These Lhasa-made rifles seem to have been distinguished from other foreign
arms that Younghusband encountered among the Tibetans, but he could not
trace their provenance with certainty back to the Russians.[38] In any case, these
efforts, along with a new military drill, mark the first real signs of Tibet's modernization along the lines of Western nations. However, without substantial
Russian assistance, this was too little and too late to stop the British advances.
The Dalai Lama had backed the wrong faction by relying on Dorjiev and fled
Tibet, leaving affairs to be worked out by the British and Qing representatives
in conjunction with his representative.

The Tibetan elites then fell back on their second option: relying on the Qing
empire. The Lhasa authorities insisted that the Manchu *amban* negotiate on their
behalf, pleading—according to Younghusband—that they were "ignorant of the
ways of great nations."[39] Younghusband's settlement was quintessentially commercial: the British demanded, among other things, "the advantage of being able
to come to Tibet to buy wool and other things which were produced more
cheaply here than in India, and of selling to the Tibetans the surplus of articles

produced more cheaply in India.'[40] The dream of opening one of the last "closed" markets in the world network of trade had been realized. As Younghusband put it: "trade relations, which were no less advantageous to themselves than to us, [were] established with them as they had been with every other country in the world."[41] However, this forceful integration of Tibet into Britain's global commerce led to grave consequences for the Tibetans.

Chinese Nationalist Strategies: Designs on Tibet and the Tibetan Response

In fact, the Lhasa elites had all along recognized the disadvantages to themselves of such free commercial relations with British India. They had decided to limit such trade because they benefited far more from the loose oversight and support of the Qing empire. As mentioned above, participation in the Qing empire conferred the dual rewards of imperial support for monks and monasteries and the continued devotion of the Tibetan and Mongolian adherents of Tibetan Buddhism who inhabited the Inner Asian frontiers dominated by the Qing. However, the British invasion spelled the beginning of the end of these advantages. With internal challenges to Qing rule occurring all over China in the late nineteenth century, ethnic Chinese were playing an ever greater role in running the empire's affairs. Now, with the British encroaching on Tibet, Chinese were to gain the upper hand in the control of Tibetan affairs. In so doing, they fundamentally changed the nature of Qing-Tibetan relations.

Prior to the British invasion nearly all the *ambans* of Tibet had been either ethnic Manchus or Mongols. After the British had withdrawn from Tibet, the Manchu *amban* and other officials who had brokered the agreement between the British and Tibetans were cashiered and arrested at the insistence of the new Chinese assistant *amban*.[42] The chief Manchu *amban* was replaced by his former assistant (also a Manchu). However, the continuing negotiations between the British and the Qing governments were carried out by Zhang Yintang, the first Chinese civil official to be appointed to Tibet (as an assistant *amban*) in the history of Sino-Tibetan relations.

In the actions of this assistant *amban,* the defense of a modernizing Chinese nation was evident. In negotiating the Qing adhesion to the Anglo-Tibetan Convention of 1904, Zhang succeeded in securing a provision that the British would neither annex Tibetan territory nor interfere with the internal administration of Tibet, as well as a clause stating that China was not considered to be a "foreign power" in relation to Tibet. That such issues were on the table demonstrates just how weak Qing influence was in Tibet at this time. As opposed to the loose oversight that the Manchus had maintained up to now, this Anglo-Chinese Convention of 1906 allowed Zhang to assert Qing sovereignty over Tibet. Zhang also played a crucial role in negotiating the repayment of the indemnity that Younghusband had so carefully constructed to fulfill the aims of British traders. The treaty had been written to allow the Tibetans to slowly pay off the indemnity over a long period in order to ensure British India's continued trade relations with Tibet. Instead, Zhang arranged for a three-year payment plan, to be fulfilled by the province of Sichuan. The British home government—less concerned about the Indian tea trade in Tibet and more concerned about British trade with the much more populous Chinese—agreed to let the Qing government accept the responsibility for the indemnity. In addition, the Trade Regulations of 1908, originally to have been negotiated directly with the Tibetans, were decided by the British and Qing governments, without Tibetan participation.[43] By dint of his persistence, Zhang had diplomatically recovered what the Manchu authorities had very nearly lost to the British: the territorial integrity of the most weakly controlled dependency of the Qing empire.

I call this a nationalist strategy because, with the involvement of ethnic Chinese in Tibetan affairs, a modern territorial policy took shape that has continued to the present day. According to Stein Tønneson and Hans Antlöv, nationalism is "an ideological movement for attaining and maintaining a nation-state."[44] Anthony Smith adds that one of the most important aspects of the nation-state is "compact territory, preferably with 'natural' defensible borders, in a world of similar compact nations."[45] The Chinese were trying to construct just such a nation-state in the early twentieth century. Upon the founding of the Chinese Republic, the governors of Sichuan expressed their concern about Tibet's status: "Tibet is a buttress on our national frontiers—the hand, as it were, which protects the face—and its prosperity or otherwise is of the most vital importance to China."[46] Only the British aggression could have produced this attitude. None of the other southern neighbors of Tibet had ever made the Chinese feel threatened from this direction, although there had certainly been attacks on Tibet from this direction in the past. The point here is that, previously, Qing rule of Tibet had been governed by an Inner Asian (not international) system of interstate relations; that is, Tibet had a separate administrative structure that was only loosely integrated with that of the Qing empire, principally through Manchu institutions. Under the new framework, which accepted the Western model of nation-state relations, Chinese officials used the British acknowledgment of Qing suzerainty to claim Qing sovereignty of Tibet.

Feeling that they had successfully established Qing sovereignty over Tibet in the field of international relations, Chinese officials now hoped to realize this territorial sovereignty on the ground. As early as December 1903, just as the

English were invading Central Tibet, the provincial governor of Sichuan had sent a communication to the throne regarding plans to develop the Tibetan borderlands of Sichuan, called Kham. The governor's main development objectives were agriculture and mining. However, the Sichuan authorities knew that the Tibetans would be of no assistance in these projects and suggested that Chinese settlers be brought in to fuel these initiatives. This project had just started when the British exacted their right to free trade with Tibetans in 1904. In response, this program was expanded to shore up the Sino-Tibetan borderland against possible British encroachment. The area under development was to be taken out of the control of local leaders (*tusi*) and placed directly under Chinese rule.[47] Again, this marked a drastic change in Qing relations with Tibetan leadership. Only a decade before, when the same region had risen in rebellion, the Chinese governor of Sichuan had suggested that the administration be taken over by Chinese officials. At that time, both the Manchu *amban* in Lhasa and the Manchu commander in chief in Chengdu had successfully opposed this administrative change.[48] These Manchus may well have anticipated the results of extending Chinese administration into Tibetan regions that were to occur in 1905.

Tibetans were not amenable to the changes the Sichuan authorities planned to implement in Tibetan regions. When the assistant *amban* tried to used his troops to enforce these administrative changes, he sparked a riot. This was partly because of the new, colonial approach taken by troops "newly trained and organized according to foreign military methods."[49] The monastic community, whose membership he had tried to limit the previous year, joined with the aristocrats who were unwilling to be displaced, and the populace who felt threatened by the development plans and the Catholic mission under Chinese protection. In the spring of 1905 the agricultural project and the Catholic church were destroyed. Church missionaries and all representatives of Qing authority were killed.[50] A decade earlier the Manchus had sided with the Tibetans in keeping Chinese officials out of the region. However, the new British challenge in Tibet led the Qing court to accept Chinese officials' advice this time.

The Qing court now expedited the Chinese suggestion of a forward policy that advocated the colonization and development of Tibet. Again, the similarities to the Korean situation some decades earlier were striking. There the Qing responded to Japanese military and economic influence in Korea by interfering "boldly in Korea's internal affairs, claiming the authority to do so on the basis of the traditional suzerain relationship."[51] The Qing resident in Korea, Yuan Shikai, succeeded in tightening "China's control of Korea," but the similarity to the Tibetan situation changed after the outbreak of the Sino-Japanese War, which concluded with a treaty declaring Korea independent of China.[52] In Tibet two Chinese bannermen were put in charge of the expedition to restore Qing control. One of these men—Zhao Erfeng—was to play a major role in the attempt to transform Tibet from its former status as a loose dependency of the Qing empire into a firmly integrated territory of the nascent nation-state. His first job was to subdue the rebellion in Kham, which he did in short order, replacing local Tibetan leaders with Chinese magistrates and furthering plans for Chinese colonization. After this success he was awarded with the newly created position of Frontier Commissioner for Sichuan and Yunnan and submitted his plans for controlling Kham. These plans embodied the domestic corollary of the diplomat Zhang's international agreements. The problem was stated most clearly by Zhao's subordinate in a 1911 memorial: "[Kham] was formerly divided up into twenty Native States and Tribes, the inhabitants of which, while paying tribute to the Emperor, were not actually Chinese subjects."[53] Only by integrating these diverse polities into the compact territory of China could the security of the boundaries of the Qing empire, functioning as a nation-state, be maintained.

Zhao intended to use modern modes of colonization and administration to transform the Tibetan regions into Chinese territory. He explicitly declared that Kham was a part of China and that the Tibetans were subjects of the emperor. He provided protection and assistance to Chinese settlers to develop agriculture, mines, and other mineral resources, as well as commerce capable of supporting Chinese inhabitants without dependence on shipments from China Proper. He promoted education to change Tibetan customs and regulated those customs that differed from the customs of China, from marriage and funeral arrangements to sexual relations, clothing, and hygiene. He especially attempted to control the monasteries by placing them under the control of Chinese officials, forbidding the building of new monasteries (he had destroyed many while putting down the rebellion), and restricting the number of monks. He compared his activities to the colonization taking place by the "British in Australia, the French in Madagascar, the Americans in the Philippines and the Japanese in Hokkaido," and employed foreign engineers to help with technical aspects of the colonization of Kham.[54]

In 1908 Zhao's appointment as *amban* of Tibet allowed him to start to extend this incorporation of Tibetan territory beyond Kham and into Central Tibet. He was directed to carry out measures similar to those executed in Kham: to extend the control of the Qing administration over Central Tibet; develop mining, industry, and agriculture; train troops; and promote modern education there.[55] Although this appointment was withdrawn in 1909, Zhao had already expanded his area of control to almost all the Tibetan regions in Sichuan, incorporating them as regular Chinese administrative divisions for the first time in history. By this time, even the Manchu *amban* in Lhasa was convinced of the necessity of such reforms for Central Tibet and requested additional troops to help enact them. These troops were held back by Tibetan troops at the frontier between Tibet and Sichuan, and Zhao was called in to assist them. When his troops crossed into what the Central Tibetans considered to be their territory, Zhao pushed the Central Tibetans beyond the point of accommodation with Qing rule.

The Tibetan Response to Chinese Nationalist Aggression

As long as Central Tibetan Buddhist institutions were not threatened, the Tibetan elites had put up no concerted resistance to Qing overlordship (whether suzerain or sovereign). However, word of Zhao Erfeng's methods had preceded him to Central Tibet. Thus the moment his troops and the strategies he had pioneered in Tibetan regions in the east were threatening to overtake Central Tibet, the Tibetan elites elected to try a new strategy. On December 4, 1909, Zhao left his base in Sichuan to assist the Chinese troops entering Tibet. On December 7, 1909, the Dalai Lama dispatched telegrams requesting assistance to "Great Britain and all the Ministers of Europe" via the British trade agent in Tibet. Younghusband summarized the message as follows: "They [Zhao and the Lhasa *amban*] had brought many troops into Tibet, and wished to abolish the Tibetans' religion; the Dalai Lama asked, therefore, that 'all the other countries should intervene and kindly withdraw the Chinese troops.'"[56] The Tibetan leader was at last appealing to the community of nations, rather than merely seeking the support of a single empire, to protect Tibet's interests.

As a result of the thirteenth Dalai Lama's firsthand experiences with Europeans during the years of his exile, this mode of communication was entirely different from that conducted between the Russia tsar and the Dalai Lama at the turn of the century. Early on, Dorjiev had been able to play the roles of both Tibetan Buddhist adviser to the Dalai Lama and Russian citizen, depending on the context. The Russian government was able to claim that he was merely a religious (and therefore nonpolitical) representative of the Dalai Lama, and the Russian newspapers had described him as Extraordinary Envoy of Tibet.[57] But in 1904 the Dalai Lama had started to communicate directly with foreign ministers in Urga, meeting with the Russian consul to Mongolia and the Russian minister to China. There, in 1905, he also met the Japanese monk Teramoto Enga, who later traveled to Tibet and became his trusted adviser.[58] Later, in the early months of 1908, he met other foreigners at the Buddhist sanctuary of Mount Wutai, where he was at some liberty to handle his own affairs. There he hosted a German, a Japanese Buddhist (who arranged for him to the meet the Japanese ambassador in Beijing), the American minister to China (W. W. Rockhill), a British officer of the Colonial Service, and a representative sent by the tsar especially to convey the tsar's support of Tibetan Buddhism and the news that a Tibetan Buddhist temple had been built at the capital, St. Petersburg. The relationship that the Dalai Lama established with Rockhill, a student of Tibetan Buddhism, grew from their meeting at Mount Wutai.[59] It was also from Mount Wutai that the Dalai Lama sent his first letter to the British minister in China, which attested to his desire to maintain friendship with the British.[60]

When the Dalai Lama went to Beijing later that year, the Chinese tried to restrict his access to foreigners. Zhang Yintang, who had been so instrumental in interposing the Chinese in the negotiation of British relations with Tibet, was on hand to mediate visits between the Russian and British ministers and the Dalai Lama. The Dalai Lama met with a Japanese military attaché, which eventually led to the assignment of a Japanese military drill instructor in Tibet. However, the Dalai Lama generally found himself at odds with the Qing Foreign Affairs Office that was handling his complaints of Chinese incursions in Kham.[61] In addition, the Dalai Lama's request for the restoration of direct communication with the throne, rather than mediation through the *amban*, was denied. At the same time the court issued a decree which clearly stated that henceforth the Dalai Lama was "to carefully obey the laws and ordinances of the sovereign State." Both the British and the Dalai Lama recognized in this a new order of affairs.[62]

The Dalai Lama had hoped that the option of relying on the Qing was still a viable one, but his time at court and the rumors of Zhao's activities were ominous signs that this alternative was no longer an option. No doubt the Dalai Lama had heard from Dorjiev of the assimilation drive (1902–1904) that had affected Dorjiev's home region among the Buriats, overturning the old policies of independence and opening the way for Russian colonization and administration.[63] In 1908 and 1909, as the Dalai Lama made his way back to Central Tibet, he heard similar reports of Zhao Erfeng's activities in eastern Tibet. These Chinese attempts to colonize Tibetan regions made a nationalist of the Dalai Lama. He had tried to pin Tibetan fortune onto the Russian empire, but the war with Japan and impending revolution had destroyed any chance of support from that quarter. He had turned to the Qing empire and found that, despite promises, the treatment of Tibetans that was being recommended by Chinese officials was worse than anything threatened by the British. The assurances of continued Qing support for Tibetan Buddhism that he had received from the emperor and empress dowager died with them, even before he had left Beijing for Tibet.[64]

Thus, once he was safely within the borders of Tibet, the Dalai Lama tried to reach out to the representatives of other nations for assistance. On November 7, 1909, the Dalai Lama, in separate letters, requested the aid of the British,

Russians, French, and Japanese against the aggression of the Chinese. However, since the letters were sent to the foreign missions of these countries in Beijing via Calcutta, they did not arrive at their destinations until February 21. In December, on news of Zhao's advance into Central Tibet, a more desperate plea was sent abroad via telegram.[65] These efforts can be considered the first effective instance of a proactive Tibetan attempt at acting as a member of the international community. Until this moment the Tibetan Buddhist elites had kept alive the hope, however slight, that the Qing government would remain the protector of their religion which it had so effectively, if at times passively, served for nearly two centuries.

Clearly the Dalai Lama no longer trusted the Qing representatives in Tibet. On February 9, 1910, he met with the new assistant *amban,* also Chinese, who assured him that "the Lamas would not be harmed or their monasteries destroyed." But three days later, when the troops Zhao had assisted marched into Lhasa, the Dalai Lama fled into exile under British protection.[66] The Dalai Lama's request for British aid was based especially upon the threat to Tibetan Buddhism and the Tibetan government with which the religion was so intimately linked. He expressed the fear that Chinese officials would now govern Tibet. In order to acquire the status of the undisputed head of a Tibetan state, he asked the British for assistance in driving the Chinese completely out of Tibet so that his "position may be that of the Fifth Dalai Lama, who was an independent sovereign."[67] To the Tibetans' surprise, Britain provided little aid against the Chinese, aside from informing Chinese officials that Tibet's transformation into a province of China, as was being reported in Chinese newspapers, would be a violation of previous treaties.[68]

Despite the lack of effective British support for Tibet, the two and a half years spent in exile in British territory (mostly in Darjeeling) no doubt had a profound impact on the Dalai Lama's perception of the workings of the modern world. Whereas formerly his best opportunity to acquaint himself with foreigners had been a few short months at Urga and Mount Wutai, he was now exposed to a range of different influences. The royal families of Sikkim and Bhutan had had long experience with the British. When the Dalai Lama first went into exile, "in Darjeeling, with its Westernised ideas, meetings of protest [against the Chinese] were held by the Buddhists of Tibet and Darjeeling and the neighboring Buddhist States. However, these did not have much effect on public opinion, for those assembled were neither numerous nor skilled in the organisation of protests."[69]

Charles Bell, one of the longest-serving officers of the British Government of India who dealt with Tibet, recorded that he had some fifty conversations with the Dalai Lama. These included discussions of both the affairs of China and

Tibet and those of the rest of the world, as well as "events in Britain, Ireland, Germany, India and Japan, and the inner meaning of these events."[70] The Dalai Lama was especially interested in "the military strength of other nations" and in "the Great Powers, and learned all he could about the kings and different nations of the world."[71] A Russian Tibetan Buddhist carrying a letter from Dorjiev and a Russian consul (declining aid to Tibet) visited him. From Dorjiev, he regularly received news and proceeds from a bank account in Mongolia. He secured the assistance of one of Bell's clerks in translating newspaper articles about Sino-Tibetan affairs and the disturbances in China at the time. As he did not write an autobiography, it is uncertain what he thought of all these affairs. Nevertheless he was certainly made aware of early Indian efforts at seeking independence and one of his ministers expressed the belief that "all nations should govern themselves."[72]

With the fall of the Qing empire, the Tibetans were able to regain control of their country, and the Dalai Lama hoped finally to bring to completion the third and last of his options, cooperation with the British. The Anglo-Bhutanese treaty of 1910 formed the basis for the best hope of the Tibetans at this point. In this treaty the Bhutanese agreed to give up power over external affairs in exchange for Britain's protection.[73] Since under such an agreement internal affairs would still have been under the control of the Tibetans, this would have provided them with much more control than they could have exercised under the Qing reforms pushed through by the Chinese.[74] Why was it that the Tibetans could accept accommodation with an aggressor motivated by commercial interests so much better than the nationalist one? The problem was essentially that the Tibetans "considered the Chinese an irreligious people"; thus as long as the Chinese officials wanted to directly control affairs in Tibet, there would be trouble.[75] Yet the Chinese felt that they had few options. Through the antiquated institutions of the Qing empire, they, too, were negotiating their own relationship with the other nations of the world. The new territorial expectations required that the state control Tibet much more tightly than the Manchus had done for most of the previous two centuries or risk losing the region to British imperial interests.

On the other hand, the Dalai Lama's time with the British directly exposed him to their religious tolerance, which was exercised as long as their trade interests were protected. In this respect, the British Empire shared more in common with the Russian empire or the pre-reform Qing empire than it did with the nascent Chinese nation. The British wanted only free trade and were not interested in directly administering Tibet, as were the Chinese. This was similar to the Russian and the former Qing imperial interests in employing Tibetan Buddhist leaders' assistance in securing the allegiance of their Mongolian subjects. Yet because of the restrictions of the Anglo-Russian convention, signed in 1907, the British could not grant the Tibetans the status accorded Bhutan.[76] The British sources, generally sympathetic to the cause of Tibetan independence, fail to mention the overwhelming British interest in not jeopardizing their trade interests in China. The China trade was essential to Britain, especially British India, and this could not be threatened merely on the basis of helping an economically insignificant country such as Tibet.

Thus caught between the commercial and national forces of globalization, when the Dalai Lama returned to Tibet in 1912 he felt that he had little choice but to seek to establish Tibet as an independent nation-state. This he did to the best of his ability, acting as the main supporter of what Bell called "the national party [that was] fighting for the independence of Tibet."[77] Here the catalogues of the advocates of Tibetan independence make easy the task of finding the outward signs of a modern nation-state, although there are few signs that any real transformation of identity or consciousness (the hallmark of nationalism) took place. Dorjiev was purported to have negotiated a treaty on behalf of Tibet in 1913 with the newly independent Mongolia.[78] The Dalai Lama reorganized the Tibetan army along the lines of the British army.[79] He even offered the British one thousand soldiers in the First World War.[80] He "introduced new paper currency, gold and silver coins, and postage stamps,"[81] and oversaw the creation of a national flag, apparently with the assistance of a visiting Japanese.[82] Probably the most convincing testimony to this independence is that of one of the last of the Chinese Republic's own representatives to Tibet, Shen Tsung-Lien (who finished his term in 1947). His summary of Tibet's status was that "since 1911 Lhasa has to all practical purposes enjoyed full independence. It has its own currency and customs; it runs its own telegraph and postal service; it maintains a civil service different from any other part of China; it even keeps its own army."[83]

Although de facto independence was achieved, Tibetans failed to create a nation. No real effort was made to promote an "imagined community" or to develop a concept of citizenship. To do so would have altered the relationship between the monastic and noble elites and a populace that was more or less their subjects. Much like the imperial elite during the reforms of the self-strengthening movement in late nineteenth-century Qing China, the Tibetan leadership seemed to feel that they could become a nation-state by using international tools without changing the fundamental structure of Tibetan society. Decades later, in 1943, one Tibetan revolutionary would complain about the failure to develop a feeling of shared citizenship: "Tibet was not unified. There was no sense of a common Tibetan people. The Kham and Amdo people did not trust the Tibetan government [in Lhasa], which in turn did not trust the officials of the Panchen Lama."[84] Besides failing to create a citizenry, the Tibetan leadership was frustrated by unsuccessful reliance on Britain in their efforts to gain international recognition. In the Simla convention of 1914 the British desired the participation of the Chinese and, without it, refused to recognize more than Tibetan autonomy. Within Tibet the Dalai Lama was master of affairs and went about consolidating the state, but he was not able to gain international recognition of this status.

At the same time, however, his efforts at creating a compact national territory caused internal troubles. Just as Tibet had broken with China when the Chinese attempted to administer Tibet directly, the leaders of heretofore self-governing Tibetan regions resisted the authority of a centralized Tibetan government. Their efforts at seeking the aid of their enemy's enemy, China, were critical in negotiating China's future relations with Tibet. The problem here was that both the Qing dynasty (at least with respect to its Inner Asian dependencies) and the Lhasa-based Tibetan administration (with respect to outlying Tibetan polities) were undergoing a major realignment of power, from an interstate system similar to what Stanley Tambiah has called a "Galactic Polity" or, in this case, nested galactic polities, to the model of competing nation-states.[85] Tambiah describes this system as follows:

> The concentric-circle system [of Galactic Polities], representing the center-periphery relations was ordered thus: In the center was the king's capital and the region of its direct control, which was surrounded by a circle of provinces ruled by princes or governors appointed by the king, and these again were surrounded by more or less independent "tributary" polities.[86]

Neither the Qing nor the Tibetan administration exactly fit this model, but they both shared a problem in their efforts to incorporate those third-tier polities that exercised significant independence. Whereas the Qing lost control of or influence over Korea, Tibet, and Mongolia, the Tibetan government in Lhasa was more successful in dominating the polities that tried to challenge its authority.

The Tibetan Nationalist Administration

When the Tibetan elites tried to modernize their rule and transform Tibet into an independent nation-state, the effort to implement a centralized administration characteristic of such states created tensions in the larger Tibetan cultural world, parts of which did not necessarily recognize the full authority of a Central Tibetan government. Resisting the Lhasa administration and the military forces that supported it, several local Tibetan leaders tried to counter these efforts at nation building by seeking aid from the Chinese. In this respect, the effort to create a compact nation-state was one shared by the rival Chinese and Tibetan administrations. The reaction these efforts provoked among formerly autonomous regions was likewise similar. The 1909 appearance of a Chinese army bent on redefining the relations of power in the very heartland of Tibet had forced the Tibetans to take a more active role in the world of nations. Similarly the incursions, in the 1920s and 1930s, of Lhasa authority into the formerly self-ruling polities in the Tibetan cultural area caused the leaders of the most threatened of these polities to flee to China. By tightening control over Tibet and modernizing the Tibetan administration as much as was possible, the Dalai Lama hoped to maintain Tibet's independence. At the same time the aggressiveness with which Central Tibetan forces extended their control sowed the seeds for future discord.[87]

At least partially the Chinese Republican and Communist aggression toward Tibet throughout the twentieth century has reflected a similar contestation of power. Whereas the thirteenth Dalai Lama felt that he should exercise dominion over all culturally Tibetan regions, the Chinese believed they had rightful dominion over all the former Qing dependencies, which included Tibet. In the end, whether the aggressor was Tibetan or Chinese, the military ability to enforce a set of claims has been the deciding factor in who would rule Tibetan regions. For example, the Tibetans' current claim to independence is based on the fact that Central Tibetans succeeded in driving out the Chinese forces at the end of the Qing empire. In contrast, the monastic polities that tried to resist the centralization of Tibet under the rule of the thirteenth Dalai Lama were not successful in resisting Central Tibetan aggression. They were therefore forced to seek support outside Tibet proper.

The impetus of nationalism that drove the Tibetans to consolidate a Tibetan state in the first half of the twentieth century is thus not entirely different from the forces of nationalism that impelled the Chinese to exert control over Tibet in the second half of the century. In both cases, smaller polities that wished to be separate and independent (but were not recognized as such by the international community) were forcibly incorporated into a larger community on the basis of nationalistic feelings. The similarity of these two situations is not so surprising, because in both cases, to use John King Fairbank's famous model, there was a similar stimulus (the incursion of imperial commercial interests and nationalism) which produced a parallel response. As Fairbank and Goldman note in *China: A New History*, "by 1901 the Qing court had got the message that it could become modern only by centralizing power at Beijing."[88] Only a decade later the Tibetan elites understood the same logic and overthrew Chinese power in Tibet, trying to replace it with their own centralized administration.

Challenges to Local Tibetan Polities

Despite their successful invasion in 1904, after the British had their trade agreement they had no interest in direct colonial control of Tibet. Nevertheless the Chinese felt threatened by this new encroachment at the hands of an imperialist power that had been constantly eroding the Qing empire's sovereignty since the Opium War in the 1840s. The thirteenth Dalai Lama had sought Qing protection from the British, but failing to secure it, he took matters into his own hands. The Dalai Lama's first step in making Tibet a modern nation-state was taken before he had even returned to Central Tibet. Shortly after the revolutionary elements in the Qing garrison had overthrown the imperial representatives in Lhasa, he created a War Department. Over the course of one year this War Department was able to take control of Central Tibet (by August 1912), eliminating the last Chinese military presence in Central Tibet by January 1913. The Dalai Lama immediately set out to discipline those Tibetans who had aided the Chinese forces in Tibet after the fall of the Qing. Tengyeling monastery, in Lhasa, which had sheltered and provisioned Chinese troops in the previous year, was the first institution to fall to the process of centralization in modern Tibet.[89] In the meantime, the Dalai Lama continued to build up the Tibetan army along modern lines. After experimenting with Mongol, Manchu, Japanese, Russian, and British systems of military training, he settled on the British system and sent young Tibetans abroad to be educated in the use of artillery and machine gun warfare.[90]

Funding the development and expansion of a modern military severely strained the financial resources of the Lhasa government. Again, the situation in Tibet ran parallel to that in China some decades earlier: "Beijing tried in 1884 to regularize and secure control of central revenue from the various provincial measures for military financing, [but] the provinces objected to so many details."[91] In seeking to generate new revenues, the Lhasa government turned to an eighteenth-century precedent that had required the Panchen Lama's estate to pay one-quarter of the military expenses of the central government. In 1792 this had been acceptable to the estate because the Panchen Lama's monastery had been directly under attack, but in 1912 this application of precedent was clearly an attempt both to develop the revenues and to extend the power of the Lhasa government at the expense of the Panchen Lama.[92] The Panchen Lama's extensive landholdings represented the largest single corporate estate in Central Tibet not directly administered by the Lhasa administration. This estate, based at Trashi Lhünpo monastery, was ruled by a government bureaucracy separate from and independent of that of Lhasa. Moreover, the Panchen Lama was perceived as a rival, as he appeared to have attempted to gain further autonomy with both

British and Chinese help, in 1904–5 and in 1910–11, respectively, while the Dalai Lama was in exile.[93] Although the Panchen Lama had never actually tried to replace the Dalai Lama, his continued control of large estates and his status as the second most important incarnate lama in the hierarchy of the ruling Gelukpa school made his status and independent administration a challenge to the Dalai Lama's efforts to centralize control of Tibet.

A modern Tibetan nation-state required a different relation between the central government and the outlying—and formerly fairly autonomous—religious and aristocratic estates.[94] After the Lhasa government created the Revenue Investigation Office, which was responsible for reassessing estate taxes to fund the new military, relations between the Panchen Lama's estate and the Central Tibetan government worsened. In Lhasa the Dalai Lama limited the assignment of religious administrative posts to monks from the three large monasteries around Lhasa, thereby eliminating this avenue of advancement and representation that had been open previously to monks from Trashi Lhünpo.[95] Likewise the local representative of the Lhasa administration in the vicinity of Trashi Lhünpo monastery was given a higher status and the power to demand corvée labor from the peasants of the Panchen Lama's estate. By 1922 the Panchen Lama had appealed to the British for aid, stating that "officials of the Tashi Lhumpo [i.e., the Panchen Lama's monastic] Government . . . are undergoing imprisonment at the Potala Palace [the seat of the Dalai Lama's government]" and were apparently to be held there until the revenue demands were met.[96] The imprisonment of these officials was the direct cause of the Panchen Lama's flight from Tibet in November 1923. Thus, within a decade of his return from exile, the Dalai Lama's efforts to centralize and militarily maintain a Tibetan nation-state resulted in the alienation of one of the most important figures in the Tibetan Buddhist world. The Chinese were happy to receive the Panchen Lama when he arrived in Chinese territory and provided for his basic needs for many years to come.[97]

Another lama driven into exile did not entirely share the Panchen Lama's relative good fortune. The Norlha Qutughtu (Ch. Nuona *huofo,* Sönam Rapten; 1865–1936),[98] who was the spiritual and political leader of a small territory in Riwoché, Kham, near Chamdo, was actually imprisoned by the Tibetan government and only went into exile after he escaped from his captors.[99] When the Dalai Lama had secured control of Central Tibet, the new Tibetan army fought with some success against the Chinese forces on the eastern frontiers of Central Tibet using the arms bought from the British and captured from the departing Chinese. Just as the Chinese had fought to preserve the territorial integrity of the Qing empire in the face of what they saw as British interference in Tibet, now the Central Tibetans struggled to secure the territorial integrity of Tibetan regions from the interference of the Chinese. They planned to do this by retaking the eastern Tibetan regions that had been subjugated by the Chinese just before the fall of the Qing empire. In 1917 and 1918, as these Central Tibetan forces successfully occupied Tibetan principalities in the region of Kham, they imprisoned those Tibetan leaders who had cooperated with the Chinese. The Norlha Qutughtu was one such figure captured in the Central Tibetan advances that overran the region. He was brought to Central Tibet early in 1919, where he remained in prison for some years. He avoided being poisoned, a common fate in Tibetan prisons, by refusing to eat at certain times. Finally, in 1923, after being transferred to southern Tibet, he managed to escape across the Nepalese border. From there he traveled to India and eventually to Shanghai, becoming the second exiled lama to flee to China in the face of Tibetan nationalist forces. He arrived in Beijing in late 1924, just as the Panchen Lama himself was making his way to the Chinese capital over land.[100]

When these two figures arrived in China, the period of competing warlords was at its height. The northern government was still recognized as the legitimate government of China but was soon to be under attack from the southern Nationalist Party. Although these opposing forces agreed that Tibet and other Inner Asian dependencies of the former Qing empire should remain part of the Chinese nation-state, the institutions for achieving this goal were not very strong at that time. The northern government office responsible for interacting with Inner Asians was called the Mongolian and Tibetan Bureau (Meng Zang yuan). Members of the bureau greeted the Panchen Lama upon his arrival in Beijing and made arrangements to house him at government expense but did little else.[101] The Norlha Qutughtu's reception was much less lavish, no doubt because of his lower status. One source says that when he called on the director of the bureau he was not even received, because they had no common language through which to communicate.[102] As these details demonstrate, at that time the Chinese government was not prepared to take full advantage of the presence of these Tibetan lamas in exile from their native land.

Nor was the Chinese government capable of effective communication through Chinese envoys to Tibet. After the expulsion of the remnants of the Qing garrisons in Tibet in 1913, the first official effort of the Chinese to renew contact was largely ignored by the Dalai Lama and the government of Tibet. Official envoys sent by the Chinese government in early years were limited to the 1920 mission from Gansu. Governor Zhang Guangjian sent Zhu Xiu, Gulang cang (Gurongtsang), and others from Qinghai to Tibet to meet with the Dalai Lama.[103] Charles Bell, the British agent in Tibet at the time, compared his reception with that of the Chinese mission:

The Chinese Mission was in Lhasa for four and half months in 1920. During that period they were permitted only two interviews with the Dalai Lama; and, before going into the presence of His Holiness, each member's person was unceremoniously searched to make sure that he was not secreting arms. . . . When I took my mission to Lhasa in 1921, I frequently visited the Dalai Lama, who used to rise from his seat, grasp my hand cordially, and make me sit at the same table as himself. The contrast could not have been stronger.[104]

Thus the Chinese government was under no illusions about its status in Tibet; official missions were not of interest to the Tibetans. Bell, a trade representative himself, reported that the "trade connexion with China is the only strong connexion that Tibet as a whole desires. Both countries realize its value. Many a time have Tibetans said to me, 'We want no Chinese officials; the only man we want from that side is the Chinese trader.'" For some years then, Chinese merchants were to be almost the sole source of Chinese information on the situation in Tibet.[105] In this way, the persistent influence of commercial and nationalist forces on the rest of Asia were manifest in Tibet as well. The idea that Tibet was somehow isolated from these modern forces can only be maintained if we ignore both the Chinese and British commercial interests in Tibet and the effects that Tibetan centralization efforts had on regional autonomy in Tibet.

Racial Ideology in China

Another element of the process of globalization was sweeping through intellectual circles in China with results that would influence Chinese perceptions of their relations with Tibetans in the coming decades. Racial ideology arrived simultaneously with the discourse of nationalism in China and was hotly debated by prominent reformers and revolutionaries.[106] As John Fitzgerald explained, "There is no one word in the Chinese language referring to 'nation,' as distinct from state (*guo*), and the want of a definitive name has encouraged state-builders to define the nation in ways consistent with their state-building efforts. . . . Words in common usage have included 'citizen' (*guomin, gongmin*), 'people' (*renmin*) and 'race' (*minzu*), along with the derivatives 'Han race' (*Hanzu*) and 'Chinese race' (*Zhonghua minzu*). Each implies a different nation."[107] One thing was certain: in the final years of the Qing empire there was little talk of the glories of a multiracial China that included all the frontier races. This was because of the origins of racial ideology in Asia and the usefulness of this ideology in the hands of

Chinese revolutionaries seeking ways to free their race-nation from the Manchus. Michael Weiner has argued that "'race' and nation inhabited the same ideological space" in Japan, where many Chinese students were introduced to racial and national ideas.[108] Frank Dikötter makes much the same point about the phrase "*Minzuzhuyi*" that most scholars now translate as "nationalism," the first of Sun Yat-sen's "Three Principles of the People": "*Minzuzhuyi*, from the Japanese *minzokushugi*, exerted a lasting influence on the political terminology of the Chinese students. The term literally meant 'racism,' and expressed a nationalist vision of race."[109] Of the students who had gone from Qing China to Japan, many Chinese were busy fomenting anti-Manchu revolution, while the Manchus—and the Chinese who still supported them—emphasized instead their efforts to promote equality of relations between Manchus and Chinese.[110]

Prior to the fall of the Qing empire a real diversity of ideas characterized the debate about who should be included in the Chinese nation. Liang Qichao recognized the weakness of an ethnic definition of the nation for a multiethnic empire like the Qing and embraced the model of citizenship instead. According to Pamela Crossley, Liang Qichao was aware that, "without an emperor, the cultural simultaneities, the coexistence of historicized constituencies, had little chance of being coherent. . . . The Qianlong emperor may have been able to create the sensation of being all-in-one. But a republic would demand one-in-all."[111] In order to accomplish this goal Liang insisted that "the interests of state required nationalists to sever the connection between ethnicity and national identity in order to maintain the territorial integrity of the empire which was home to many ethnic groups."[112] But as Fitzgerald has pointed out, the revolutionary nationalists could not accept this proposition. Their best hope for fomenting revolution was to play on the anti-Manchu tension in China Proper. They were hardly concerned with what happened on the Qing frontiers, at least until they had control of China Proper. And ultimately, despite the misgivings about the future coherence of the nation described by Crossely, Liang Qichao, like the revolutionaries, could not accept that the empire's frontier peoples were part of the same race-nation. He distinguished the Chinese (*Han*) race from the Tibetan, among others.[113]

The best known of such revolutionary figures was Sun Yat-sen. His principle of race-based nationalism (*minzu zhuyi*) could be interpreted as supportive of the national liberation of the Qing empire's frontier peoples. As Crossley summarized the logical outcome of this position: "If Manchus, Mongols, Uigurs, Tibetans and even Chinese Muslims were to be 'races' with moral and cultural destinies distinct from that of the Chinese, it would be inevitable for them to seek (with, logically, Chinese encouragement) homelands equally distinct from China."[114] Despite the logic of this argument, ultimately Sun's conception of

Chinese territory as synonymous with the Qing empire would threaten the nascent nationalist movements in Inner Asia.

Zhang Binglin was the only prominent nationalist revolutionary to explicitly eschew any interest in the non-Chinese peoples or their territories on the empire's margins. He found strength in the idea of limiting the nation to a single ethnic or racial group, the (Han) Chinese.[115] In order to free the new nation from imperial traditions, he was willing to relinquish claims to large portions of Qing territory. According to Crossley,

> Zhang wished to see China completely purged of the imperial process, even at the cost of great territorial sway. In this way, he escaped the strategic dilemma out of which Sun Yat-sen and Wang Jingwei had found no graceful exit. He had no wish to prevent the alien peoples from splitting off and forming their own countries. He foresaw them as buffer states.[116]

Anyone who has tried to read Sun's corpus for indications of his approach to the borderland peoples will sympathize with the fact that Zhang "lost patience with the obfuscations of Sun's racial and cultural positions, which only recalled the forced integration under the Qing empire."[117] Of course, with Zhang's premature death, most of these ideas fell by the wayside before the Tibetans were considering racial ideology and their place in modern Asia, but remnants of this discourse were even embedded in the often inconsistent work of Sun Yat-sen.

The solution to the tensions between Sun's anti-Manchu stance and the need to keep the empire intact in the form of the Chinese nation was provided by a group of Manchus educated in Japan. These Manchus were eager to guarantee a safe place for themselves and their people in the rising tide of anti-Manchu Chinese nationalism. Their bargaining chips were the domains of the Qing frontier peoples (Tibetans, Muslims, and Mongols).

Modern Origins of the "Five Races" Concept

Although tracing the idea of *racial* unity back to the Qianlong period is anachronistic, as this concept was not current in the eighteenth-century Qing empire, twentieth-century Manchus do indeed seem to be the originators of the concept of the five races in unity (*wuzu gonghe*). The fivefold division may have originated in the mid-Qing, but it was intended to divide imperial constituencies, not unite them into a single nation. Although all five constituencies were under the Manchu Qing emperors, they were not unified with one another. In fact, the concept of unifying "Manchus, Han, Mongol, Muslims and Tibetans as one citizenry" was not articulated until 1907 by the imperial clansman, Hengjun, and other Manchu intellectuals.[118] As recounted by Edward Rhoads in *Manchus & Han,* the Manchu editors of the *Great Harmony Journal* (*Datongbao*) based in Japan were the first modern figures to conceive of a new China based on the equality and unity of these five distinct ethnic groups:

> *Great Harmony Journal* . . . recognized the existence of different "races" (*zu*) within China, specifically five—Manchus, Han, Mongol, Muslims (Hui), and Tibetans. This may seem no more than a restatement of the Qianlong emperor's self-image as the all-encompassing ruler of these same five peoples, but it had been modified in one significant way: these peoples now owed their loyalty not to the Qing empire but to China.[119]

It had also been modified in another and more telling way. The transformation of these imperial constituencies into races was significant. Where the Qianlong emperor had merely used the scripts of five civilizations to designate the constituencies under his rule, these modern Manchus accepted Western racial discourse and applied it to their domains. For example, Kai-wing Chow has argued,

> the conceptualisation of the Manchus and the Chinese as "Manchu people" (*Manren*) and "Han people" (*Hanren*) had been a standard practice in the political language of the Qing regime. Both terms denoted no more than loosely related groups of people without specifying the nature of the bond as kinship.[120]

The greatest impact of this transformation was to come when the Chinese gained control of China's government. With a demographic majority in power, this racialized conception of China's constituent elements allowed for the sort of abuses that have typically accompanied the use of racial discourse.

In 1907 Hengjun brought this radical message directly to Beijing as part of a delegation representing thousands of Qing students in Japan. He was sent to Beijing to advocate on behalf of the Manchu-founded Association for Constitutional Government. The language of equality and unity among the five races was an important part of the association's message. Hengjun stayed in Beijing to continue this mission by founding the daily newspaper the *Central Great Harmony Daily* (*Zhongyang datong ribao*).[121] However, his idea of defining Qing China as a union of five races was not readily adopted by the Qing government. If we look at the selection criterion for the National Assembly in 1909, this particular concept had clearly not gained acceptance, even among the Manchus. Instead, imperial appointees (which made up half the body of the assembly) were drawn from seven categories, which were not limited merely to racial divisions. Status distinctions within "racial" groups were equally important. For example, Manchus were categorized differently depending on their ancestry and position. As for the idea of equality among the five races, it was nowhere to be found. The Chinese comprised three-fourths of the assembly, Manchus were awarded around 20 percent of the seats, and the Mongols, Muslims, and Tibetans together shared fourteen of two hundred slots.[122] Until the very end of the dynasty, those Manchus who actually held power declined to even articulate the rhetoric of the "five races in unity."

Modern Appropriation of Imperial Qing Narratives

We now turn to answering the question posed by Crossley in the introduction to her *Translucent Mirror:* "Whether and under what circumstances have those aspiring to lead 'national' republics appropriated . . . imperial narratives and agenda?" Rhoads's work in *Manchus & Han* provided part of the answer: twentieth-century Manchus, in both the imperial family and the officialdom, invented the idea of harmony between the empire's races when threatened with extermination by Chinese revolutionaries. Once the Manchus abdicated, reformist and revolutionary Chinese also appropriated this "imperial" narrative under the threat of losing the Qing dynasty's frontier dependencies. How did this new rhetoric enter the corridors of power from a place at the margins of political discourse in Japan and later in Beijing? In 1911 Yang Du, the Manchu founder of the Association for Constitutional Government and the Society for the Advancement of Republicanism, drew close to Yuan Shikai and Wang Jingwei.[123] This network of organizations, supporting newspapers, and personal contacts must have been responsible for bringing the idea of the "five races" further into the mainstream of those who were soon to hold power in China.

Once the revolution looked like it would succeed, the Chinese were willing to embrace Manchu reformist rhetoric. The Republican negotiator for Qing abdication was the first to commit to these ideals, proposing that "with regard to the 'Manchus, Mongols, Muslims, and Tibetans' (*Man-Meng-Hui-Zang*), they would be treated on a basis of equality with the Han." The aggregation of the Manchus with the other four groups continued throughout the negotiations. For example, Duan Qirui and other Qing generals threatened a hesitant court that "if fighting broke out and the Qing forces were defeated, it would be difficult to provide for 'the honor of the imperial household and the livelihood of the imperial clan and the colonial [literally, frontier] peoples' (*huangshi zunrong zongfan shengji*)."[124] For the Qing dynasty, being treated equally with their former subjects was not an idea they could easily embrace. It certainly cannot be equated with the Qianlong emperor's dominion over subjugated peoples. When the empress dowager, as the head of the Qing court, responded to Duan's threat by indicating the imperial desire to proceed with the negotiations, she asked Yuan Shikai "to arrange in advance the terms for the future treatment of the imperial household, the imperial lineage, the Eight Banners, and the Mongols, Muslims, and Tibetans."[125] She still considered the divisions between the status groups of the Manchus at least as important as the ethnic divisions between the frontier peoples, and the order of these groups very likely indicates their order of relative importance to the dynasty.

Only when the dynasty was being ousted and terms were forced on its leaders did the Qing imperial government finally "acknowledge" the equality and unity of the five peoples, and then only at the insistence of the Republican negotiator Wu Tingfang and the dynastic adviser Yuan Shikai. Yuan's influence and future plans were evident in the final gestures of the outgoing Qing court. The smooth transition from the Qing empire to the Chinese Republic was clearly one of his primary goals. Thus on the very day in February 1912 that power was transferred to the Chinese nation-state, the rhetoric of the five peoples was officially invoked for the first time. Drafted by the Republicans, edited by Yuan, and issued by Empress Dowager Longyu, the formal abdication edict concluded with "the hope that the 'territories of the five ethnic groups [*wuzu*]—Manchu, Mongol, Han, Muslim, and Tibetan—would unite to form one great Republic of China.'"[126] The image of the new Chinese nation—one with multiethnic unity—had been officially articulated, but it was a novelty and not a mere continuation of the Qing empire under a new name.

Yuan Shikai was, however, careful to ensure the continuity of certain imperial policies toward Inner Asia. Yuan, unlike intellectuals such as Zhang Binglin, had little hesitancy about continuing the imperialism of the Qing under Chinese leadership.[127] Yuan added two critical clauses to the Republicans' proposals for dealing with the Manchus, Mongols, Muslims, and Tibetans: that the nobility would be supported and that "non-Han peoples would enjoy religious freedom."[128] Unlike the Republican negotiator, Yuan was an insider to the court who had his own plans for the future of the country. He knew that both noble prerogative (of Manchus, Tibetans, and Mongols) and religions (Tibetan Buddhism and Islam) had to be respected if any new formation of the state was to maintain all the Qing territory. For example, he invited the Changja Qutughtu (Lozang Penden Tenpé Drönmé, 1890–1957) to the capital twice in 1912, granting the Tibetan Buddhist prelate a new title.[129] However, the current Changja incarnation was of little use to the various Republican governments, as the incarnation series had no real influence in Tibet after centuries of residing in China Proper. Recognizing this, the lama would later decline a 1929 request from Nationalist government officials to go to Tibet to try to restore relations between the Dalai Lama and the exiled Panchen Lama.[130]

Yuan also preserved the imperial tradition of appointing Inner Asians (mostly Manchus and Mongols) to handle relations with Inner Asians.[131] Qing relations with Tibet had always been directly handled by the Manchu dynasty (mediated by the Imperial Household Department and the Court for Managing the Frontiers) with the assistance of a handful of Mongolian, Monguor, and Tibetan Buddhist religious leaders and Tibetan nobility. This established relationship could not simply be reconfigured as a relation of five (in principle) united and equal peoples. The primary raison d'être and the institutional basis for the relationship had vanished with the imperial family's abdication. By April 1912 Tibetans under the leadership of the Dalai Lama overwhelmed and repatriated the remaining Chinese garrison troops in Tibet through India. In a weak attempt, on April 21, to avert this reality with rhetoric, President Yuan issued an order that stated:

> Now that the five races are joined in democratic union, the lands comprised within the confines of Mongolia, Tibet, and Turkestan all become part of a territory of the Republic of China. . . . For the future all administrative matters in connection with these territories will come within the sphere of internal administration.[132]

As Melvyn Goldstein noted in his history of modern Tibet, Yuan Shikai did not hesitate to try to back up his rhetoric of unity with military force, sending troops well into Tibetan territory in the summer of 1912. In 1913–14 they were engaged by the Central Tibetan military and driven back to Kham.[133] Because the Tibetans had successfully driven the Chinese out of Tibet and there was no immediate military solution in sight, Yuan returned to diplomatic efforts using a new rhetoric.

Modern Innovations: Five Races as One Family

As described by Rhoads, the Republicans developed the idea of racial equality by adding "the phrase 'The five ethnic groups are as one family' (*Wuzu yijia*). This was a constant refrain in the first years of the republic. A significant extension of the Qing idea of 'Manchus and Han as one family' (*Man-Han yijia*), it was espoused in 1912 by such diverse figures as Longyu, Yuan Shikai, and Sun Yat-sen."[134] Yuan's presidential mandate of October 28, 1912 (published in the *Peking Gazette*), was the first modern diplomatic use of the "family of five races" rhetoric targeted specifically at Tibet:

> Now that the Republic has been firmly established and the Five Races deeply united into one family, the Dalai Lama is naturally moved with a feeling of deep attachment to the mother country. Under the circumstances, his

former errors should be overlooked, and his Title of Loyal and Submissive Vice-Regent, Great, Good, and Self-Existent Buddha is hereby restored to him, in the hope that he may prove . . . a help to the Republic.[135]

According to Charles Bell, Yuan also apologized for the excesses of the Chinese soldiers in the telegram to the Dalai Lama that "restored" his title. The Dalai Lama's response has not been reproduced by either the Chinese government (for obvious reasons) or, surprisingly, the Tibetan government-in-exile. Although hardly an unbiased source, Bell reported that the Dalai Lama replied "that he was not asking the Chinese Government for any rank, as he intended to exercise both temporal and ecclesiastical rule in Tibet."[136] In any case, the Dalai Lama clearly did not recognize the authority or validity of this earliest instance of the rhetoric of the five races applied to the Tibetans. He pointedly refused to prove "a help to the Republic." Instead he ordered his forces to attack and drive back the Chinese advance on the Tibetan borderlands.

While this new Chinese rhetoric was essential to conceptually holding the old empire together as the new nation-state, it could not hide the contradictions inherent in Chinese nationalist thought. The abdication agreement called the five peoples "*minzu,*" meaning races or nations.[137] Chinese revolutionaries had used the term as a way to divide one race from another in the hopes of freeing themselves from the Manchus.[138] The idea was best known in Sun Yat-sen's formulation, "*minzuzhuyi,*" typically translated as "nationalism." However, well after the fall of the Qing this phrase continued to have strong racial overtones. The centrality of race in the Chinese understanding of nationalism would last well into the twentieth century, as demonstrated by a lone 1937 article that tried to distinguish between race and nation but failed to convince or change the discourse on this topic.[139] If each "*minzu,*" be it nation or race, was to determine its own fate and not be ruled over by another, as the revolutionaries had long been arguing, then the rhetoric would have to be altered to keep the empire intact. Thus, as Crossley argues, "*Minzu zhuyi* was retained as one of Sun Yat-sen's Three People's Principles (*san min zhuyi*), though its racial intentions were mitigated by a new language of nationalism manifested by the Brotherhood of the Five Races of China."[140]

Sun was a master at ignoring the contradictions in his own evolving rhetoric. Once he was assured that the Manchus would no longer control China, he was ready to drop the idea of racial divisions in the nation. As described by Mark Elliot, "Sun Yat-sen, in a volte-face from his previous promotion of 'monoracial unity,' began in 1912 to argue instead for multiracial national unity: 'The root of a nation is its people. National unity means unifying the areas where Han, Manchus, Mongols, Muslims, and Tibetans live as a single nation, and the union of these peoples as one people.'"[141] This was hopeful language but not very realistic. What Yuan thought to accomplish by issuing edicts, Sun hoped to achieve by altering his nationalist strategy. Fitzgerald described Sun's views as

> an assertion of the racial unity of the Chinese people which seemed to defy the evidence of the senses. . . . When Sun insisted that the Chinese people were racially distinct from all other "races" of the world, he drew the boundaries of race along the borders of the Chinese state and would allow no comparable ethnic distinctions to be drawn within China itself. The gene-pool of the race, in other words, happened to coincide with the borders of the state. Minority peoples were asked *to adjust their belief and behaviour* accordingly.[142]

The Qing emperors had certainly never envisioned their empire as unified in this way. Nor had they asked the Inner Asian peoples to change many of their beliefs or behaviors. The Mongol and Tibetan rejection of the new state could not be overcome merely by issuing edicts—whether from the Qing dynasty or from the new Republican authority—or by changing revolutionary rhetoric. The fall of the Qing empire and the challenges of unifying even the provinces of China Proper left the former frontiers of the empire virtually independent. Sun Yat-sen acknowledged the distinction between the Chinese provinces and the former Qing frontier territory in a speech given in September 1912:

> I believe . . . that the nation's *internal* problems are now satisfactorily resolved. What concerns me is that Mongolia and Tibet do not yet fully understand the true meaning of a republic, so they are inclined to oppose it. That fact, however, stems from the discord between them and the rest of the country, which has produced estrangement at every turn. Because of inadequate communications between the interior and Mongolia and Tibet, the situation has always existed, even during the Ch'ing period. The situation is more serious today, and for the moment cannot be easily resolved. Although a domestic affair, this matter is in reality inextricable from the diplomatic issue.[143]

Sun recognized that relations with Tibet and Mongolia were more or less external affairs, despite his assertion to the contrary. He knew that the desired recognition of the new Chinese government by the British could be affected by how the Chinese dealt with Tibet. He and Yuan Shikai could do little to remedy the loss of Tibet without endangering China's weak international status.

Sun also recognized the practical reality that Qing Inner Asia had already been disaggregated from China Proper, carved into spheres of foreign influence.

His comments on the border peoples in his *Memoirs of a Revolutionary* reveal his awareness of the real difficulties facing the Chinese who wanted to reunite the Qing territory under Chinese rule:

> After the overthrow of the monarchy and the establishment of the republican system in the territory populated by the five nationalities (Chinese, Manchus, Mongols, Tartars and Tibetans), a vast number of reactionary and religious elements appeared. And here lies the root of the evil. Numerically, these nationalities stand as follows: there are several million Tibetans, less than a million Mongols, about ten million Tartars, and the most insignificant number of Manchus. Politically their distribution is as follows: Manchuria is in the sphere of Japanese influence, Mongolia, according to recent reports, is under the influence of Russia, and *Tibet is the booty of Great Britain. These races have not sufficient strength for self-defense but they might unite with China to form a single state.*[144]

Shifting the blame for this situation to the imperialist powers, Sun offered the hope that the non-Chinese "races" might choose to join the new China. He also offered a prescription to speed this process:

> The name "Republic of Five Nationalities" [*wuzu gongheguo*] exists only because there exists a certain racial distinction which distorts the meaning of a single Republic. We must facilitate the dying out of all the names of individual people inhabiting China, i.e. Manchus, Tibetans, etc. In this respect we must follow the example of the United States of America, i.e. *satisfy the demands and requirements of all races* and unite them in a single and political whole.[145]

Although often quoted to demonstrate Sun's interest in assimilating the borderland peoples, the reference to following an American strategy of fulfilling the desires of all the people in order to incorporate them is generally ignored. This two-part strategy, seeking to assimilate while satisfying the borderland people's interests, ultimately became the goal of the Nationalist Party.

Even Sun's successor Chiang Kai-shek (1887–1975) eventually adapted to the realities of trying to work with recalcitrant borderland peoples once he came to power. But in 1912 Chiang was a little known Chinese military man who was critical of the government's apparent apathy with regard to the former Qing frontiers. He criticized the British and Russian presence in Tibet and Mongolia, and argued that the Chinese government "should demand the restoration of our sovereignty. Why does our government not act in this way, instead of repeatedly tolerating this oppression, and willingly retreating and withdrawing?"[146] As he did not hold a high post in the government, he did not have to face the international reality that the British and Russian presence in Inner Asia was the least of China's problems. Once he had to grapple with these issues as China's leader, he was more accommodating. Like Sun, Chiang would come to understand that efforts to include Tibet in the new Republic would require accommodation from both sides.

In fact, as Sun had acknowledged, the lack of communication between China and Tibet, and the concomitant lack of understanding, was the root of the problem. Despite the rapid spread of Sun Yat-sen's ideology in China, Tibetans heard almost nothing of it until 1925, when the Panchen Lama came to Beijing. For the next quarter of the century, many of China's political and intellectual leaders—from Dai Jitao to Chiang Kai-shek—invoked the ideology of the founding father of the Republic to include Tibetans in the new China. But, as Liang Qichao had feared, the Chinese were initially unable to maintain the imperial relationship with the Tibetans that the Manchus had preserved for two centuries. Russian and British commercial interests had succeeded in staking claims to Tibetan Buddhist regions of Inner Asia. Late Qing nationalist-inspired development plans for Tibet only encouraged Tibetans to take a strong stand against the new Chinese state. Fortunately for the Chinese, the centralized administration of a nationalist Tibetan government drove disgruntled lamas into exile in China. There they encountered another feature of globalization: the rise of the conception of pan-Asian Buddhism. This modern understanding of religion gave these lamas an unprecedented opportunity to establish connections with the Buddhists in China.

3. Buddhism as a Pan-Asian Religion (1890s–1928)

AN ARTIFICIAL UNITY based on nationalist or racial ideology would never have succeeded in linking Tibet with China without force, and the Republican government lacked the necessary military capabilities. However, other effects of globalization in Asia began to change Chinese perceptions of the Buddhist religion at roughly the same time as ideas of nationalism and race were altering the Chinese conception of the state's constituent elements. In China the idea of Buddhism as a single pan-Asian religion with ethnic variants developed first among modernizing monks and laity but was eventually adopted by the government as well. The end result of this process was similar to that described by Derek R. Peterson and Daren R. Walhof in their introduction to *The Invention of Religion:* "Creating, redefining, and standardizing religion has long been a political strategy linked to the making of national identities and the exercise of colonial power."[1] In the absence of other common cultural features, the pan-Asian conception of Buddhism was critical to linking Chinese and Tibetans. Yet the origins of such strategies are not always located in state plans, nor are they always linked to hegemonic power. In the case examined here, Buddhists redefined themselves and their tradition in an attempt to cope with threats to their religious institutions (whether from secular nationalists in China or religious nationalists in Tibet). For this reason I agree with Peterson and Walhof that reinventing religion is "an act of power," but I would argue that it is not always one that "truncated the social and political meanings of certain human practices."[2] In this case, religious agents also expanded the definition of religion in order to exercise power over politicians, nationalists, and colonialists.

How did modern Chinese Buddhists become less Sinocentric and willing to embrace a respect for Tibetan Buddhism? This came about through a gradual process from the late nineteenth century to the early twentieth century.[3] Lay Buddhists with international connections to the global scholarly community became involved in a renewal of Chinese Buddhism through finding and printing texts absent from the Chinese Buddhist canon, particularly in Japan. In addition, the enthusiastic reception of esoteric Tibetan Buddhism by the Chinese in the Republican period (1912–1949) was an essential vehicle for spreading such an interest among the Chinese. This scarcely studied phenomenon had important consequences for modern Tibetan and Chinese relations. As Peterson and Walhof assert, the "making and remaking of religion is a political enterprise, intimately linked to the imagination of new social and intellectual communities."[4] I would add that the inclusion of Tibet in the modern Chinese imagination of the nation was dependent on this redefined religious community, embodied in the tremendous popular support for Tibetan Buddhist teachers and practices by Chinese Buddhists.[5] This potent, though unintended, consequence of the popularity of Tibetan Buddhism in Republican China was not easily accomplished. The main challenge to this reception was convincing Chinese Buddhists that Tibetan Buddhist teachings were part of the teachings of a more grandly conceived "Buddhism." For those swayed by this argument, Tibetan Buddhist teachers and the rituals they led for the Chinese were a powerful source of hope during the distressing times of the Chinese Republic. Chinese Buddhist monks entertained the possibility that the addition of Tibetan Buddhist teachings would help save their religion (*jiu jiao*), and lay Buddhists turned to Tibetan Buddhist ritual practices to save the country (*jiu guo*).

But how did this change in attitude play a role in Tibet's incorporation into the modern Chinese nation-state? Few Tibetans, as inhabitants of the least integrated region of the former Qing empire, had any concept of belonging to a nation at all, much less the modern Chinese nation. The principal unifying identity in Tibet was that of being an "insider" (*nang pa*), as the Tibetans translate being Buddhist.[6] Given this distinction, the few Chinese Buddhists who sought to learn from Tibetan Buddhists were generally welcomed in Central Tibetan monasteries, but Tibetans felt little connection to non-Buddhist Chinese. Of course, few if any Chinese identified primarily as Buddhists, but most Chinese had some exposure to Buddhism, and it was by far the strongest institutional religion in modern China. Yet Chinese, even Buddhists, typically looked down on Tibetan Buddhism as a corrupt religion not even deserving of the name of Buddhism. Only the Western perspective that Buddhism was a single unified religion with variant forms all deserving of equal respect could provide a neutral conceptual context for relaxing this condescending view. Not all Western Buddhologists thought that Tibetan Buddhism was an equal to all other forms of Buddhism; nevertheless, conceptually the innovation was adapted, by Taixu at least, to the Chinese context. Thus this novel perspective introduced into China by lay and monastic Chinese Buddhists proved essential in providing a logic of inclusion for Tibetans in the modern Chinese nation-state; they were co-religionists.

The modern conception of Buddhism as a single global religion with related "ethnic" branches also helped bring individual Chinese Buddhists and Tibetan lamas together. This important change allowed Chinese monks to seek the renewal of traditional Chinese Buddhism in the vitality of Tibetan Buddhist textual and ritual practices. This new conception of Buddhism also opened the way for lay Chinese Buddhist interest in Tibetan Buddhist esoteric rituals. The combination of this monastic and lay interest led to a great popularization of Tibetan Buddhism in China. The Chinese Buddhist laity provided essential financial support for Tibetan Buddhist lamas in China and Chinese monks in Tibet. These pioneering Buddhists were the first Chinese and Tibetans to bridge the gap between these two very different cultures.

Religious Differences in Republican China

The distinction between these traditions is best reflected in the names they gave each other, even well into the twentieth century. These terminological differences do not mean that the two traditions did not recognize some shared origins but rather that they wanted to emphasize their differences. For example, Tibetan Buddhism was still disparaged in China as the "teachings of the lamas" (*lama jiao*), often translated as "Lamaism." In the Tibetan tradition, lama (*bla ma*) is a term used to refer to respected teachers, whether prominent religious laymen, monks, or reincarnation series, such as those of the Dalai and Panchen Lamas. However, the term is also applied to any teacher whom a disciple accepts as his personal master. The prominence of such figures in the Tibetan tradition led the Chinese, and also some Westerners, to call all Tibetan monks "lamas"; by extension, the tradition was called Lamaism. Taking a distinct religious practice to (mis)represent the entire tradition is similar to calling Catholics "Papists." In both cases the common origins of the traditions may be recognized as tracing back to the Buddha or Christ, but the variant traditions within each of these "world religions" are sufficiently different that adherents often viewed one another with great disdain, or at least as differing in critical beliefs and practices.

For their part, some twentieth-century Tibetans such as the ninth Panchen Lama adopted the Chinese term for Buddhism (Ch. *Fo jiao*, Tib. *Bu ja'o*) directly into Tibetan to refer to Chinese Buddhism. This term at least reflected what the Chinese called their religion, but it failed to draw any link between Tibetan and Chinese Buddhism. For example, the Tibetans could have literally translated the term as the "Buddha's teaching" (*Sangs rgyas kyi bstan pa*), a standard term in Tibetan, but they did not, preserving instead its foreignness.[7] Similarly, the Tibetans adopted phonetic versions of Chinese Buddhist terms to describe

Chinese monks (Ch. *heshang,* Tib. *hwa shang*) and their monasteries (Ch. *si,* Tib. *hwa shang dgon*).[8] Again, the Tibetans did not translate the terms into their Tibetan equivalents (*grwa pa* and *dgon pa,* respectively).

This terminological divide would eventually be bridged, at least by the Chinese who respected Tibetan Buddhism. They took to using the phrase Tibetan Buddhism (*Xizang Fojiao*), putting it on an equal footing with Chinese Buddhism (*Zhongguo Fojiao*).[9] Under the Communists these terms would be altered to accord with minority nationality theory. Just as all citizens were considered "Chinese," whatever their ethnicity, all variants of Buddhism had to be included in Chinese Buddhism (*Zhongguo Fojiao*). Thus, the various traditions were named after their ethnicity, for example, the Chinese tradition of Buddhism (*Hanchuan Fojiao*) and the Tibetan tradition of Buddhism (*Zangchuan Fojiao*). Of course, these terminological sleights of hand cannot erase the real differences that still exist, but they do indicate the dramatic mental shift that was necessary to see these different traditions as part of a single world religion.

The majority of Chinese and Tibetan Buddhists were oriented toward different centers of authority (in the lower Yangtze River region and around Lhasa, respectively)[10] and had different standards for training and practice that scarcely overlapped. The traditional Chinese disdain for "the teachings of the lamas" was reciprocated by Tibetan Buddhists, who generally saw Chinese Buddhism as impure. They considered the funerary practice of the burning of paper money, houses and boats, as well as the addition of Chinese musical instruments to Buddhist chanting, unwarranted accretions.[11] Furthermore, the Chan (Zen) meditation practice was generally considered worse than useless by the ruling Gelukpa order in Central Tibet, to judge by the orthodox work of the order's founder.[12] These lamas valued instead rigorous scholastic training in logic and analytical philosophy, hardly a strong point of the Chinese tradition. Monguor and Mongolian Tibetan Buddhists from the borderlands and even Tibetans of different traditions, such as the Nyingmapa, may have felt differently about these matters, but they did not represent the powerful Gelukpa centers of religious learning.[13] The seventeenth- and eighteenth-century Mongol and Monguor lamas who served at the court, or with Qing support in Köke nor—including Sumpa Khenpo Yeshé Penjor (1704–1788; an Oirat Mongol or a Monguor), Changja Rölpé dorjé (1717–1786, a Monguor), Tukwan Lozang Chökyi Nyima (1737–1802, a Monguor), Gönpo Kyap (fl. eighteenth century, a Mongol)— tended to have a better understanding and more sympathy for Chinese Buddhists and their practices.[14]

One of the most discussed contrasts between the "Buddhisms" of China and Tibet was the diet. A Chinese monk living in Tibet in the 1940s was told that the Tibetans saw no scriptural basis for Chinese Buddhists' vegetarianism, while

Tibetan teachers' appetites for meat appalled the Chinese Buddhists in the Republican period. Even the clothing worn by monks of the two traditions differed greatly, with the Tibetans claiming the higher ground by adhering to Indian traditions.[15] Reflecting these differences, in a letter to the Panchen Lama, Dai Jitao once referred to Chinese monks as "Central lands black[-clothed] vegetarians" (*Zhongtu zisu*).[16] Clearly, viewing Chinese and Tibetan Buddhists as part of the same tradition challenged the accepted perceptions of both traditions.

The Origins of Modern Pan-Asian Buddhism

The globalization of world religions, as signaled by the Parliament of World Religions held in Chicago in 1893, made possible the inclusion of Tibetan Buddhist teachers and practices within a formerly hostile Chinese Buddhist context. The globalization of religious traditions meant that, for the first time in history, the many different traditions that traced their origins to the Buddha were conceived of as a single religious tradition called "Buddhism." Differences were described according to their national (or ethnic) divisions, as detailed above. Jonathan Walters, author of the American Historical Association booklet entitled *Finding Buddhists in World History*, has called this modern innovation the Buddhological Construct, an appropriate name which emphasizes both the role that Buddhologists have played in this construction as well as the contingent nature of this recent creation.[17]

In China the adoption of just such a modern conception of Buddhism can be traced back to the literatus Yang Wenhui (1837–1911).[18] Yang was the first Chinese Buddhist scholar to assign equal validity and positive value to Buddhist traditions outside the mainstream of Chinese Buddhism. Yang worked in the Chinese Embassy in London for some six years during the late nineteenth century and there came in contact with foreigners from Europe, Japan, and the United States.

On his first tour of duty Yang was exposed to scholars of "Oriental" religion and was so impressed by their work that he called Paris "the capital of Buddhism."[19] He made the acquaintance of the Oxford professor of Asian religion Max Müller and his Japanese assistant, Nanjio Bunyiu. Müller was then compiling his series, *Sacred Books of the East,* which included much besides Buddhist texts, while Nanjio prepared a catalogue of the Chinese Buddhist canon. Müller, as a pioneer Orientalist, was studying East Asian religions just as the field of Buddhology was coming into existence. His series perfectly exemplified the view of a single religion (Buddhism) with various forms (generally associated with nations: Sri Lanka, India, China, and Japan). Müller himself translated Buddhist texts from Pali and Sanskrit, which were understood in Europe as the most authentic Buddhist sources. He also introduced other scholars' translations of Burmese, Chinese, and Japanese Buddhist works to the Western world.

Yang Wenhui's friendship with Nanjio led to the start of an important new trend in the Chinese Buddhist world: a respect for sources of Buddhist teachings other than original Indian texts. After Nanjio told Yang that Japanese Buddhists had access to many texts not found in the Chinese Buddhist canon, Yang arranged for Nanjio to send him more than two hundred volumes that were missing in China.[20] This was one of the first times since the Tang dynasty that Chinese Buddhists had sought out new Buddhist texts, and this time the Chinese did not merely turn to India as the source for authentic Buddhism. Instead, Yang turned to the Japanese, who had themselves received Buddhism from the Chinese. While still in Europe Yang also followed the "progress of critical editions of Buddhist texts in Sanskrit, Pali and Tibetan."[21] Yang's innovation was to have lasting repercussions for Chinese Buddhists, especially through the schools later established by his student Taixu.

Borrowing Buddhist texts from other segments of a Buddhist world was not Yang's only innovation, for even the fact that a lay Buddhist would have a monastic student such as Taixu was extraordinary at this time. Yang started a school in 1908 that seems to have been inspired by another of the great figures in the formation of the Buddhological Construct, Anagarika Dharmapala (1864–1933). Dharmapala stopped in China on his return from the 1893 Parliament of World Religions in Chicago and was introduced to Yang by the Christian missionary Timothy Richards. Dharmapala informed the Chinese of his hopes to create a pan-Asian Buddhism with their help.[22] Although nothing conclusive came of their first meeting, the year that Yang opened his school he and Dharmapala exchanged letters about "making a common effort to revive Buddhism in order to spread it throughout the world." Yang had already been taking note of Christian proselytizing methods and had helped Richards translate the Buddhist text *Awakening of Faith* into English in 1894. By 1906 he had completed a textbook "for the express purpose of training monks for missionary work abroad."[23] Taixu, famed reviver of Chinese Buddhism, was the best known of the students who attended the short-lived school that Yang set up. Although Taixu had little success in spreading Buddhism to other countries, he was more successful in supporting Chinese Buddhists in bringing other "Buddhisms" (Japanese, Tibetan, and Sri Lankan) to China.

Although Yang was most interested in the rich additions that Japanese Buddhism could make to the effort to restore Chinese Buddhism, his open-minded attitude led the way to greater acceptance of non-Chinese Buddhist traditions including the Sri Lankan and Tibetan traditions. Taixu extended and gave institutional backing to many of Yang's ideas. For example, according to Holmes

Welch, Taixu conceived of unifying Chinese and Tibetan Buddhism in the following manner:

> He wanted to unite the component parts of Buddhism itself. He felt that it would be incomplete without its Tantric component, which he therefore decided to revive. He planned to modify it and then combine it with the existing schools *so as to produce a new, unified Buddhism, both esoteric and exoteric,* in which adepts who knew the secrets of Tibetan lamas would live the pure life of Chinese monks. That is why, for example, although lamas are permitted to eat meat, the food served at his Tibetan College was strictly vegetarian.[24]

The root of such expansive ideas can be found in the interest in pan-Asian Buddhism that Yang shared with Dharmapala. In the early years of the twentieth century the conception of Buddhism as a unified religion spread to a handful of new institutions in China. Taixu's Wuchang Buddhist Studies Institute and later his World Buddhist Institute, the Buddhist Institute for the Study of Tibetan Language in Beijing, the Metaphysical Institute and the Academia Sinica in Nanjing, as well as Beijing University—all more or less embraced Tibetan Buddhism as a part of the world religion of Buddhism. The same was true of many of the Buddhist lay practitioners who started the less academic study associations dedicated to Tibetan Buddhism in most of China's major cities, including Nanjing, Beijing (Beiping), Tianjin, Shanghai, Canton, Hong Kong, Hankou, Changshou, Suzhou, Hangzhou, Chongqing, Kaifeng, and Chengdu.[25] Such academic and popular institutions were enough of a foothold to change the way that many Chinese Buddhists understood their religion by the 1930s and thereafter. This groundswell of support for Tibetan Buddhism is thus a defining aspect of Tibetan Buddhism's place in Republican China.

The Shared Interests of Chinese and Tibetan Buddhists

The economic and political importance of Tibetan Buddhism to the Chinese Buddhist community may also help to explain why Tibetan Buddhists were, for the first time in Chinese history, accepted as equal partners in the Buddhist establishments of Republican China. Conservative Chinese Buddhists were initially resistant to such a broad (and to them denigrating) conception of Buddhism, but most ultimately accepted elements of it in order to survive. This new understanding of Buddhism would eventually help these conservative Chinese Buddhists reckon with the forces of globalization—imperial commercial interests and secular nationalism—which swept across China. Western impe-

W. commerce &

rialist commerce brought with it the challenge of Christian missionaries and ultimately the overthrow of the state that had protected the status of Buddhist establishments. The secular nationalists sought to appropriate the vast Buddhist landholdings for a variety of new projects, especially schools. Many monasteries responded to these threats by opening their own schools, and the modernization of the Buddhist social world was accelerated in these new seminaries. At the same time, traditional Buddhists scrambling for new standing in the secular state became willing to accept association with Tibetan Buddhists if this unity would help to protect their assets.

The de facto independence of Tibet raised the role of Tibetan Buddhists in China from the margins of the Chinese Buddhist community to the center of this community's efforts at self-preservation. Tibetan Buddhists were accorded a special status in China because of the perceived role that they could have in reconfiguring the relations between newly independent Mongolia and Tibet and the Chinese republic. Tibetan Buddhists in China were thus able to play a role in the protection of institutional Buddhism out of proportion to their small numbers. Much of Welch's *Buddhist Revival in China* summarized the efforts of Chinese Buddhist monks to protect their land holdings and temples. He described how the effort to protect Buddhist property played a critical role in the modernization of Chinese Buddhism, from the formation of national associations and lay societies that functioned as lobby groups for Buddhism to the new educational systems that countered the criticism of secular educators.[26]

Early Efforts to Protect Buddhist Resources in China

Buddhists in China were quick to respond to the threats to their property occasioned by the secularization that accompanied revolution in China. For example, in 1912 the government official in charge of religious affairs carried out a survey of monastic property in order to begin confiscation. By securing a charter for the first Chinese Buddhist Association from the central government by the end of 1912, the Buddhists managed to outflank this first attack. Welch clearly outlined what was at stake in the political and economic relations among Chinese Buddhism, Tibetan Buddhism, and the Chinese state. Yuan Shikai's support for this association's charter was credited to the intervention of the most prominent Tibetan Buddhist lama in China at the time, the Changja Qutughtu. When this Tibetan Buddhist hierarch met with Yuan Shikai in the fall of 1912,

[he] urged Yuan to give equal protection to Buddhism of every sect and suggested that the problem of Mongolia and Tibet could be solved through reli-

gion. Later he was given a warm welcome by the Chinese sangha [monastic community], whose members appreciated the leverage he had provided toward securing government protection of the monasteries. That is, the government could not successfully use Buddhism as a tool for cementing relations with Tibet if it allowed Buddhism to be persecuted on China's own territory.[27]

Welch's argument is convincing, although he failed to explain why this Tibetan Buddhist would be so concerned with Chinese affairs in the first place.

To understand why the Changja Qutughtu would participate in this conflict between China and Tibet, we must look to Qing precedents and the lama's own material interests in China. The Changja Qutughtu was the latest in a series of incarnate lamas that originated among the Monguor people in Qinghai. The Monguors were remnants of Yuan dynasty Mongols stationed in Qinghai who had largely adopted Tibetan culture over the centuries while remaining under Chinese administration. Because they were ethnically of Mongol descent, culturally Tibetan, and subjects of China, the Monguors were ideal intermediaries for the multiethnic empire of the Manchus.[28] The first Changja Qutughtu was granted a title by the Kangxi emperor in the seventeenth century and helped negotiate relations with the Mongols. As the second Changja Qutughtu was more or less kidnapped as a child and raised at the Qing court, he was a personal friend and religious instructor of the Qianlong emperor. He was sent to Tibet to assist with settling affairs in the turbulent eighteenth century, when the Qing empire was extending its rule there. But despite their Mongol and Tibetan background, the Changja Qutughtus became almost entirely dependent on the Qing court for financial support. They presided over temples and landholdings in Gansu and Inner Mongolia, as well as at Mount Wutai, Beijing, and Rehe. Moreover, the prestige conferred by the Qing court on this incarnation series ranked it the highest outside Tibet or Mongolia proper.

As the leading luminary of Tibetan Buddhists living in China Proper, the Changja Qutughtu represented a host of intermediary figures who had grown dependent upon the Manchu court for their status and upkeep. Elite Manchu support for Tibetan Buddhism had led to a significant presence of officially recognized Tibetan Buddhist monks and temples in Beijing during the Qing. Susan Naquin's study of Beijing listed fifty-three Tibetan Buddhist temples in and around Beijing, with some forty-two receiving regular imperial support.[29] As Naquin noted, "these Tibetan Buddhist temples enjoyed a condition of special dependency. With a limited constituency among the local population, they were usually both founded and funded by the throne."[30] Although imperial support for these Tibetan Buddhist temples waned with the challenges to the dynasty in the latter half of the nineteenth century, the ultimate challenge came with the success of the 1911 Revolution.[31] As support for these monks and their temples dwindled, they were exposed to the same threats as the Chinese Buddhists. It was natural for figures such as the Changja Qutughtu to turn to the new government of China to try to preserve their wealth and status.

Although the Changja Qutughtu may have convinced Yuan Shikai with his reasoning in 1912, he was not able to deliver on his promise to help solve the problem of Tibet's independence through religion. By the end of 1914 the Dalai Lama had sent the Tibetan army to resist Chinese forces in Kham. In addition, the Simla Convention held in India in 1914 went poorly for China. The British and the Tibetans agreed to bilaterally recognize the terms of the convention, the chief of which was Tibetan autonomy, without Chinese concurrence. To show its support, the Government of India "had adopted a policy of assisting the Tibetans in the preservation of their de facto independence by the provision of arms and ammunition."[32] With this turn of events, by 1915 Yuan's support for Buddhism had eroded so far that he supported a bill to regulate and control monasteries and disbanded the lobby group that tried to oppose the bill. Because the protection of Buddhism in China had resulted in no concrete gains in Tibet, Tibetan Buddhists at this time had no more power than the Chinese Buddhists to change the government's new regulations on Buddhism.

Fortunately for Buddhists in China, Yuan's abdication and death made the bill a dead letter, and for some years there was no serious threat to Buddhist property. In 1917 the Changja Qutughtu and a Chinese monk revived the Chinese Buddhist Association in Beijing. The abysmal state of Chinese–Tibetan relations may explain why the government failed to honor this Buddhist cooperation. In 1918 the Tibetans successfully repelled a Chinese attack on Tibetan borderland garrisons and then advanced into Chinese-held territory in Sichuan. By 1919 the government declared this new organization illegal and ordered it dissolved.[33]

Some Republican-era threats to Buddhist landholdings were averted without the involvement of Tibetan Buddhists. For example, in 1928 the Ministry of the Interior planned to confiscate monastic property for the purpose of financing modern education. The Chinese Buddhists again organized an association to protect their interests and succeeded in temporarily getting the ministry to abandon its plans. When overseas-educated college officials renewed their attempts to promote the confiscation of temple property for educational purposes in 1929, the monks once again succeeded at delaying this plan. However, positive and secure national protection of Buddhist property was only offered in return for solid political commitments made by the Panchen Lama in the 1930s.

These are discussed in chapter 5. Until the Chinese government had such a commitment, Chinese and Tibetan monasteries in China were equally threatened by the secular state.

Esoteric Techniques: Religious Salvation for Chinese Buddhists

Quite aside from the financial interests of the monastic communities, many Chinese hoped to find a source of power in esoteric (*mizong*) Buddhism to help them cope with the difficulties of the Republican period—revolution, civil wars, natural disasters, imperialism, and modernization. The perceived benefit of the esoteric traditions was twofold. First, the actual conferral of an initiation as a public ceremony was considered a powerful blessing for the hosting locality and even the country. This was because the merit accumulated during the ceremony was most frequently dedicated to ending the difficulties of the country and the people, and sometimes even to achieving world peace. Second, after a ceremony was over, those who had actually received the initiation were bound by vows to continue to perform daily the prescribed ritual practices (recitation of scripture, repetition of a certain number of mantras, and particular visualizations). For people powerless to control the chaotic external situation, these rituals conferred a sense of being able to do something potent but personal to resolve their own and their country's problems.

Coincident with the collapse of the Manchu dynasty was a growing attraction to esoteric Buddhism among the Chinese. Esoteric mantras, vows, and collected teachings from the Tang and Song dynasties were reprinted in Chinese in the early decades of the twentieth century. The Tibetan Sakya tradition's "Path and Result" texts (Tib. *lam 'bras*, Ch. *dao guo*), originally translated into Chinese in the Yuan period, were also rediscovered in the early decades of the century and reprinted.[34] A few Chinese monks pioneered the study of esoteric Buddhism. At first, they went to study the esoteric tradition that had been transmitted from China to Japan in the Tang dynasty and had been maintained there. Later, many more went to Tibet to pursue Tibetan Buddhist teachings that were absent from Chinese Buddhism.

The extent of the popularity of Tibetan Buddhism is best revealed by the contemporary commentators on Chinese Buddhism in the Republican era who were critical of these esoteric practices. A Taiwanese researcher, Mei Jingshun, wrote about the considerable amount of criticism and distrust of Tibetan Buddhists and their "gullible" followers. As Mei's sources were drawn from Taixu's magazine, *Haichaoyin*, they demonstrated a continued tension between the Chinese and Tibetan Buddhist traditions—even in the publication of the man who helped initiate this interest. Chinese monks were exhorted not to pursue

Tibetan Buddhism, and Chinese laity were ridiculed for assuming every Tibetan monk was an incarnate lama. The lamas were attacked for not being vegetarian, and some critics suspected them of performing the rituals for financial gain.[35] The monk Weihuan ridiculed those who took part in esoteric initiations, "from high officials of the government down to the old ladies who frequent Buddhist temples." He lampooned the teachers who proclaimed that "they can fix anything from national catastrophes to influenza" and described their disciples as "ambitious" and "avaricious" in seeking to use these mystical techniques to gain what they wanted—from government jobs to lucky lottery tickets. He proceeded to describe in some detail, and unsympathetically, the verbal, physical, and mental aspects of esoteric practice.[36] From his descriptions it is obvious that Chinese from all walks of life had direct and practical problems that they hoped esoteric Buddhism could ameliorate.

The scholar Wing-tsit Chan more sympathetically described this interest in what he called "Mysticism," as a response to the fact that Chinese Buddhism had lost its vitality and spirituality. Like Weihuan, he was critical of what he perceived as superstition; nevertheless, he noted that a Tibetan Buddhist emphasis on practice, as opposed to what he saw as the theoretical teachings of Chinese traditions, appealed to the Chinese in those difficult times.[37] John Blofeld, an English Buddhist living in China during this time, concurred with Chan's evaluation of the limitations of Chinese Buddhism and added an important insight. In his experience the lamas understood the precise purposes and meanings of their ritual practices and could explain them. He contrasted this with the ignorance of most Chinese Buddhist monks he encountered. As a participant in both the Chinese and the Tibetan Buddhist communities, Blofeld was able to compare them and found the latter the more vital. He credited the attraction of its religious practices to the combination of practice grounded in a knowledge of the supporting theory.[38]

The Origins of Chinese Interest in Tibetan Buddhist Teachers and Practices

Two events in the early years of the twentieth century illustrate the transformation that linked the Tibetan and Chinese adherents of the Buddhist religion in China. In 1914 a Mongol lama named Bai Puren (1870–1927), born in Rehe but residing in Beijing, used special rituals to protect the capital from a flood.[39] Although Tibetan Buddhist protection had been invoked by the Mongol Yuan and Manchu Qing dynasties for centuries, this was the first instance of such Buddhist protection being conferred on the new nation-state. The Mongol ethnicity of the lama was significant because, despite his non-Chinese origin, he chose to embrace the Chinese state. Yet the continuity with the past was not quite complete. Although Bai Puren had committed to protecting the new state, there is no indication that the state had sponsored or requested his protection. The new state had yet to embrace a traditional role of supporting Buddhist institutions and practices.

Only a year later, in 1915, Taixu issued his plans for reforming the Buddhist establishment in China. In line with the revolutionary ideas of his times, Taixu saw the need to radically overhaul Chinese Buddhism, and his proposals included plans to send people to Japan and Tibet to study their esoteric (tantric) traditions. This was the first articulation of an idea that would have an enduring impact not just on Chinese Buddhism but also on the very composition of the Chinese nation-state. Although the state was not ready to embrace Tibetan Buddhism at this early date, the chain of events that Bai Puren and Taixu started in these years would eventually provide a crucial link between China and an independent Tibet, which was otherwise alienated from the modern Chinese nation-state.

The work of these two monks from such different backgrounds started to weave together the two strands (as we now see them) of Chinese and Tibetan Buddhism. Each monk, trying to meet the demands of the times according to his own tradition, soon found himself working toward a common goal: the study and propagation of esoteric and Tibetan Buddhist teachings in China. Since his debut in 1914, Bai Lama had frequently exercised himself—as well as powerful beings in the Buddhist pantheon known as Yakshas—to save and protect the country (*jiu hu guo*). In this effort, a Tang dynasty quasi-esoteric scripture called the *Sutra of Golden Light* (*Jin guang ming jing*) especially inspired him.[40] A portion of this Buddhist sutra was known for bringing the celestial kings of the four directions (also known as world-protectors) to guard and protect one's country and other this-worldly interests (*zhenhu guojia ji xianshi liyi*).[41] Teaching this text, Bai Lama made quite an impact in his native region of Rehe (northeast of Beijing), counting some seventeen thousand people as his disciples. One county seat in particular, Pingquan, just to the east of Chengde (Jehol), was particularly faithful to him, and its populace practiced the recitation of the *Sutra of Golden Light*.[42] When routed warlord armies ransacked Rehe in 1922, Pingquan remarkably escaped unscathed. For this reason, the sutra and its advocate gained some renown, and others seeking to eliminate disaster adopted the practice of reciting the text.

Having demonstrated his power, this (Mongolian) Tibetan Buddhist lama received the first request for spiritual aid from a leader of the modern Chinese state. Early in 1925 Duan Qirui was restored as titular head of the Beijing government and sought ways to resolve the political situation in northern China in his favor, including sponsoring a ritual led by Bai Lama at Yonghegong. This temple was located in the former palace of the Yongzheng emperor and had relied on the support of the imperial household since it had served as the seat of imperially sponsored Tibetan Buddhist training at the capital under the Qianlong emperor. When imperial patronage for the temple collapsed (in 1923 apparently),[43] the resident monks must have been eager to ensure continued support for their activities. Bai Lama led 108 of the temple's residents in a twenty-one-day Golden Light Dharma ritual based on the *Sutra of Golden Light*. By sponsoring this ritual, the Chinese state embraced the same Buddhist establishment that had protected the interests of the Qing dynasty.

In the new era the Chinese people were not as segregated from the state's interests as they had been in the Qing. Whereas the Manchu court had patronized Tibetan Buddhism exclusively through imperial household institutions, Duan's support was a public phenomenon. This was a marked contrast with earlier times, fueled no doubt by the development of the media which more closely linked the government with the people. Within months of Duan's sponsorship, Shanghai Buddhists invited the lama and twenty-eight assistants south to perform the same ritual, again for twenty-one days. From there Bai Lama went to Hangzhou where he performed a portion of the *Sutra of Golden Light* ritual involving a great white parasol, initiating three hundred people in the process. He also initiated a smaller group of eighty-one people into an unspecified Tibetan Buddhist esoteric tradition. That same year the newly arrived Panchen Lama granted him the distinguished title of *khenpo*.[44] The Panchen Lama must have recognized that Bai Lama had laid the foundations of interest in Tibetan Buddhist practices in some of the most important cities in China: Beijing, Shanghai, and Hangzhou.

Monks Pursue Esoteric Buddhism

In these same years Taixu was realizing his ambitious reforms as best he could. In 1919 he ordained a former military man named Li Jinzhang (1893–1929), giving him the religious name Dayong. As one of Taixu's earliest disciples, Dayong was sent, in 1921, to fulfill that part of Taixu's mission involving the study of Japanese esoteric Buddhism. A Norwegian missionary in China at the time discussed the impetus for Taixu's encouragement:

T'ai-hsü has sent one of his ablest disciples to Japan to study the [esoteric] school. . . . The monk has been sent to Japan not so much to bring back scriptures belonging to this special school (although many such scriptures still exist), but rather *to get into personal contact with the masters who have received the traditional sayings, rules and mysteries from the old masters.* It is always stated that the real meaning of Mi-tsung [*mizong*: the esoteric school] can never be apprehended through study alone, but personal contact with the masters is the main thing.[45]

Dayong returned in 1923, having earned from his Japanese masters the right to transmit the secret teachings to others. It would not be long before he applied the same approach to Tibetan Buddhist esoteric teachings.

The early 1920s also marked the commencement of modern Buddhist education, which included an interest in esoteric and Tibetan Buddhist teachings. While Dayong was studying in Japan, Taixu successfully started another aspect of his planned reforms by opening a modern school for monks called the Wuchang Buddhist Studies Institute (Wuchang Foxue yuan). This institution was funded by the laity, as neither the government nor the traditional monasteries would support such an endeavor. Dayong taught some of what he had learned in Japan to the students at the seminary before heading north to Beijing. There, in the spring of 1924, he met Bai Lama, who inspired him to take up the study of Tibetan Buddhist esoterica and became his teacher.[46] When the first class of students graduated from the Wuchang academy that summer, one eager student named Fazun met Dayong at Mount Wutai and followed him to Beijing to join a new school.

In the fall of 1924 Dayong started the first Sino-Tibetan educational institution, the Buddhist Institute for the Study of the Tibetan Language (Fojiao Zangwen xueyuan). Several other recent graduates from the Wuchang academy joined Fazun and the Beijing laymen who made up some fifty students—both monks and laypeople—who lived, ate, and studied Tibetan language and Tibetan Buddhism together. Bai Lama and Hu Zihu, the Chinese layman and Tibetan Buddhist practitioner who had introduced Bai Lama to Dayong, sponsored the school.[47] The Tibetan language teacher was a Chinese layman from Sichuan, and visiting lamas in Beijing also came to teach.[48] As Dayong was Taixu's disciple, when Taixu was in Beijing he also came and lectured on Chinese Buddhist topics.[49]

Tibetan Lamas in China, Chinese Monks in Tibet

The watershed year for the modern diffusion of esoteric Buddhist teaching in China was 1925, marked especially by the arrival of the Panchen Lama at the capital. Dayong's Tibetan school was in its first year, Bai Lama led a ceremony at the state's behest, and the Panchen Lama went to Beijing at President Duan's

Photo 3.1 Master Dayong, *Ācârya* (1893–1929), from a 1930 issue of *Haichaoyin*

invitation. Also in that year, Taixu—no doubt inspired by Bai Lama's successes—started teaching another Tang dynasty esoteric scripture called the *Scripture for Humane Kings Who Wish to Protect Their States (Renwang huguo jing)* to thousands of people.[50] This text would eventually become very popular, partially with the assistance of a lay advocate, the politician Dai Jitao. Shortly after the Panchen Lama arrived, Taixu was in the capital to teach the sutra and invited the Panchen Lama to join him, "to practice the exoteric and the esoteric traditions together, in order to save the country, pacifically control [the situation], and eliminate people's hardships, disasters, suffering and danger" *(xian mi shuang xiu, jiuguo heping zhi, xiaochu renmin zai nan ku wei).*[51] The Panchen Lama's presence also attracted another Tibetan Buddhist teacher who was to have a profound impact on the development of Tibetan Buddhism in China, Dorjé Chöpa (1874–?).[52]

Dorjé Chöpa's importance derived from the fact that he was the first fully trained Tibetan teacher in the Republican period to regularly teach the Chinese Tibetan Buddhism. He had spent twenty years at Drepung, the largest monastery in Lhasa, earning an advanced degree in Buddhist philosophy before undertaking three years of tantric studies at a monastic school dedicated to these practices. For years afterward he lived in Mongolia and must have become familiar with Chinese Buddhists on his five trips to Mount Wutai in the first decades of the twentieth century. All this prepared him well for the budding interest in Tibetan Buddhist teachings in China. He quickly became Dayong's teacher and even taught at the new school. Most important, he gave Dayong the idea to go to Tibet to study Tibetan Buddhism.[53] Before the school year ended Dayong transformed his Beijing school into a twenty-member expedition, the Team to Study the Dharma Abroad in Tibet (Liu Zang xuefa tuan). As Dorjé Chöpa was a native of the important border town of Dartsedo (Ch. Daqianlu, now known as Kangding)[54] west of Chengdu, he was able to provide the introductions to the first temple (Tib. Ngachö Gön, Ch. Anjue si)[55] in which the study team lived.[56] The expedition was once again funded by the Beijing layman Hu Zihu and others who created an "association of those left behind" (Liu Zang xuefa tuan huoyuan hui) to help bankroll the venture. While Dayong fulfilled Taixu's original plan by following Dorjé Chöpa's advice, Dorjé Chöpa followed the interest in Tibetan Buddhist teachings south to Hangzhou. By the year's end he had given initiations into ten different Tibetan Buddhist tantric cycles and had translated more than twenty different types of Tibetan esoteric texts into Chinese.[57]

The following year saw all these trends continue. Dayong's group was diligently studying Tibetan in Daqianlu. Bai Lama won the respect of so many military figures that one article named the one military officer who did *not* believe in Bai and then gave a sample listing of those who had taken Buddhist precepts, calling them a monk army (heshang zhun).[58] Dorjé Chöpa was invited to

Photo 3.2 Dorjé Chöpa Geshé (1874–?), from a 1932 publication for the Southwestern Dharma-Assembly for Peace

Hankou, where the warlord Wu Peifu took refuge with him in the spring of 1926, as did the former Nationalist officer Zhao Hengdi.[59] Dorjé Chöpa also started the Tantrayana Study Society (Micheng xuehui) in Wuchang.[60] In this way Dorjé Chöpa launched his career as the single most active Tibetan Buddhist teacher for many years in China.

After more than a decade of cherishing the same goals, the only documented record of Taixu and Bai Lama working together was in 1926, when Bai taught at Taixu's Wuchang Buddhist Studies Institute. This was part of Bai Lama's last southern tour, put together by an enthusiastic preparation committee based in Nanjing. On this tour Bai performed the Golden Light Dharma (*Jin guang ming fa*) ceremony in five of the southern provinces: Jiangsu, Jiangxi, Zhejiang, Anhui, and Fujian. In Hunan some five hundred or six hundred people studied the Golden Light Dharma with the lama. In 1927 Bai Lama died in Beijing and, despite his obvious importance in initiating interest in esoteric and Tibetan Buddhism among the Chinese, he is largely forgotten today.

While the study team was in the field the fame of Bai Puren and Dorjé Chöpa had spread throughout the country. Bai's burgeoning fame fittingly ended with a nationally oriented ritual called the "ceremony for averting disaster for the entire country" (*quanguo xiaozai daochang*), which he performed before his death in 1927. Thereafter the meteoric rise in the demand for Dorjé Chöpa's services indicated that he filled the gap left at Bai's death. The range of his activities, described in the next chapter, demonstrates the widespread awareness of and interest in Tibetan Buddhist esoteric practices. For example, a Sichuan warlord who had retreated to Guangdong asked Dorjé Chöpa for help and had several esoteric rituals performed on his behalf. When Beijing was experiencing a serious drought early in 1927, Dorjé Chöpa was asked to pray for rain. The Buddhist Mantra Association (Fojiao zhenyan hui) in Shandong invited Dorjé Chöpa to teach for seven days. In early 1928 he was invited to Liaodong to perform a forty-nine-day "Northeastern Dharma-Assembly for Peace" (Dongbei heping fahui).[61] These examples demonstrate that interest in Tibetan Buddhism spanned China, from the southernmost and easternmost provinces to the far north.

To a degree, the Chinese monks and lay adherents of Tibetan Buddhism were always on different trajectories toward the linked goals of saving Buddhism and saving the country. However, in the period after 1926 they became more separate, as the different groups were in distinct geographical locations pursuing separate aspects of Tibetan Buddhism. The monks studying abroad wanted to improve Chinese Buddhism, while the Chinese Buddhist laity wanted effective rituals and practices to solve their own and their country's problems. This distinction is complicated by the fact that the monks depended on the laity for their support, so at least some of the laymen were supportive of the monastic goals. However, the fact remains that no prominent layman went to Tibet to study in this period. Likewise, no prominent Chinese monk devoted himself to supporting Tibetan teachers and their ritual activities in China; this was left to the laity. Here we will look first at the attention the Chinese laity showered on the Tibetan lamas who fled Tibet for political reasons, and then turn to the Chinese monks who went to Tibet to study Buddhism there.

Tibetan Lamas Teach in China

Although I mainly consider the reception the Chinese laity gave these Tibetan lamas, it is important at the start to place these events into a broader context. An examination of the activities of Tibetan lamas in China in the early decades of the twentieth century reveals the repetition of centuries-old traditions as well as innovations associated with modernity. In the West, and among contemporary Tibetans in exile, lamas who worked with the Chinese government are often viewed as dupes at best, collaborators at worst.[62] I contend that these lamas exercised an active agency that elevated their role above that of mere pawns in someone else's game. At the same time I recognize the very real context of events that did limit these actors' choices.

During their early years in China, two Tibetan lamas in exile—the Panchen Lama and the Norlha Qutughtu—were involved almost exclusively in spreading Tibetan Buddhist teachings. As I describe below, the Panchen Lama was careful to maintain a low political profile at first. Part of the tension between the Dalai Lama and the Panchen Lama had been over the Panchen Lama's relations with the Qing state and the British in India. During his early years in China—while the Panchen Lama was still hoping to quickly return to Tibet—he did not want to add to the accusations that could be leveled against him. For this reason, at first the Panchen Lama mostly sent representatives to deal with government officials and to attend political gatherings, while he himself propagated Tibetan Buddhism.

The Panchen Lama's first teachings were directed at Mongolian, Tibetan, and Chinese adherents of Tibetan Buddhism at the sites of the old imperially supported Tibetan Buddhist temples in and around the capital. However, he quickly moved into contexts that were purely Chinese, both ethnically and in terms of the form of Buddhism practiced. In these communities the Panchen Lama largely focused on teaching about Buddhist figures that were shared with his Chinese Buddhist brethren. At the same time he infused his teachings with elements unique to Tibetan Buddhism, especially emphasizing the esoteric aspects of the Buddhist figures about whom he taught.

Meanwhile, the Norlha Qutughtu sought Chinese government assistance in retaking his domains but failed to secure it. At best he was given permission to try, but without substantial resources this was an impossible task. As there was no way to return to the combined political and religious position that had formerly been his, the Norlha Qutughtu was also limited temporarily to religious activities among the Chinese. Unlike the Panchen Lama, however, he seems to have focused on presiding over rituals whose precedents were long-standing in imperial China. As the Qing elite was no longer a viable audience, he adapted these traditions by making them available to the Chinese Buddhist laity. Although a prominent local politician eventually came to his aid, his actual support appears to have come from a very broad base of the Chinese Buddhist community in Sichuan Province. In these early years in China, then, these two Tibetan Buddhist religious rulers focused their attention primarily on spreading Tibetan Buddhism among the Chinese, without ever losing sight of their longer-term goals.

The Panchen Lama Avoids Politics and Teaches Buddhism to the Chinese

By any society's standards, the Panchen Lama's first activities in China were perfectly consonant with his being a prominent religious leader. Seeing the death and destruction caused by the ravages of warlord battles, he offered prayers for those killed. Shortly thereafter he sent an open telegram to all the warlords of China, requesting that they cease fighting one another so that peace and prosperity might return to China.[63] He favored no side and only made vague statements about his support of the central government based in Beijing.

Moreover, when the government invited the Panchen Lama to the National Reconstruction Conference (Shanhuo huiyi) in 1925—which brought together the rulers of northern China with the "father" of Republican China, Sun Yat-sen—the Panchen Lama studiously avoided becoming too involved in Chinese politics. He sent a representative to express his concern that Chinese rhetoric regarding the unity of the five nationalities was premature given the mutual incomprehension and regional conflicts that afflicted the country at that time. The Panchen Lama himself stopped at the sacred Buddhist pilgrimage site called Mount Wutai and gave Buddhist teachings there until the conference ended.[64] This mountain complex was an ancient center for Sino-Tibetan contact. As such, it had traditionally provided a liminal zone for Tibetan Buddhist religious rulers approaching the Chinese government.

This instance of first contact with the central Chinese government set the pattern that the Panchen Lama was to follow for several years. He would send representatives to deal with political matters while he frequented temples and expounded on Buddhist topics, eschewing direct involvement in politics. Aside from considering how the Tibetan government would respond to his having dealings with the Chinese government, the Panchen Lama also might have been aware of the Chinese condemnation of monks who were involved in political affairs. Unlike Tibetan society, Chinese culture left little room for religious figures to participate in politics.[65] Upon his arrival in China the Panchen Lama visited local political leaders wherever he went but took no direct role in politics for several years.

When the Panchen Lama arrived in Beijing he taught first at Yonghegong. While there he transmitted the samaya precepts and the intitiation of the long-life Buddha, and explicated in detail teachings on Green Tara and the Kâlacakra tantra.[66] Although some ethnic Chinese were pursuing studies of Tibetan Buddhism at Yonghegong at that time, the audience would have been primarily ethnic Mongolian Tibetan Buddhists, as this group comprised the principal monastic population of the temple. This instance demonstrates the subtle yet significant role that the presence of Mongols in China continued to play in linking Chinese and Tibetan culture. Just as Bai Lama had been the first to teach Chinese laymen, the earliest Chinese scholar of Tibetan Buddhism (Yu Daoquan) studied at this ethnically Mongol Tibetan Buddhist monastery in the early twentieth century.[67]

BUILDING A FOLLOWING. The Panchen Lama's first contact with a purely ethnic Chinese audience seems to have taken place in the first few months of 1925. Holmes Welch, in his *The Buddhist Revival in China,* indicated that the Panchen Lama occasionally lectured at the Buddhist Institute for the Study of Tibetan Language which had been founded by Chinese Buddhists in the fall of the previous year. Because this school was transformed into a study expedition headed for Tibet by June 1925—closing its doors in Beijing—the Panchen Lama taught there in March of 1925. Unfortunately Welch says only that he taught Tibetan Buddhist "verses," providing no further details. But the Panchen Lama's involvement with this early instance of Sino-Tibetan Buddhist educational exchange was recorded in Taixu's *Haichaoyin.*[68]

Definitive references to the Panchen Lama teaching Chinese are also found in the record of the Panchen Lama's journey into the heartland of Chinese culture in Jiangnan, south of the Yangtze River. The Panchen Lama's southern tour, which lasted two and a half months, marked a rare instance of a lama from Central Tibet reaching large ethnically Chinese audiences. His visit to Jiangsu and Zhejiang was especially significant because this region was the heart of Chinese Buddhist education and training. Welch described how these two provinces represented the best and the brightest of Chinese Buddhism. In fact, according to his figures, the number of Buddhist monks and laity in these two provinces outnumbered those in most of the other provinces combined.[69]

In April 1925 the Panchen Lama went to the cultural centers of this region, Shanghai and Hangzhou. In Hangzhou he taught Chinese audiences esoteric Buddhism for the first time, at the famous Lingyin Temple.[70] He transmitted the long-life Buddha's mantra according to the esoteric tradition. The long-life Buddha (Amitayus) cycle of teachings was especially significant coming from the Panchen Lama, as he was understood to be an emanation of Amitabha, who is closely associated with Amitayus. Thus this transmission, especially when given as an initiation, linked the recipients to the Panchen Lama through a powerful set of religious beliefs; he was the master and they the disciples.

The Panchen Lama was clearly building a religious following oriented toward Tibetan Buddhist practice, although initially he did this through Buddhist teachings and deities which Tibetan and Chinese Buddhism shared. In mid-April, at the request of the Hangzhou Buddhist Study Association, he transmitted the "heart mantras" (*xinzhou*) of the long-life Buddha, the bodhisattvas Manjusri (*Wenshu pusa*), Avalokitesvara (*Guanyin pusa*), and Vajrapani (*Jingang pusa*).[71] These buddhas and bodhisattvas were well known in China (with the exception of Vajrapani), but the Panchen Lama was able to create a special link to himself, both as an emanation of the long-life Buddha as well as through his knowledge of the esoteric aspects of such teachings. He was also able to connect to the Chinese Buddhists by lecturing on the five vows for the laity.

At that time, support for the Panchen Lama was steadily growing. Some Chinese Buddhists gathered funds and planned to build a stupa in memory of the Panchen Lama's visit. On his return to Shanghai, he was welcomed by the monastic and lay Buddhist community. He lectured on the meaning of taking refuge in Buddhist teachings and once again transmitted the heart mantra of Sakyamuni Buddha. In early May, after meeting with a group of monks, he recited Buddhist scriptures to bring prosperity to Zhejiang Province.[72]

Shortly thereafter, the Panchen Lama traveled to another of the four Buddhist sacred mountains in China: an island called Mount Putuo. The island was home to a very concentrated Chinese Buddhist monastic population that was well known for the intensity of its study and practice.[73] His visit to this island was also important because this site was understood to be the home of the bodhisattva Avalokitesvara, called Putuo in Chinese (or Potala—as in the Potala Palace built by the fifth Dalai Lama in Lhasa—in Tibetan).[74] The Dalai Lama is understood to be an emanation of the bodhisattva Avalokitesvara, who is in turn an emanation of Amitabha in the Tibetan tradition. Yet no Dalai Lama had ever visited Mount Putuo. When the thirteenth Dalai Lama came to the Qing capital in 1908 he had gone no farther than the environs of Beijing to minister to the faithful. Thus the Panchen Lama was on new terrain here, and the significance of this visit would not have been lost on him.

In mid-May he blessed with the touch of his hand the fourteen hundred monks who had gathered to see him, a rare honor from a Tibetan hierarch. He also gave two silver dollars to each monk. Welch notes that a Chinese silver dollar was generally worth one-quarter to one-half of an American dollar during the Republican period.[75] Whether his donations totaled U.S.$700 or U.S.$1,400, this was a significant financial contribution at the time, especially for a refugee who had fled home owing to lack of funds.[76] On the next day he lectured to two thousand monks on the Buddhist theories of birth, old age, sickness, and death, as well as the three trainings in ethics, meditation, and wisdom. He also transmitted the heart mantra of Tara and the mantra of Avalokitesvara. This gathering was a historic occasion, as it probably marked the first time since the Yuan dynasty that a lama from Tibet taught so many Chinese monks.

The Panchen Lama's visit to this island sanctuary may well be the first clearly recorded occasion of Chinese Buddhist monks learning an explicitly Tibetan Buddhist practice: the recitation of the mantra associated with Tara, a female bodhisattva not part of the mainstream practice in the world of Chinese Buddhism.[77] From the Panchen Lama's perspective, Mount Putuo may have been an especially auspicious place to teach Chinese monks about Tara. In the Tibetan tradition Tara's origins are traced back to tears cried by Avalokitesvara. The ability to link himself to this cultic center through three cycles of teachings: of Amitabha, Avalokitesvara, and Tara made for a powerful connection to these Chinese Buddhists.

Before he left, the Panchen Lama also made a large donation to the monastery that had hosted his teaching. Buddhist doctrine accords the highest praise to the gift of Buddhist teachings, but surely the monastic officials were also favorably impressed by the three thousand silver dollars given to the temple.[78] Thus, in his brief tour of the south, the Panchen Lama made his first contact with the center of Chinese Buddhist learning and practice—the laity as well as the monastic community—and no doubt impressed both the faithful and the more worldly in these communities.

By mid-May southern China had become uncomfortably hot for the Panchen Lama, so he returned to Mount Wutai via Beijing. Mount Wutai was as much a part of the Inner Asian steppe as Mount Putuo was part of the Chinese seaboard. Reaching a height of ten thousand feet above sea level, the site was named after five flat grass-covered terraces above the tree line. Although only some 150 miles west of Beijing, the ecology of this mountain range is close to that of the Tibetan plateau, which helps to explain why Mongolians and Tibetans had been going there for centuries. This was especially true of Tibetan Buddhist lamas who came to visit the empire's capital. The mountain had been an escape from the summer heat for Pakpa, Karma Pakshi (1206–1283), Jamchen Chöjé Shakya Yeshé (1354–1435), Changja Rölpé dorjé (1717–1786), and many less famous Tibetan Buddhists over the centuries. The thirteenth Dalai Lama had stayed there for more than five months on his way to the Qing capital in 1907. He taught the resident monks, hosted a tea ceremony for them, and distributed alms. Such activities were a Tibetan tradition, and the Dalai Lama had treated Mount Wutai as the Tibetan Buddhist sanctuary that it was.[79]

traditional visits by the Dalai Lama

In light of this tradition it is interesting how little the Chinese sources on the Panchen Lama have to say about the three months he stayed on the mountain in 1925. They note that he spent twenty-one days in retreat, recited the sutra of White Tara, and gave gifts to the assembled monks.[80] The dearth of information indicates the relative lack of importance the Chinese attached to this visit, as opposed to the trip to the south. In any case, the end of the Panchen Lama's stay on Mount Wutai marked the beginning of a new level of participation in the world of Chinese politics and culture.

BEIJING'S GOVERNMENT GRANTS RELIGIOUS RECOGNITION. In late July 1925 the provisional president of China, Duan Qirui, sent envoys to Mount Wutai to invite the Panchen Lama back to the capital to receive the government's official recognition. Duan embodied a combination of the old and the new in China. He had studied military science at the Qing empire's top academy and in Berlin and became a chief protégé of China's president, Yuan Shikai. Like Yuan, who tried to reinstate the Chinese monarchy under his own family's rule, Duan was unimaginative in his rule of China. He had been trained in the "self-strengthening" thought of late nineteenth-century China which held that modernization could come about through the adoption of Western science and techniques without fundamental changes in the traditional ways of governance. Thus, when considering how to honor the Panchen Lama's presence in China, he resorted to rather old-fashioned methods.

In fact, Duan's recognition of the Panchen Lama was based on earlier models dating back as far as the Yuan dynasty. The tradition since the Mongol rule of China had been that rulers of China—whether Mongol, Chinese, or Manchu— would award respected Tibetan Buddhist religious leaders with eloquent religious titles and accompanying symbols of respect.[81] The most recent example, which Duan followed fairly closely, was the Qing court's treatment of the thirteenth Dalai Lama: "The Qing court, by imperial decree, conferred on him an additional title, inscribed in a gold leaf album."[82] In August Duan bestowed the title "Propagator of Honesty, Savior of the World" on the Panchen Lama and gave him a certificate printed on plates of gold and a golden seal as symbols of his new honor.[83] Thus Duan demonstrated no new way to "utilize" the Panchen Lama's presence in China in the service of the struggling Chinese nation-state. Although aware of the need to preserve the integrity of the former Qing empire's borders, he was unable to conceive of any modern methods of employing Tibet's second most famous hierarch to this end. In fact, the only innovation that came about as a result of the Panchen Lama's interaction with this conservative leader of China was undertaken at the Panchen Lama's request. After receiving the aforementioned honors, the Panchen Lama requested that he be permitted to set up his own offices within China, which are described in the next chapter.

The Norlha Qutughtu Pursues Politics but Teaches Buddhism Instead

Unlike the Panchen Lama, the Norlha Qutughtu had little success either in gaining assistance from the government or in teaching the Chinese in his early years in exile. As mentioned above, his lack of a common language seems to have hindered his ability to communicate, especially in north China. He was from Kham, which had its own dialect, and he was trained in the Nyingma school of Tibetan Buddhism, whereas most of the Tibetans living in China Proper at that time were adherents of the Gelukpa school. The combination of these differences may well have made it difficult for the Norlha Qutughtu to find disciples or venues in which to teach. Like the Panchen Lama, the Norlha Qutughtu visited the two famous Buddhist mountains, Mount Putuo and Mount Wutai. However, he apparently gave no teachings at either of these sites but was merely a pilgrim there venerating the resident bodhisattvas. In this capacity the Norlha Qutughtu was unable to gather any appreciable following among the Chinese.

The Norlha Qutughtu's one successful contact with a Chinese politician while living in Beijing was noted in his biography (or hagiography, as it was written by his Chinese disciples). This biography described how he reached the president of China, Duan Qirui, through the practice of a great "dharma" which was "in response to a need" (*ganying dafa*).[84] Duan was said to be very surprised by this, and this event apparently increased his respect for the Norlha Qutughtu. The biography also implied that Duan studied Buddhist teachings with the Norlha Qutughtu, although it does not state this directly nor is it confirmed by any other source.

In addition, Duan apparently "gave the Norlha Qutughtu permission to return to Kham to try to retake his lost territory."[85] The language of the biography suggests that the Norlha Qutughtu was seeking support for his former rule, rather than that the Chinese were seeking to utilize his good services to retake the area. The northern Chinese had their own problems at the time, and Tibet was far away and far from a priority. His biography adds that Duan gave him one thousand Chinese *yuan* in cash.[86] In any event, by the autumn of 1925 Duan was already losing the support of the warlords who had placed him in control of the Beijing government.[87] When Duan resigned his office in April 1926 the Norlha Qutughtu was left without even this weak patronage.

New patron

TEACHING IN SICHUAN. This problem was solved when a regional militarist leader of Sichuan Province, named Liu Xiang, heard about the Norlha Qutughtu from one of his officials in Beijing.[88] Liu Xiang's devotion to spirituality was documented by Robert Kapp in *Szechwan and the Chinese Republic*. Kapp noted rumors that "Liu consulted the spirits on every matter relating to the armies, from the order of battle down to the most auspicious hour for cooking meals." His dependence on the Taoist adept Liu Zongyun ("Liu of the Clouds") cost him the support of several of his officers. He does not seem to have limited his interest to the Taoist religion. His mother was a devout Buddhist, and his current descendants insist that he (as they are now) was an adherent of the Nyingma school of Tibetan Buddhism.[89] Given his predilection for spiritual advisers, it is not surprising that Liu Xiang invited the monk of the Nyingma tradition of Tibetan Buddhism to Chongqing in 1927. This tradition was the most famous for its magical powers and the least associated with scholastic studies of all the Tibetan traditions. This well suited Liu Xiang, as Kapp described him as the "least cultivated" of the Sichuan warlords. He did not even have a middle school education and had never left Sichuan.[90] Did Liu Xiang have ulterior motives for inviting a Tibetan lama from the borderlands between independent Tibet and Sichuan-claimed Tibetan territory? This seems unlikely in 1927, when Liu Xiang's recently established territory hardly extended west of Chongqing, leaving hundreds of miles of a rival warlord's territory between his own and the Tibetan frontier. Certainly no overt mention is made of even linking Chinese and Tibetan cultures (to say nothing of territory) in reference to the Norlha Qutughtu's sojourn in Sichuan.

Instead, all the extant sources focus entirely on the Norlha Qutughtu's Buddhist activities, whether teaching, performing rituals, or doing charitable work. At one point, the Norlha Qutughtu recited sutras for 120 days. He also announced that his teachings had been heard only once before in China, at the Mongol Yuan capital of Dadu (modern-day Beijing).[91] In 1928 he held a Great Dharma Assembly for Prayers (*Qidao da fahui*).[92] That same year the Norlha Qutughtu established a sort of "dharma center" (in modern-day American parl-

Photo 3.3 Norlha Qutughtu (1865–1936), illustration from the biography written by his student Han Dazai

ance; Ch. *daochang*. lit. "Hall for [practicing] the Way) called the Harmonious Association for World Buddhism (Shijie Fojiao datong hui). The purpose of this establishment was to "spread the Buddhist teachings, benefit the masses, and advance the great harmony of the world" (*hongyang Fofa, liji renqun, zujin shijie datong wei zongzhi*). To this end, internal divisions were set up to handle lectures on the scriptures, the recitation of the Buddha's name, research, and the practice of the *zhenyan* (Sanskrit, *mantra*) esoteric tradition. A Buddhist studies library and offices to print scriptures and circulate materials were also established. The center even seemed to have been influenced by Christian missions, as charity, assisting disaster victims, and support for peasant enterprises were added to the traditional Buddhist practice of liberating beings (such as captive fish).[93]

In comparison with the Panchen Lama's teachings, the Norlha Qutughtu's religious ceremonies were closer to the traditional rituals that had been performed in China over the past centuries. For example, the Norlha Qutughtu's ritual activities included both forty-nine- and one-hundred-day "dharma assemblies to avert disaster and bring benefit."[94] Such rituals had been practiced by Tibetan Buddhists associated with the court of China continuously since at least the Ming dynasty (1368–1644). However, this Tibetan lama's practice of these rituals does seem to mark the first time they were performed in, and especially for the benefit of, the modern Chinese nation.

The Norlha Qutughtu was also prominent in merging these traditions with modern practices. In the spring of 1927 he held a forty-nine-day Dharma-Assembly for Peace (*Heping fahui*). The event was held on the second floor of a Chinese company's office in Chongqing. Laypeople were permitted to attend the esoteric ceremony.[95] Both these conditions were new in the realm of Sino-Tibetan relations. Under the auspices of the Qing dynasty, such rituals had been performed at court-supported temples dedicated to the practice of Tibetan Buddhism. Only the Buddhist elite and the imperial family would have taken part in such ceremonies, although they, too, had been for the benefit of both the dynasty (and, by extension, the country) and the people. In the words of his biographer, "the Guru went from none to an abundance [of students]." The one English-language biography for the Norlha Qutughtu simply states that he "was invited to Szechuan by Gen. Liu Hsiang to preach Buddhism, 1926 and won many converts to the faith."[96]

The next spring, in 1928, the Norlha Qutughtu held a one-hundred-day "Great Dharma Assembly for Prayers" (*Qidao da fa hui*).[97] At this assembly a vajra-mandala was constructed. This became somewhat of a regular practice in China. Moreover, this activity did not merely draw an anonymous fringe of Chinese Buddhists. Many officials either cabled telegrams or sent representatives to attend

the ceremonies. The two ceremonies described here also included a ritual reading of scripture for which a special platform was built. Again, although the recitation of scripture was a standard practice in both Tibetan and Chinese Buddhism,
these events marked the first known instance in which scripture was recited by a
Tibetan lama for a Chinese audience. At both ceremonies miraculous events were
observed, such as the frequent sounding of thunder for no explicable reason. The
Norlha Qutughtu's ability to gather what was said to be more than ten thousand
disciples within three years is credited to these ceremonies and the impression
they made on the Chinese people.

   If the Norlha Qutughtu's main goal in coming to China was to regain power
in his native region of Kham, he made little progress in this direction during his
first five years of exile. He gained permission to make the attempt, and limited
financial support, far from the contested region, from a warlord who was on his
way out of power. When he was invited to move closer to his home he still had
no opportunity to realize his dreams. Nevertheless, his time was not entirely
wasted, as he built up a large following among the Chinese in Sichuan. In the
end, the Norlha Qutughtu's efforts at cultivating Chinese Buddhists as his disciples had the positive result of bringing him to the attention of the central government (described in chapter 5). As was the case for the Panchen Lama, only
after all of China was united under the single banner of the Nationalist government was the Norlha Qutughtu's influence actually brought to bear on political questions.

Chinese Monks Study in Tibet

   While these Tibetan lamas were teaching the Chinese laity, for the first time
in Chinese history groups of Chinese monks ventured out of China and into
Tibet to pursue a Tibetan Buddhist education. They traveled abroad with the
support of what Prasenjit Duara has called the "public sphere," in the form of
lay Buddhist associations, as distinguished from institutionalized governmental
support, which would only come later.[98] Starting with Dayong's "Team to Study
the Dharma Abroad in Tibet,"[99] dozens of Chinese monks went to Tibet,
although few of them left very complete biographical records. Fortunately the
two most prominent Chinese students of Tibetan Buddhism, Nenghai Lama
(1886–1967) and Master Fazun (1902–1980), for whom biographies exist, provide a window into the experiences of the first wave of Chinese monks who
went to Tibet. Fazun was included in the group of Taixu's students who followed
Dayong to study in Tibet, while Nenghai led his own groups of Sichuanese

monks to Tibet. Both Nenghai and Fazun went so far as to make Tibetan Buddhism central to their teaching of Buddhism in China.

Motivations for Studying Tibetan Buddhism

What motivated these monks to learn Tibetan, travel and live in a foreign land for years, and study and translate Tibetan Buddhist texts? According to their biographies, both Nenghai and Fazun embraced Tibetan Buddhism as a source of authentic and potent teachings in order to redress perceived inadequacies of Chinese Buddhism. Their motives for going to Tibet are described in detail in Fazun's autobiographical writings from the 1930s and in Nenghai's biography (by his disciple) written in the early 1980s.

Fazun's collected writings include an essay entitled "My Purpose for Going to Tibet." He explained how he was inspired by the challenges overcome by the Tang monk Yijing (635–713 AD) who traveled to India and studied at the top monastery for years so that he could translate (into Chinese) scriptures unavailable in China. Fazun also compared the difficulties of going to Tibet to the journeys of Faxian (in the fifth century) and Xuanzang (in the seventh century), both of whom had gone to India to bring scriptures back to China. By extension, these role models indicate something of the way Fazun imagined Tibet—as a source of authentic religious teachings on a par with medieval India. In the medieval period Buddhism still flourished in the monastic universities of India; in the twentieth century only Tibet remained such a bastion of religious authority. Fazun declared that,

> Tibet has the perfect Buddha-Dharma for studying, translating and transmitting. . . . With respect to Tibetan Buddhist scriptures, I vowed that all those, which China Proper (*neidi*) did not have, I would study and translate in order to supplement that which was lacking. I very strongly wanted to supplement and make complete Master Yijing's translations of Vinaya-pitika [the canon of monastic precepts]. Tibet's esoteric dharma was of course not something that was excepted from the list of that which I desired to study—that is, worldly matters of geography and history as well as handicrafts, medicine, politics and literary knowledge.[100]

Thus, prior to going to Tibet, Fazun said that his interests differed from those of his teacher Dayong. He was not only attracted to the esoteric tradition of Tibet but also wanted to seek valuable additions to exoteric Chinese Buddhist teachings, such as those dedicated to the monastic precepts.

Photo 3.4 Master Fazun (1902–1980), from a 1936 issue of *Haichaoyin*

Photo 3.5 Nenghai Lama (1886–1967), from an image still circulated by disciples

In contrast, Nenghai's disciple explicitly described his master's interest as the study of esoteric Buddhism. The third chapter of Nenghai's biography, entitled "Going to Tibet to Study the Dharma," opened with the following lines:

> The master had studied Buddhism, studied the essentials diligently and inten-sively—probing deeply and studying in detail each of the exoteric sects of China (*Handi*)—and still felt unsatisfied. Furthermore, having once looked over the Tibetan catalogue in Beijing's Yonghegong, he had become aware that [it] contained many esoteric sutras and commentaries and had developed the desire to study esoteric teachings. Having received the monastic precepts, he arrived in Chongqing to teach the scriptures and planned to go east to Japan to study the Buddha-Dharma abroad. . . . [However,] a student from Nanjing said: "Tibet's Buddha-Dharma is extremely rich. Tibet has every-thing that has not been translated in China, while that which Tibet lacks, but which has already been translated in China, is very limited. Therefore, to study the Dharma, one should go to Tibet." . . . When Dayong returned home from Japan, he confirmed that Japanese esoteric Dharma could not come close to comparing with Tibet's plenitude. Following this, Nenghai decided to go to Tibet to study esoteric teachings.[101]

Nenghai was willing to go wherever the most complete esoteric Buddhism was being taught. Unlike Fazun, going to Tibet was not a substitute for the lost pos-sibility of traveling to Buddhist India. For Nenghai, Tibetan Buddhism became central to his interests because it was the repository of the richest esoteric Buddhism.

Given the Republican government's refusal to relinquish claims on Tibet, even during this period of Tibetan independence, some might suspect ulterior motives for these monks' interest in Tibetan Buddhism. In an effort to query the sources, we must ask what might be hidden, why, and from whom. If these monks were working for the government, would they hide it from their fellow countrymen? If Buddhists were ashamed of serving such political goals in the Republican period, would that shame still have been a factor in the Communist period when the works were published? I believe that the answer to both these questions is no. After they gained their knowledge in Tibet, these monks were willing enough to assist their country's government in its efforts to persuade the Tibetans to accept the official Chinese view that Tibet was a part of China. Neither Nenghai nor Fazun hid their later engagement with the Republican and Communist governments, which demonstrates that they would have had no reason to hide government support for their early studies. I have also found other Chinese Buddhist sources from both the Republican and the Communist periods that openly discuss the subsequent cooperation of some Buddhists with the Chinese government's attempts to incorporate Tibet. Thus, when no mention is made of the government being involved, these sources appear to be reliable on this count.

Furthermore, recent official Communist Party publications memorializing the great figures of the twentieth century do not offer different accounts of the lives of Fazun and Nenghai. If information on their involvement with the government's plans to incorporate Tibet were available, it would surely be celebrated in these sources. Far from being embarrassed by these activities, the Communist Party would see such cooperation as a testament to the usefulness of Buddhism. Similarly, Buddhists would be likely to emphasize such an instance of their helpfulness to a government that sees their religion as merely "an opiate of the people." Thus, although these accounts are obviously after-the-fact reports, I do not believe that they hide an ulterior motive of serving the interest of the Republican government. Although they cannot serve as mirrors of historical fact, they can serve as guides that are corroborated by other evidence.

These men and their motivations can be taken as representative of the others who joined Dayong's expedition. Even Nenghai, who had not previously studied at the Beijing school, briefly joined Dayong's group to study the Tibetan language in Daqianlu. Together the expedition team vowed that "going to Tibet to seek the Dharma is our group's intent; the more difficult the circumstances, the more steady our intent—even if it shatters our bones and grinds our bodies to powder!"[102] Yet only a few of the group were actually able to fulfill this vow. Dayong died in Kham in 1929, and, over the years, most of his students turned back. Of those who reached Central Tibet, only Nenghai and Fazun returned to China to teach Tibetan Buddhism.

By 1929 the presence of Tibetan lamas in China and Chinese monks in Tibet marked a new era of pan-Asian Buddhist relations between Chinese and Tibetans. Going beyond the mere idea of linking Chinese to Japanese and Tibetan Buddhism through texts, Taixu's students entered cultural Tibet to further their understanding and practice. At the same time Taixu and the Chinese laity welcomed Tibetan Buddhists as co-religionists. The differences of doctrine, practice, and society that had kept Chinese and Tibetans apart in previous centuries started to break down in the face of shared interests. Chinese and Tibetan Buddhists in China joined forces for their common protection. Tibetan lamas willingly taught the Chinese the esoteric techniques so eagerly sought for salvation in those trying times. Initially government officials had no interest in assisting these Buddhists in pursuing their goals, but this would change in the coming decades, as different politicians realized that they, too, shared common goals with some Buddhists.

4. Overcoming Barriers Between China and Tibet (1929–1931)

THE PREVIOUS CHAPTERS introduced the regional and global factors that created the conditions of alienation and tension between the central governments of China and Tibet. They also indicated some of the potential ways that these two nations might forge new links, in particular a conception of Buddhism that could unite Chinese and Tibetans through a single religion. The chapters that follow demonstrate the importance of this new conception of Buddhism as it was advocated by the Nationalist government of China in an attempt to bring Tibet under its control. The earliest links between this concept and its practical application, initiated in Sichuan Province in 1930, were built on Chinese and Tibetan Buddhist contact there. But before the Nationalist government could turn this pan-Asian Buddhism to its own ends, this idea needed a wider currency.

However, this process was not one that could easily be deliberately directed by the Nationalist government, especially in Sichuan's distant territory. Sichuan's leaders, largely independent of central Chinese governments for nearly a quarter of a century, attended to their own agenda without catering to the interests of the distant Republican governments in Beijing or later Nanjing. Sichuan Province had declared its independence from China early in the Republic and only submitted to the Nationalist government in Nanjing with hollow formality in 1927. Yet because of the province's proximity to Tibet, the provincial leadership was more concerned about relations with Tibet than the Beijing government had been. In addition, several of these leaders had strong religious inclinations and were hardly driven by the same ideology as the Nationalist leaders. Thus they were more responsive to the religious developments occurring around them and could more easily imagine a role for religion in state matters than most central government leaders could. The sheer numbers of lay Buddhists interested in Tibetan Buddhism helped to draw Sichuanese political leaders into supporting Tibetan Buddhist ceremonies for peace. At the same time the persistence of Chinese monks pursuing Tibetan Buddhist studies gradually overcame the numerous barriers that separated Chinese and Tibetan cultures. Probably inspired by these developments, the Sichuan provincial leader Liu Xiang tried to recruit monks drawn from eastern Sichuan's Buddhist temples to serve as emissaries along the Sino–Tibetan border. By informing Liu of the difficulties Chinese monks had encountered in Tibetan regions, Master Taixu altered this idea. He convinced Liu that a Sino–Tibetan Buddhist school in Sichuan would produce better-trained "goodwill" envoys. Thus, whereas in central China the government continued to try to keep religion and politics separate, the Sichuanese led the way in uniting these two concerns.

Barriers to Chinese Studying Tibetan Buddhism

The challenges encountered by Dayong's Team to Study the Dharma Abroad in Tibet (*Liu Zang xuefa tuan*) demonstrate the tenuous nature of Chinese and Tibetan social and political networks after a decade of Tibetan independence. The difficulties this group faced indicate the practical barriers that had to be overcome for Chinese to learn about Tibet in this new era. In order to gain a better understanding of why Chinese access to Tibet was so limited at this time, I will describe the financial, linguistic, cultural, physical, and political obstacles these Chinese monks had to face to build their knowledge of Tibet. The relative ease, safety, and respect accorded Qing official missions was not an option for these students. However, their nonofficial capacity allowed them to live among Tibetans and learn from and about Tibetan life in an entirely unprecedented way.

Financial Barriers

The first obstacle to Chinese monks studying in Tibet was that this was an expensive proposition. Beijing laymen planned to support the group that set off from the Buddhist Institute for the Study of the Tibetan Language in 1925, as no government support of Chinese studying in Tibet was evident before 1930. But as early as the end of 1926 the expedition was cut off from its Beijing backers, no doubt by the ongoing civil war between the northern and southern governments. Dayong told the students that they should pursue their own studies in a monastery with a lama, as a formal school-like setting was no longer possible with their limited funds.[1] Nevertheless, as long as Dayong was alive, Fazun apparently had little need to worry about where his next meal was coming from.[2] Dayong was a native of Sichuan and a respected teacher in China Proper, so Sichuan donors continued to support the expedition for years. However, when he died in 1929, Fazun became more dependent on sympathetic Tibetan lamas.

Upon Dayong's death the expedition was reorganized into an organization with the long-winded name of the Daqianlu Association of Students of the Beiping Buddhist Institute for the Study of the Tibetan Language's 1925 Team to Study the Dharma Abroad in Tibet (Beiping Fojiao Zangwen xueyuan yizhou liu Zang xuefa tuan zhu [Daqian]lu tongxuehui). The reputation of the group was apparently enough to maintain a minimal sort of support from lay sponsors: each person received a paltry 96 *yuan* each year.[3] Fazun never mentioned this association in his biographical writings. Possibly because he no longer resided in Daqianlu, he was unable to receive these funds. Toward the end of 1931 a one-time windfall came to the Daqianlu monks and to Nenghai and others in Lhasa at the completion of Chengdu's Southwestern Dharma-Assembly for Peace. Each group was sent a donation of 1,000 *yuan*.[4] This boon was not mentioned in the biographies of Fazun or Nenghai, so it is difficult to say what kind of role such irregular, though generous, support played in their daily lives. Nenghai, like Dayong, was Sichuanese and had a following in Chengdu to which he could turn. Once he had lined up an introduction to a Lhasa-based lama, he returned in 1927 for a final fund-raising tour in Sichuan. Nenghai brought back some ten monks on his return journey. Six apparently stayed in Daqianlu, and four continued on with Nenghai.[5]

The absence of government funds to assist Chinese studying in Tibet is documented into the 1930s. In a 1931 letter to Hu Zihu, the former sponsor of Dayong's school and study group, Fazun sought funds to stay on in Tibet. He had already been forced to borrow more than two hundred silver dollars in order to try to complete his studies.[6] He remarked that he did not want to become like his fellow students, forced to return to China out of financial difficulty. He specifically asked that funds in Tibetan currency be sent through Daqianlu.[7] In the meantime, Fazun, like other poor monks in Tibetan monasteries, was dependent on the daily donations doled out in the assembly halls of the monastery.[8] Nenghai seemed to have been better off, but he still benefited from lamas who, "sympathizing with the difficulties of Chinese pursuing the Dharma, especially provided [him] conveniences."[9] The implication is that the lamas gave Nenghai financial or material assistance. Thus the first wave of Chinese monks who studied in Tibet were supported by fellow Buddhists, whether Chinese laymen or Tibetan monks, and not by the Chinese government.

The Language Barrier

The second and most basic problem was the linguistic barrier between Chinese and Tibetans. These monks had set out to remedy this problem, but there was no easy solution. The school in Beijing had been inadequate,[10] as their principal teacher was a Chinese man from Kangding.[11] The one monk sent by the Tibetan government to live in Beijing as a translator was apparently not a good teacher, even if the Chinese students had been able to gain access to his services.[12] As late as 1909 Chengdu had apparently had a government school that taught the Tibetan language (Zangwen xue tang).[13] However, there are no records of the school having continued into the Republican period. Had it still been active, these monks would no doubt have stopped first in Chengdu to continue their training. Instead, they continued on into Tibetan regions to study the language with only the most rudimentary of glossaries. Fazun mentioned only one set of reference materials at their disposal, and even these were not of Chinese provenance. They relied on hand-copied Japanese publications of Buddhist and secular terminology (four volumes each) which included both Chinese and Tibetan languages.[14] This explicit reference to the lack of Chinese language resources was to be remedied later by Fazun. Such a deficiency of linguistic resources is remarkable given the two centuries that the Qing empire supervised affairs in Tibet.[15] Rockhill mentioned a short list of basic terms in one of the Qing gazetteers of Tibet but found it of little practical use and so did not translate it. In addition, some quintilingual works were produced by and for the Qing imperial court for government or religious purposes. However, none of the Chinese monks mentioned having access to any of these works.[16]

A comparison of these meager resources with even a cursory examination of the work of European scholars, missionaries, and colonial servants with an interest in Tibetan language demonstrates how weak the Chinese knowledge of Tibetan was at this time. I have compiled a list of some of the most prominent linguistic works published before the 1930s. In some of the more interesting cases I have included the publication information to indicate the locus of motivation (trade, missionizing) that seems to have inspired these early compilations.

1. Schröter, *Tibetan-English Dictionary* (Serampore: East India Company, 1826).

2. Alexander Csomo de Körös, *Essay towards a Dictionary, Tibetan and English* (Calcutta: Baptist Mission Press, 1834).

3. Alexander Csomo de Körös, *A Grammar of the Tibetan Language* (Calcutta, 1834).

4. I. J. Schmidt, *Lexicon: A Tibetan-German Dictionary* (prior to 1881).

5. I. J. Schmidt, *Tibetan Grammar* (prior to 1881).

6. H. Jäschke, *Tibetan-German Dictionary*: lithograph (1876).

7. H. Jäschke, *A Tibetan-English Dictionary, with special reference to the prevailing dialects (to which is added an English-Tibetan vocabulary)* (London, 1881).

8. Auguste Desgodins, *Dictionnaire thibetain-latin-français* (1899).

9. Sarat Chandra Das, *Yig kur nam shag: Being a Collection of Letters, Both Official and Private, and Illustrating the Different Forms of Correspondence Used in Tibet* (Calcutta: Bengal Secretariat Press, 1901).

10. Graham Sandberg, *A Hand-book of Colloquial Tibetan* (prior to 1902).

11. Graham Sandberg, *Manual of the Sikkim-Bhutia [Tibetan] Language* (prior to 1902).

12. Sarat Chandra Das, *A Tibetan-English Dictionary, with Sanskrit Synonyms* (Calcutta: Bengal Secretariat Book Depot, 1902).

13. Sarat Chandra Das, *An Introduction to the Grammar of the Tibetan Language, with the Texts of the Situ sum-tag, Dag-je sal wai melong and Situ Shal lung* (Delhi: Motilal Banarsidass, 1915).

14. Charles Bell, *Grammar of Colloquial Tibetan* (prior to 1924).

15. Charles Bell, *English-Tibetan Colloquial Dictionary* (prior to 1924).

As this list clearly demonstrates, the Chinese were at quite a disadvantage in learning the Tibetan language, at least from textual sources. No doubt there were some Tibetans who spoke Chinese, but none of the biographies I have examined explicitly states that this was the case. Fazun related that, when they first arrived in Daqianlu, they lived in Ngachö monastery and studied Tibetan from "a half-Tibetan, non-Han local Tibetan language teacher." Fazun complained that "though his spoken Tibetan was better than ours, he hardly knew any more literary Tibetan than us."[17]

In fact, it seems that these monks had to rely principally on Chinese from Daqianlu (Tib. Dartsedo) to gain access to Tibetan language instruction. As mentioned above, the teacher at the Beijing school was from Daqianlu, and he returned to his home shortly after the study group arrived there. As the disciple of a monk at Daqianlu's Baomashan temple (Tib. Lha mo rtse),[18] he was able to arrange for Dayong, Fazun, and Liangchan to study Tibetan with his master there. The master appears to have been bilingual, as indicated by his having two names, in Chinese Master Cigu (*fashi*) and in Tibetan Jampa Mönlam.[19] With his assistance Dayong, Fazun, and Liangchan were able to study Tibetan grammar from original Tibetan treatises for the first time. For example, they studied the *locus classicus* of Tibetan grammar, the "Sumchupa" (*San shi song*), said to have been composed by the inventor of the Tibetan script in the seventh century. While studying this and other Tibetan grammatical works, they also studied religious works. When Nenghai arrived in Daqianlu with his group of preceptmates, they, too, settled at this temple. His biography recorded that he studied there with a man named Jiangba gege (Jampa Gegen, meaning, Teacher Jampa).

Although the dates in this biography are not entirely in agreement with those of Fazun, Nenghai's biographer also mentioned that Fazun and Dayong came to this site and studied with the same teacher.[20] Later, Fazun would publish a Chinese language text for a class on Buddhism edited by a Jiangba Lama (Jampa Lama).[21] Assuming this was the same person, it appears that not only was this monk bilingual but he was also bicultural, possessing a knowledge of both Tibetan and Chinese Buddhism. As such, by sharing his knowledge with these Chinese monks, he provided a crucial link in the social network that allowed the monks to expand Chinese knowledge about Tibet. Just as the interface of Chinese and Tibetan trade relations was located in Daqianlu, so was that of the cultural worlds. However, the linguistic problem was only the beginning of the obstacles to these monks' pursuit of knowledge about Tibet.

Cultural and Physical Barriers

The third problem the Chinese faced was that Tibet was an alien culture and environment. Even the basic elements of life such as food, clothing, and shelter were very different in Tibet.[22] At the time these monks sought to enter Tibet, Chinese cultural outposts there were basically nonexistent. The sparse military outposts of the Qing era had all been swept away after the dynasty abdicated.[23] These monks thus had no obvious guides to aid them in making their way to Tibet. Chinese trade establishments seem to have been almost entirely limited to Daqianlu, which was the center of a rich and active trade of Chinese tea for Tibetan animal products. Chinese merchants had their warehouses there, and the Chinese had some temples east of town. Eventually Fazun and Liangchan had the opportunity to travel to Tibet along with a Chinese merchant's mule train. They succeeded in reaching Kardzé (Ch. Ganzi), the first major town beyond Daqianlu, disguised as ordinary monks.[24] Aside from this, the biographies of these Republican Chinese monks make only vague references to a Chinese presence beyond Daqianlu.[25]

This sharp cultural divide was not just a psychological challenge to the Chinese monks; it also had physical ramifications. The monks' bodies were affected by the quality of food and housing, and the generally unfamiliar environment. Fazun indicated that it took him a year to "become accustomed to Tibetan people's lifestyle" which he did by experimenting with eating *tsampa* (roasted barley flour) instead of rice and noodles.[26] Elsewhere he discussed in detail the challenges of poor clothing, shelter, and food.[27] Other physical challenges were more directly a result of the geography of this part of Tibet. Nenghai detailed the difficulties he experienced with snow and frozen rivers;[28] Fazun mentioned that flooding was so bad that "[Chinese] officers and soldiers would not dare guarantee [our safety]."[29] One biographer blames the breakdown and death of the study team's leader, Master Dayong, on the climate and environment (literally water and earth, *shui tu*) of Tibet, so different from that of China, combined with the master's excessive diligence in his studies. By the fall of 1929, four years into their tour of study, the group had dropped from more than thirty members to fewer than twenty. Some had returned to China, and several had died.[30] Similarly, of the five monks that joined Nenghai in entering Tibet, four turned back after living for half a year in Litang.[31] In 1931 Fazun and another monk managed to buy a horse and push on from Kardzé to Chamdo (Ch. Changdou), a town directly administered by the Tibetan government in Lhasa. In a letter he wrote later that year, he explained, "the reason I came to Changdou was really the desire to invite this *geshe* (Tib. *geshê*) to return to China (*Zhongguo*), to gradually study, translate, and transmit [Buddhist teachings] *in order to avoid many years of suffering staying in the Tibetan regions*."[32] These sufferings were such that Fazun feared he would die in Xikang, so it is no wonder that he wished to solve this dilemma by bringing a knowledgeable Tibetan monk back to China.[33] He failed in this effort because of Tibetan officials' resistance to his plan.

Political Barriers

The final and almost insurmountable obstacle was that created by the political situation in the Sino-Tibetan borderlands. First, the ethnically Chinese side of this cultural frontier had completely fallen to bandits, such that Dayong had to hire the bandits themselves as bodyguards to get his study group through to Ya'an. Similarly, Nenghai and his group were held up in Ya'an by fighting. The ongoing struggle between the Chinese and Tibetan forces in this area heightened the traditional local suspicion of Chinese.[34] As early as 1878 the governor of Sichuan ordered a man to explore the route to India via Tibet. He was able to travel no farther than Batang, because "the natives beyond that locality became suspicious and he was unable to enter [Central Tibet]."[35] In this region Tibetan suspicion of Chinese was a long-standing problem not easily overcome.

As soon as these Chinese monks reached the Tibetan cultural region they were accused of political motives, and their progress was blocked by Tibetan officials.[36] This explains why Fazun and Liangchan had surreptitiously joined a trade caravan to reach Kardzé. Fazun complained that this suspicion was because of Dayong's particular approach to entering Tibet. Rather than behaving in a subtle manner, as Fazun and Liangchan learned to do, Dayong paid Chinese government envoys to use their officers and soldiers to allow him and his group to enter Tibet under protection. Thus, all along the route, this group made quite a production and appeared to have the support of the Chinese government. Fazun stated:

"Precisely because Master [Da]yong was safely delivered by the officers and soldiers, the Tibetans suspected that the [Chinese] state had especially sent an important person." This led the Tibetan government (*Xizang zhengfu*) to send a letter to Kardzé ordering that Chinese people be prevented from entering Tibet.[37]

The Tibetan restrictions on ethnic movements in these regions were also applied to Tibetans planning to go to China. Although Fazun convinced one accomplished lama (a *geshê*) to return to China to teach Tibetan Buddhism to the Chinese, the Tibetan authorities in Chamdo blocked this move, forbidding him to travel to China. For the time being, this put an end to Fazun's attempts to free himself from the trials of living in Tibet to learn Tibetan Buddhism. Instead, he and several other Chinese monks pushed farther, to Lhasa—the center of Tibetan culture—to expand their knowledge of Tibet.

Forging New Links: Lamas Assist Chinese Monks

Once Dayong passed away in 1929, these Chinese monks lost their last symbol of Chinese superiority in this senior and ex-military man. Although Fazun doubted the wisdom of Dayong's approach to entering Tibet, Fazun was always protected and well fed when under Dayong's care.[38] Without Dayong's aid, Fazun, Nenghai, and the handful of other monks who reached Tibet in this period did so by submitting themselves fully to the Tibetan way of life. These Chinese monks became dependent on the goodwill of local Tibetan lamas to assist them in their efforts to study the Tibetan language and Buddhism. In so doing, the Chinese monks created unprecedented personal links with individual Tibetan lamas.

The principal reason these Chinese monks sought out close, cooperative relationships, rather than the coercive relationships so characteristic of Chinese officials in Tibetan regions, was that they needed information from, and not control of, the Tibetans. This is an obvious point that the biographies do not explicitly address. Nevertheless, the need for Tibetan assistance in learning about the culture and in building networks is clear throughout the biographical works. Aside from teaching the Chinese, Tibetan lamas provided the crucial social network that gave these monks access to Tibetan knowledge. Only those Chinese monks who took the time to cultivate the proper connections were able to go to Tibet, build their knowledge, and return to share what they had learned with other Chinese.[39]

The connections the Chinese monks had made with the Tibetans in Daqianlu seem to have yielded little assistance in bringing them in contact with other Tibetan teachers. Instead, the Chinese monks had to go deeper into

Tibetan regions in order to connect with a Lhasa-centered network of social relations. At the next major Tibetan towns on the way to Lhasa (Kardzé, on the northern route, and Litang, on the southern route) these Chinese monks were able to gain access to a fully articulated Tibetan social network. Although Fazun had arrived in Kardzé with the help of Chinese merchants, he followed Dayong into a local monastery. We do not know precisely how Dayong was admitted to this monastery, but Fazun's critique of his methods implies that he may have bought his way into the good graces of the local Tibetans. Be that as it may, on this basis Fazun managed to build long-term and successful relationships. He stayed at Drakkar monastery south of Kardzé under the tutelage of the head lama there, Drakkar Lama.[40] The lama's disciples assumed the task of teaching Fazun about Tibetan Buddhism, and Fazun extensively praised his main teacher Getuo zhugu (Tib. *Getok Trülku). Through this teacher, Fazun was able to make the acquaintance of another teacher he had long hoped to meet: Amdo Geshé Jamröl Rölpé Dorjé (Ch. Andong Geshe Jiang re, 1888–1935).[41] When they met in 1928, the lama had many questions for Fazun. Later, he was to become Fazun's principal teacher, Fazun's main source for the transmission of Tibetan Buddhism.

In like manner, Nenghai secured access to the prestigious Lhasa social network through the mediation of a lama of similar status. A locally high-ranked lama in the town of Litang, by the name of Jamyang Chöpel Rinpoché (Jiangyang qingbu Rinboqie, d. 1927), befriended Nenghai.[42] This reincarnated lama had lived at Mount Wutai for several years and recognized the difficulties of living in a foreign land. He encouraged Nenghai to study Tibetan Buddhism in Central Tibet in order to bring it back to the Chinese. His letter of introduction to an important lama in Tibet, Khangsar Rinpoché (1888/90–1941, Ch. Kang sa), smoothed Nenghai's way.[43] As with Fazun, this Lhasa-educated lama was to become his principal teacher. One of this lama's Tibetan disciples remarked on his lama's dedication to teaching Buddhism without regard for worldly affairs: "If someone asked him for religious teachings, Rinpoche would answer in great detail, but if someone asked him about worldly things his answers were very brief."[44] As these instances demonstrate, some lamas were willing to work with dedicated Chinese students of Tibetan Buddhism in the interest of spreading Tibetan Buddhism among the Chinese.

The peak of these Chinese monks' learning experience in Tibet was in the last years they spent there, at the center of Tibetan culture in Lhasa. Both their teachers arranged for them to study at the preeminent monastic institution, Drepung Monastery. Of the three main monasteries in Tibet, this was the largest, with some ten thousand monks. Melvyn Goldstein's introduction to *A History of Modern Tibet* describes these central monasteries as resembling "the

Photo 4.1 Fazun's Tibetan lama: Amdo Geshé, Jamröl Rölpé Dorjé
(1888–1935), from a 1936 issue of *Haichaoyin*

classic British universities such as Oxford, in that the overall entity, the monastery, was in reality a combination of semi-autonomous subunits known in Tibetan as *tratsang* [Tib. *grwa tshang*]." Extending the analogy, these subunits are typically called colleges. Within these subunits were further divisions called *khangtsen*, which might be compared to fraternity houses, except that membership was automatic based on native place association. These smaller units actually housed, and to some degree looked after, the monks from a particular area, as they shared common features such as dialect, familial and social connections, and so forth. Typically any Chinese monk would be placed in Drepung monastery, Loselling college, in the Gyarong (Ch. *Jinchuan*) house. The Gyarong region borders Chinese cultural areas in Sichuan and had a distinct dialect only distantly related to Tibetan. Loseling was composed largely of monks from Kham, which was partially under Chinese control.[45] Nenghai initially joined this unit but had a conflict with a scholar there and secured the support of the monastic community to transfer to Gomang college.[46] The ability of these Chinese monks to gain entry into this highest institution of Tibetan learning is a remarkable testament to their persistence, as well as the willingness of the Tibetans to work with serious students of Tibetan Buddhism, of whatever ethnic origin.[47] Japanese monks and agents who had lived among the Mongols before coming to Tibet were given similar access to Tibetan Buddhist learning. One of these, Hisao Kimura, summarized the lack of national divisions in the face of a shared Buddhist culture: "In this part of the world religion is far more important than nationality, and men are regarded as brothers because of the way they behave rather than where they were born."[48]

Sichuan Laity Elicits Government Involvement

While Chinese monks went to Tibet to study, Buddhist laity in China Proper pursued a different course. The most persistent interest in Tibetan Buddhism came from the laity of Sichuan, whose province had suffered devastating civil wars since the end of the 1911 Revolution. Sichuanese residing in Beijing had informed people in their home province about the lamas in the national capital in the mid-1920s. Convinced of the efficacy of Bai Lama's practices, Sichuanese lay Buddhists invited both Bai Lama and Dorjé Chöpa to come to Sichuan to perform rituals. Efforts to bring these lamas to Sichuan focused on the religious powers they had to offer the Chinese in this turbulent period. Because the language of contemporary sources does not mention any interest in Tibet proper, I argue that considerations of Tibet's independence were not involved in the earliest years of Chinese interest in esoteric Tibetan Buddhism. Not until 1930, and then only sparsely in the extant literature, did the more or less political goal of "linking Tibetan and Chinese cultures" even begin to be a consideration.

Early Lay Interest (1926–1929)

The existing sources demonstrate that the Sichuan laity were responsible for inviting lamas for the purpose of bringing peace to China and the world. The most detailed historical document available from the efflorescence of Tibetan Buddhism in Republican China is the special issue of Chengdu's Southwestern Dharma-Assembly for Peace (*Chengdu Xi'nan heping fahui tekan*). The multiple prefaces of this work are dated December 1931, but the chain of events leading up to the assembly is recorded back to the year 1926. When Buddhists in Sichuan Province heard of the Golden Light Dharma rituals that Bai Lama was performing on the east coast, they invited him and Dorjé Chöpa to come to their war-torn province to perform the same ritual in order to avert disaster there. Although the funds they were willing to provide (some two thousand gold coins, Ch. *jin*) were insufficient to attract the lamas, the text of the invitation revealed the way these Chinese Buddhists originally conceived of their interests in esoteric Buddhism. They traced the initial Chinese practice of esoteric Buddhism back to the Tang but added that, in Tibet, these traditions had been maintained without interruption from that time. Like Fazun, these lay Buddhists simultaneously linked their interest in Tibetan Buddhism to both their own history of (Chinese) Buddhism and a broader conception of Buddhism, which allowed for the inclusion of Tibetan Buddhist traditions in their own lives. When a native of Sichuan returned with tales of seeing Bai Lama's supernatural powers (*shentong*) with his own eyes, the Sichuanese Buddhists again sent Bai a letter urging him to come to Sichuan and included a donation of 1,000 *yuan* (roughly U.S.$300). Early in 1927, when Bai Lama declined the invitation, he assured the Sichuan laity that he would include Sichuan in his "ceremony for averting disaster for the entire country."[49] When Bai died later that year, these Sichuanese sent money to help build his memorial stupa (Tibetan-style pagoda). In the meantime, they kept up the effort to attract Dorjé Chöpa to the province.

After Dorjé Chöpa finally agreed to come to Sichuan in 1929, the hosting Buddhists contacted the military and political leaders to arrange for their support and assistance. The detailed account of the prolonged process of inviting Dorjé Chöpa clearly indicated that the hosts waited to contact the "famous and virtuous generals and leaders of each army" until they were assured that the Tibetan lama would come. Had some prominent civil or military leader masterminded this invitation from the beginning, we can be sure that his role would have been recorded in the special memorial volume. As it stands, however, those

Buddhist militarists who were members of the hosting association in 1929 were not even important provincial leaders. Truly prominent Chinese leaders—and even these were active Buddhists such as Liu Wenhui—did not join the effort until after Dorjé Chöpa had arrived in Sichuan, when his popularity had become clear to all.[50] Thus I would argue that if some motive beyond religious interest was involved in the calculations of provincial leaders, it was domestic interest (supporting a cause popular with the local people) and not external matters (such as influencing Chinese and Tibetan relations).

Praying for Peace (1929–1931)

When Dorjé Chöpa first came to Sichuan he lived in Liu Xiang's base of Chongqing for one year. The Chengdu memorial volume recorded few details of his time there, only mentioning that the first Southwestern Dharma-Assembly for Peace, lasting forty-nine days, had been held there early in 1930. Dorjé Chöpa enjoyed immense popularity in Chongqing. The mayor of Chongqing and other local notables were initiated into Tibetan esoteric practices at the first Southwestern Dharma-Assembly for Peace. To commemorate Dorjé Chöpa's visit they built an enduring monument: an enormous stupa set on a hill in the center of the city.

The stupa, known as the Bodhivajra Stupa (Putijingang ta), was built toward the end of 1930 under the direction of the mayor, the Public Security Bureau chief of Chongqing He Beiwei, and several others. The stupa represented a substantial investment on the part of Chongqing's residents and officials. The pagoda stood about 30 feet tall, was filled with Tibetan scriptures, and was inscribed with Chinese Buddhist scriptural passages and mantras in Chinese and Tibetan. The structure was said to have cost more than 40,000 *yuan* (around U.S.$13,000), a tremendous sum at the time. The "Paean to the Bodhivajra Stupa" (*Puti jingang ta song*), inscribed on the stupa, explained that the precious offerings that accompanied the stupa were all made on behalf of "benefiting the country and enriching the people" (*wei guoli minfu*). Dorjé Chöpa was praised as "the world's best hope" (*shijie di yi xi*).[51] The attention and funds spent on this visiting lama indicate the importance attributed to Tibetan Buddhist efforts at bringing peace to Sichuan Province.

Dorjé Chöpa's increasing popularity meant that his public appearances had become charged with competition among the militarists who controlled Sichuan. For example, the Chengdu Buddhists who were still eagerly awaiting Dorjé Chöpa after four years of invitations sent a representative to Chongqing, but Dorjé Chöpa only responded to a telegram sent by Liu Xiang's uncle, Liu Wenhui, who controlled Chengdu. The period in which Dorjé Chöpa lived in

Photo 4.2 The 1930 Bodhivajra Stupa in Chongqing in 1999 (photo by the author)

Sichuan was full of the tense struggle of rival, if related, military leaders. This rivalry would culminate in civil war between Liu Xiang and Liu Wenhui in December 1932. To safeguard their interests, both the militarists and the lay Buddhists hedged their bets, and the list of the famous sponsors of the Chengdu event started with the four militarists who divided control of Sichuan Province among them: Liu Wenhui, Deng Xihou, Tian Sungyao, and Liu Xiang. From other indications, however, Liu Wenhui and Tian Sungyao were actually the most prominent sponsors of the event. For example, both men were present at various parts of the assembly and both wrote prefaces to the memorial publication. They also made large and apparently competing financial contributions to the proceedings (Liu, 3,300 *yuan*, and Tian 3,000 *yuan*, roughly U.S.$1,000 each). Deng also wrote a preface and contributed 1,000 *yuan* but was neither personally present nor otherwise represented at the Chengdu events. Liu Xiang seemed to have been listed only out of respectful (or fearful) courtesy, as he contributed neither a preface, money, nor his presence.[52]

Early in 1931, when the long-awaited Southwest Dharma-Assembly for Peace at last took place in Chengdu, the military and government representatives publicly acknowledged the assembly and its goal of Buddhist-inspired peace. The day before the public ceremony began, the provincial chairman Liu Wenhui, with representatives of many of the armies that controlled Sichuan in attendance, invited Dorjé Chöpa to consecrate the altar and offered him a silk scarf as a sign of respect (in the Tibetan Buddhist tradition).[53] The next day the banners read "Eliminate the Southwest's Disasters / Pray for World Peace" (*Xiaochu Xi'nan zaili / Qidao shijie heping*).[54] When the public ceremony started, the head of the Buddhist association was first on the program and introduced Dorjé Chöpa as the master to more than one hundred thousand disciples and proclaimed that he had come to Sichuan "to avert disaster and pacify conflicts" (*xiaozai xizheng*). His comments were followed by those of the warlord Tian Sungyao, who launched into a detailed account of the disasters from which the Chinese needed saving. Surprisingly, he started the list with the military problems in Sichuan, adding that,

> The government and the people all have one wish: that is, society wants sustainable peace, a way for the people to be able to benefit from good fortune. For this reason, with the agreement of all, the Master [Dorjé Chöpa] was invited to preside over the dharma-assembly, to avert and eradicate disasters and troubles, and to say prayers for peace. Given the current natural disasters and military troubles—on the grand scale throughout the country, on the small scale in Sichuan—none are without suffering. . . . The Master's words

will smash the darkness and march along the bright path, saving the country and saving the people.

He even addressed himself to those who doubted the efficacy of such rituals, saying, "All worldly people mistakenly believe this affair is superstition, doing something negative, [but] they do not know that the Buddha-Dharma has the real truth, and is certainly not superstitious." Although Deng's speech was the most elaborate praise and justification for the event, the provincial government representative also discussed the usefulness of esoteric teachings and Buddhist compassion as offering hope for an end to society's ills. A representative from another Sichuan army praised the ability of Buddhism to bring out the buddha-nature in all beings.[55] All these militarists talking about peace and compassion must have been a moving sight for the troubled people of Sichuan, though their difficulties were not to end very soon.

However, my effort here is not to examine the efficacy of the ritual; rather, it is to describe what motivated these events and how they were conceived, organized, and funded. Interest in Tibet proper, cultivating relations with Tibet, or linking Chinese and Tibetan cultures was nowhere mentioned in any of the literature—not even in the militarists' prefaces and letters included in the memorial volume. Instead, Buddhists—laymen and militarists alike—refer back to Bai Puren at Beijing's Yonghegong and the Golden Light Dharma ceremonies he performed. In fact, the organizers of the Sichuan dharma-assembly had planned to invoke this same name for the ritual, but Dorjé Chöpa provided the new title: the "Dharma-Assembly for Peace."[56] In his opening remarks, Dorjé Chöpa concurred with the assessment of the Sichuanese militarists: "Buddhism originally emphasized saving the world. Today, having arranged this assembly, we desire that all the disasters and difficulties in the world will thereby be annihilated. Our Buddha-Dharma is a precious jewel having unimaginable powers."[57] Publicly, then, the principal Chinese sponsors and the Tibetan presiding over the event concurred on the motives of the assembly.

Donors and Beneficiaries

Despite the high profile given to the political sponsors, this assembly was not merely an affair for the Sichuanese elite. The names and donations of almost 4,500 people were recorded in the final section of the memorial volume, which constitutes more than half the book. The smallest donations were those of a single 100 *wen* coin (worth much less than $1.00). The attention paid to these seemingly miniscule donations is surprising until one considers the tally: more than one-third of the total donations (16,322 silver dollars out of 48,240) was given by people whose contributions could be counted in small change: 1,000 or 100 *wen* coins. The balance of the rest of the patrons each gave less than 10 silver dollars, with only about 1 percent of donors contributing more than 100 silver dollars. This is hardly surprising when we realize that a typical salary at the time, roughly 8 *yuan* per month, was sufficient to live on comfortably.[58] The three militarists mentioned above gave substantial amounts (totaling some 5,500 silver dollars) and reaped the benefit of being associated with this pacifist assembly in the eyes of the thousands of people who attended and heard about the event. But, in the final analysis, they contributed only a little over 10 percent of the donations.[59]

Almost all the nonmilitarist donations are listed in groups that open with the heading "On behalf of . . ." and then list individual donors, the amount of the donation, and, at the end of each group, the total amount donated. For example, modest donations were made on behalf of a county or a county government (Loujiang county government: 41 *dayuan*),[60] an individual (the elder, Mrs. Yu: 36 *jiao yangyuan*),[61] an association (Minzhu Buddhist Association: 1 *yangyuan* and 41,000 coins), or a temple (such as Wenshu yuan where the event was held: 61 *yangyuan* and 15,000 coins).[62] The only nonmilitarist entry that differs from this pattern is that of pawnshops, which are grouped under the heading: "assistance from pawnshops."[63] I suspect that the huge number of common people supportive of this ceremony was precisely what drew the pawnshops and politicians to patronize this event.

Although no explicit mention is made of attempting to forge links between Chinese and Tibetan cultures, the economic dimension of the assembly revealed an ongoing exchange of resources. In the expense account, the association that organized the ceremony carefully detailed its expenditures. As for the Tibetan lamas involved in the ceremony, 2,200 *yuan* were offered to Dorjé Chöpa and 100 *yuan* to each of 20 Tibetan monks who assisted.[64] Compared to the fees paid to two Chinese Buddhist laymen to recite scriptures for the ceremony (totaling 3,200 *yuan*), such donations to the Tibetan principals were modest. The offerings made to groups and individuals peripheral to the assembly were the greatest expense (more than 12,000 *yuan*). These offerings were disbursed as far away as Beijing (for Bai Lama's stupa) and as close as several temples and a Buddhist society in Chengdu. However, most of these funds appear to have gone to support Chinese monks studying Tibetan Buddhism. An offering of 1,000 *yuan* was sent to the various Chinese monks in Lhasa, care of Master Nenghai. Equal amounts were sent to pay the tuition (*xuefei*) of both the 1925 and the 1929 Expeditions to Enter Tibet to Study Abroad (Ru Zang liuxue tuan), care of Master Dagang in Daqianlu.[65] Finally, a negligible amount of 150 *yuan* was sent to three anonymous monks who were "following their master to Tibet to study the dharma."[66]

The assembly organizers also made offerings to the Tibetan Buddhist monasteries at which the Chinese monks were studying. For example, 1,000 *yuan* were offered to the three great monasteries (*san da si*) of Lhasa where Nenghai and Fazun were studying. Another 1,000 *yuan* was also given to each of two temples in Daqianlu: Baomashan (the monastery at which many of the Chinese monks going to study in Tibet were first taught Tibetan) and Ngachö monastery (Dorjé Chöpa's home institution and the first stop of Dayong's expedition some five years earlier). Although these donations might on the surface seem to demonstrate some parity between Chinese support of Tibetan temples in Central Tibet and in eastern Tibet, in fact the division of these donations indicates the relatively weak links between China and Central Tibet at this time. Whereas the three largest and most prominent monasteries in Tibet divided 1,000 *yuan* between them, two tiny Tibetan borderland monasteries with no academic standing were honored with substantial donations.

Other expenditures demonstrate that Tibetan material culture was gaining increasing recognition in Southwest China. Tibetan incense, ritual clothing, butter to make altar lamps, and even cow's milk for the lamas were all listed in the expense account. The tremendous amount (more than 10,000 *yuan*) spent on transporting Dorjé Chöpa and his ritual paraphernalia from Beijing and ultimately to Daqianlu included a military escort and should remind us of the number of Chinese people (from soldiers to innkeepers to porters) who would have been exposed to this group of Tibetans traveling so lavishly in war-torn China.

For those who had not yet been exposed to Tibetan cultural practices, Dorjé Chöpa's weeks of teachings after the ceremony provided further opportunities to learn. The section of the memorial volume entitled "Dharma Treasures" (*fabao*) detailed the dates and content of Dorjé Chöpa's teachings, rituals, and initiations. The teachings consisted of such basics as taking refuge in Buddhism and the vows of the three Buddhist vehicles (Hinayana, Mahayana, and Tantrayana) up to the most esoteric practices. Rituals included mandala offerings and burnt offerings (*homa*), rituals in which a special altar was set up for the purpose of "removing sins, restoring broken vows, and eliminating disaster."[67] The initiations included those into the practices of various forms of Manjusri (Red, Yellow, White, four-armed), four-armed Avalokitesvara, and the Medicine Buddha.

The end of Dorjé Chöpa's teaching in Chengdu marked the end of such major events led by Tibetans in Sichuan. Other ethnic Tibetan monks would come to Sichuan, but they did not have the status or charisma of Dorjé Chöpa, and so never drew such a large following. Likewise, although other Tibetan Buddhist practitioners would later teach in Sichuan, they were ethnically Mongol or Chinese and did not engender the same level of interest. After Dorjé

Chöpa's departure, the Buddhist laity's enthusiasm or resources ebbed low. This presented a remarkable contrast to the situation in central China in 1931, which exploded with Tibetan Buddhist activity fueled by the combination of the despair over deteriorating relations with Japan and the presence of the exiled Tibetan lamas, the Norlha Qutughtu and the ninth Panchen Lama (discussed in the next chapter). Meanwhile, Sichuan's strongest militarist, Liu Xiang, considered ways to take advantage of the local interest in Tibetan Buddhism.

The Political Monk: Taixu

While Sichuanese laity hosted Tibetan Buddhist lamas and Chinese monks studied in Tibet to gain the religious knowledge they were seeking, one activist monk had focused his energy on organizing national and international Buddhist groups in China. The most prominent Buddhist reformer in modern China, Master Taixu, has been the principal subject of two Western scholarly works. Both Holmes Welch, in *The Buddhist Revival in China,* and Don Pittman, in *Towards a Modern Chinese Buddhism: Taixu's Reforms,* detailed Taixu's efforts to transform Chinese Buddhism, principally through educational reforms.[68] The most successful modern Buddhist educational institution was Taixu's Wuchang Buddhist Studies Institute (1923–1934). One Western missionary sympathetic to Buddhism said of the school: "The curriculum is practical and includes the study of some of the most urgent secular questions of today. The chief point, however, is that the students are inspired to revive Buddhism and preach the 'law of salvation' in such a way that they can meet the needs of the new China."[69] Yet meeting the needs of the new China and the needs of new Buddhism led Taixu to work more closely with Chinese politicians than most of his conservative peers were willing to do and earned him the dubious distinction of being a "political monk."[70]

Taixu's Rhetoric: Meeting the Needs of New China with a New Buddhism

Taixu spent many fruitless years trying to secure adequate government funds to support a modern Chinese Buddhism. He adopted Christian tactics such as creating a Young Man's Buddhist Association and engaging in charitable work. He used scientific language to explain Buddhism and advocated modern schooling for monks. Yet most of his organizations or initiatives came to little, because funding for these nontraditional Buddhist activities was extremely difficult to generate among conservative Buddhists.[71] Turning to the state for funding was the one option that ultimately worked for Taixu. In 1929 Taixu secured funding from Chiang Kai-shek for an international Buddhist tour. Lasting more than a year, this tour inspired him to make the idea that Buddhism was a world religion a reality in China. On his return to China, he renamed the Wuchang Buddhist Studies Institute the headquarters of the World Buddhist Institute (Shijie Foxueyuan). Eventually this institute had branch "campuses" in urban centers around China: Beijing, Xi'an, Chongqing, Amoy, and Zhaozhou.[72] However, the only branch that actually fulfilled Taixu's grand expectations was the school devoted to Tibetan studies, because this branch was supported by the government.

LINKING BUDDHISM AND THE STATE: MUTUAL AID.   Taixu gradually developed a rhetoric to encourage government support for Chinese Buddhist institutions. However, rather than directly serving the Republican government's irredentist goals, in these early years Taixu was primarily interested in demonstrating that Buddhist teachings (including the esoteric tradition) could assist with the social and political difficulties China faced. Welch's assessment that the "reason for his interest in Tantrism was his eagerness to prove that the Buddhist religion was not a mere relic of the past, but could serve the cause of national reconstruction" remains valid. Yet, whereas Welch implied a colonial aspect to this national reconstruction, Taixu intended instead to assist the state by making Buddhism an integral part of governance.[73]

Taixu's adoption of the *Scripture for Humane Kings Who Wish to Protect Their States (Renwang huguo jing)* revealed much about how he expected Buddhists to work with the modern nation-state. In the 1920s Taixu gave regular teachings on the *Scripture for Humane Kings Who Wish to Protect Their States* to large audiences.[74] Charles Orzech, who has studied this scripture in detail, explained that, "as an alternative to Buddhism's serving the state, the *Scripture for Humane Kings* proposes that the state and Buddhism serve each other." Such a goal was precisely what Taixu sought to achieve. Thus Taixu's revival of the scripture on which the Tang emperors had relied for the protection of their state (*huguo*) can be considered his initial contribution to making Buddhism truly relevant to the modern Chinese state.[75] This scripture was particularly important for its "forceful advocacy of the essential unity of Buddhists and Chinese and of a Buddhist and Confucian polity." By linking the Chinese homophones for the key Confucian term of humaneness (*ren*) and the key Buddhist term of forbearance (*ren*), this scripture managed to link good leadership with Buddhist virtues.[76] Through the medium of this scripture, modern Chinese Buddhism could thus be linked to Sun Yat-sen's revival of the Confucian concept of humaneness and Dai Jitao's continuation of this ethical basis for nationalism.[77]

This attempt to link Buddhism to the state was a doctrinally valid and historically proven option open to Buddhists and not merely an attempt to preserve Buddhism through demonstrating its usefulness to the state. Orzech's interpretation of the scripture could equally be applied to Taixu's relationship to the state:"On a cursory reading one is tempted to regard the *Scripture for Humane Kings Who Wish to Protect Their States* as a bald attempt to curry favor with rulers, an attempt to make Buddhism useful and attractive to people concerned with the very real and often intractable problems of war, famine, and disease. Careful study of the scripture soon disabuses us of this facile opinion." Orzech's more considered reading was based on the fact that Buddhist notions of rulership and the proper relation between Buddhists and rulers were not "mere appendages or compromises necessary for the survival of the faith in the world, but integral parts of Buddhism." Likewise, Taixu's interest in working out a mutually beneficial relationship with the state was not a betrayal of Buddhist principles, at least according to some doctrines.[78]

Yet Taixu was aware of the weakness inherent in being dependent on the state and wished also to make the state dependent on Buddhism. One reason Taixu felt that esoteric Buddhism was essential to a new Chinese Buddhism was that this branch of Buddhist doctrine had a very successful record in working with polities without becoming subsumed by them. Orzech described this success in the following way: "It was in the East Asian Esoteric Buddhism and Tibetan Vajrayana that the full political implications of the Mahayana insistence upon the identity of this world and nirvana were developed and deployed in a comprehensive rhetoric and practice of 'National Protection' (*hu-kuo*)."[79] When these doctrinal implications were played out to their fullest, Buddhism was politically potent and flourished as it had in Tang China and Heian Japan, and as it continued to do in Tibet. For Taixu, then, the goal was to unite the Japanese and Tibetan esoteric Buddhisms within a Chinese Buddhism that was integrated with the state in a mutually supportive relationship.[80]

Although Taixu had foreseen the need for Chinese Buddhists to study Tibetan (and Japanese) Buddhism as early as 1914, no government figure expressed any interest in or support for this idea until 1930. By this time Taixu's disciples had already been studying Tibetan Buddhism in a Tibetan cultural context for years. After Taixu's disciple Dayong died in 1929, he was memorialized by one of his Sichuan disciples in Taixu's Buddhist monthly *Haichaoyin*. Having praised Dayong for his travels to Japan to recover Tang and Sung esoterica, the memorial commended Dayong for "going west [to Tibet], to consult with those who are good and knowledgeable (Ch. *shan zhi*, Tib. *geshê*) and initiating communication between the estranged cultures of the Chinese (*Han*) and Tibetans (*Zang*)." In an ironic description of this improved communication, the author said that Dayong had established "feelings of affection and mutual confidence between the Chinese (*Han*) and the barbarians (*Yi*)."[81] This article, which appeared in January 1930, was the first time that Chinese Buddhists discussed the role of the students of Tibetan Buddhism as goodwill intermediaries between the Chinese and the Tibetans.

Turning Religious Capital Into Financial Capital

The earliest government support for Chinese studying Tibetan Buddhism as a policy tool was to come in Sichuan Province under the direction of Liu Xiang. In 1929 the Nationalist government's Mongolian and Tibetan Affairs Commission had apparently made plans to send monks to study abroad in Tibet,[82] but these plans were opposed by the Ministry of the Interior (Neizheng bu) under the Executive Yuan and were not implemented.[83] However, by September 1930 Liu Xiang had independently struck on this idea and proposed that "Sichuan send monks to enter Tibet to study scriptures."[84] When Taixu visited Chongqing in November 1930 he learned that Liu Xiang had undertaken to send young Chinese monks to Tibet with funding extracted from county Buddhist establishments.[85] This was a surprising initiative, because Liu Xiang was still only one among many militarists in Sichuan and the one farthest from the Tibetan border. This activity may mark the start of his campaign to be recognized as the governor of Sichuan by the Nationalist government.[86] Hoping to take control of the entire province, Liu Xiang appeared to be planning to make the Buddhist establishments do their part by assisting with the integration of Tibetan regions in western Sichuan. Because Taixu's disciples had already faced some difficulty in their efforts to study Tibetan Buddhism, Taixu was interested to learn of a government proposal to generate funds to send Chinese monks to study Tibetan Buddhism. Based on the experiences of his disciples, he proposed that,

> Sending monks to study abroad in Tibet would not be as good as setting up a Tibetan language college to train Chinese monks in the study of Tibetan language, in order to prepare them for entry into Tibet. At the same time, Buddhist incarnations and lamas could come to Sichuan and, aside from lecturing, studying and being hosted, they would link up Chinese and Tibetan culture and serve as liaisons for Chinese and Tibetan goodwill.[87]

To make this proposal a reality, Taixu joined with the head of Chongqing's Buddhist Studies Society as well as with his disciple, the mayor of Chongqing, to apply to Liu Xiang for support in opening such an institute.[88] Having gained

Liu's approval and access to funds, they set up a committee to organize the World Buddhist Institute's Sino-Tibetan Buddhist Institute (Shijie Fojiao xueyuan Han-Zang jiaoli yuan). Although Taixu would at last have the opportunity to make Buddhism useful to the government, he had also altered the immediate purposes of the militarist who supported this idea.

By cooperating with this militarist, Taixu finally found the necessary government support to put his idealistic plans into action. Yet even after expressing his interest in Liu Xiang's plan, Taixu did not immediately alter the way he conceived of and discussed the role of Chinese students of Tibetan Buddhism. In the fall of 1930 Taixu described the significance of Chinese Buddhists studying Tibetan Buddhism only in terms of the doctrinal aspects of Tibetan Buddhism that were being added to Chinese Buddhism. The students' most important contribution was still the knowledge they had gained about esoteric Buddhism, which would help to "reestablish China's esoteric tradition" (*zhong jian Zhongguo mizong*).[89] Even in a December 1930 letter sent to Sichuan, Taixu still phrased his support of Liu Xiang's idea in purely Buddhist, as opposed to politicized, language. First, he addressed his letter to Liu Xiang *and* the Buddhist faithful of eastern Sichuan. Second, he praised Sichuanese Buddhist activities collectively: building a stupa and holding a peace assembly were listed alongside sending monks to study abroad in Kham and Tibet. And, finally, when he discussed the benefits of Liu Xiang's new plan, he merely said that the young monks would "improve themselves through discussions with [the Tibetans]" (*huxiang qiecuo*).[90] Moreover, when Taixu wrote to encourage Fazun to return from Tibet to run the new school, he focused on Buddhist, rather than any political, objectives of the school.[91] In describing the school's purpose to Fazun, he stated that "the purpose of the school was to bring together the fundamental principles of Chinese and Tibetan Buddhist teachings" (*huitong Han-Zang Fojiao zhi li wei mudi*).[92] However, the discourse about training this second wave of Chinese monks to enter Tibet would not remain politically neutral for long.

The man Taixu put in charge of working out the details of forming this school was eager to demonstrate the national and global benefits of creating it. This man, a monk by the name of Manzhi, wrote a short article, dated January 1931, describing the mission of the new school.[93] This was one of the earliest documents about the school. Manzhi explicitly stated that Taixu's actions followed Liu Xiang's lead and had been taken to maximize the benefit to Chinese Buddhism. Taixu had at last found the ideal espoused in the *Scripture for Humane Kings Who Wish to Protect Their States*: a ruler who protects Buddhism and thereby protects the state.[94] At the same time Manzhi acknowledged the more or less political motive of creating goodwill between Chinese and Tibetans.

Manzhi's article also emphasized both the global and national benefits of the proposed school. Globally the school would "cause the world's people to hear the Buddha-Dharma and improve their minds, thereby promoting the world's great harmony" (*shi shiren de wen Fofa er gaishan qixindi, yi zujin shijie zhi datong*). On the national level Manzhi referred to Chinese citizens' demands for peace, especially regarding the national defense of the Mongolian and Tibetan frontiers. He also invoked the *Scripture for Humane Kings* in reference to the Tibetan tradition of joining politics and religion (*Xizang zhu zhengzhi heyi*).[95] This may have been a subtle justification for Chinese Buddhists working with the Sichuanese militarist. However, in this first mission statement, Manzhi stopped short of saying that the new school was dedicated to government service.

When Taixu saw a rare opportunity to redirect government initiative to the benefit of Chinese Buddhists, he did not hesitate over concerns about the source of the funding or the nature of the task. After all, when Liu Xiang's Twenty-first Army assigned a temple complex and its associated properties to the new school, this was a grand reversal of a trend of property confiscation that had been working against Chinese Buddhists for more than a decade. The school's landholdings eventually included two separate temple compounds and associated rent-producing lands; but these assets had a price.

The Buddhist school was directed to link Chinese and Tibetan cultures. An army order dated March 1931 contained the earliest reference to the school's responsibility "to link up cultures" (*goutong wenhua*), which Liu Xiang explained as "causing the Chinese and Tibetan Buddhist vehicles [that is, their doctrines] to unite as a single family" (*shi Han-Zang Focheng, he wei yi jia*).[96] As Taixu had been working for some time to bring Tibetan Buddhist teachings into a reformulation of Chinese Buddhism, he had no problem adopting the specific new rhetoric of linking Chinese and Tibetan cultures as well. This was especially true because the army order also contained a clause providing for the disbursement of 600 *yuan* a month for the school from the provincial educational funds. By reformulating the power base of Chinese Buddhism, Taixu had used the "religious capital" of Buddhism to obtain the financial capital to run a school for Chinese Buddhists. Furthermore, the army had ordered county governments to ensure that local Buddhist institutions (associations, study groups, and temples) send a total of one hundred students to attend the school.[97] The Sino-Tibetan Buddhist Institute thus became the first modern Buddhist school in China to receive government funds and a government mandate.

As always, Taixu's prime interest was to advance the role of and support for Buddhism in modern China, and he felt that helping the state to resolve the Tibet problem was the best hope for promoting such interests. By linking Tibetan Buddhism to Chinese Buddhism in this way, Chinese Buddhists did serve the state in trying to maintain the Qing imperial border regions. Nevertheless, because Chinese Buddhist interest in Tibetan Buddhism preceded government support, the role of Tibetan Buddhism in China and the direction of this interest could not be entirely determined by government priorities or subsidies. I have discussed here the principles behind the formation of the school in order to examine Taixu's deployment of government rhetoric for the benefit of Chinese Buddhists. Later developments at the school and the actual details of its operation involved a certain amount of rhetorical struggle over the application of the general principles outlined in the mission statement. Taixu and the military trustees of the school did not always discuss Tibet in the same terms, but this is a subject for a later chapter (chapter 7), which describes the institutionalization of Tibetan Buddhist education in China.

Summary

Sichuan thus served as the first site for Chinese and Tibetan Buddhists to develop new networks and secure some political support for their religious activities. These trends eventually served as models for Nationalist government efforts at building goodwill with the Tibetans. Sichuan, as a middle ground between the centralized administrations of China and Tibet, proved more capable of flexible innovation than the cultural centers of either nation. For example, the Tibetan Buddhists in Kham were willing to appreciate the religious interests of Chinese monks, and thereby facilitate their entry into Tibet, even against the directives of the Lhasa government. The Chinese political leaders in Sichuan were likewise willing to consider religion a viable option, both for their own citizens and for building better relations with Tibet. The critical catalyst for realizing both possible scenarios was the serious interest that Chinese Buddhists, both lay and monastic, took in the Tibetan Buddhist religion.

religious capital = Sichuan
↳ refers to geographical meaning NOT $

5. The Failure of Racial and Nationalist Ideologies (1928–1932)

WHILE TIBETAN BUDDHIST rituals and education were already being sponsored by the political leaders of Sichuan Province, modernist secular policies continued to govern the decisions of most of the political leaders in central China. Under the leadership of the Nationalist Party, the Northern Expedition had seized power in central and north China in 1927–28, replacing the Beijing government with the Nationalist government in Nanjing. Unlike the Beijing government, which had focused its concerns mainly on retaining power in north China, the new leaders sought to realize centralized rule of all of China, a China that included the former frontiers of the Qing empire. Through the party-state system and a rational reorganization of the government structure, the Nationalist Party led a government more unified than China had seen for decades. Sun Yat-sen's work, especially the *Three Principles of the People,* was elevated to the guiding ideology of the new state. The idea of the harmonious unity of the five races (*wuzu gonghe*) took second place to a Sinocentric nationalism. This shift was marked by such signs as the replacement of the five-barred flag of the Beijing government (symbolizing the equality of the central "races" of China) with the Nationalist government's flag (a single white star on a blue and red background). Nevertheless, the Nanjing administration continued to find the racial (*wuzu*) rhetoric useful when dealing with the borderland peoples outside its control.

Unlike the Sichuan provincial governments, the Nationalist government initially pursued only political, and not religious, ways of relating with the Tibetans. Thus the ideologies of racial unity and nationalism described by Sun Yat-sen carried over from earlier times were central to the government's efforts to work with exiled Tibetans to bring an end to Tibet's independence. In contrast to the Beijing government, the Nationalist government's ability to include prominent Tibetans within its political system marked a significant development that has had lasting effects to the present day. By incorporating Tibetan Buddhists living in exile into the national political administration, the Chinese government drew representatives from Central Tibet into a complicated network of political relations.

Inclusion of Tibetans in the Chinese administration, although part of the multiracial nationalist rhetoric of the Chinese Republic from its early years, only started to become a reality in the late 1920s. Initially the context through which Tibetan exiles understood nationalism predisposed them to opposition to such modernist ideologies. For the Tibetan Buddhist leaders of small polities not directly controlled by the Tibetan government in Lhasa, the arrival of nationalism in their homeland had constituted a particular challenge. The Lhasa government had refused to accommodate their interests and ousted those who resisted the imposition of the extension of the nascent Tibetan nation-state's power. Thus, when Tibetans such as the Panchen Lama and the Norlha Qutughtu went into exile in China, they were wary of ideologies that would subordinate their interests as the centralizing Tibetan administration had done. Partially to circumvent this resistance from Tibet's traditional elite, the Chinese government developed educational institutions to train Tibetan youth in the prevailing secular ideologies.[1] The historic record shows a cautious acceptance of some of these ideological principles by some Tibetans. However, the Chinese government's refusal to grant even regional autonomy to Tibetans in Kham finally gave the lie to the rhetoric. Ultimately the secular ideologies of nationalism and racial equality alone were insufficient to persuade powerful Tibetan lamas to join the Chinese nation.

Despite their eventual cooperation with Chinese politicians, these Tibetan Buddhists were also pursuing their own goals. In order to return to their previous positions of power in Tibet, they sought the financial and military backing that only the Chinese government could have provided. In fact, as religious figures cooperating with the Chinese government, they established an important pattern for the future of Sino-Tibetan relations. As is still the case today, Chinese politicians were forced to work with the religious leaders of Tibet to try to maintain control over the populace in the region. At the same time these men invented and adapted strategies for dealing with the new challenges of a globalized world. They dealt with Chinese government ideology by judiciously employing the government's multiracial or nationalist rhetoric when addressing the Chinese. However, there is little indication that this rhetoric made much of an impact on the lives or thoughts of the leading Tibetan lamas in exile. Successful dialogue with the Chinese government would only come after the Nationalist government embraced the dual religious and political system these lamas represented, as is detailed in the next chapter. Until that time the effort to engage prominent Tibetans solely as political figures who could be incorporated in a secular Chinese nation-state merely set the stage for the substantive Sino-Tibetan dialogue that followed in the 1930s.

The Panchen Lama's Early Offices in China

Before the Nationalist Party controlled northern China, the Beijing government had basically treated the Panchen Lama as a religious figure without official civil standing in China. After Duan Qirui granted the visiting lama a new religious title and honors, the Panchen Lama had requested the right to set up offices to handle his affairs. In 1926, when the first such office was opened in a temple in Beijing, the government permitted its establishment but neither funded nor otherwise oversaw the offices.[2] Initially the Panchen Lama seems to have established offices in China simply to handle the routine activities associated with being a prominent personality. Far from being part of a government ploy to enlist the services of this prominent Tibetan Buddhist in Chinese schemes, these offices were the result of Tibetan initiative. I suspect that their principal reason for existence was to handle the business affairs that accompanied the donations of the Panchen Lama's Buddhist followers. For most of 1926 the Panchen Lama was teaching in Buddhist temples around the capital. In mid-September he gave an initiation into the tantric practice of the Amitabha Buddha to lay and monastic Buddhists. One feature of tantric initiation is the often substantial donations made to the teacher of such liberating techniques. It seems likely that these initiates' donations provided both the need and the funds for creating offices that would handle the Panchen Lama's affairs.

Shortly after September some sources state that he sent representatives to set up local offices in Sichuan and Qinghai provinces (both bordering on Tibet), as well as in the city of Fengtian (Shenyang in Manchuria) and as far away as India. All the offices were described as "the Panchen's offices to handle affairs" with the exception of the Indian office, which was described as a "communications office."[3] No doubt the logic behind the founding of these offices was, on the one hand, to process the donations coming in from north China, and, on the other, to redistribute them to the supporters of the Panchen Lama in Tibetan regions. However, the only evidence that these offices were actually successfully established at that early date was a later reference to the translation of Sun Yat-sen's *Three Principles of the People* undertaken in the Xining, Qinghai office in 1927.[4]

For the next two years the Panchen Lama's only recorded contact with the Nationalist government occurred in March 1928, when he sent representatives to congratulate Chiang Kai-shek on his successful conclusion of the Northern Expedition that united China. It is also only in this year that we have further confirmation that the Panchen Lama's representatives had actually been sent out to the various provinces. For example, on March 4, 1928, the Qinghai branch office was said to have been "formally" set up. Similarly, in the southwest of China, the Panchen Lama sent an ethnically Tibetan Sichuanese representative to petition the Chinese government in 1928.[5] Whether the initiative for this contact was wholly from the Panchen Lama's side, as the sources seem to indicate, or whether there was some effort to involve him in politics from the new Nationalist government is difficult to judge. Of the more than four hundred published archival documents dealing with the Panchen Lama's time in China, only three are dated prior to his contact with the Nationalist government, and none of these is concerned with setting up the offices.[6]

Thus, during the early years of his time in China, no Chinese politician tried to engage the Panchen Lama in political activities. In fact, from late 1926 until early 1929 the Panchen Lama lived among the Mongol adherents of Tibetan Buddhism in Inner Mongolia. His religious activities for a Mongolian audience provide a useful point of comparison with the Panchen Lama's southern tour in China (discussed in chapter 3). Most of the teachings that he gave in Inner Mongolia were associated with the tantric tradition, and figures such as Avalokitesvara and even Sakyamuni Buddha were rarely recorded as being topics of teaching. Instead, during this period, he gave many initiations into the messianic Kâlacakra tantra. The ceremonies that conferred these initiations attracted enormous crowds (eighty thousand Mongols were said to have attended each of the first three initiations into this tantra) and brought the Panchen Lama much prestige and rich donations. As Andresen noted in researching the Kâlacakra tantra in America: "economically . . . patronage of Kâlacakra provides an important source of financial support for exiled Tibetans."[7] The growth in the number and the formality of the foundation of the Panchen Lama's offices was no doubt given great impetus by similar donations.

How did the Panchen Lama conceive of these "offices" to handle his finances and affairs in China and in relation to Tibetan regions? Nowhere is the answer stated explicitly. He could not follow the Dalai Lama's example, because the Dalai Lama's representatives in China were drawn from the temples (in the former capital, now called Beiping and Mount Wutai) that had handled religious affairs under the Qing dynasty. The abbots of these temples were later appointed as the Dalai Lama's representatives to China without major administrative changes taking place in the Tibetan government. Did the Panchen Lama observe modern businesses or the diplomacy of the international community and adopt their central and branch office structure or consulates as his model? This seems unlikely given his limited contact with Westerners in China.

The most likely explanation, and one that is supported by linguistic evidence, is that the Panchen Lama adapted an old Qing institution to his own purposes. The leading Qing representative to Tibet, generally known as the chief *amban,* had been given the title "Grand Minister Resident in Tibet to Handle Affairs" (zhu [Xi]zang banshi dachen). The Panchen Lama's bureaucratic structure added his own title (*Banchan*) to the phrase to indicate that this was not a government bureau, substituted the word *office* (*chu*) for *official* (*dachen;* Manchu, *amban*), and inserted whichever place name was appropriate. Thus he adapted the older Qing model to his new creations: the "Office of the Panchen's Resident in Sichuan to Handle Affairs" (Banchan zhu [Si]chuan banshi chu) and the "Office of the Panchen's Resident in Qinghai to Handle Affairs" (Banchan zhu Qing[hai] banshi chu). His employment of this bureaucratic model was not surprising, as it was the primary model through which he had interacted with the Qing government prior to coming to China. More surprising is that he decided he needed to create such offices at all. To extend the comparison, the Panchen Lama's modeling his offices on those of the Qing representative in Tibet may suggest that he was trying to assert himself as a Tibetan representative to Republican China. Although he was given permission to set up these offices prior to 1929, they were not part of the Chinese administration during this early period. At best, the Panchen Lama was an unofficial representative of Tibet in the Chinese heartland.

The Politicization of Lamas' Roles in China (1929–1930)

The real politicization of the Tibetan Buddhist leaders in China did not occur until 1929, after the success of Chiang Kai-shek's Northern Expedition allowed for the establishment of a more centralized government. Although the Beijing government had had a Mongolian and Tibetan Office (Meng Zang yuan), it had been a very weak version of the Qing empire's Court/Board for Managing the Frontiers (Lifanyuan/Lifanbu). The Chinese borderland scholar Wu Fengpei reported that the early Republican government in Beijing basically continued handling Tibetan affairs according to the Qing precedents as laid down in the *Precedents for the Board for Managing the Frontiers* (*Lifanbu zeli*).[8] Under the central government of Nationalist China, a new bureau, the Mongolian and Tibetan Affairs Commission (Meng Zang weiyuanhui), was created to handle the relations with the peoples on China's borderlands. The new government entity, although ranking lower in the bureaucracy of the Republic than its Qing predecessor, was nonetheless a much more effective political body than it had been under the Beijing government.

The Panchen Lama's Political Offices

Under the Nationalist government, the previously religious nature of the Panchen Lama's role in exile was initially transformed into a secular official one, with a political administration. The government responded positively to the Panchen Lama's congratulatory initiative in the spring of 1928. By January 11 of the following year, the "Office of the Panchen's Resident in [the Capital] Nanjing to Handle Official Affairs" (Banchan zhu [Nan]jing bangong chu)[9] was officially established. For the first time in the history of modern China the government had created a special office for a Tibetan Buddhist hierarch. To mark the establishment of this office, the government issued a proclamation of its opening, a chart of its organization, and detailed rules and regulations to guide how affairs were to be managed in the office.[10] Fabienne Jagou, who has devoted much research to the life of the Panchen Lama, has argued that all the Panchen Lama's offices were incorporated into the structure of the Mongolian and Tibetan Affairs Commission.[11] Nevertheless, the chief role of these offices seems to have continued to be that of serving the Panchen Lama's needs, including that of communication with the central government. In the meantime, the Panchen Lama established additional offices, one in Taiyuan (located on the main road between Inner Mongolia and Nanjing) and one in Kham (which suggests that the previously mentioned office in Sichuan may never have been very effectively established).[12] When the Panchen Lama obtained government permission to set up the first office in the capital, Lozang Gyentsen was the man he put in charge of this central office. He was responsible for presenting the Panchen Lama's views to the Chinese government. For example, when the Dalai Lama's representatives complained about a title given to the Panchen Lama in 1931, Lozang Gyentsen delivered the response on behalf of the Panchen Lama.

Having established these offices, the Panchen Lama remained in Inner Mongolia for two more years. According to Jagou, "the Nationalist government's intention was to use the 6th Panchen Lama as an instrument to pacify Mon-gol princes anxious to establish their own autonomy." The Panchen Lama did apparently counsel the Mongols that "they would do well to ally themselves with the Chinese government" in the face of Japanese aggression.[13] Whether this was at the government's behest or on the Panchen Lama's own initiative remains to be demonstrated. It is certainly true that the Panchen Lama communicated during this period with Chiang Kai-shek, the leader of China. However, judging from the content of the letters exchanged between the two men, it seems that the Panchen Lama was trying to see what sort of support he could gain from Chiang Kai-shek before he made any promises. Despite the official cooperation and ongoing communication between these two men, neither the Nationalist government nor the Panchen Lama was to have their wishes fulfilled at that time.

The Norlha Qutughtu's Official Appointments and Offices

In 1929, just months after establishing the Panchen Lama's office in the capital, the central government summoned the exiled Norlha Qutughtu from Sichuan Province to the capital in Nanjing.[14] Once there, he was made a member of the Mongolian and Tibetan Affairs Commission. An office similar to the Panchen Lama's, called the "Office of the Qutughtu's Resident in Nanjing to Handle Affairs (*Hutuketu zhu [Nan]jing banshi chu*)," was established at that time, while three branch offices were eventually set up in Chongqing, Chengdu, and Kangding. The concentration of these latter three offices in the single province of Sichuan demonstrated the more limited scope of the Norlha Qutughtu's influence compared to that of the Panchen Lama.[15] Because his influence was seen as critical for securing the loyalty of the Tibetans in Kham, he was also made a member of the commission to establish the province of Xikang.

His presence in the capital was important window dressing for the foreign community. The Nationalist government could counter Central Tibetan claims to the contested region of Kham if they had a spokesman from that region within their own government. In the 1933 supplement to *Who's Who in China*, the compilers gullibly reported that the Norlha Qutughtu was the "former secular and religious ruler of Hsikang [Kham]."[16] This was an obvious error of fact; the Norlha Qutughtu had only ruled a rather small portion of Kham. Nevertheless, the ignorance of Westerners living in China and the prestige conferred on this individual by the Chinese government were a powerful combination. Not only was the Norlha Qutughtu given positions within institutions that dealt with Inner Asia, he was also made a member of the national legislature (*lifa weiyuan*). Although this government body was actually powerless in the Nationalist party-state, foreigners may have been impressed by the presence of a Tibetan in such "governing" bodies. Thus, after an initial period of avoidance or exclusion from the political realm, both the Panchen Lama and the Norlha Qutughtu had been welcomed into the secular Chinese government bureaucracy.

The Dalai Lama's Offices in China

In responding to the increased official recognition granted the Panchen Lama and the Norlha Qutughtu, the Dalai Lama was fortunate to have his traditional representatives at Mount Wutai and Yonghegong. Although the early Republican governments had failed to take advantage of this vital link between China and Tibet,[17] Chiang Kai-shek was quick to engage with Yonghegong's Tibetan representatives after the success of the Northern Expedition. He visited Yonghegong when the Nationalist Party forces took Beijing in 1928.[18] At this time, the Nationalist government claimed that it would remain true to Sun Yat-sen's policy of "equality for all nationalities of the country." Encouraged by this stance, that winter the Dalai Lama sent his resident representative at Mount Wutai to Nanjing to serve as an intermediary with Chiang Kai-shek. This exchange, which has been heralded as "the beginning of contact between Tibet and the KMT [Kuomintang, or Nationalist Party] government," followed the congratulatory envoy of the Panchen Lama by almost half a year, giving the impression that the Central Tibetans were trying to keep up with the Panchen Lama's efforts.[19]

This impression is confirmed by the fact that it was only after the Panchen Lama's office in the capital had been set up in early 1929 that the Dalai Lama regularized Tibet's relations with the Republican government. After the Panchen Lama had established his office, the Dalai Lama sent the Tibetan abbot of Yonghegong, Könchok Jungné, to Nanjing to let Chiang Kai-shek know that the Tibetan government was friendly to China and welcomed the Panchen Lama's return. At Chiang's request, Könchok Jungné continued on to Tibet with "a good communiqué for improving Sino-Tibetan relations."[20] According to one source, as early as 1929 the residence of one of the incarnation series in Yonghegong had been transformed into the "Office of the Tibetan Resident in Beiping to Handle Affairs" (*Xizang zhu [Bei]ping banshi chu*).[21] In any case, by 1930 Könchok Jungné had returned to China with four assistants to serve as the Dalai Lama's representative in Nanjing. Thus the Tibetan Representative Office (*Bod kyi don gcod khang*),[22] also known as "Tibet Office to Handle Affairs" (Tib. *Shi tsang ben hre tru'u;* from the Chinese, *Xizang banshi chu*) was set up in Nanjing, with a branch office in Beiping.[23] Könchok Jungné was said to have had a good understanding of the Chinese government and global politics, and he and two of the other representatives were at least somewhat fluent in Chinese.[24] Although the Tibetan appointees who served in these offices were monk-officials, this was a thoroughly secular office as far as the Nationalist government was concerned.

Secular Educational Institutions

Aside from the overtly political role that some Tibetan lamas took in dealing with the government of China, a small group of Tibetans also enrolled in modern Chinese government schools and were thereby exposed to official Nationalist government ideology. For instance, Tibetans residing in the Chinese Republic were constantly being informed that they were one of the five races that constituted modern China. The Chinese political and intellectual climate, especially Chinese views on their neighboring nations and races, obviously affected the decision making of important Tibetan figures such as the Panchen Lama. For the period I am examining, the single most important source of the Chinese attitudes to other races was the work of Sun Yat-sen, especially his *Three Principles of the People*. Although Sun died shortly after the Panchen Lama arrived in China, his work continued to play a major role in the ideology of Republican China, especially after the success of the Northern Expedition in 1927. Sun's work was reprinted, translated at least partially into Tibetan, and made available to the Tibetans living in exile in China. As Heather Stoddard has demonstrated in her *Le mendiant de l'Amdo,* some Tibetans were able to find a liberating message in Sun's ideology.[25]

Sun's ideas were also further developed by such Nationalist politicians as Dai Jitao and Chiang Kai-shek. Both these men met personally with the Panchen Lama while he was in China. Contrary to June Dreyer's arguments, in *China's Forty Millions,* that the Republican approach to other ethnic groups was purely assimilationist, there is evidence that, at least in the Tibetan case, a respect for Tibetan culture and autonomy (though not independence) was predominant in Chinese communications with Tibetans. In fact, Chiang's upbringing, like Dai Jitao's, had been as a Buddhist. By the time he met with the Panchen Lama, he had been baptized as a Christian, but he may have been able to speak of his mother's devotion to Buddhism or his own time spent in retreat at a Buddhist monastery as a point of reference with this visiting lama.[26] Meanwhile, Gu Jiegang waged his own campaign to respectfully include the borderland peoples within the modern Chinese nation-state and did much to develop the idea that the so-called barbarians were, in fact, Chinese.

Pan-Asian Educational Plans Include Tibetans

The origin of Nationalist Chinese schools open to Tibetans can be traced back to Sun's revolutionary comrade Dai Jitao.[27] Dai had been the translator for one of Sun's last lectures, which espoused Pan-Asianism (*Da Yazhou zhuyi*).[28] Possibly this lecture, or other discussions Dai had with Sun, partially inspired Dai's later efforts. On the other hand, he may have been influenced by Gu Jiegang's ideas, published in the summer of 1926: "instead of saying that such elements of our population as the Mohammedans and Tibetans have reached a state of decline . . . one should say that they have not yet reached their maturity. True education will take cognizance of this state of affairs and inject a new potency into our national life."[29] As the president of Canton's Zhongshan University in 1927, Dai was the first public figure to formally organize research on and education of non-Chinese peoples. Although Dai's proposed Eastern Races' College (Dongfang minzu yuan) never became a reality, in his plans for this school we see the earliest model for the current "minority nationality" schools in China.

Dai's ideas for this pan-Asian educational institution are recorded in his *Path for Youth* (*Qingnian zhi lu*), which was published late in 1927, after his year of serving as president of Zhongshan University.[30] Dai seemed to be directing this publication at the graduating students, who were being sent back to their respective provinces as Dai moved north following the success of the Northern Expedition. The timing and audience of this delivery seems to have been crucial to raising an awareness and sense of urgency about the condition of China's borderlands.

In this landmark publication Dai informed China's youth that he had set forth a program to establish the Eastern Races' College as part of Zhongshan University. The scope of this school's target population included both "internal" (*guonei*) races, including those in Mongolia, Xinjiang, Qinghai, and Tibet, and races with which the Chinese had "intermarried" (*yinqin*), including Koreans, Burmese, Vietnamese, Malaysians, and Indians. Here I only examine the "internal" populations.[31] The school would "accept students of the weak and small races (*ruo xiao minzu;* i.e., non-Chinese) who had the desire to be social science and historical researchers."[32] Gu Jiegang, a prominent educator who would have frequent disagreements with Dai over the years, envisioned a very different role for educating the other races of China. As early as 1926 Gu Jiegang had written that "there is hope for the future of China if we see to it that all the racial elements are given educational advantages, by the aid of which they can work out their own salvation."[33] Dai's plan was less altruistic and more self-serving. Aware that knowledge was required to exercise dominion over others, Dai envisioned research on different races' "languages and literatures," "customs and habits," and "history and geography" as the goal of the school.

The model for this school was Soviet, as Russia had set up an Eastern University (Dongfang daxue) to accept students of various Asian nationalities in 1922.[34] However, Dai had several suggestions as to how the Chinese school could improve on that of its neighbor. Most interesting was Dai's insistence that, as followers of Sun Yat-sen and his "Three Principles," it was important that "they were against any different race's oppression." Thus he intended not to limit the school's focus to international training. Instead, he insisted that students maintain a sense of the importance of their own country and people. No doubt this was a jab at the Soviet attitude toward China as just one more Comintern project.

Of course, for those races that Dai determined were internal to China, the goal was to make Chinese citizens of them. He planned to educate them into seeing China as their nation:

> We want to recover China's races (*Zhonghua minzu*).... At the same time that we lend them ability and knowledge, [they] can help us with the materials necessary for [answering] many academic questions.... China can [thus] soon transform into a [single] body sharing a common lifestyle of [all] the people

within the country—including the barbarian tribes (*miaowan*) of Mongolia, Xinjiang, Qinghai, Tibet as well as the southern provinces. We hope to make them reach the awakening of higher humanity and with our China's race (*wo Zhongguo minzu*) join in the common effort and single-heartedly establish China's new culture.[35]

Although China had lost control of large portions of the former Qing empire, Dai was offering the youth a new vision. After a decade and a half of division—which would have been all these students had ever really known—Dai painted in the broad strokes worthy of any imperialist. Still, Dai brought them back to reality:

> The organization of the Eastern Races' College requires much preparation time. It is not possible to establish the school this year, but within the liberal arts, we have already started much of the work. Next semester we thus wish to start research on Tibetan literary and philosophic studies. [We] have already invited a suitable Tibetan scholar [*Xizang xuezhe*—ethnicity and name not specified] to serve as the lecturer on Tibetan literature and Tibetan Buddhist Studies. Aside from this work, there are a lot of plans which we hope to implement by 1928.[36]

Chen Tianxi's biography of Dai described how, aside from planning this innovative new school, Dai "devoted himself to soliciting students" in order to make these plans a reality.[37] He commissioned the commander in chief of Sichuan's armies in Xikang, Liu Chengxun (b. 1879), to recruit Kham-Tibetan (*Kang-Zang*) students who wanted to go to China to pursue their studies. All expenses were to be borne by the government in Guangdong. According to Chen, this initiative was totally misunderstood because of the situation in Kham and Tibet (i.e., the Sino-Tibetan warfare), and the quality of this first round of recruiting was not all that had been hoped. I assume this means that no students of any caliber showed up.

Despite all Dai's planning, the idea collapsed with the success of the Northern Expedition. He went north to head the Examination Ministry, and, despite his continued role in encouraging borderland studies, it would be decades before such a school (*minzu xueyuan*) would live up to this dramatic rhetoric. Although the school itself never materialized, Dai's ideas demonstrate the continuing anxiety over having lost the Qing imperial borderlands. The immediate focus on Tibet also indicates that this was the locality of greatest concern, a trend that would be repeated in most of the official schools for borderland peoples in the Republican and Communist periods.

Nationalist Government Institutions for Sino-Tibet Exchange

In spite of this false start in Canton, with Liu Chengxun's help the first students went instead to Nanjing (the new capital) in 1928. As the Eastern Races' College in Canton had not materialized, a special class was organized within the Party Affairs School (Dangwu xuexiao) to accommodate these students. Chen asserts that this was the beginning of borderland students studying in China. Certainly it seems to have been the first modern school organized by Nationalist authorities to make citizens of borderland peoples. As such, it was the predecessor of the Minority Nationalities College and may even have been the model for the Yen'an minority school.[38] In 1929 the Party Affairs School became the Central Political School (Zhongyang zhengzhi xueyuan) and there was again a special class for borderland students, although it appears to have been remedial, in order to advance these students' learning. Then, in 1930, this special class became the Mongolia and Tibetan School (Meng-Zang xuexiao), and the comparatively remedial nature of the class became the standard.[39] Sometime later, the school also established satellite schools sited in the borderlands (Meng-Zang xuexiao bianjiang fenxiao): at Jiuchuan in Gansu, Xining in Qinghai, Kangding in Xikang, and Dali in Yunnan. Thereafter the Mongolia and Tibetan School at the capital changed its name to the Borderlands School (Bianjiang xuexiao). During this time Dai served variously as director or committee member of the Central Party Affairs School (Zhongyang dangwu xuexiao) and the Political School (Zhengzhi xuexiao), so he was able to continue to advance his ideas. He must have been disquieted by the fact that so many of the students from Xikang wanted to study Western languages, no doubt owing to the presence of French missionaries and English envoys in Tibetan regions.[40] He must also have been disappointed at the failure of these schools to produce Tibetan cadres obedient to the Nationalist Party. The sparse information on the few Tibetans who studied at these secular institutions is discussed below in the context of the exiled Tibetans' understanding of the racial and nationalist ideology of Republican China.

Sino-Tibetan Dialogue on Chinese Terms

In the early twentieth century Tibetan Buddhists from Amdo and Kham were in a tight spot. They were caught between the Muslim and Chinese warlords only loosely connected to the struggling Chinese nation-state and the independent Central Tibetan government with which they shared cultural ties but which could not protect them from the warlords. Tibetan Buddhists from the borderlands between China Proper and Central Tibet had traditionally played an important role in mediating between the central governments of China and Tibet. The Republican period of Chinese history was no exception to this tradition.[41] Prominent Tibetan Buddhists from Amdo and Kham clashed with the leadership of Central Tibet and came to China seeking to pursue their own interests and those of their native regions. Through their willingness to adapt to the modern conception of a multiethnic Chinese nation-state, these individuals were essential to the negotiation of modern Sino-Tibetan relations.

Although the Panchen Lama was from Central Tibet, he was joined by many Tibetans from the borderlands who served as his interpreters and staff. His prominence lent power to these lesser figures who provided the living interface between the Chinese and Tibetan cultures. The centrality of the Panchen Lama as the focal point of Sino-Tibetan negotiation is signaled by the publishing activity of the current Communist government of China. From 1912 to 1924 the only official contact between China and Tibet was a 1920 government party sent by the Gansu provincial government to Tibet. The Dalai Lama kept them at a distance while they were in Lhasa, as observed by Charles Bell, and the mission was viewed as a failure by the Chinese, who rarely even mention the event in modern histories of Sino-Tibetan relations.[42] On the other hand, numerous books, articles, and chronologies have been devoted to the activities of the Panchen Lama in exile from 1924 to 1937. As an important political and religious figure and a major landholder in Tibet, his presence in China offered the various Chinese governments that ruled in these years their best chance at favorably influencing Tibetan opinion.

The chief obstacle impeding Tibetan Buddhist lamas from gaining knowledge and understanding of modern Chinese political ideology was linguistic.[43] Yet unlike the Chinese who were trying to learn about Tibetan culture and religious ideology at this time, these Tibetan monks were comparatively well financed and looked after. They had Nationalist government funding, interpreters who accompanied them, and devoted disciples to assist them. They did not have to learn the Chinese language or worry about day-to-day survival. Yet the modern Chinese political discourse presented its own challenge just because it was so alien to Tibetan Buddhist cultural conceptions.

As I examined the Chinese ideology to which exiled Tibetans were exposed, I focused primarily on the occurrence of racial terms, such as the "five races" (*wuzu*) or the politically charged neologism, *minzu* (race/nation/people), as well as the rhetoric of nationalism drawn from Sun Yat-sen's *Three Principles of the People*. When trying to discern what was communicated by Chinese politicians to the prominent Tibetans in exile in China, we are constrained by the limitations of the source material. Since the Panchen Lama did not know Chinese, he

→ *linguistic issues in trying to mediate relations*

had to rely on the Tibetan language. To state the obvious, this means that verbal communications had to be interpreted for him and texts had to be translated. The published archival documents of communiqués, letters, and telegrams between Chinese politicians and these Tibetans are entirely in Chinese. Thus we know what was said in Chinese but not how it was translated into Tibetan. This is significant because so many of the terms that were found in the Chinese were modern political concepts that had no ready analogues in classical Tibetan. The way these terms were translated was of the utmost importance in shaping the Tibetans' understanding of Chinese political conceptions. Upon his arrival in China the Panchen Lama was exposed to the thought of Sun Yat-sen and, before 1932, apparently even studied a translation of the *Three Principles of the People*.[44] The earliest recorded instance of any Tibetan translating the works of Sun Yat-sen was in 1927, when the Panchen Lama's representatives in Xining undertook the task. According to a letter from his Qinghai office in 1929, the office had been established in Xining "especially in order to translate the Director's noble instructions, and in turn publicize them, so that the Mongol and Tibetan masses would quickly awaken to the principles and unite."[45] However, this translation does not appear to survive. Instead, only a few short references to Chinese nationalist ideology survive in the enormous Tibetan language corpus of the Panchen Lama.

The Chinese Language Record

Given these limitations, what can we learn from the Chinese language communications attributed to the Panchen Lama? First, and most significant, even in the Chinese language materials issued by the Panchen Lama's representatives during the decade he was in China Proper (1925–34), the two kinds of Chinese political rhetoric that I sought were mentioned only occasionally. The racial rhetoric of the "five races" occurred in only ten of the eighty-four published archival documents from those ten years, while only seven explicit references were made to Sun Yat-sen or to his *Three Principles of the People*. In these materials the "five races" rhetoric occurred in three distinct periods—early (1925–26), middle (1929–31), and late (1931–34)—when the Panchen Lama was interacting with Chinese political authorities. The references to Sun clustered only around the latter two of these periods. My analysis of the timing and use of Chinese rhetoric demonstrates that the Panchen Lama (or his interpreters) carefully deployed such rhetoric almost exclusively when addressing the Chinese, often to accomplish specific goals in negotiating a beneficial relationship with the Republican government.

These findings have significant repercussions for the Chinese language sources that are attributed to the Panchen Lama. Since certain terms appeared in the Chinese language sources translated by or issued from the representatives of the Panchen Lama, we might expect to find them somewhere in the corpus of the Panchen Lama's Tibetan language works.[46] Having tested this expectation for two sets of ideas in particular—the thought of Sun Yat-sen and the racial discourse (*wuzu gonghe*) of the Republican period—in examining hundreds of pages of the Panchen Lama's autobiography and religious writings, I have found little to confirm the presence of these discourses in the Panchen Lama's own writings. Such an absence makes me approach the Communist-published Chinese language archives attributed to the Panchen Lama with a hermeneutic of suspicion. If these are indeed valid sources, then the Panchen Lama's representatives appear to have employed Chinese political ideology only to please a certain audience (which financed the lama and his entourage) without this rhetoric penetrating the Panchen Lama's own (Tibetan) discourse.

Early Tibetan Responses to Racial Rhetoric (1925–1926)

The Panchen Lama's early contact with Chinese political figures was cautious, and although the published documents from that time invoked the rhetoric of the "five races," they reflected this caution rather than an immediate embracing of the concept of racial harmony. When we examine what the Chinese officials communicated to him in Chinese and the text of "his" responses, we have to consider who interpreted for and represented the Panchen Lama in China. Because he did not know Chinese, although the Panchen Lama was physically present in China, he nevertheless still depended on others to represent him to the Chinese. At the same time he relied on others to represent the Chinese and their political ideology to him. Currently we only have knowledge of a handful of these intermediary figures. One of the most important, Lozang Gyentsen, was the Panchen Lama's chief representative to the Chinese from the start.[47] He delivered the Panchen Lama's speech to the National Reconstruction Conference in 1925. This public address demonstrated an early critique of Chinese racial rhetoric compared to the grim reality of ongoing ethnic warfare.

The first two Chinese language documents to discuss the "five races" were the letter and speech that Lozang Gyentsen delivered to the 1925 National Reconstruction Conference organized by Duan Qirui.[48] The letter hopefully encouraged the natural tendency for "the five races to assist one another" (*wuzu gongzhu*) but fell short of suggesting that the harmony of the five races (*wuzu gonghe*) already existed. The text of the speech clarified Tibetan doubts about this harmony, indicating that "these days, China claims the five races are in harmony (*wuzu gonghe*), yet in reality one sees that usually misunderstandings are not yet avoided in the frontier regions."[49] Here we must remember that the Panchen

Lama had just traveled through an area of intense ethnic conflict between the Muslims and Tibetans, with the Chinese frequently switching sides, on the Qinghai and Gansu border. The conflict was described thus: "The Tibetans and Muslims were engaged in ethnic slaughter, not modern warfare. Ma [a Muslim warlord] is said to have offered a reward for every Tibetan head his soldiers could bring in."[50] The speech delivered at the conference rhetorically asked, "Where is the fruit of the true meaning of the five races in harmony?" The equality for all, the end of disparity between the noble and the lowly, the poor and the rich, and the common progress of civilization that government propaganda suggested were clearly nowhere to be found in those days.[51] Although this speech used the phrases "the five races in harmony" and "the peoples of the five races" (*wuzu renmin*) more frequently than later documents would, the text repeatedly points to the absence of unity and the failure of harmony to materialize.

In fact, the northern militarists who controlled China's central government until 1927 were scarcely concerned with borderland issues or realizing the harmony of the five races. As previously discussed, the Panchen Lama had minimal interaction with this turbulent government. Nevertheless, portions of another Chinese language letter from the Panchen Lama suggest that he or his representatives were prepared to use this racial rhetoric when addressing Chinese leaders. In a 1926 letter to Wu Peifu, one of the leading warlords of North China, the following passage was attributed to the Panchen Lama: "[I], the Panchen Lama, care for the fatherland. . . . Therefore braving 10,000 dangers and crossing 10,000 *li* to come to China Proper (*neidi*) was really for the sake of the harmony of the five races."[52] Although we do not know the full context of this letter, clearly more of an effort was being made to show a positive view of the Republican racial rhetoric compared to the critical speech of 1925. These first three documents demonstrate that, at the very least, the Panchen Lama's representatives and translators were aware of the importance of the Chinese conception of the harmony of the five races and were willing to deploy it in their limited communications with Chinese politicians.

The Tibetan Language Record

The influence of this racial rhetoric was more difficult to detect in Tibetan documents. By examining how the Panchen Lama deployed terms of human typology I probed whether this modern Chinese discourse influenced the Panchen Lama's thinking. The idea that there were five races as part of China never occurs in the Tibetan texts I have seen. In the Panchen Lama's works, this seems to be to the result of the fact that Muslims were never included with the other "races" (Tibetan, Manchu, Mongol, and Chinese) that were associated with Buddhism. As Dai Jitao would argue (see chapter 6), Buddhism was the uniting factor in the eyes of Tibetans such as the Panchen Lama. Thus, even though the lama and his representatives dealt with Muslims, such as those who held power in the Mongolian and Tibetan Affairs Commission or in the regions of Qinghai and Ningxia, they declined to explicitly include this group in any references to racial or ethnic unity.[53] And although Manchus are mentioned occasionally in the Panchen Lama's biography, they, too, seemed to matter remarkably little to Tibetans in Republican China. Instead, the most common collective reference is not to a group of five races but rather to the three races or ethnicities best known for their adherence to Buddhism: the Chinese, Mongol, and Tibetan. This is reflected in the phrase, "the three, Chinese, Tibetan, and Mongolian" (*Rgya Bod Sog gsum*), which occurs at least six times in the Panchen Lama's biography.[54]

As this phrasing demonstrated, the new racial and ethnic divisions introduced to East Asia in this period were rarely incorporated into the Panchen Lama's work. Instead, a generic term for "beings" is typically paired with what we would think of as ethnic categories. The Tibetan word *skye bo*, meaning "one who was born," has a strong Buddhist flavor and is applied equally to humans and all other living creatures. In the Panchen Lama's biography, this word was paired to create words for Chinese, Mongolians, and Manchus (*Rgya Sog skye bo* and *Rgya Manju'i skye bo*).[55] Aside from this phrase, the biography usually discussed groups according to their affiliations: Chinese and Mongol monastics and laymen (*Rgya Sog ser skya*),[56] representatives (*'thus mi*) of some geographical region, or as Chinese Buddhists (*Bu ca'o rnams*).

A term (*mi rigs*) that is now the standard Tibetan translation of the modern Chinese term *minzu* occurred rarely in the Panchen Lama's works. Moreover, in the Panchen Lama's biography this term was rarely used as the Chinese would have used it; that is, the term does not regularly appear to be a direct translation of the Chinese, at least not in this text, one of the earliest published instances of this term in Tibetan.[57] In early 1925 the Panchen Lama visited Yonghegong and the Dalai Lama's officials there. On this occasion he also met people he described with the phrase "*Rgya Sog gi mi rigs rnams*" (Chinese and Mongols).[58] This usage could certainly be a literal translation of the Chinese "*Han Meng minzu*." At times when the Panchen Lama addressed a Chinese audience, he clearly used the term as the Chinese would (Tib. *Krug sgo'i mi rigs*, equivalent to Ch. *Zhongguo minzu*).[59] However, three other instances where this phrase is used do not replicate this straightforward "translation."[60]

The first instance of this term is paired with the term for "foreign nationalities" (*Phyi gling mi rigs*) who attended the Beijing Kâlacakra ceremony in 1932.[61] To my knowledge, Chinese would not have used a translation of this term (such as *waiguo minzu*) to indicate a generic foreign "nationality." The second use occurred in the phrase "Chinese, Mongols, and foreigners" (*Rgya Sog phyi gyi mi rigs*).[62] Again, the insertion of "foreigners" problematizes what would otherwise look like a Chinese ethno-racial term. The third occurrence complicates matters further, as it refers to three different groups from the Tibetan cultural world: the peoples from Kham, Tibet, and Köke nor (*Kham Bod Mtsho sngon kyi mi rigs*).[63] Could the Panchen Lama be intending to imply that there were three separate races, ethnicities, or nations within the Tibetan cultural region? Possibly, but he did not adapt this idea from Chinese Nationalist discourse because the Chinese did not generally distinguish between Tibetans in this way.[64] In any case, I think these various examples demonstrate that these uses of the term *mi rigs* cannot be understood strictly as a Tibetan translation of the Chinese term *minzu*.

So what were Tibetan conceptions of human typology, and were they altered by exposure to the modern concepts expressed in racial and nationalist ideologies in China? The Tibetan term *rigs* has two meanings, one indicating lineage and the other type or kind. In the above four instances, the term may well be inflected toward the sense of lineage, which would indicate a more racial conception of persons similar to the Chinese term *zu*. On the other hand, the references to foreign lands and the division of the Tibetan cultural world into three regions as a typology for the peoples from those regions may indicate that this usage just specified geographical, and not genealogical, origins. For most of the biography, in any case, this term was simply being used as an indicator of a type of person. For example, by far the most common appearance of the term was in the phrase "*dpon rigs*," meaning official type, or simply "official."[65] Likewise, the term *rigs* was associated with other designations of peoples' professions, such as monks or businessmen (Chinese and Mongolian monks: *Rgya Sog grwa rigs*, merchants: *tshong rigs*). Only twice does an equivalent to the Chinese model of ethnic designation (*Han, Meng, Zang* paired with the lineage marker *zu,* as in *Hanzu,* etc.) occur. Both times this involved the term "Mongol type or lineage" (*Sog rigs*), which could be a literal translation of Chinese *Mengzu* (Mongol ethnicity or race). The phrase "Chinese person" (*Rgya mi,* equivalent to Ch. *Hanren*) occurs only once,[66] and similar equivalents of the Chinese term are not applied at all to other groups.[67]

Why is this so significant? Because the stark absence of an adoption of Chinese conceptions of racial terminology indicates the weak influence that Chinese conceptions of race and ethnicity had on Tibetans at this time. In the Panchen Lama's collected writings there are almost no instances when he uses terminology which closely follows that of the Nationalist ideology to which he was exposed for more than a decade. Moreover, aside from these rare and ambivalent uses, the Tibetan language would not be transformed to embody the idea of ethnic distinctions along the lines of Western conceptions in a consistent manner until the Communist period.

Chinese Language Presentations of Republican Rhetoric

The Chinese language materials concerning the information about Chinese politics that was presented to the Panchen Lama are not very abundant. Again, I sought sources that would have informed the Panchen Lama about two key sets of ideas in Chinese Nationalist political discourse: the "*wuzu*" Republican racial rhetoric and Sun Yat-sen's ideology. Although the Panchen Lama was obviously exposed to these two discourses just by virtue of being in China, I could find only a handful of text-based instances to compare to the Panchen Lama's responses to these discourses. The earliest published archival document that mentions these ideas was sent from Chiang Kai-shek to the Panchen Lama in November 1930. This letter is the only one from a Nationalist source that used aggressive assimilationist terminology to discuss race relations in China. Chiang told the Panchen Lama that, "hereafter, the center, based on the *Three Principles of the People,* will smelt the five great races (*wu da minzu*) in one furnace, forming one Chinese race (*Zhonghua minzu*)."[68] Assuming that this Chinese language letter was translated accurately for the Panchen Lama, he would have been warned of the manner in which Chiang intended to apply Sun's "Three Principles" to the borderlands. However, the Panchen Lama never indicated his acceptance of this approach by using such terminology in his own writings. Even the Chinese language material associated with the Panchen Lama's offices in China never repeated this language.

Later Chinese Texts Attributed to the Panchen Lama (1928–1930)

The second period in which Chinese language documents attributed to the Panchen Lama contained Republican rhetoric occurred after 1927. At that time the Nationalist Party succeeded in replacing the Beijing militarists as the legitimate rulers of China and started broadcasting the ideology of Sun Yat-sen. The Nationalist Party enshrined Sun's ideas as party doctrine, and the Panchen Lama's letters and those of his representatives reflect an awareness of this change. From 1928 to 1930 these Chinese language materials suggest a concerted effort to use both the Republican racial rhetoric and Sun's ideology when addressing a Chinese political audience. As is discussed in chapter 6, this period was marked by an effort to build a working relationship between the Panchen Lama and Chiang's Nationalist government. In this context, the Panchen Lama's use of Chinese political rhetoric may well have served as "tokens of exchange" which indicated to the Chinese that the Panchen Lama and his entourage accepted the Chinese political view of the Sino-Tibetan relations.[69] Rather than examining each of these communications individually, I attend only to the first and last and summarize those that were exchanged in 1929 and 1930. In a 1928 letter addressed by the Panchen Lama to Chiang Kai-shek, mention was made of the "Three Principles of the People illuminating all of Asia" (*San min zhuyi zhao bian Yazhou*). This letter also used the new Chinese term for Tibetans (*Xizang minzu*) for the first time in these diplomatic exchanges. Such statements could indicate Tibetan knowledge of Republican ideology without indicating specifically how the Tibetans understood these new ideas.[70]

Throughout 1929 and early in 1930 the Panchen Lama and his representatives continued to exchange letters and telegrams, which showed an increasing willingness to use both elements of the political rhetoric under analysis here, with the Chinese government. Letters from the Nanjing and the Beiping offices included both the discourse of the five races and Sun's ideology.[71] A telegram sent to all branches of the government, military leaders, provincial governments, and newspapers from the Panchen Lama employed the phrase "the five races are one family" (*wuzu yijia*) in an appeal to end the disastrous military struggles that were tearing China apart.[72] A 1930 letter to Chiang contained frank reference to the "division of the five races" (*wuzu fenlie*) as well as the harmony of the five races.[73] As in 1925 the Tibetan representatives of the Panchen Lama seemed unable to speak uncritically or unrealistically about there being harmony among the five races that the Chinese recognized as significant constituent elements to the new Republic.[74]

Failed Rhetoric: Tibetan Autonomy Denied

Two of the most significant secularly oriented intermediaries between the Chinese and the Tibetans were also loosely affiliated with the Panchen Lama. They came from the town of Batang in Kham, which sat just east of the line of control between the Chinese and Tibetan armed forces. Batang had long received Chinese influences, as it was on the main official route to Tibet during the Qing dynasty. At the end of the Qing, Zhao Erfeng had enacted certain reforms in Batang, and the Chinese Republic saw fit to continue to try to develop this area. Two men, Kelzang Tsering (1899–1941) and Kelzang Chönjor (Ch. Liu Jiaju; 1900–1977), who were later associated with the Panchen Lama, grew up in this town and received their education from Chinese schools set up in Kham.[75]

Kelzang Tsering went to the Xikang Military Academy (Xikang zhunguan xuexiao) in 1924 and then served in the Xikang army under Liu Wenhui for several years. Somehow he ended up in the entourage of the exiled Panchen Lama by 1927. When the Nationalist government invited the Panchen Lama's official

Gongkar Trashi to Nanjing, Kelzang Tsering accompanied him as his interpreter. He must have impressed the Chinese officials, because Dai Jitao recommended him for official posts in the Mongolian and Tibetan Affairs Commission. In those days bilingual Tibetans were a rarity, so he was appointed a member of the commission and the head of the Tibetan Affairs Office (Zangshi chu) within it.[76] Later, he became the associate editor of the *Mongolian and Tibetan Weekly* (*Meng Zang zhou bao*). In this capacity he would certainly have been exposed to a barrage of information about Chinese political ideology. He also appears to have remained in close contact with the Panchen Lama and his representatives in the capital, as I demonstrate below. This man, having gone from working for the Chinese military to serving the Panchen Lama's entourage as an interpreter, was now situated in the heart of Tibetan policy making in the Chinese government.

Kelzang Tsering would play a key role in the doomed attempt to adapt Sun Yat-sen's ideology to the Tibetan context. Although the details of this endeavor are far from complete, I will try to sketch the general picture as best as I can.[77] In the Nanjing schools described above, the Chinese Nationalist Party appears to have been trying to train Tibetan cadres for the purpose of returning to Xikang and weakening the influence of the warlord Liu Wenhui there. The experiment was a complete failure. The Chinese seemed to have assumed that indoctrination in Sun Yat-sen's thought would make the Tibetans loyal only to China's interests. Instead, they read Sun's work in light of their own interests. Frank Dikötter has argued that, "[Sun's principle of] racial nationalism . . . embodied the discourse of race as lineage as well as the discourse of race as nation."[78] The Tibetans could more easily apply both these discourses to their own understanding of Tibetan ethnicity than they could apply these theories to link Tibetans with the Chinese ethnicity. In effect, the Tibetans applied the logic of "liberation from oppressors" and "national autonomy" to their own situation and ethnic group. Although this is hardly surprising, Tibetan agency in redeploying ideology is often overlooked by Western sympathizers as it was by the Republican Chinese. This would be harder to do if we remember the words of Cynthia Bell:

> Ideology is not a coherent set of ideas, statements or attitudes imposed on a people who duly internalize them. Any ideology is always in dialogue with, and thus shaped and constrained by, the voices it is suppressing, manipulating, echoing. In other words, ideology exists only in concrete historical forms and in specific relations to other ideologies.[79]

In 1931 plans were formulated to send Kelzang Tsering, as Commissioner for Goumindang Affairs of Xikang, to start the work of establishing a Nationalist

Party organization in the region. When the Central Political Institute graduated a class of fifty Tibetan students in 1932,[80] Kelzang Tsering led them back to Xikang to initiate this party directive. These students divided themselves into two groups; one headed to Batang via Kunming with their leader, while the other set up a Party Affairs Office in Kangding. When Kelzang Tsering arrived in his hometown of Batang, he joined with the local people to disarm Liu Wenhui's garrison there.[81] They demanded autonomy, employing the slogan "Khampa rule for Kham" (*Kangren zhi Kang*).[82] This slogan may reflect local experiences as much as Sun Yat-sen's ideology. In the early twenties, while Kelzang Tsering was training under Liu Wenhui, the Sichuanese warlords had successfully advocated for provincial autonomy using the slogan "Sichuan for the Sichuanese."[83]

The Kham Tibetans seem to have linked Sun Yat-sen's discussions of nationalism with this local precedent. Like the Sichuanese, at first these Tibetans were initially not so much trying to secede from China as to gain real military and political control over their own region. In a telegram to the Nationalist government, Kelzang Tsering informed the government that representatives from the thirty-three counties of Xikang had been organized into the Commission to Establish Xikang Province. This commission had elected him their political leader (*weiyuanhui zhang*) as well as the leader (*ciling*) of the Xikang Provincial Defense Army. It seems that he did not get the support from the Nationalist government that he expected, because he is said to have eventually declared independence (*xuanbu duli*), against the party's wishes.[84] However, without Chinese support, this independence movement seems to have collapsed within months, when Kelzang Tsering accepted an order recalling him to Nanjing in October.

The relations between the Panchen Lama and Kelzang Tsering during this period are discussed in a memorandum sent by the Dalai Lama's representative Könchok Jungné to the Central Executive Board of the Nationalist government in August 1932. Far from being pleased with the proclamation of independence by a group of Kham Tibetans, Könchok Jungné explained that the Panchen Lama and the Mongolian and Tibetan Affairs Commission were conspiring together, implying that these veiled actions were contrary to what the Nationalist government intended. Specifically the memo charged that Kelzang Tsering had forcibly occupied the area of Batang according to the plan and with the assistance of Shi Qingyang, the director of the Mongolian and Tibetan Affairs Commission.[85] If this information was correct, then the Panchen Lama would have been aware of the plans to establish an autonomous Kham (*Xikang*). Even if the Panchen Lama had not conspired with Kelzang Tsering, the fact that such men had served as interpreters and informants to the Panchen Lama indicates that some Tibetans chose to understand Chinese political ideology as a way to liberate their own domains from outside oppression. Kelzang Tsering was not the only vital intermediary between the Panchen Lama and the Chinese government to be influenced by modern Chinese political ideology in this way.

The second such intermediary was Kelzang Chönjor.[86] This man was also from Batang and, like his friend Kelzang Tsering, had been educated in Chinese schools that had been set up there. From 1918 until 1929 he was given various responsibilities within these Chinese schools. In 1929 he was invited by Kelzang Tsering to come to Nanjing and edit the Tibetan language portion of the *Mongolian and Tibetan Weekly*. In 1931 he was given a position within the Mongolian and Tibetan Affairs Commission's Tibetan Affairs Office and was made a full member of the commission. Kelzang Chönjor later served the Panchen Lama as his secretary-general from 1932 until the latter's death in 1937. Even after the Panchen Lama's death in the Tibetan borderlands, Kelzang Chönjor continued to use the Panchen Lama's field headquarters (*xingyuan*) to influence Kham politics. Reminiscent of Kelzang Tsering's attempt, he cooperated with local Tibetans to take control of a number of Xikang counties.[87] As before, ending Liu Wenhui's control of the region was the chief goal of the movement, and the slogan "Khampa rule for Kham" was again the rallying call. Yet, just as before, the movement seems to have fizzled and Kelzang Chönjor eventually returned to work in the Chongqing office of the Panchen Lama.[88] The basic problem with all these movements, aside from logistic and strategic issues, was that only Tibetans who had left their home territory and lived among the Chinese seemed to view all Tibetans, or even all Khampas, as a single group that needed to be unified. But local Tibetans were concerned primarily with local matters and could rarely even be convinced that all of Kham needed to be unified to resist the Chinese.[89]

Despite the failure of these two autonomy movements to achieve their long-term goals, the mere fact that two figures closely associated with the Panchen Lama were involved in such projects helps us to comprehend how Chinese political concepts were understood by Tibetans. These men were bilingual, had been educated in Chinese schools, and had worked in Chinese government organs that created Tibetan policies. Yet the moment they had the opportunity, they took what they had learned of Sun Yat-sen's nationalist liberation ideology and applied it to their own localities. The Panchen Lama might also have shared such an interpretation of these new ideas. Possibly he despaired of ever being allowed to return to Central Tibet and hoped that he could play a prominent role in an autonomous Tibetan regions outside Tibet's control. According to a German who was in northwest China in the mid-1930s, "The story was that the Tashi Lama had an idea of establishing his reign in north Tibet, in the hope later to be summoned to Lhasa as head of the Lamaist church."[90]

Several other Tibetans associated with the Panchen Lama and Kham autonomy movements attended various Chinese institutions of higher education, and
some of these manifested the same tendency to understand Sun's philosophy as
a blueprint for liberating Tibet. The Panchen Lama's nephew Wangdü Norbu
was raised in China and attended the Goumindang Military Academy.[91]
Although little is known about this man, he joined the Chinese Nationalist
Party and was closely associated with the radical Tibetan, Pomdatsang Rapga.[92]
Other associates of the Panchen Lama who attended the Central Political
Institute include Meru Samshak, and the monk-official (*rtse drung*) Lozang
Püntsok.[93] According to Heather Stoddard, other Tibetans attended the Baoding
Military University (Baoding junguan daxuexiao) and the Whampoa Military
Academy (Huangpu junguan xuexiao).[94] Of these Tibetan students of Chinese
Nationalist political ideology who might have influenced the Panchen Lama, we
only have detailed information on two men. Although these men's links to the
Panchen Lama were not as intimate as the Batang intermediaries examined
above, they were part of a close-knit Tibetan community in exile in China. One,
known to Stoddard only by his Chinese name Jiang Xinxi, was the uncle of
Kelzang Tsering. From Goldstein, Dawei Sherap, and Sieberschuh's account, this
must be Lobsang Thundrup (Tib. Blo bzang don grub).[95] The other, Rapga,
knew the Panchen Lama's nephew. Both these men were strong proponents of
Sun Yat-sen's "Three Principles of the People." Jiang graduated at the top of his
class at the Central Political Institute, was given the title "Liaison Officer to the
Tibet Garrison," and was assigned to the Department of National Defense
(Guofang bu). Despite these bright prospects, Stoddard presented the frustrating
reality that such Tibetans faced in Nationalist China:

> He had no real power, either in Tibetan territory under the control of the
> Chinese or in Nanjing. Also, while praising the *Sanmin Zhuyi* (*Three Principles
> of the People*) of Sun Yat-sen, Jiang Xinxi bemoaned the gap between theory
> and practice because, in the end, in spite of the theory of the equality of the
> "five races," the Guomindang had never yet placed anyone of non-Chinese
> origin in a position of power.[96]

No doubt the failure of his nephew's efforts at establishing an autonomous
Kham in 1932 colored his assessment of the prospects of actually applying Sun
Yat-sen's ideology in Tibetan regions. Did Kelzang Tsering communicate his
uncle's opinions of Nationalist rhetoric to the Panchen Lama? We will probably
never know.

Linking Rapga's thoughts on Sun's ideology to the Panchen Lama is equally
difficult, but his association with the Panchen Lama's nephew predates the

Panchen Lama's death, so he may have shared his enthusiasm for Sun's work with his friend, Wangdü Norbu, and his uncle, the Panchen Lama. Even if he did not, Rapga's experiences make an interesting comparison with other Tibetans in exile. The first notice of Rapga coincides with yet another attempt by the Khampas to attain autonomy, this time from Central Tibetan forces in Markham, just west of Batang. Although no Chinese influence has been linked to what Goldstein, Dawei Sherap, and Sieberschuh called this "abortive nationalist revolt," some members of the defeated Pomdatsang family fled to China to be sheltered by the Chinese. Moreover, although Goldstein, Dawei Sherap, and Sieberschuh were not specific about the date, it may be that, as early as the 1934 revolt, Rapga "was a devout believer in the political ideology of Sun Yat-sen and had translated some of Sun's more important writings into Tibetan."[97] If so, the Panchen Lama may have even read Rapga's translation; at present, no such translation appears to be in circulation. Until other sources become available, it remains unclear how and just when Rapga developed a thorough knowledge of the "Three Principles of the People." In 1936 Rapga met the Chinese official Huang Musong in India and was persuaded to go to China. That same year Rapga was made a member of the Mongolian and Tibetan Affairs Commission.[98] For the next decade Rapga would be involved with the Chinese, eventually securing their assistance in establishing a new political party to transform Tibet. Although their efforts were eventually blocked by the effective cooperation of British and Tibetan policing, Goldstein concluded that, by 1946, this new party had "a hundred or so sympathizers among Khamba traders."[99]

The attempt to apply Sun Yat-sen's ideology in a Tibetan context failed precisely because those who supported this activity were not at the center of elite Tibetan religious culture. Revolutionary Tibetans realized and were often frustrated by this problem.[100] In a sense they were trying to change Tibet from the outside, through secular means. Despite this failure, from Stoddard's interviews, we learn that even in 1975 Rapga still held to his beliefs that Sun's theories were valuable:

> The *San min zhuyi* was intended for all peoples under the domination of foreigners, for all those who had been deprived of the rights of man. But it was conceived especially for the Asians. It is for this reason that I translated it. At that time, a lot of new ideas were spreading in Tibet.[101]

If the Panchen Lama had been willing to personally and publicly support these early efforts at seeking local Tibetan autonomy (in particular among Chinese Buddhists and the media that followed his ritual activities), might the movement have had more success? We will never know the answer to this question. However, the very fact that so many of the bilingual Tibetans who understood modern Chinese political ideology saw it as a way to liberate all or parts of Tibet suggests that this was the message the Panchen Lama would have received through his interpreters. As will be clear in the next chapter, once the Panchen Lama had negotiated a relationship with the Chinese government on mutually agreeable terms (from 1931 on), he too embraced aspects of Sun Yat-sen's ideology.

In pointed contrast to these Chinese-educated Tibetans' interpretations of Chinese Republican ideology, the Chinese language materials attributed to the Panchen Lama never suggest a redeployment of this ideology directed toward seeking an autonomous Tibet. The experiences and activities of the bilingual Tibetan intermediaries in the Republican period demonstrate the contrast between what these men did and said, and what the Chinese language texts attributed to the Panchen Lama communicate. The disparity between the two is surprising, but, of course, the published archival documents were sanctioned by the authorities, and no independent researcher has gained access to unpublished archival material. The Panchen Lama's own interpreter, Kelzang Tsering, sought Kham independence, albeit some years after he had left the lama's service. Then, after the death of the Panchen Lama, his secretary-general tried again to claim autonomy for the Khampas. In the intervening years the Panchen Lama's nephew was associated with a third Khampa who also sought Kham independence. Yet aside from the memo from the Dalai Lama's representative accusing the Panchen Lama of conspiring with Kelzang Tsering, no mention was made of the Panchen Lama ever advocating such ideas of autonomy or independence.

From analyzing the Chinese language documents attributed to the Panchen Lama prior to 1931, it is clear that the Panchen Lama's representatives chose to employ the Chinese racial and nationalist rhetoric of the day to communicate with Chinese politicians in ways that the Panchen Lama never chose to do in his own writings. It is possible that the Panchen Lama personally dictated some of these letters, transcribed speeches, or memorandums to his representatives. However, unless the original Tibetan versions of these Chinese sources become available, scholars should treat these documents with particular care. Instead of granting us access to what the Panchen Lama understood about Chinese political ideology, these sources indicate merely what the Panchen Lama's representatives communicated with the Chinese government.[102] Furthermore, as I demonstrate in the next chapter, the Panchen Lama pointedly refused to use Sun Yat-sen's rhetoric until he had been recognized as a religious *and* a political leader by the Chinese government and was assured of Chinese respect for the Buddhist religion.

The Weakness of Chinese Rhetoric

The failure of Chinese Republican rhetoric to significantly influence powerful Tibetans should hardly be a surprise, as even nationalist Chinese intellectuals found much of it unconvincing. The greatest critic of the official Goumindang (GMD) ideology was the educator, Gu Jiegang. Although Gu agreed with the Nationalist Party that China's borderland peoples (and their territories) were a vital component of the modern nation-state, he was unwavering in his intellectual honesty about the history of these people's relations with China. Gu's biographer Laurence Schneider stated that "because of his belief in multi-ethnicity, Gu regarded Pan-Hanism, advocated by the GMD in the late 1920s under the motto 'The Five Races in Harmony' (*wuzu gonghe*), as both historically untrue and morally irresponsible."[103] He also ridiculed the Nationalist Party "spokesmen who sometimes suggested that all the racial groups in contemporary China (the Mongols, the Manchus, Tibetans, and Muslims, etc.) were descendants of the Yellow Emperor."[104] But really these arguments were for the benefit of the Chinese, not the other races, for whom the Yellow Emperor meant nothing. Frank Dikötter described this strategy, arguing that "racial discourse, which has sometimes been more about imagined social inclusions than about real social encounters, has shaped the identity of millions of people."[105] Although China's racial discourse did not widely penetrate Tibetan society, Tibetans were nonetheless affected by it.

This is because the Nationalist government was bent first on educating a domestic audience, never mind the historical or contemporary reality. Again Dikötter has best summarized this approach: "racial knowledge has been deployed to subordinate and dominate entire groups of people."[106] Thus Gu, too, was unconcerned about how the Tibetans or other races would understand this propaganda. However, he was worried that the Chinese people would see through the weakness of the government's arguments. Then, like Zhang Binglin, they might decide that China was actually better off without these "barbarian" border peoples holding back the nation's progress. Just as Taixu felt that Tibetan Buddhism would help to revive Chinese Buddhism, Gu believed that an infusion of "barbarian" peoples was precisely what China needed to reinvigorate its dying culture.[107] He was determined not to let misleading propaganda destroy the possibility of alliances with China's borderland peoples. Therefore, according to Schneider:

What Gu undertook was to unmask the political agenda behind the GMD's claim that it was fulfilling the historic mission of unifying the country. . . . [H]e took the GMD to task for lying to the Chinese people: "In this world, a thousand empty claims cannot compete with one solid truth. . . . If we develop a good method of <u>unifying the nation, we shall have no difficulty in staying together.</u> The government does not need to lie, telling us that we all have descended from the same ancestors. Even if the government is successful in unifying the country with lies, this unity will be flimsy. Once the people become intelligent, can this trick still deceive them?"[108]

Although history is still used to accomplish government aims in China today, Gu's influence may be present in the attempt to maintain the appearance of scholarship regarding China's "minority nationalities."[109]

Of course, the Tibetans never accepted the Sinocentric myths of the Nationalist government, if indeed they were even aware of them. The Tibetans in exile were too busy trying to attending to the needs of their own regions to worry about abstruse historical debates between Chinese intellectuals. But even Tibetan attempts to work out secular liberation techniques from Chinese nationalist rhetoric ultimately failed. The Chinese government was unwilling to live up to its rhetoric by truly assisting the Tibetans who sought its support for regional autonomy. Thus ended the attempt to use secular ideology alone to convince the Tibetans to join the Chinese nation-state. Once Dai had to deal with real (and not merely mythological) Tibetans, and maybe because he had not even convinced Chinese like Gu, he changed his tone dramatically. Dropping Chinese foundation myths, he turned to shared historical and cultural factors of Sino-Tibetan connections such as Buddhism.

6. The Merging of Secular and Religious Systems (1931–1935)

IN CHINA, the early growth in popularity of Tibetan Buddhism from 1924 to 1930 had been based on the spiritual comfort that could be derived from the new practices and rituals that Tibetan Buddhists offered the Chinese. The later development of interest in Tibetan Buddhism, from 1931 to 1940, differed from these early years. Some earlier traditions were carried over into this new decade, but Nationalist government support of and involvement with Tibetan Buddhists greatly increased. From the thirteenth Dalai Lama's visit to Beijing in 1908 until the 1930s, the governments of China had, in general, tried to depoliticize the role of Tibetan lamas. Whereas the monks active in the early period were supported largely by lay Buddhists and only marginally by powerful politicians, in the later period Tibetan Buddhists were integrated into the government structure as paid official protectors of China and publicists for the Nationalist government. Starting in 1931 the Panchen Lama, the Norlha Qutughtu, and the Changja Qutughtu were awarded titles that included the epithet "protector of the country" (*huguo*). When the Nationalist government sought Buddhist protection for China, it was continuing a traditional relationship that affirmed the mutual interests shared by the state and religious institutions. To fully integrate these lamas into the state structure, all three men were also awarded commissions as envoys to the peoples of China's frontiers. From the perspective of the Nationalist government, acceptance of such titles and the accompanying responsibilities indicated an acknowledgment of China's sovereignty over these regions. From a Buddhist perspective, such recognition was a sign that the Tibetan Buddhists had succeeded in convincing the Chinese government that religious and state power were naturally linked.

The Chinese Nationalist government, led by Dai Jitao's efforts, reached out to Tibetan Buddhists on their own terms, combining aspects of religious and political roles in the positions these leading lamas were offered. Dai, Chiang Kai-shek, and Lin Sen met with the Panchen Lama to negotiate a mutually agree-

Photo 6.1 Dai Jitao (1891–1949) and the Changja Qutughtu (1890–1957)

able relationship. The central government thereby eschewed the military solution to the "Tibet problem" advocated by the borderland militarists Liu Wenhui and Ma Bufang. Having gained certain concessions from the Panchen Lama, the government advocated forcefully for his return to Tibet. Following the lead of Chinese politicians and Tibetan lamas, Taixu also offered his services and those of his students to the cause of improving relations without recourse to violence.

Dai and Taixu both publicly broadcast the idea that only the Buddhist religion could unify all of China's peoples, in contrast to the early secular ideals of the Chinese government. This period marked the political transition from anti-superstition, antireligion policies to the embracing of an officially approved Buddhism, which included Tibetan Buddhism, that has continued to the present day with only a single interruption (the period from the Anti-Rightist Campaign to the Cultural Revolution). As discussed by Duara in *Rescuing History from the Nation*, between 1928 and 1930 religion in China became defined and Buddhism became a legal entity.[1] In the process of being defined, Chinese Buddhism could be expanded to included Tibetan Buddhism. In this way these Buddhists and Chinese politicians participated in an Asiawide phenomenon described by Peterson and Daren R. Walhof in their introduction to *The Invention of Religion:* "By divesting religions of their divisive or heterodox elements, nation builders crafted templates for nationalism, unifying sets of rituals and ideas that defined new political communities."[2] Politicians and political monks joined forces against modern secularists and the conservative elements of Chinese Buddhism to define just such a new Chinese Buddhism, which would receive state protection and support.

Ironically, laws addressed to religions that the Nationalist government was using elsewhere to "exclude those whom it found difficult to bring under its political control" were used in a completely different way for Tibetans.[3] Precisely because the state found Tibet impossible to bring under its political control, the Nationalist government was willing to include Tibetan Buddhists within its new definition of Buddhism in China. One Chinese writing in 1934 noted that the explosive growth of interest in Tibetan Buddhism dated back to the Panchen Lama's arrival in China. He suggested that "private individuals and Buddhist disciples" (*geren yu [Fo]mentu*) had been able to pursue their interest in Tibetan esoterica precisely because "the government, in order to try to control the borderlands, does not restrict or stop Mongolian-Tibetan Buddhism and for the last year or two has also really encouraged it. This is one reason why the transmission of Tibetan esoterica flourishes so at the moment."[4] This was the only element of "control," an ideological one limited to China Proper, that the state could exercise over Tibet.

The Chinese government's claims on Tibetan territory were thus strengthened domestically by the popularity of the Tibetan cultural presence in China and confirmed by specific government support for Tibetan Buddhists and their rituals. The very real de facto independence of Tibet could not compete, at least not within China Proper, with the forces backing the powerful Chinese imagination of their modern nation. The Tibet represented in China—through exiled lamas, esoteric rituals, and state-sponsored activities—was one integrated with the modern Chinese nation-state. The well-publicized participation of Tibetan Buddhists in Chinese popular and political culture in the mid-twentieth century firmly grounded this Chinese Republican "imagined community" in undeniably concrete events.

Buddhist accounts of the Tibetan rituals sponsored in China certainly seemed optimistic about the role Tibetan Buddhism could play in the Republic, but how could some Chinese have found solace in the heretofore "barbarian" civilization of their neighbors? Rob Weller argued in his *Resistance, Chaos, and Control in China* that the "most heavily overloaded situations . . . occur where the social organization of interpretation has broken down."[5] This precisely describes the period in which Tibetan Buddhism became prominent in China. The first surge of Tibetan ritual activity in China had coincided with the final dismantling of the Qing imperial household and the height of internal political struggle. With the demise of the previous imperial structure and the instability of the new political establishment, the Chinese sought solutions and solace in a great variety of alternative worldviews. Meanwhile, the government campaigns against popular religion had undermined the usual religious options of many Chinese. As Duara has illustrated, such campaigns were carried out with some success by both the northern (Beijing) and southern (Nanjing) Republican governments from 1912 to 1915 and from 1927 to 1930, respectively.[6] It is no surprise, then, that the peaks of Tibetan Buddhist activity in China (from 1915 to 1927 and from 1930 to 1942) coincided with the intervals between these campaigns against popular religion.

Moreover, the incursions of the Japanese throughout the 1930s and the Chinese failure or inability to turn aside this threat also led some Chinese to seek solutions outside the mainstream of secular state power. The extent to which some Chinese turned to Tibetan Buddhism in this period is difficult to believe and might be dismissed as hagiographic flourishes if our sources were limited to those of Buddhists memorializing these events. However, in 1935, one of China's most articulate cultural spokesmen and critic of Chinese Buddhist belief in lamas, Lin Yutang, described the attention given to Tibetan lamas in the following terms:

As late as 1933–4 the Panchen Lama of Thibet sprinkled holy water over tens of thousands of people in Peiping and Nanking, including high government personages like Taun Ch'ijui [Duan Qirui] and Tai Chit'ao [Dai Jitao], and was royally entertained by the Central and local governments in Nanking, Shanghai, Hangchow and Canton. As late as May, 1934, Nola Kotuhutu [Norlha Qutughtu], another Tibetan lama, as official guest of the Canton Government, publicly declared his ability to protect the people against poison gas by incantations, and actually was able to influence a certain general to change the position of his guns at his fort through his superior knowledge of astrology and necromancy. Their influence would not be so great, if the Chinese could see a clear way to repel Japanese attacks by modern military science. The Chinese reason here falters, and therefore turns to religion. Since the Chinese army cannot help the Chinese, they are willing to be helped by the Buddha.[7]

In a word, with their own religious systems and the country in general besieged and no secular interpretative system offering much hope (as communism would later), Tibetan Buddhism became loaded with messianic expectations.

Renewed Sino-Tibetan Dialogue on Tibetan Terms

The success of this religious activity was grounded in the real dialogue that took place between Chinese and Tibetan leaders in the 1930s. Unlike the secular Tibetans who tried to adopt nationalist strategies to free their home regions, the Panchen Lama had real influence in the Tibetan cultural world. Since the seventeenth century, when this incarnation series was first recognized, the Panchen Lama had been seen as one of the most important figures in Tibet and beyond. Although the Dalai Lama was universally recognized as the preeminent Gelukpa lama, the Panchen Lama was also greatly respected and was at times in Tibetan history even a more prominent figure than a young and often powerless Dalai Lamas. The sixth Panchen Lama, Penden Yeshé, most famous for traveling to Qianlong's court and dying there, was courted by both the British in India and the Manchu rulers of China. Much the same strategy was repeated in the early twentieth century when the Dalai Lama had fled into exile. The British first invited the Panchen Lama to India, and later the Chinese offered him additional secular power in Tibet during the Dalai Lama's exile in India.[8]

Thus the Panchen Lama had more leverage to negotiate the terms by which he would cooperate with the Chinese than the secular students from the Tibetan borderlands. In particular, he used his position to convince the Chinese government to recognize his joint political and religious role, a long-standing tradition in Tibetan society.[9] Although I often categorize the activities of Tibetan lamas as either "religious" or "political," the figures examined here would probably not have compartmentalized their lives in the same way. Neither would they have felt that they were using religion to achieve political ends nor that their involvement in politics was merely some "expedient means" to be employed in the spread of religion. Instead, they would have understood that the political and religious concerns were linked in a most natural way. They were Buddhist leaders who had been ousted from their rightful place in the cultural context in which they were raised. Given these circumstances, they intended to do whatever was necessary and appropriate within the confines of the situation and their worldview to restore themselves to power. For example, in April 1930 the Panchen Lama had requested military supplies—five thousand rifles, a quarter of a million rounds of ammunition, five thousand uniforms, and funds to pay soldiers—to be used against a bogus Nepalese "invasion" of Tibet.[10] Chiang, who understood this request as an attempt to create a private army, linked the supply of these items to the Panchen Lama's agreement to a position of renouncing Tibetan independence entirely, at least in principle, since he had no real power to decide these matters in any case.[11] The Panchen Lama refused these conditions at that time and received no military aid.

Rather than arming the Panchen Lama, the Nationalist government sought to negotiate his participation in their efforts to incorporate Tibet in public discourse, if not in reality. In these efforts the government was represented by the senior party member, the political leader, and, most important, the Buddhist Dai Jitao. Even as he reached his pinnacle of power in the late 1920s, Dai had furthered his interest in and commitment to Buddhist practice. Dai credited his mother with his Buddhist upbringing, and his wife had aspired to the life of a nun before they were married. Although he was raised as a Buddhist, he said that he had forgotten religion in the thick of his involvement with revolutionary politics from 1911, when he met Sun Yat-sen and became one of his closest friends and supporters. However, when he was sent to Sichuan on party business in 1922, he lost hope in the revolutionary cause and attempted to drown himself in a river. He saw a white light and was saved by fishermen. Through this experience he returned to his religious faith.[12] He spent most of the next eight months in Chengdu with his mother, at which time he renewed his interest in Buddhism. One biographical source reported that in the 1930s he receded into the political background, increasingly studying Buddhism: "to many in Nanjing who knew him well, he seemed more concerned with Buddhist sutras than party affairs and ideology. His interest in Buddhism and its origins in India led to efforts to promote Sino-Tibetan cultural relations."[13] Yet Dai did not disappear entirely from the political scene.

Dai's first interaction with the Panchen Lama in 1930 was an official one. Following orders, Dai wrote a telegram inviting the Panchen Lama to come to the capital to teach Buddhism and rescue the multitudes.[14] This was the first time that a Nationalist government official had requested Buddhist teachings from a Tibetan lama. This initial contact laid the groundwork for what would grow to be a serious and committed interest in the Panchen Lama on the part of Dai, the Chinese Buddhist community, and the government in central China. Thus even as Dai's participation in the exercise of governance appeared (to Westerners) to be declining, he became the government's most powerful and sincere advocate of Buddhism and an important intermediary with China's borderland peoples.[15]

The differences between the Panchen Lama and Chiang Kai-shek had been resolved by February 1931, when the Nationalist government invited the Panchen Lama to the National People's Convention (Guomin huiyi) to be held later that year.[16] He accepted and on May 4 was welcomed to Nanjing by a huge crowd of people—official representatives from all government ministries, councils, and commissions as well as "several tens of thousands of citizens and students." He was housed in Chiang Kai-shek's headquarters, and the next day Dai accompanied him to a meeting with Chiang Kai-shek. Later, he met with Hu Hanmin and other top government officials.[17] This was the lama's first face-to-face interaction with Nationalist government politicians. For this reason, the content of the Panchen Lama's public message is of special interest. As demonstrated by the Chinese text of the Panchen Lama's congratulatory address to the National People's Convention, given the day after he arrived, the lama referred positively to Sun's ideology but not to the rhetoric of the five races. The speech described Sun's ideology as the "noble teachings" (*guijiao*) and specifically mentioned Sun's "Three Principles of the People and Five Powers" (*san min wu quan*). He concluded his speech by invoking Sun Yat-sen's ideas of assisting oppressed people in seeking liberation: "I pray for [the fulfillment of] . . . the director-general [Sun Yat-sen]'s instructions to save the weak and support them whole-heartedly."[18] Ironically this kind of statement could be taken as support for the very kind of autonomy movement that the Khampa Kelzang Tsering was soon to undertake. Thus, even when the Panchen Lama did employ the rhetoric of the Chinese Republicans, he could use it skillfully in ways that did not necessarily foreclose pursuing Tibetan goals.

The Panchen Lama apparently made other public pronouncements over the course of the convention, which lasted until May 17, but none of these has been reprinted in full. On May 5 the Panchen Lama attended the Central Party Memorial Conference for Sun Yat-sen (Zhongyang dangbu Zongli jinian zhou yanjiang hui), where he lectured on the topic: "Hoping the Country's Citizens Will Understand Tibet" (*Xiwang guoren renshi Xizang*).[19] This lecture has not been reproduced, but one can imagine that the Panchen Lama emphasized the importance of religion to the Tibetan society.[20] The preface to Li and Fang's archival collection, dedicated to the Panchen Lama's activities in China, also specifically mentioned a May 10 lecture delivered to Nanjing's New Asia Society. Unfortunately the collection only reproduced a short section of the lecture, an often quoted passage concerning Tibet being part of Chinese territory.[21] Ya Hanzhang, who cites part of the same passage in his biography of the Panchen Lama, would have us believe that this was the central topic of the lecture.[22] However, a *Tibet Studies* article by Guo Qing indicated that the title of the talk was "Cultivate One's Own Moral Qualities before Governing a Country." Guo also quotes the same passage about Tibet being a part of China, but the title he gave reveals that the Panchen Lama was gently chastising China's leaders at the same time.[23] In fact, this may have been a subtle way of suggesting that spiritual persons such as himself were more appropriate to rule Tibet than any Chinese politician. That these speeches have not been made available in their entirety suggests that the specifics of the Panchen Lama's "imagined community" did not completely overlap with the PRC government's editorial dictates. Similarly, the Panchen Lama's "Perspective on Resolving the Tibet Problem" (*Jiejue Xizang wenti yijian shu*), presented to the government on May 16, is only partially quoted in Li and Fang's archival collection.[24] Those portions cited bear a striking resemblance to Chiang's 1930 proposal, which the Panchen Lama had rejected earlier.[25] Although I do not doubt that the Panchen Lama invoked certain elements of Chinese rhetoric in the context of this convention, I suspect that his statements were vague and noncommittal when taken in context. Otherwise, why else would so few of them have been made available in their entirety in recent publications? In any case, these two weeks were clearly an essential period of negotiating and making public a new relationship between this Tibetan leader and Chinese politicians.

Buddhist Protectors of the State

Despite the obvious trend toward a modern secular polity in China, the Nationalist government would come to share several features with earlier multiethnic dynasties such as the Tang or the Yuan, in which Buddhists were officials of the state and charged with protecting the country (*huguo*).[26] Shortly after the convention, Nationalist government representatives persisted in their efforts to engage the Panchen Lama as a Buddhist teacher. In June 1931 Dai Jitao fulfilled this task, assigned him in 1930, by arranging for the Panchen Lama to teach at a monastery outside Nanjing. Although the Panchen Lama had taught Chinese monks in his southern tour in the mid-twenties, this event was his first time teaching Chinese in Nationalist Party–controlled territory. The session was dedicated to the six-syllable mantra (*zhengyan*), "Om Mani Padme Hum," famed for its salvific power. With a crowd of some four hundred monks and laity, this was the first of many public teachings that Dai would sponsor to introduce the lama to the Chinese public.[27]

Also at this ceremony, Dai and his wife took esoteric initiations and received Buddhist names from the Panchen Lama.[28] Dai was given the name Bukong, which suggests that the Panchen Lama knew of Dai's interest in *Scripture for Humane Kings Who Wish to Protect Their States* (*Renwang huguo jing*). Bukong (better known as Amoghavajra) was a central figure in the Tang court's adoption of tantric Buddhist techniques for protecting the country, especially the *Scripture for Humane Kings* cited above. Patricia Berger described the context of Bukong's rise as follows:

> In 765, when Tibetan troops led by Trisong Detsen threatened the Tang capital at Chang'an, two cartloads of the sutra were hauled to Ximing Temple. Amoghavajra was ordered to discourse on it; the emperor himself attended and offered incense. These actions were apparently effective, because after the Tibetan troops withdrew, Emperor Daizong ordered Amoghavajra to make a new translation of the sutra and appended his own imperial preface.[29]

And just as Amoghavajra's temple headquarters at the Tang capital had been dedicated to the protection of the country,[30] so was the monastery (Huguo shenghua Longchan si) where the Panchen Lama taught at this and other times, outside the Republican Chinese capital. The historic antecedents are very suggestive, although there is no evidence that the Panchen Lama was aware of the specific history of this scripture's origins. In any case, after this event, Dai considered himself a disciple of the Panchen Lama and made great effort to assist him, especially to spread Buddhist teachings. The Panchen Lama's biography related that "Dai Jitao had extremely great faith in the Buddha-dharma."[31] Given this faith and support, a relationship much like the traditional patron-priest relationship so central to the Tibetan understanding of Sino-Tibetan relations was renewed in the modern context.

Less than a week after the public teaching, Dai Jitao recommended that both the Dalai and the Panchen Lamas receive new titles starting with the phrase "Protectors of the Country" (*Huguo*). The irony of giving the Dalai Lama such a title was more than the government could accept. On June 24, however, the Panchen Lama was given the new title that Dai had recommended: "Protector of the Country, Propagator of Transformation, Great Master of Infinite Wisdom" (Huguo xuanhua guanghui dashi).[32] From the Panchen Lama's acceptance letter, we learn that at that time he embraced the responsibility of "eternally protecting the basis of the country's salvation" (*wei you jiuguo ji zhi yonghu*).[33] In this way the Panchen Lama became the first monk in modern times to formally be assigned the ancient role of protecting China.

Secretly the Chinese government simultaneously created a special propaganda position for the Panchen Lama. On June 21 a confidential memorandum was sent from the Mongolian and Tibetan Affairs Commission to the executive branch of the government. This memo laid the groundwork for granting the Panchen Lama a political title, the Western Borderlands Propagation Commissioner (Ch. Xichui xuanhua shi). In the appendix to this memorandum the Panchen Lama was assigned the responsibility of spreading the "Three Principles of the People" to the lamas and Buddhists of Qinghai and Kham. Again, no mention was made of publicizing the "*wuzu*" racial rhetoric.[34] Although the public conferral of this title was delayed until the end of 1932, the Panchen Lama appears to have accepted in principle the rights and responsibilities of this position. In return for his efforts, the Mongolian and Tibetan Affairs Commission provided substantial financial rewards to the lama: a monthly stipend of 30,000 *yuan* for routine expenses for the position and an annual subsidy of 120,000 *yuan* to the Panchen Lama.[35]

Possibly as a cover for this clandestine propaganda role, the public conferral of the religious title was held on June 30 in the presence of Chinese officials, including Chiang Kai-shek, and newspaper reporters. The accompanying gold album again mentioned Sun Yat-sen's "Three Principles of the People and Five Powers" (*San min wu quan*). The Panchen Lama's acceptance of this album may well demonstrate his embracing of Sun's ideology. If this is the case, the absence of any of the earlier racial rhetoric indicates that this rhetoric was not central to this interaction.[36] In other words, the Panchen Lama was participating in Chinese politics in the modern context of both nationalism and the autonomy that Sun had promised to each nation within the former Qing empire but did not accept the imagined community of a harmonious relation of races as defining new China. Following this public event, the Panchen Lama's early efforts on the borderlands were directed at the Inner Mongolians whose dependence on China waned as the Japanese forces in northeast China became more aggressive in the summer of 1931.[37] Just over a week after being granted his new religious title, the Panchen Lama left Nanjing for Inner Mongolia, where he was hosted by a number of prominent Mongol princes.[38]

The circumstances surrounding the Norlha Qutughtu's rise to national prominence are remarkably similar to those of the Panchen Lama, although on a smaller scale. Sometime after the Norlha Qutughtu was invited to Nanjing in 1930, he was also given a title that granted him the status of protector of the country.[39] In addition, he was assigned leadership roles in religious associations formed under the Nationalist government. He played official roles in both the Chinese Buddhist Studies Association and the Chinese Bodhi Study Association. In these capacities he led "dharma assemblies to protect the country and avert disaster" in Shanghai, Wuhan, Changsha, and Guangzhou.[40] His move to the capital and this official support thus made him the object of attention of Chinese Buddhists from all over the country. Reports of his success in quelling disaster on both the national and individual level swelled the ranks of the Norlha Qutughtu's disciples. The first recorded instance of these powers is dated to the summer of 1931, when heavy rains caused flooding in eastern China. At the request of a Nanjing lay Buddhist association, the Norlha Qutughtu performed a "*homa* ritual to avert disaster," which stopped the rain.[41] This event harks back to the first Tibetan Buddhist protective rite performed for the new Chinese state, by the Mongol lama Bai Puren in 1914. The principal difference was that the Nationalist government—although campaigning against superstition on other fronts—had made the Norlha Qutughtu a government official before he had performed this ceremony.

He also healed the illnesses of individual Buddhists starting in 1931. He took on this responsibility in addition to his teaching of the dharma. Some days he was visited by more than one hundred people seeking to be healed. Later, he was called on to treat an illness in Shanghai that had resisted treatment by both Chinese and Western medicine. The news of his effective rituals and healing helped spread his fame far and wide. Buddhists groups from Sichuan, Hunan, Yunnan, and Guizhou provinces sent representatives to him to request that he practice the dharma that would avert disaster for their benefit.[42]

Although these events were normal religious practices for a Buddhist said to possess such powers, these activities must also be understood within the context of national politics. Prior to 1930 the Norlha Qutughtu had had a decidedly local influence tied closely to his home region, as it was nominally controlled from the Sichuan provincial capital in which he lived. After 1930 the Norlha Qutughtu became a national figure for the Chinese, representing the interests of the nation and not just the local concerns of an exiled Tibetan Buddhist leader. By embracing this role, he gave the Nationalist government his religious and political support, and also earned their trust. For this reason the government sanctioned the lama, tacitly approving of the religious practices he used to protect the country.

State Protection of Buddhists

While the Tibetan lamas assisted the country, the Nationalist government finally moved to guarantee the protection of Buddhist land holdings. After decades of efforts by various Chinese Buddhist groups to gain such protection, a proposal, which Welch called "the high-water mark in governmental recognition of Buddhist property rights," was pushed through the Chinese National Assembly by a Tibetan, Losang Chuchen.[43] In August 1931 Chiang Kai-shek approved this proposal and sent out an executive order (*xun ling*) to inform all government organs "that infringement of monastic property rights by any government units or individuals, including the police or army, was punishable by law." This Tibetan-sponsored initiative effectively ended the periodic attempts to confiscate monastic property on a national level.[44] That such a law could only have come at the insistence of a Tibetan Buddhist demonstrates the central importance of Tibetan Buddhists in the state's agenda for dealing with Buddhists in general.

At the same time Dai Jitao developed strategies that asserted the importance of Buddhist culture in modern China. Dai saw the goals of saving the state and saving Buddhism as intertwined. Moreover, he felt that the inclusion of Tibetan Buddhism in a redefinition of Chinese Buddhism was essential to the dual project of saving the state and saving the religion. He argued that Buddhism was the only real link joining the Chinese to the borderland peoples in Manchuria, Mongolia, and Tibet. Thus supporting Buddhist teachers and institutions was necessary to retain the full extent of territory that the Qing dynasty had governed. Dai's recognition of this shared culture is reminiscent of the Kangxi and Qianlong emperors' efforts at key imperial sites such as Chengde, Beijing, and Mount Wutai.[45] Dai, as one of the founders of the modern Chinese nation-state, thought first of promoting the nation and advocated Buddhism precisely because he saw the benefits it could bring to the new state. At the same time, he was a Buddhist and hoped to support and improve the Buddhist religion with state resources.

After 1930 Dai's work on borderland issues, his efforts at reforming Chinese Buddhism, and his promotion of Tibetan Buddhism went hand in hand, united by his interest in saving the country. Dai felt that Asian races (*minzu*), especially those in China, were linked by Buddhism and that realizing this would save both the country and the religion. Dai wrote that "our country is the leader of the nations of Asia; this is already commonly acknowledged throughout the world. Internally, the regions of Mongolia, Tibet, Qinghai and Kham, and externally, the regions of Indo-Burma, Thailand and Indonesia—these nations are all united really by having Buddhism as their center. . . . [If] we don't respect Buddhism, who will respect us?"[46] He attempted to make this theory a reality through public talks and private correspondence on certain key issues. For example, in a July 1931 "Letter to Fellow-countrymen in Mongolia, Tibet, Qinghai, and Kham," Dai tried to link Buddhist ethics with Sun Yat-sen's ideology.[47]

He insisted that the country's continued existence could only come through saving Buddhism in China and linking up with the borderland races through the ethics of religion. After the Japanese attack in Manchuria, known as the Mukden Incident, in September 1931, he was quoted in the *Current Affairs Newspaper* (*Shishi xinbao*) as saying, "Scriptures and mantras will save the country" (*Jing zhou jiuguo*).[48] By November Dai had helped organize a dharma-assembly featuring the *Scripture for Humane Kings Who Wish to Protect Their States*.[49]

One of the earliest manifestations of Dai's efforts to link saving the country with both Buddhism and Tibet was in his 1931 essay, "Ideas on Reforming the Monastic System." In that work he argued that, "in disastrous times, [only] religion has the power to change people and pacify the country."[50] He then tried to convince Buddhists that they should accept the revolutionary ideas of Sun Yat-sen:

> Buddhist disciples ... should understand ... and realize the "Three Principles of the People." ... Following this teaching is the correct Buddhist teaching. Thus through this great expedient means, the whole country's people can be rescued and saved [by putting them] onto the correct path, and all of China's races (*minzu*) can be united, becoming a single great race believing in Buddhism.[51]

Having linked Sun's ideology to Buddhism, he explained why only Buddhism had the power to unite China. First he described the potential barriers to such unity:

> From the Himalayas in a great arc—Qinghai, Ili [in Chinese Turkestan, inhabited by the Buddhist Jungar Mongols], Mongolia, and Manchuria—this great expanse is several times greater than China Proper, the races (*minzu*) [there] are complex, with no less than several tens of hundreds of lineages (*zu*), the language of each is particular [to them], their customs are all different from [one another], the development of writing is especially backward.[52]

However, he argued that over the course of the past thousand years, these races' martial spirit had been pacified and dispersed through their relations with the Chinese, and the end product was the greater China of his day. He explained that this feat had not been accomplished through the force of politics, military might, or Chinese literature and philosophy. Instead, he argued, the force of Buddhism had transformed these races.[53] Since Buddhism was the only historic factor unifying and pacifying China's races, it was imperative that the government include Buddhist ethics as part of state ideology.

Merging the Secular and the Religious Realms

This elite validation of Buddhism contributed to an enormous increase in the popularity of Tibetan lamas among the Chinese in central and eastern China. The Mongol Bai Lama had enjoyed some renown in these areas, and Dorjé Chöpa had taught large crowds in the outlying provinces in northeast and southwest China, but the broad-based adherence to Tibetan Buddhism that developed in China's heartland after 1931 was unprecedented in Chinese history. Both the Panchen Lama and the Norlha Qutughtu saw a dramatic increase in requests for and attendance at their teachings.

In the spring of 1931 Beiping Buddhists had invited the Panchen Lama to preside over an esoteric ritual and practice based on messianic concepts of a pure land called Shambhala and its militaristic king who would bring peace to the world. We are fortunate that the announcements detailing the reasons for holding this Kâlacakra tantra ritual were reprinted in Taixu's magazine, *Haichaoyin*. In "A Call to Sponsor the Kâlacakra Dharma Assembly" (*Shilun fahui quan faqi wen*), the organizers of the event drew an explicit parallel between this ceremony and similar ones held during the preceding three dynasties: "In the past, during the Yuan, Ming and Qing dynasties, lamas were worshiped and presided over prayers for the country's affairs" (*Xi Yuan Ming Qing shi, lama gongfeng, zhute guojia zhi shi*). The announcement also used similar language to announce that in the coming ceremony, "The State Preceptor, the Panchen Lama, will preside over prayers for the country" (*Banchan guoshi zhute guojia*). The location for the ritual emphasized the historical continuity with previous dynastic traditions. The Panchen Lama led the ceremony from the Hall of Great Peace (*Taihe dian*) within the Forbidden City, which hosted numerous Tibetan lamas in the Ming and Qing periods. That the Chinese government had recognized the Panchen Lama with government titles was significant to the Chinese Buddhists. The presence of State Preceptors (*guoshi*) in the governments of China dated back to the period of division in the fourth and fifth centuries, when Kumarajiva was first honored with this title, but was especially prominent in the Tang and Yuan. In all these periods, non-Chinese rulers of China embraced the power of Buddhist ritual as support for their states. The continuation of this tradition was clearly important to the sponsors of this Beiping ceremony, as they noted that, "at present, the Panchen Lama has already proceeded to the capital and received the State Preceptorship."[54] It seemed to matter little to these Chinese Buddhists that the Panchen Lama had not actually been given this exact title. They remained undeterred in connecting the government's recognition with such earlier traditions. Merely the traditional gifts of title, album, and seal were enough to make him a State Preceptor in their eyes.

According to the announcement, the Beiping Kâlacakra had been organized especially to deal with current difficulties that the Chinese were experiencing. In a text detailing the lives of the successive Panchen Lamas, entitled *Saviours of Mankind*, one Swedish observer of the Beiping ceremonies noted that the "political situation was more than disquieting. The loss of Manchuria was a severe blow. Salvation was sought in all quarters. Even many Chinese hoped that a return to the beliefs and customs of ancient times would lead to a national renascence."[55] The sponsors specifically mention "natural disasters in over ten provinces" and the fact that "since the revolution of 1911, no year had been without military calamities." Their hope was that the Kâlacakra tantra could transform this situation then and into the future: "Having received this scripture, what the country lacks and has lost can be restored." The Panchen Lama was "to make great prayers to release the spirits of the dead, to bless the living, and on behalf of the past, present, and future of this [Chinese] land and other lands, in this and other worlds, and for all types of beings in all realms." The ceremony was explicitly linked to the messianic realm of Shambhala, which was described in an appendix to the announcement of the ritual. Those who were to receive the initiation into the Kâlacakra tantra were said to be creating the conditions for being reborn in Shambhala. These hopes were shared by many, as the estimates for the attendees of the Beiping ceremony range from sixty thousand to one hundred thousand. Finally, the organizers looked toward a future in which such unexcelled tantra (Ch. *wushang mifa*) would gradually come to the land of the Chinese. They planned to further this goal by publicizing and translating esoteric texts, thereby further linking Tibet to China in the discourse and imagination of Chinese Buddhists.[56]

Although recent Chinese publications emphasize the role of government officials (such as Dai Jitao and Zhang Xueliang) or retired officials (such as Duan Qirui) in organizing this tantric ritual, the contemporary Chinese language documents do not.[57] In fact, in the organizers' literature, the only prominent leader listed among the three hundred sponsors of this first Kâlacakra ceremony held in China was the militarist Wu Peifu. Instead, "Beiping's Buddhist disciples" (*Beiping Fojiao tu*) were credited with sponsoring the assembly, and no individual was thanked for their assistance in the general literature.[58] Quite the opposite is true, as the reference to public figures is only general: "The attending and sponsoring public figures were from all over; many came on behalf of the famous from all circles." In their corporate capacity they could thus stand in for all of China: "Supposing each set their heart on being a person of ideals and integrity, they could represent the country's people and piously repent, thereby eliminating disasters and disorder." The tone gently chastised these public figures, suggesting that China's troubles lay with their behavior and only such a ritual could help them remedy the current state of affairs. Such language demonstrates just how far this ritual was from serving as a government plan to demonstrate China's connection to Tibet, at least on the level of deliberate public discourse. Rather than the government directing this assembly, the organizers had to publicize their event to all levels of government—national (including the heads of all the branches of government and generals), provincial, and municipal.[59]

In this respect, the government was treated no differently from Buddhist associations and newspaper offices. The circular sent to the general public reiterates that the organizers had "invited the Panchen Lama to give initiations and practice the dharma in order to provide protection for the country and eliminate disasters."[60] The sponsors of the Panchen Lama's public teachings in Beiping in 1932 provided an excellent example of Chinese Buddhists trying to see Tibetan Buddhism as a part of a larger Buddhist world. They informed the Buddhist associations throughout the country of the event but, in so doing, found it necessary to explain why lamas ate meat (as Chinese monks would not) and why some lamas were not celibate (because they were not actually ordained monks). They concluded this apologia with a reference to "Shakyamuni's teachings" which placed both Chinese and Tibetan traditions under the figurehead of the founder, Shakyamuni Buddha.[61] Speaking of the Kâlacakra tantra, the organizers said that "the country relies on it for peace, and the people provide the funds in order to be blessed."[62] In this way the Beiping ceremony was remarkably similar to the Sichuan Dharma Assemblies for Peace, albeit on a much larger scale.

While the Chinese organizers were clearly lay Buddhists with minimal government connections, the Panchen Lama nevertheless used this occasion to demonstrate his knowledge of Sun Yat-sen's ideology and its connections with Buddhist ideas. For example, the Panchen Lama explained that, "according to the instructions of the *San min zhuyi* [Tib. *San min krul yis*], good qualities should be gathered together and negative qualities should be given up." This advice is typical of traditional Buddhist teachings, and this similarity may indicate why the Panchen Lama felt positively toward Sun's teachings. On the other hand, to summarize the "Three Principles of the People" in such simplistic terms could also indicate that the Panchen Lama had not grasped much of Sun's message. In any case, at that time the extent of the Panchen Lama's interface with Sun Yat-sen's ideology seemed to have been to see in it advice similar to that which Buddhists regularly counsel.

Yet at the same time the Panchen Lama was also trying to influence Chinese ideology with Tibetan expectations. He warned of the potential problems that would arise if religion and politics were not united in China (*chos srid zung 'brel du ma byung na re re sa phan sdo thogs pa dka' bas*), thereby advocating the adoption of this Tibetan system of governance.[63] In the coming months the Panchen

Lama made a concerted effort to broadcast this idea to the Chinese people. For example, in the fall of 1932 he received newspaper reporters to present a talk on the topic: "Religion and Government Must Develop Together" (*Zongjiao yu zhengzhi bixu tongbu fazhan*).[64] This approach was eventually embraced by the Nationalist government, at least in their dealings with the Panchen Lama and the government of Central Tibet.

Borderland Warfare

Only days after the Japanese initiated their occupation of Manchuria in September 1931, provincial military leaders in Sichuan sought Nationalist government support to "settle the Tibetan issue by force" by mobilizing troops from Yunnan, Sichuan, and Qinghai.[65] The government advised a negotiated settlement with the Tibetans, but China's northeastern troubles emboldened the Tibetans to make demands to which the Chinese government could not agree. By February 1932 the Nationalist government recalled their negotiator and left local affairs to Liu Wenhui. Having been driven into Kham by Liu Xiang, Liu Wenhui had hoped that an influx of Nationalist government forces would help restore his strength. At the same time, he thought he could prove his usefulness to the central government by resolving the "Tibet problem."

When Tibetan forces advanced into Yul shul (Ch. Yushu; considered by Chinese to be part of the recently formed Qinghai Province), Liu was able to convince Qinghai's governor, Ma Bufang, to coordinate an attack, which proved successful, on the Tibetans. However, pressure from the British to resolve the situation peacefully and concern over the situation in Manchuria led the government to order a cessation of hostilities by August 1932.[66] Li Tieh-tseng's Chinese nationalistic history of Tibet's relations with China, written in the 1950s in America, articulated the tensions that existed between the local leaders and the central government: "From a theoretical point of view, it would be self-defeating if the Nationalist government, which stood for the equality of all nations within the Republic and for harmony and peace, should use force to subdue the Tibetan people and impose a certain status."[67] This attitude conformed to Sun Yat-sen's distinctions between countries created by natural forces (*ziran li*), of which he approved, versus those created by military force (*wuli*), to which he was opposed.[68]

Dai's Buddhist Diplomacy

Taking another approach, Dai Jitao was busy trying to resolve the situation through a shared Buddhist faith, as communicated in letters to the Dalai and Panchen Lamas. For most of 1932, in an effort to improve China's troubled relationship with Tibet, Dai attempted to convince Tibetan Buddhist leaders that China could respect Buddhism. At the same time he tried to convince the Chinese of the importance of Buddhism to unifying the country. As only Buddhism, and not some element indigenous to Chinese society, had allowed for previous multiethnic polities, Dai felt that Buddhism was still crucial to uniting China's various peoples.

Dai's communications with the Dalai and Panchen Lamas were worthy of his early experiences in the propaganda department of the Nationalist Party government in Canton, yet they were also clearly the work of a Buddhist. Dai carefully built a case for restoring a positive Sino-Tibetan relationship. First, he established himself as a Buddhist who shared a faith in Tibetan Buddhism. Then he portrayed China as the protector of Tibetan Buddhism. Finally, he warned of the potential for harm to Buddhism if the Dalai Lama continued to resist rapprochement with the Panchen Lama and his Chinese backers.

In writing to the thirteenth Dalai Lama, Dai referred to himself as a Buddhist disciple and to Tibet as "a treasure-house of the true Buddhist Dharma." Yet he went beyond suggesting that he and the Dalai Lama were co-religionists in a general Buddhist sense. He inserted himself into the Tibetan Buddhist tradition by referring to the founder of the Dalai Lama's Gelukpa tradition as "our lineage master Tsongkhapa." He went beyond his personal interest in Tibetan Buddhism by arguing that China was Tibet's friend: "China's government is really the only external protector of [Tibetan Buddhism]."

Having established these connections with the Dalai Lama, he outlined his main concern: "If each of the races of our China do not bring about unity, the Buddha-dharma cannot realistically prosper vigorously." Essentially Dai was arguing that unless Buddhism proved useful to the modern Chinese nation-state, harm would come to the religion. He then reinforced the idea that the Dalai Lama was beholden to China and the Chinese precisely because he was a Buddhist. He brought the weight of the wishes of the Chinese government and the (more than four hundred million) Chinese people to bear on the question of the restoration of relations with the Panchen Lama. He cajoled the Dalai Lama, saying, "saving the country, saving the people, saving the [Buddhist] religion—such is a great responsibility and a heavy duty, yet the master [the Dalai Lama] is dependable." He went on to argue that making up with the Panchen Lama and bringing peace to the people would "establish the basis for the eternal integration of the five races."[69] At the end of the letter he again reminded the Dalai Lama that he was a "Buddhist believer."[70] Because we do not have the Dalai Lama's reply, we cannot judge the effect this letter had on him. What is clear is that Dai made a strong case for a shared Buddhist interest, which emphasized a special respect for Tibetan Buddhism.

Within the month Dai was to extend similar sentiments to the Panchen Lama, clarifying in the process that the Panchen Lama returning to Tibet was essential to saving the country and the Buddhist religion. In his letter he echoes the language directed at the Dalai Lama:"Today, saving the country, saving the people, saving [the Buddhist] religion, is entirely up to Buddhist disciples awakening themselves.... Moreover, saving the country and saving religion are actually one and the same, and are definitely not two [separate issues]."[71] And just in case the Panchen Lama was not sure what Tibet had to do with all of this, Dai made the connection for him:"Benefiting belief [and] making Tibetan religious civilization prosperous is the number one matter in saving the country and saving religion. And the basis of this is in the two great masters—the Panchen Lama and the Dalai Lama—cherishing and upholding each other."[72] He continued in this vein with six more letters to the Panchen Lama over the next four months, threatening that "Mongolia and Tibet would lose an external protector" one month and sending Buddhist images in the next.[73] The fourth letter focused on religious teachings, the fifth returned to the topic of "saving the country, saving people, and saving the world" while invoking the rhetoric of the deceased Sun Yat-sen and his *Three Principles of the People*. His concluding letter in this series announced the imminent meeting of Chiang Kai-shek and other important figures prepared to resolve Tibetan affairs. Dai urged the Panchen Lama to attend this meeting in the capital, saying,"I have done all I can in order to help the master [the Panchen Lama] attain complete success—on the one hand, to respond to the country's [need to settle the Tibetan affairs] and, on the other, to bring peace to the Tibetan people—and, moreover, to protect our Buddhist religion's existence and infinite progress."[74] Dai succeeded in his efforts, as the Panchen Lama returned to Nanjing in December 1932.

Upon his return the Panchen Lama was publicly granted a political position for the first time. He was to serve openly as the Western Borderlands Propagation Commissioner (Ch. Xichui xuanhua shi). From the Panchen Lama's biography it is clear that the Tibetan understanding of this position also included the government's recognition of his religious status as a reincarnate lama. The Tibetan transliteration of the Chinese title included the phrase "the Panchen [Lama], living Buddha" (Tib. *PaN kran ho phu*, Ch. *Banchan houfo*). This phrasing is also reflected in the Tibetan translation of the title, which included the phrase, "the Panchen [Lama], an actual Buddha" (Tib. *PaN chen sang rgyas mngon sum*).[75] This additional phrase in the title clearly indicated that, at least as the Tibetans understood it, the Chinese government was acknowledging the union of religious and political leadership in this new position. That the Chinese also understood the position in this way is confirmed by Lin Sen's description of the Panchen Lama's task: "to publicize the desires of the central government to the borderland . . . to propagate, *with the help of religious belief,* the Three People's Principles, the teachings of the late Director-General Sun Yat-sen."[76] At the same time the Changja Qutughtu was also given a similar title. In describing such government initiatives, the Mongol scholar Sechin Jagchid commented that "it was unprecedented for a lama to be openly appointed as a governmental official with a legal status that could let him interfere in . . . politics."[77] However, this perspective was limited by Sechin Jagchid's nationalistic and secular upbringing. In fact, the Mongols had been the first rulers of China to grant lamas political appointments, in the Yuan dynasty, and Mongol lamas had continued to be appointed as political leaders under the Qing and even into the twentieth century. The Republican government was merely adapting to the exigencies of the times, as had previous dynasties ruling China. In this way Tibetan Buddhists brought the leaders of China around to their perspective: religion and politics had to go hand in hand when trying to settle relations between China and Tibet.

As for the Panchen Lama's acceptance of Chinese government rhetoric, various authors cite conflicting sources to represent how the Panchen Lama phrased his acceptance of this title. The undocumented and thus less reliable of the two, found in Ya Hanzhang's biography of the Panchen Lama, was said to have been read by the bilingual Tibetan Kelzang Chönjor: "I will spare no effort to be loyal, to propagate virtuous ideas; I will exert myself to lead the way to auspicious peace and the unity of the five races in order to repay the central [government]."[78] If we could trust a Chinese Communist era report of the Panchen Lama's speech, this occasion would have marked the first and only time that the Panchen Lama personally used both Sun's ideology and the racial rhetoric simultaneously.

However, the Taiwanese Buddhist monk Shi Dongchu located a contemporary, and therefore more reliable, source that recorded a significantly different exchange. The speeches, which were recorded in the Buddhist magazine *Haichaoyin,* indicate that these discourses of race and ideology were invoked by China's President Lin Sen, but they were not repeated by the Panchen Lama in his reply.[79] Later in the ceremony a minor official in the Education Department by the name of Lei Cheng went so far as to associate Sun Yat-sen's principles with Buddhism and the salvation of the world and its peoples. Whereas the Panchen Lama had not echoed the calls of higher officials for the "unity of the country's peoples [*tuanjie guozu*]," he was willing to respond positively to Lei Cheng's vision of Sun's ideas serving to create harmony in the world (*Zongli shijie datong de mudi*). To this he responded, through Kelzang Chönjor: "Although I do not know Chinese, I studied the *Three Principles of the People* once several years ago from a translation and know that these principles can really save the country."[80] He added that religion would also play an important role in saving the country but again did not mention any unity of peoples.

Taixu Offers the Services of Chinese Buddhists

Following the example set by Dai Jitao and the Panchen Lama, Taixu offered his own suggestions for merging the political and religious systems. In response to a public letter sent by Tibetan monks, Taixu wrote an open letter to the Chinese government and the public to explain his suggestions for increasing communication between Chinese and Tibetans.[81] Just as he had altered Liu Xiang's plans in 1930, so he hoped to influence the Nationalist government to maintain its peaceful approach to handling Chinese relations with Tibet. First, he suggested that his many students in Lhasa, Chamdo, and Daqianlu could provide information on the situation in Tibet. Second, he asserted that certain Chinese monks were known to the Dalai Lama, the Panchen Lama, and the Tibetan people as faithful Buddhists who were knowledgeable about Tibetan Buddhism and had honored the lamas with offerings. He argued that cultivating these cultural connections was more valuable than attacking the Tibetans. Moreover, his hope was that the Chinese monks in Tibet could "publicize the central government's and the entire citizenry's public sentiment of respect for, belief in, as well as protection and maintenance of Tibetan Buddhism" (*xuanbiao zhongyang zhengfu ji quanguo guomin duiyu Xizang Fojiao zunyang huchi zhi gongyi*). In so doing, these Chinese would thereby gain the sympathy of the Dalai Lama and the lamas of each monastery.

No doubt Taixu at least partially welcomed the opportunity to develop ideas he had long espoused, although he had to broaden the concept of uniting Chinese and Tibetan Buddhist teachings to include the merging of the Chinese and Tibetan peoples. Taixu argued that his disciples' publicity would "improve the desired merging of Chinese and Tibetans" (*hao Han-Zang ronghe zhi xuyao*). Yet Taixu was also concerned about how Buddhism in Tibet would fare and felt that his monks' efforts would help to assure "the protection and maintenance of Tibet's Buddhism" (*huchi Xizang Fojiao*). He even had visions of "the Dalai and Panchen Lamas joining on good terms with the Chinese and Tibetans to protect and maintain Tibet's Buddhism" (*Da[lai] Ban[chan] Han Zang he he huchi Xizang Fojiao*). His proposal included the recommendation of making enormous donations to the Panchen and Dalai Lamas, as well as to their important followers and the great monasteries of Tibet. The lowest figure he thought would suffice was 200,000 *yuan*, but when he compared this to the cost of supporting armies in Kham and Qinghai, he calculated it would be less than 1 percent of the cost of such militarization. Such were Taixu's peaceful suggestions for heading off a Chinese invasion of Tibet.[82] By 1934 the Nationalist government would adopt this strategy when they sent their envoy, Huang Musong, to the Dalai Lama's funeral ceremony richly endowed to make donations.

Aside from this open letter, Taixu and his disciple, Manzhi, also publicized a new description of the purpose of the Sino-Tibetan Buddhist Institute. Manzhi's second contribution to the pamphlet, entitled "The Mission of the World Buddhist Institute's Sino-Tibetan Buddhist Institute" (*Shijie Fojiao xuefan Han-Zang jiaoli yuan zhi shiming*), was written in Shanghai at the end of 1932. This article demonstrated a much greater comfort with the idea of a Buddhist institution serving the government's needs, as long as Buddhist interests were served as well. Manzhi's lengthy article concluded with a clear breakdown of the school's negotiation of the relationship between the state and religion by listing its two main responsibilities. With regard to the country, the school "bore the mission to unite in good faith China's races" (*yi guojia de lichang yan zhi, Han Zang jiaoli yuan fu you jingcheng tuanjie Zhongguo minzu zhi shiming*). This statement was historic in marking the first definite link between a modern Buddhist institution and nationalist racial rhetoric. The rhetoric of "*minzu tuanjie*" was continued under the Communist regime, although it is now typically translated as "unity [of China's] nationalities" and is no longer associated with a phrase indicating that "good faith" is an essential ingredient. Likewise, with regard to the Buddhist religion, parallel language was used: the school "bore the mission to develop and expand all Buddhist teachings" (*yi Fojiao de lichang yan zhi, Han Zang jiaoli yuan fu youfazhan guangda zhengge Fofa zhi zhiming*).[83] This phrase demonstrated the awareness that creating such an institution was necessary to a form of Buddhism that included both Tibetan and Chinese aspects. This also continues to be a feature of state-approved Buddhism under the Communist Party today.

Taixu's contribution to this 1932 pamphlet explaining the mission of the new school was less obviously oriented to the country's service but represented a sophisticated use of historical and cultural rhetoric to make the case that Buddhism was essential to the constitution of modern China. Taixu opened his "Origin of the World Buddhist Institute's Sino-Tibetan Buddhist Institute" with the assertion that the Chinese and Tibetan races had been intimately related by blood and culture since the Tang dynasty. Yet he also argued that "the most important connection was the [common] bond of esteem and respect for Buddhism." He emphasized this point by explaining that all Tibetans were Buddhists, as were three-quarters of Chinese.[84]

He then turned to historical precedents to create the appearance of greater unity than actually existed between Chinese and Tibetans. He mentioned the presence of a Tang princess at the Tibetan court to explain why a small portion of the writings of Chinese Buddhists had been translated into Tibetan and preserved in the Tibetan canon. On this flimsy historical basis, he concluded that Chinese and Tibetan Buddhist cultures were deeply related.[85] Turning to more relevant history, Taixu noted the historic flourishing of Tibetan Buddhism among the Manchus and the Mongols, and its continuing prosperity even in the current troubled times. The success of Tibetan Buddhism presented quite a contrast to the beleaguered state of Chinese Buddhism. He concluded, therefore, that "the return of prosperity to Chinese Buddhism would be provided by Tibetan Buddhism." Furthermore, he explained that the Tibetan, Mongol, and Manchu cultures extended from Tibet to the provinces of Kham (Kang), Qinghai, and Ningxia and "really constituted [part of] the greater Chinese race and formed a pillar of the greater Chinese Republic." Despite arguing that these cultures were so intimately related, in order to justify the purpose of the school Taixu was forced to pose the need for developing further connections in the form of a rhetorical question: "Now, given that Buddhist as well as Chinese and Tibetan cultures are as intimate as they are, and that Chinese and Tibetan Buddhism as well as the construction of the Chinese country's race are also as important as they are, how could we not communicate and link up [with the Tibetans] to demonstrate this?"[86] Ignoring the obvious irony of the Chinese having to convince the Tibetans of their intimate cultural connections, Taixu rhetorically wove Tibetan and Chinese Buddhism into the fabric of the new Chinese nation.

The Zenith of Tibetan Buddhist Activity in China

After the success of the Panchen Lama's Beiping religious ceremony and the Nanjing political ceremony, the level of Tibetan Buddhist activity in the major central Chinese cities such as Nanjing, Shanghai, and Hangzhou increased enormously for the next couple of years. At Dai's invitation, the Panchen Lama performed a Buddhist ritual attended by more than one hundred people in one of the Nationalist government auditoriums on Christmas Eve, 1932.[87] The Norlha Qutughtu also enjoyed his greatest popularity at the same time, counting disciples from nearly every province in China. While the Chinese government was embracing the Buddhist religion within its administration and in the halls of governance, the lamas made greater effort to integrate Chinese rhetoric in their public teachings and lectures. In this respect, they, like Taixu, were active participants in a government-supported effort to link Chinese and Tibetan cultures.

Racial Rhetoric in Religious Contexts

In January 1933, again at Dai's invitation, the Panchen Lama taught a crowd of three hundred for three days at the same monastery dedicated to the protection of the country where he had taught previously (Huguo shenghua Longchan si).[88] This assembly was called the "Ceremony of the Seven Medicine Buddhas to Protect the Country, Save the People, Propagate the Dharma, and Benefit Beings" (*Huguo jimin hongfa lisheng Yaoshi qi Fo daochang*).[89] The Medicine Buddhas are particularly associated with assistance in worldly matters.[90] As the Medicine Buddhas were important to both the Tibetan and Chinese Buddhist traditions, such teachings served as a convenient bridge between these different traditions.

This event marked the Panchen Lama's first recorded participation in a public acknowledgment of the "five races" rhetoric. In addition to the Chinese in the audience, this ceremony apparently included "several scores" of Mongolian dukes and princes as well as abbots from prominent Tibetan Buddhist temples in Qinghai, eastern Kham (*Xikang*), Tibet, and Yunnan.[91] One of the vows from the ceremony revealed the depths of the commitments that the Panchen Lama, Dai, and the other participants were making at this event. These twelve vows were each directed at a specific audience, be it the nation's people, young men, young women, the Nationalist Party, or the central government. The ninth vow was directed toward the five races imagined to constitute the modern Chinese nation-state: "[We] vow to the entire country's compatriots—Chinese, Manchu, Mongol, Tibetan, and Hui, including the Muslim territory [of Xinjiang] and even the mountain peoples of the southwestern provinces—by means of a common great heart toward all under heaven, to abide together and jointly develop the great vow to unite the country's races. We vow, using the Three Principles of the People as the model, to establish this shared belief."[92] As the Panchen Lama did not know Chinese, he could not have spoken this vow aloud in unison as the participants of the ceremony had been directed to do.[93] Yet he must have had some idea of the contents of the vows, as they were being administered under his religious authority. Thus, in the context of religion, the Panchen Lama appeared ready to approve both Sun's ideology and the unity of the five races. Because the Panchen Lama was presiding over this ceremony, these vows would have been binding on the Tibetan Buddhists attending.[94] This was a powerful "use" of religion on behalf of the Nationalist government.

From this time on, Chinese language materials attributed to the Panchen Lama continued to use the racial rhetoric he had eschewed up to this point. He gave a speech entitled "Tibetan History and the Five Races United" (*Xizang lishi yu wuzu lianhe*) to the Mongolian and Tibetan Affairs Commission in January 1933. In the speech he commented that, "although in the past the Mongolian and Tibetan regions have had nothing to offer to the center [i.e., China], nevertheless the five races are one family."[95] From internal evidence, such as the use of Qing emperors' regnal titles as a way to date events, I doubt that the Panchen Lama could have written this speech, although he may have delivered a Tibetan version. Even in Chinese, the disparity between conventional Chinese rhetoric and the terms used in this speech was striking. For the most part, this text employs the term *minzhong* (multitudes) to refer to Mongols and Tibetans (*Meng Zang minzhong*), or Khampas and Tibetans (*Kang Zang minzhong*). However, in the last paragraph, the ideologically charged term *minzu* is attached to regional terms to indicate the employment of marked racial or ethnic categories: the Kham ethnic group (*Xikang minzu*) and the Mongol ethnic group (*Menggu minzu*). The speech also used modern features characterizing ethnic groups, such as religion, culture, and script (which were shared by Tibetans and some Mongols) to argue that the Khampas in Xikang and the Mongols in Qinghai were part of greater Tibet. By this time, after almost a decade in Chinese territory, the Panchen Lama had at last deigned to employ the terminology of ethnic classification, even if he did not prepare the speech himself.

Who wrote this speech then?

Tibetan Buddhist Influence in Inner Mongolia

When the Panchen Lama publicly received the position of Western Borderlands Propagation Commissioner, the Nationalist government granted a similar title to the Changja Qutughtu. Sechin Jagchid has argued that such strategies would only have alienated the Mongol elites who had been influenced by modern conceptions of the separation of religious and secular power.[96] However, Jagchid's own account makes it clear that the Panchen Lama had a great influence on the decisions of many Mongol leaders. Some of the most important princes of Inner Mongolia were devoted followers of the Tibetan lama, including Prince So (Sodnamrabdan) and Prince De (Demchudongrub, 1902–1966).[97] The Panchen spent more than a year with the Inner Mongolians, according to one source, helping persuade them to resist the Japanese and ally themselves with the Chinese.[98] Moreover, the Mongol princes knew that the Panchen Lama's support was critical for their own efforts to promote autonomy for Inner Mongolia. When they convened their autonomy conference at Beile-yin sume (Ch. Bailing miao) in the fall of 1933, they arranged for the Panchen Lama to perform the Kâlacakra initiation at the same time, because "the presence of the Panchen Lama would attract thousands of Mongols to Beile-yin sume to pay homage and attend the ceremonies, and that would increase the momentum of the movement." Far from offending the Mongols with his involvement in such a political affair, Jagchid stated that the "presence of this high lama and his sympathetic attitude had great impact on the decisions of the conservative attendees."[99] Jagchid implied that the Panchen Lama was fully behind the Mongols' pursuit of autonomy, although he offered no evidence one way or the other. On the other hand, the Chinese certainly felt that the Panchen Lama would be a potent representative for their interests.

The persuasiveness of a Tibetan Buddhist leader in spreading Nationalist government rhetoric among adherents of his religion had not been lost on Chinese politicians.[100] In the middle of the convention Dai sent a telegram to the Panchen Lama to encourage his efforts.[101] In late October the lama lectured to the Mongolian princes and dukes assembled at the temple. The Chinese text of his speech records that the reason he had stayed in China Proper and the Mongol territory for almost ten years without returning to Tibet was "in order to seek the five races' sincere unity, living together, and flourishing together" (*wei yiju wuzu jingcheng tuanjie, gong zun gong rong*).[102] Fabienne Jagou, working with contemporary though possibly biased sources, reported that with "the Panchen Lama acting as a mediator, the Mongols and the [Chinese] government agents agreed on abandoning the principle of a completely autonomous [Inner Mongolia] government in favor of regional autonomy under the control of the Chinese Republican government."[103] The Chinese were not the only ones to perceive that the Panchen Lama was an important influence on the Mongols. The former head of the American Legation in Beijing (during 1912) and a keen observer of Chinese relations with its borderlands neighbors, E. T. Williams, also concluded that, "the success of the central government in its efforts to retain the support of the Mongol princes was undoubtedly due to the influence of the Panshen [*sic*] Lama as he traveled about among his coreligionists."[104]

For this period the Panchen Lama's propaganda efforts were thus directed not at ethnic Tibetans as specified in the 1931 secret memorandum but rather to the Tibetan Buddhist elements of Inner Mongolia. Possibly the Panchen Lama saw some progress in these Sino-Mongolian relations that encouraged him to think that there was hope for Tibetans to be able to work with the Chinese in a similar fashion. Possibly the Panchen Lama felt that a Tibet with regional autonomy under the Chinese Nationalist government was a better option than a Tibet to which he could not safely return.

The Norlha Qutughtu's Activities in Eastern China

While the Panchen Lama was in Inner Mongolia, the Norlha Qutughtu became the principal Tibetan teacher among the Chinese. In fact, 1933 was his busiest year, as he taught and performed ceremonies in Nanjing, Shanghai, and Hangzhou (see Table 6.1). Over the next several years, the Norlha Qutughtu was asked to perform six more rituals to avert disaster in different cities in south China.[105] The Buddhist laity initiated these assemblies and rituals. Although prominent politicians could have been members of the local lay societies (*jushilin, Foxue hui*) that arranged these teachings, no individual is given credit for sponsoring these events. Thus, once again, lay interests in solving immediate and regional problems were the principal impetus behind these Tibetan

Table 6.1 The Norlha Qutughtu's Peak Year of Teaching[1]

April 1933	Shanghai: practiced great dharma to eliminate disaster and prayed for peace (*xiaozai dafa, jidao heping*) and held *homa* ritual.
May 1933	Shanghai: Guangdong Buddhists came to ask for help.
May 1933	Shanghai: practiced great vajra-dharma to eliminate disasters in Beiping and Tianjin (*xiaozai Ping Jin zai*), more than 300 attendees.
July 1933	Nanjing: held Long-life Buddha assembly, 400 attendees.
Summer 1933	Shanghai Buddhists invited him to teach on nearby mountain.
Fall 1933	Hangzhou Buddhists invited him to West Lake for 10 days.
October 1933	Nanjing: gave Padmasambhava initiation.
November 1933	Nanjing Buddhists invited him to consecrate Medicine Buddha, 200 attendees.
November 1933	Shanghai: instructed disciples.
December 1933	Nanjing: Sichuan, Hunan, Yunnan, Guizhou Buddhists asked Nor lha to come practice the dharma to eliminate disaster (*xiu fa xiaozai*).
December 1933	Nanjing: practiced the great vajra-dharma to eliminate disaster and pray for peace (*Jingang xiaozai jidao heping dafa*) and a *homa* ritual to avert great and small disasters (*da xiao xiaozai huma*).
April 1934	Guangdong: performed dharma-assembly to eliminate disaster and benefit the people (*Guangdong xiaozai limin fahui*).[2]

[1]Han, *Kang Zang Fojiao*, 6a–7a; Shi Dongchu, *Zhongguo Fojiao jindai shi*, 401.
[2]*Haichaoyin* 15 (1934): 524.

Buddhist activities in eastern China. We are told that the Norlha Qutughtu initiated twenty thousand disciples into the esoteric teachings of Tibetan Buddhism. His biography states that he had disciples from all provinces of China.[106] Given that he traveled and taught in Beiping, Tianjin, Chongqing, Shanghai, Hangzhou, Guangzhou, Nanchang, Wuhan, and Changsha, while being based in the capital of Nanjing, this claim seems entirely possible.[107] A list of the donors who helped sponsor the teaching and translation of the biography of the founder of Nyingma Tibetan Buddhism, Padmasambhava, in the fall of 1933 at the Nanjing Tantrayana Practice and Study Society (*Micheng xiu-xueshe*) included at the end of that text reveals modest support for this activity.[108] Some of his disciples set up the Norlha Students' Society to provide funds to support his living and travel expenses as well as for the publication of his teachings.[109] In this again, the Norlha Qutughtu's experience anticipates that of dozens of teachers who have come to America. Without the status of the Panchen or Dalai Lamas, such men have had to rely on a devoted following of students.[110] Devotees supporting their lama was certainly nothing new to the Tibetan Buddhist tradition; however, the formation of particular societies dedicated to this purpose appears to be a modern phenomenon.[111] Another modern innovation, the use of radio to spread the idea that Buddhism was essential to saving China, helped focus attention on the vital role that Tibetan lamas could play in realizing the Chinese imagination of the modern Chinese nation-state.

Broadcasting the Rhetoric and Building the Panchen Lama's Status

In a 1933 national radio broadcast entitled "China's Religious Reforms and the Enterprise of Saving the Nation," Dai reached what was probably the widest audience in his life.[112] In this talk he explained, to a national audience, his concerns for saving the nation and saving Buddhism. At the same time he clearly indicated the connection these dual projects had with integrating the Qing imperial borderlands, particularly Tibet, into a new China. Dai argued that the basis of a country was its races (*minzu*). A race was defined by certain characteristics (common bloodlines, language, literature, and customs). To this Dai added religion, because every race had a particular religion which had influenced each country's culture, education, and government. He posited that ninety-eight to ninety-nine out of one hundred people believe in a religion. Furthermore, he added that,

> In the various regions of our country's borderlands, 100 percent of the people believe in religion. For example, in Xinjiang, Qinghai, Xikang, Tibet, and Mongolia, religion is not only believed in, moreover it has a special status. Tibet's religion has a special status, holding the limits of authority not only in culture but in politics as well. . . . In summary, religion in China occupies a very important place, and in the borderlands it is even more important.

The principal content of Dai's ideas on religious reform focused on the government paying greater attention to religion. Of the five fields in which he thought the government should attend to religious matters, the fifth concerned the "problems of borderland religion." Although he did not directly name Tibet, the greatest among these "problems of borderland religions" was certainly that of how to handle the Dalai Lama's dual political and religious administration. Although Dai noted that the issue was very sensitive, he offered two suggestions drawn from Buddhist teachings. The first was that "one should not be in disagreement with self-awakening." He explained this by reference to Buddha, who fled his royal birth, giving up the possibility of kingship in order to found Buddhism. This critique seemed to be directed at the Dalai Lama, said to be enlightened like Buddha, yet ruling a country. Possibly Dai thought a reminder of Buddha's path to awakening would chasten the Dalai Lama and cause him to give up leadership of Tibet, or at least make him more amenable to compromise with China.

The second suggestion was that "one should not be in disagreement with the times." Again, he did not directly name the problem with Tibet—its unclear international status, neither part of China nor part of the established system of nation-states. Instead he suggested that one look at the situation in China and the world: "How will the world be able to permit there being a special system?" He did not want to dictate terms to the Tibetans on Chinese national radio, but he implied that the solution must come through working with China: "How could this problem be resolved? I want to invite the whole country's public figures, especially Tibetan compatriots, to attend to this."[113] Shortly thereafter, the Panchen Lama started his last and most public tour in China. For more than two years Dai had been interacting with the Panchen Lama regularly. Given the frequency of his exchanges with the Panchen Lama before this public address, the broadcast seems to have been carefully timed with the Panchen Lama's agreement to fully cooperate with the Chinese government in returning to Tibet as a government official. He thus became the single most prominent "Tibetan compatriot" attending to this issue in China, and large numbers of people witnessed him acknowledge China's sovereignty over Tibet, at least according to Chinese sources.

Throughout 1933 the Chinese government assisted the Panchen Lama in negotiating permission with the Tibetan government for the Panchen Lama's return to Tibet. Finally, at the end of 1933, Dai's efforts at reconciling the Dalai and Panchen Lamas came to an end when the thirteenth Dalai Lama died. The perfect opportunity to try to bolster the Panchen Lama's role in Tibet had finally afforded itself. Dai sent a telegram to the Panchen Lama in Inner Mongolia and urged him to make haste to return to the capital to preside over the mourning ceremonies to be held there.[114] The lama returned to Nanjing, where he led the government-sponsored prayer assemblies. With this turn of events there emerged a new possibility for the Panchen Lama to return to Tibet.

In preparation for his return home, the Panchen Lama was appointed Commissioner of the National Government (Minguo zhengfu weiyuan) at the end of January 1934. In his acceptance speech, the lama said, "I should endeavor to follow the late Director-General Sun's teachings that a public spirit and his Three People's Principles should rule everywhere under the sky, and to preach Buddhism for the country's unity, our people's well-being, and world peace."[115] In this way he publicly linked politics, in the officially accepted form of Sun's teachings, with the Buddhist religion for this Chinese audience. Having become an official representative of the Nationalist government, the Panchen Lama participated in a last burst of activity in China Proper.

These activities were an attempt to elevate the Panchen Lama's status in the eyes of the Chinese public and the world community. The Panchen Lama presided over the Dalai Lama's memorial ceremony at the capital, and funds were also distributed throughout China, Amdo (Qinghai), and Inner Mongolia for regional commemorative rites. The Nanjing memorial was held in the Examination Bureau building and was attended by the representatives from each of the five government branches.[116] While the Panchen Lama was in Nanjing, several Chinese monks representing a group of some five thousand lay and monastic Buddhists arrived from Hangzhou to invite the Panchen Lama to lead another Kâlacakra tantra assembly.[117] The Panchen Lama agreed to come teach in March. This second public Kâlacakra assembly to be held in China Proper was an impressive affair that still rivals, yet anticipates, similar events held in Europe and America by the fourteenth Dalai Lama in the late twentieth century.[118] A broad appeal to the masses and the media, a focus on ameliorating world problems, and the celebrity attendance of the event characterize this new use of Buddhist ritual.

During the ceremony the Panchen Lama "prayed for world peace and people's health and happiness."[119] Moreover, Duan Qirui's biography added that, at this event, the lama recited the *Scripture for Humane Kings Who Wish to Protect Their States.*[120] One account numbered the attendees in Hangzhou at more than seventy thousand.[121] Dai Jitao, who no doubt attended the ceremony, noted in his 1937 eulogy of the Panchen Lama that more than ten thousand took the precepts and were initiated into the Kâlacakra's tantric cycle.[122] The general, Huang Musong, and Master Taixu, who received tantric initiation at the event, are both mentioned in the Panchen Lama's biography.[123] In the Panchen Lama's view, and that of other Tibetan Buddhists, this initiation would have indicated an entry into a firmly Tibetan Buddhist world marked by vows that articulated submission to the lama and the Buddhist teachings. Presumably not everyone who attended took these more committed steps, so the true figure probably lies somewhere between the two estimates. With the level of popular attendance and elite participation, clearly the religious aspect of the event must have been seen as a great success by both the Panchen Lama and the organizers of the event.

As for the political aspect of the event, after a full decade in exile and frequent meetings with the highest government officials, the Panchen Lama's Tibetan texts finally showed signs of adopting some of Sun's discourse, which underpinned the Nationalist government. For example, at this event he said that under certain conditions, "China's peoples will be united in purpose" (*Krung sgo'i mi rigs rnams blo rtse gcig mthun la 'gro rgyu red*). This phrase appears to reflect the Chinese phrase "*Zhongguo minzu gonghe*" (China's peoples harmoniously joined).The Panchen Lama also referred to the *San min zhuyi* of the party leader (Tib. *Tsung lis,* Ch. *Tsongli;* i.e., Sun Yat-sen) and his ideology of "all the peoples in harmony and equality" (*mi rigs tshang ma blo rtse mthun cing nyoms pa*).The final and most explicit Tibetan language reference to Sun's ideology also employs the phrase "all the peoples" (*mi rigs thams cad*) in reference to their livelihood (*'tsho ba'i thabs*)—one of Sun's "Three Principles of the People." Whether Sun's ideology had transformed the Panchen Lama's own ideas or was merely being trotted out here to please the Chinese audience is difficult to determine.[124]

However, even in these public events with large Chinese audiences the Panchen Lama failed to refer to there being five racial or ethnic groups. Despite the supposed imperial origins of this concept, late Qing and Republican rhetoric emphasizing an understanding of China as consisting of five racial groups (*wuzu*) appears not to have entered the Panchen Lama's vocabulary. No Tibetan record of this phrase survives in either the Panchen Lama's collected writings or his autobiography. If the Panchen Lama was unwilling to use such terminology, why would the Chinese government allow such an event? Did it serve some other purpose?

One monk writing in Taixu's Buddhist monthly, *Haichaoyin,* spoke of the necessity to understand the background and uses of sponsoring the costly Hangzhou Kâlacakra assembly. He encouraged "the government, prominent people, and the Mongolian and Tibetan Research Institute [in Shanghai] to enthusiastically advocate the Kâlacakra vajra assembly to resolve the Tibet problem." Urging the government to support this strategy, he argued that "prominent people have undertaken difficulties that they are reluctant to bring to the attention of others," so their efforts should not be opposed. He clearly felt that this Tibetan Buddhist ceremony served a useful political purpose beyond that of eliminating disaster and bringing world peace, thereby implicating the sponsors in this utilitarian approach to Tibetan Buddhism.[125] The matter of how politicians and even monks began to use Tibetan Buddhism for ends beyond those stated in the ceremonies I have been exploring certainly deserves further study, but contemporary sources currently available reveal little of such designs.

The fact remains that the Chinese Buddhist laity sponsored most of the rituals without direct government involvement. So many Chinese became interested in Tibetan Buddhism that secular Chinese intellectuals attacked and mocked the idea that Tibetan Buddhism had a place in the Chinese cultural world. For example, the *Current Affairs Newspaper* (*Shishi xinbao*) ran an editorial criticizing the Hangzhou Kâlacakra assembly. The writer praised science over religion and condemned monks and aristocrats for using Buddhist spirits to deceive the people. Writers for the magazine *Humor* (*Lunyu*) also lampooned Tibetan Buddhist activities. Lao She wrote a piece called the "Song of Saving the Country from Difficulties" (*Jiuguo nan ge*) in which he played on Taixu's name, respect for reincarnated lamas (*huofo*), and Dai's hopes for the salvific "genuine mantra and genuine scripture" (*zhenzhou zhenjing*).[126] The editor of *Humor*, Lin Yutang, also included a sarcastic piece entitled, "A Proposal to Make the Lama Religion Our National Religion" (*Zun Lama jiao wei guojia jiao yi*) in the first volume of his magazine.[127] Although the joke never became a reality, popular lay interest and eventually government approval of Tibetan Buddhist lamas were obviously strong enough to threaten the secular guardians of Chinese civilization. These critiques of Tibetan Buddhism in China demonstrate the strength of the burgeoning interest among the Chinese. This groundswell of support for Tibetan Buddhism is thus an important aspect of Tibetan Buddhism's place in Republican China and cannot simply be dismissed as serving a utilitarian political function. Yet its very popularity and its ability to link Tibet and China in the Chinese media and popular imagination may have been the most potent of political effects.

Although the Buddhist pure lands and the peace prayed for in these ceremonies would elude the Chinese, the pervasive presence of Tibetan Buddhist teachers and rituals in China played an important role in the expanding Chinese understanding of their country. Having become convinced that Tibetan Buddhism was necessary to the salvation of their religion and their country, Chinese Buddhists came to embrace Tibetan religious culture as a necessary part of China's future. Although probably only a few score of Tibetans were aware of this perception, tens of thousands of Chinese were exposed to this powerful idea during the Republican period. The grand rituals, the media attention—whether praising or mocking—and the involvement of prominent Chinese Buddhists in all the Tibetan Buddhist activity in China did much to convince the Chinese that Tibet was, in fact, a vital part of a modern China.

Political Propaganda Missions by Lamas

Although the Panchen Lama was officially the propagation envoy for the western regions, he had an important role to play publicizing government propaganda on the eastern seaboard as well. The Panchen Lama also seems to have had his own agenda in these propaganda efforts. On April 19, 1934, when he lectured at the Central University (Zhongyang daxue) in Nanjing on the topic "The Whole Story of Tibet's Political and Religious [System]" (*Xizang zhengjiao zhi shiwei*) he was able to explain to the elite of China's educational institution the mechanism of joint political and religious (*chos srid gnyis*) rule prevalent in Tibet.[128] It may be that he hoped to return to lead this system of government now that the thirteenth Dalai Lama had died. The American diplomat E. T. Williams was aware of the system of regency during the youth of the Dalai Lamas, although he did not know about the Lhasa-based pool of lamas from whom these regents were drawn. He, like the Chinese no doubt, felt that "the official best qualified to fill the post of regent is the Panshen [*sic*] Lama."[129] His last major public appearance in China in the spring of 1934 was to be his best attended event. According to Chinese sources, he lectured in Shanghai, at the mayor's invitation, to a crowd of three hundred thousand. As with an earlier lecture, the sources disagree on the topic of the talk. The official Communist biography of the Panchen Lama again said that he lectured on territorial issues, a talk entitled "Mongolia and Tibet are China's Important Frontiers." According to Ya Hanzhang, in this speech he firmly embraced the Chinese racial rhetoric and commended the government on its support of religion.[130] On the other hand, Guo Qing, in what must be a reference to the same event, stated that at "a great greeting meeting attended by three hundred thousand people, he gave a lecture about the Buddhist idea of equality and Sun Yat-sen's teachings. Sun's Three Principles of the People, he said, contained the same idea of equality as that of Buddhism. He praised Sun's creation of the revolutionary principles and founding of the Republic of China, and asked the people to follow Dr. Sun's teachings. In the lecture he once again gave an account of the historical close relations between the Tibetan area and the central government."[131] The chronological account compiled by Danzhu Angben of the Panchen Lama's life seems to indicate that the Panchen Lama gave several different lectures at this time, which may confirm that these were separate events. However, it is hard to believe that three hundred thousand people were present on more than one occasion in so short a time without a clearer record being made of it.[132]

Unfortunately none of these authors cites his source for these lectures. In addition, the editors of the archival collection of the Panchen Lama's activities in China clearly possessed the relevant document, which they partially cite in the preface but failed to include in its entirety. One is yet again left with the distinct impression that the Panchen Lama's statements had to be tailored very carefully to accord with contemporary Chinese Communist Party political ideology. The Panchen Lama's autobiography is also of little use in this case, as it mentioned his meeting with many officials in Shanghai, but not the content of the discussions nor any such well-attended event.[133] However, the Panchen Lama was explicit about the content of discussions held just before he left China Proper. In his last days in Nanjing, the Panchen Lama met with Dai Jitao and "gave a long talk on the dual religio-political [system]" (*chos srid gnyis*).[134] He also met personally with Chiang Kai-shek to discuss his return to Tibet.[135]

The Panchen Lama's willingness to cooperate with the Nationalist government was just the support that Dai needed to argue that China should restore a special relationship with Tibet following the model of earlier dynasties. Dai presented his views to the Central Political Conference (Zhongyang zhengzhi huiyi) in late May 1934. In the document that records his presentation Dai raised the point that China had limited means to address the problem of Tibet's independence. He argued that "from today and henceforth any policy of the central [government] toward Tibet, even if it is decided from an entirely balanced perspective, will still never be able to suddenly change historical relations [between China and Tibet]. From the Yuan dynasty to the end of the Qing dynasty, central control of Tibet has often used special treatment, different from that on other frontiers." Although he does not explicitly mention the role of religion, his reference to the Yuan and Qing dynasties clearly indicate that he sought to return to the recognition of the Tibetan Buddhist religio-political system that the imperial dynasties had practiced so successfully. Anticipating objections to continuing this special treatment of Tibet, he argued about the special significance of Tibet to all of China's Inner Asian frontiers: "Tibetan relations do not end with Tibet. Kham, Qinghai, Mongolia, and Manchuria, as far south as the borders of Yunnan and north to the borders of Chinese Turkestan and Gansu, [everyone] is completely in the thrall of this center [Tibet]."[136] Dai recognized that adopting a special policy was a compromise solution for many Chinese leaders, but in this closed government meeting he pointed out that China had neither the military force nor the wealth to alter the reality in any other way.[137] Dai probably relayed some of the content of these discussions to the Panchen Lama just before the latter headed west.

The Panchen Lama's departure for Tibet in 1934 was an exciting time for those who had advocated a partnership between Buddhists and politicians. No doubt the Chinese thought that they were building a relationship with the soon-to-be-leader of Tibet, as the Panchen Lama had been formally invited back to Tibet after the Dalai Lama's death. Even the British were worried about what this meant for Tibet and sent a mission to observe the Panchen Lama's return.[138] The American E. T. Williams, writing in 1937 before news of the Panchen Lama being blocked from arriving in Tibet had reached him, reflected the views that the Chinese government had surely projected about this important lama:

> He went back to Tibet, not only as regent of that dependency, but also as representing the suzerain. This has tended, no doubt, to bring the two peoples into more friendly relations, and will probably aid in a peaceable solution of their long-standing difficulties.[139]

The imagined Buddhist unity of China and Tibet had been realized in the lives of men like Dai Jitao and the Panchen Lama, and they had high hopes of extending their example into a political reality for Tibet's relation to China. Although the Panchen Lama ultimately failed to return to Tibet, the promise of

national unity through Buddhist culture had an enduring impact on the way
Chinese Buddhists and their political supporters thought of Tibet's connection
to China for decades.

For example, the Nationalist government continued to respond to Tibetan
pressure to protect Buddhist property in China. An attempt at renewing the
enforcement of the executive order protecting Buddhist property, originally
promulgated in 1931, was made by the Shanghai-based Sino-Tibetan Buddhist
association called the Bodhi Society (Puti xuehui). Duan Qirui founded the
Bodhi Society at the behest of the Panchen Lama in 1934, and the Panchen Lama
was appointed president in absentia in November 1935.[140] If this move to make
the Panchen Lama president was intended to bolster the importance of this
Buddhist organization, the ploy seems to have worked. At the time, the Panchen
Lama was traveling on the borders of China and Tibet, ostensibly as an envoy of
the Chinese government. Yet the treatment of Buddhists that he saw there must
have made him doubt the government propaganda he was sent to spread. Armies
in the borderlands were reported to have been destroying the Buddhist statues in
Tibetan Buddhist monasteries. An article in the Buddhist journal *Haichaoyin*
described the negative impact this was having on the Tibetan and Mongolian
peoples whose reverence for Buddhism was so strong.[141] In response to complaints and the Bodhi Society's petition, in March 1936 the National Military
Council sent out a circular order to all army commanders to protect Buddhist
property.[142] Once again, Tibetan Buddhists had been critical in gaining national
support for the protection of Buddhist institutions.

Chinese efforts to convince the Tibetans of their respect for Tibetan
Buddhism were part of an ongoing propaganda struggle being waged against the
British influence in Tibet. The extent to which the British presence in Tibet
troubled the Chinese and the hope that Buddhism would play a role in cir-
cumventing this problem can be see in a 1934 review of Wang Lükang's "Self-
Criticism on the Tibet Problem," which had been published in the journal *New
China* (*Xin Zhonghua*). The author of the review, a monk named Zhizang, criticized Wang's approach to the Tibet problem as too passive. Wang's attitude
toward the place of Buddhism in resolving the Tibet problem was summarized
as follows: those among the present government officials who had an interest in
Buddhism could, as private persons, worship and be in contact with [Tibetan]
religious leaders. He argued that it was not necessary to oppose such activity. On
the contrary, Zhizang argued that because Buddhism had become a powerful
asset for managing the nation's ethnic relations, the government should actively
encourage private persons to create such contacts. Such a policy would serve as
a means of surpassing the British. Zhizang recognized that the British supported
religious freedom and respected Buddhist leaders but did not actively support

Buddhism. Thus, if the Chinese were able to be positive advocates of Buddhism and support the people's freedom of religious belief, then China would win the support of the Tibetan people.[143] This strategy was, in fact, implemented at the highest levels of the Chinese Nationalist government.

The former general and Mongolian and Tibetan Affairs Commissioner, Huang Musong, was engaged in fulfilling an official mission aimed at just such a policy when this article was published. Huang went to Tibet as a Chinese government envoy and as a Buddhist who had taken part in ceremonies conducted by the Panchen Lama in China. He even dressed as a lama for part of the trip and in Qing official-style silk jacket and skirt at other times. The caption under the photo of Huang Musong, though a modern Chinese Communist government interpolation, must reflect some of the thinking behind these deliberate attempts to use clothing to make an impression: "Photo of Huang Musong on the road to mourn the thirteenth Dalai Lama, playing the lama and acting out the part."[144] These outfits presented a sharp contrast to the military uniform that he wore for photos in China Proper.[145] To further convince the Tibetan elites of the sincerity of the Chinese government's respect for Tibetan Buddhism, he brought four hundred thousand Chinese silver dollars into Tibet as an offering to the monasteries and the individual monks of the three largest temples in Lhasa, as well as for other gifts and expenses.[146] This ploy failed to win the Tibetan government's acknowledgment of Chinese territorial claims, but it undoubtedly softened many Tibetans' attitude toward China.[147] This strategy of sending a representative to Tibet who could be recognized as an active adherent of Buddhism would again be used by the Nationalist Chinese once the Burma Road was cut off by the Japanese when the Chinese hoped to bring supplies through Tibet to the wartime capital in Sichuan.

The Chinese also relied on Tibetan lamas to spread their message among the Tibetans. From 1934 to 1937 the Panchen Lama attempted to spread Chinese Nationalist ideology in the Tibetan borderlands. Early in 1935 his offices published the first issue of the *Monthly Review of the Western Borderlands Propagation Commissioner* (*Xichui xuanhua shi yuekan*).[148] That summer the Panchen Lama "untiringly pursued his task of making propaganda for moral values, sending envoys to villages in Amdo and Kham, and printing books in Chinese and in Tibetan to explain the principles of unity and the pacification of the border regions."[149] Once again, the American diplomat E. T. Williams summarized the knowledge he could gather from Chinese sources about the Panchen Lama's activities in this regard: "The Panshen [*sic*] Lama . . . was made a Special Frontier Commissioner and did excellent service in winning for the Republic the support of the nomads of Koko Nor [Qinghai] and Mongolia."[150] The Norlha Qutughtu, too, was granted a new political title by the Nationalist government:

the Xikang Pacification Commissioner (*Xikang xuanwei shi*). One source said that the lama was given a thousand soldiers and ordered to return to Tibet (presumably to his home territory of Riwoché) but was apparently stopped by the Xikang warlord Liu Wenhui until the Communist Red Army arrived.[151] Other sources assert that the Norlha Qutughtu's abrupt assignment to this new political role was occasioned by the Communist Long March through his native Kham. In August 1935 the Norlha Qutughtu went to Daqianlu and assembled the important religious and political figures of the region to explain the position of the Nationalist government and the threat of the Communists.[152] At this meeting he spoke of "the efficacy of the Three Principles of the People." However, he was captured by the Red Army and died of an illness in their custody in 1936.[153] In the end, although the Norlha Qutughtu was able to use the influence gained during his years in China to secure the support of the Chinese government in returning to his homeland, he failed to reclaim his former domains. Like the Norlha Qutughtu, the Panchen Lama finally secured the support of the Chinese government to try to return to his former domains, but he, too, died (in 1937 in the borderlands between China and Tibet) unsuccessful in his effort to return to his former position of authority. Other missions were to follow these, but their success was largely limited to demonstrating that the Republican government was willing to continue a peaceful dialogue with the Tibetans. For example, Dai Jitao traveled to Kham to participate in the memorial ceremony of the Panchen Lama in 1938.[154]

Although the Chinese Nationalist government's new policy of embracing religious leaders as political officials failed to yield immediate and concrete results, the long-term influence of this approach was effective. First, the diminished military threat from the Chinese allowed both progressive and conservative forces in Tibet to continue to view China as a potential friend. Second, Huang's mission and his, at least outward, respect for and support of Buddhism had a great impact on Tibetan attitudes toward China. Moreover, the elevation of two Tibetan lamas to relatively high office in China must have given some of the Tibetan leadership hope of being able to work out other such positions in the future. However, after reestablishing an official presence in Tibet, the Chinese government turned to more pressing matters on their eastern borders. Thus the initiative for innovations in Chinese and Tibetan relations once again devolved to the Chinese locality that had the most at stake: Sichuan Province. Only after the Nationalist government had been driven into Sichuan by the Japanese would these local innovations become national policy.

7. Linking Chinese and Tibetan Cultures (1934–1950s)

EVEN BEFORE the propaganda missions of the exiled Tibetan lamas ended with their deaths, Chinese monks and politicians had started advocating the idea of joining Chinese and Tibetan cultures through regularly funded, institutionalized educational and religious exchanges. The most successful educational institutions were those set up by Buddhists, either to teach Chinese about Tibetan Buddhism and culture or to impart modern schooling to Tibetan monks. In this chapter I describe in some detail many of the Buddhist monks, both Tibetan and Chinese, who played important roles in these exchanges to demonstrate the importance of these individuals' interests in shaping these institutions. A host of secular private and government institutions for research and education about the borderlands also developed. These were institutions that prefigured America's regional studies university programs. And just as America's programs developed after the Second World War to address gaps in knowledge about cultures vital to national interests, the Chinese developed similar institutions in the 1930s. The faculties and students of these new organizations were later incorporated into Communist-era institutions. As before, developments in Sichuan were precursors to national programs, in part because of Sichuan's historically close relationship with Tibet and in part because the Nationalist government was driven into Sichuan by the Japanese invasion in the late 1930s. Equally important were Tibetan efforts to introduce modern schooling methods and subjects into Tibetan monasteries and communities in the borderlands, especially in Gansu and Qinghai provinces.

Aside from the educational exchanges that marked this era, a process of indigenization made Tibetan Buddhism a small but integral element of Chinese culture. Chinese monks and Buddhist politicians started to preside over Tibetan rituals for the Chinese public. One monk even founded several Chinese monastic schools following Tibetan traditions and practices. The integration achieved at the end of the Chinese Republic was eagerly embraced by the Communists as they sought allies to extend their control and legitimacy over Tibet.

Hybridized Educational Institutions

The Sino-Tibetan Buddhist Institute

Taixu's Sino-Tibetan Buddhist Institute in Sichuan was by far the most successful of the Republican educational institutions set up to link Chinese and Tibetan cultures. From its conception in 1930, this school sought to bridge the knowledge gap between Chinese and Tibetan Buddhists. However, the nature of the rhetoric devoted to this topic developed gradually in conjunction with growing state interest in this project. As noted in chapter 6, when the mission statement of the Sichuan school was announced in Shanghai in 1932, its conceptual origins were rewritten in light of the fact that the Chinese government and its Tibetan officials had since agreed that politics and religion could serve to bolster common interests. Taixu continued to integrate and advance the ideas put forward by government officials in the years that followed.

In the fall of 1932 Taixu's Sichuan school, the Chongqing branch of the World Buddhist Institute, opened its doors to the first group of students.[1] For Taixu, the importance of the Chongqing school increased as his Wuchang academy in eastern China encountered financial difficulty and eventually closed in 1934. The Wuchang buildings were occupied by Chinese soldiers, and an attempt to transfer the school to Beiping ended in 1937 owing to the scarcity of lay donations in the face of the Japanese invasion.[2] As Taixu's need for government support increased, so, too, did his adoption of assimilationist rhetoric. Meanwhile, the Chongqing school continued to attract the attention of provincial and Nationalist government leaders, as well as a host of Chinese monk-teachers trained in Tibet.

THE TEACHING STAFF.   The Sino-Tibetan Buddhist Institute was initially challenged by the lack of skilled teachers knowledgeable about Tibetan language and religious culture.[3] Since the need for qualified teachers was critical for the advent of successful hybrid institutions, here I detail the challenges of building up a competent staff for running the school. Although the government sponsored this school, none of the Chinese or Tibetan teachers had been supported by government funds or programs before coming to the school. For the first two years, aside from the regular Chinese teachers, the teaching staff included only one Tibetan and one Chinese monk who had studied in Kham and Tibet. The Chinese monk, Zhaoyi (b. 1894), had joint responsibility for managing the school and teaching Tibetan language and Buddhism. His principal skill seems to have been administrative, as he had managed the Beijing school in 1924 and the study expedition in 1925. Nevertheless he received some training in Tibetan

Photo 7.1 The Sino–Tibetan Buddhist Institute in 1999 (photo by the author)

Buddhism, having "graduated" (*biye*) from Drepung monastery in Lhasa.[4] The Tibetan, Tupten Gyatso (b. 1890; Ch. Tudeng jiangzuo), had been affiliated with Tengyeling (Ch. Dengji si), the Lhasa monastery that had sided with the Chinese troops in 1912. He had probably been in exile since the destruction of his monastery by the Dalai Lama. Although he had trained in Lhasa's largest and most prominent monastery, Drepung, he apparently did not receive the best education. For example, he could not even correctly write the name of his alma mater, which he spelled 'Bras spong, which reflected its pronunciation but not the correct Tibetan orthography: 'Bras spungs.[5] Not surprisingly he vanished from the school roster as soon as knowledgeable Chinese monks trained in Tibet had been recruited to teach.[6]

Taixu's Chongqing school was the first to resolve the problem of inadequate teachers on Tibetan topics in modern China. Taixu benefited from the fact that his students had been the first Chinese to go to Tibet to study its language, religion, and culture. The man on whom the school most depended to fulfill its educational mission was Fazun. He spoke and read Tibetan and understood the subtleties of Tibetan Buddhism; without such a person at the school it would have been difficult to fulfill the school's mission at all. Early in the winter of 1933 Fazun reluctantly left Tibet out of respect for his teacher Taixu, who had been sending him letters requesting that he come to direct the school.[7] However, Fazun did not arrive at the school until the middle of 1934 and then was frequently away—in Chengdu to translate, teach, or fund-raise to bring his Tibetan teacher to China, or at Mount Wutai raising money to publish his translation of Tsongkhapa's *Great Treatise on the Stages of the Path to Enlightenment* (*Byang chub lam rim chen mo*). He had only been acting principal for two very busy semesters when he returned to Tibet with an invitation to his Tibetan teacher to come teach in China. Because his teacher was ill, he called on many other teachers with the same request. Some were unwilling to go to China, and others were "too busy"; in the end, he could find no one to come with him and returned to the school alone in the winter of 1936.[8]

Despite this failure, the institute had hired a full complement of Chinese teachers knowledgeable about Tibet by 1936. Four of the Chinese monk-teachers had spent significant time in Tibet, as had one of the new administrators. The school's manager, Miyan, had studied at the school in Beijing and spent seven years studying abroad in Kham and Tibet (*liuxue Kang Zang qi nian*). The phrase "study abroad" is repeated for the other monk-teachers, three of whom had spent a decade or more in Tibetan regions. These three (Fazun, Yanding, and Guankong) had also graduated from Taixu's Wuchang Academy, while the fourth (Changguang) had studied in Zhaojue Temple's Buddhist Institute in Chengdu.[9] Through such training, they had the necessary background to prepare them to teach in a modern-style Buddhist school. In addition, at some point in the 1930s, Yeshé Geshé (Ch. Yuexi geshe), a classmate of Fazun's from Lhasa, taught for some time at the school. He returned to Tibet late in 1940 to invite his teacher, Dongben Dalama, also a *geshé,* to come teach at the school. Dongben Dalama apparently accepted the offer, although neither of these men were ever listed on the school's staff rosters.[10]

SCHOOL OFFICIALS AND OFFICIAL DIRECTIVES. Success in locating knowledgeable teachers about Tibet and its religion was only part of the strength of this institution. Equally important were its patrons and the support Taixu managed to secure among government officials. Although Liu Xiang and his uncle, Liu Wenhui, the commander of the Twenty-fourth Army, are said to have been struggling with each other for control of Sichuan at this time, Liu Wenhui was listed as the Honorary Director of Trustee Affairs (*yin dong shi zhang*), while Liu Xiang was listed as the Honorary Principal (*yin yuan zhang*) of the college.[11] Other prominent trustees include General Xia Douyin, commander in chief of the Twenty-first Route Army from 1930 and chairman of the Hubei provincial government in 1932, and General Wang Zanxu, commander of the Forty-fourth Army and chairman of the Sichuan provincial government after 1938.[12] The man who seems to have had the real administrative responsibility for the school was He Beiheng, the director of both the Sichuan River Control Commission and the Chongqing Public Security Bureau.[13] Thus, despite the fact that the daily activities of the school were run by Buddhist monks, the oversight of the school was in the hands of local and provincial security and military forces.

Official involvement with the school and outside efforts to direct the school's mission rose dramatically in 1935. This coincided with the arrival of the full complement of teachers, and from 1936 the school's activities were fairly regular until at least 1945.[14] This expansion accelerated with the encroachment of the Japanese into central China. As the Nationalist government was pushed into southwest China, Tibet became especially important as a route for supplies to reach the wartime capital in Chongqing. But even before the Japanese drove the Nationalist government to Chongqing, and to the school's doorstep, the provincial government was acting on the ideas initially proposed by Taixu in his 1930 meeting with Liu Xiang. Three important documents help to explain the role that this school's Tibetan Buddhist education was to play in political policy: an official letter (*gong han*) from Liu Xiang in 1935, a petition sent to the Sichuan provincial government in 1936, and the lectures of two military officials published in *Haichaoyin,* also in 1936.

Liu Xiang's letter described the purpose of the school: "to link Chinese and Tibetan culture, unite the Chinese and Tibetan spirit, consolidate the western border, and protect China's entire territory." The petition to the Sichuan government was very specific about the enemy against which these efforts were to be directed: the British. It explained that Chinese and Tibetan unity, through the linking of cultures, would keep the British from taking advantage of the current situation.[15] Equally revealing were the lectures two military officers gave to the students at the Sino-Tibetan Buddhist Institute. Their version of the school's mission was recorded in Zhou Guanren's 1936 *Haichaoyin* article. Entitled "Linking Chinese and Tibetan Culture," this article discussed the work of linking the cultures of the five races and included extracts of the generals' speeches.[16] Zhou emphasized the importance of Buddhism as a uniting factor. The only problem he raised was how to link up different Buddhist cultures. When he asked rhetorically who could fill the role, his answer was obvious: Chinese monks had already been trained and more were in training.[17]

Zhou used the generals' speeches to drive home the importance of training Buddhist monks as intermediaries with Tibet. The military officials—school trustee General Xia Douyin and General He Guoguang—came in May 1936 from the Provisional Headquarters of the President of the Military Affairs Commission (of which the aforementioned trustee, Wang, was the chief of staff).[18] They spoke of their plan and directives for opening and developing (*kaifa*) Kham and Tibet. Zhou highlighted certain parts of the speeches, such as General He's exhortations: "I really hope that everyone is extremely diligent in studying Tibetan, to use it to open and develop Kham and Tibet, to revive our Chinese races (*women Zhonghua minzu*), and to consolidate the borderlands." General Xia specifically encouraged the better-trained Buddhist monks (*ge wei fashi*), though monks only made up about half the students, and those qualified as "masters" (*fashi*) were even fewer. Zhou specified that one of their tasks was to correct the Tibetan people's conception that China was devoid of Buddhism.[19] In this effort Chinese monks applying themselves to Tibetan Buddhism would obviously have provided convincing proof to the Tibetans that China was still Buddhist.

ACADEMIC CURRICULUM. Insisting on extensive and specialized training in Chinese and Tibetan literature and Buddhism was Taixu's greatest contribution to the original government plans. Rather than serving as a crash course to prepare monks for propaganda work among the Tibetans, the school curriculum provided substantial training in Tibetan and Buddhist culture. In so doing the training deferred the immediate gains the local government sought and limited the time that could be spent on political training. Thus, despite the occasional lecture on government policy, the Sino-Tibetan Buddhist Institute seems to have been focused mostly on teaching the students Buddhism and language skills. The faculty, drawn largely from the graduates of Buddhist institutes (*Foxue yuan*) from all over China, taught history, Chinese and Tibetan literature, and various doctrinal topics from Buddhist literature. University graduates also taught literature, calligraphy, and natural science.[20] According to the curriculum, of thirty-six hours of class in the general ("undergraduate") division that lasted four years, only one hour specifically addressed party ideology, which made it comparable to physical education.[21] In the specialty ("graduate") division, which lasted two years, there were no such political classes, but one-fifth of the time was spent studying Tibetan geography.[22] Thus, although it was important to understand the government's overall goals, the main task at the school was to master Chinese and Tibetan literature and Buddhism. Obviously such classes would help produce students useful to the government's purposes, but this was not the focus of the training.

For example, when Taixu lectured at the school in 1937 on the topic of fusing Chinese and Tibetan Buddhism, he did not talk about politics. Instead, he discussed how the various doctrines that were absent in either Tibetan or Chinese Buddhism should be studied by the religious tradition that had the deficiency.[23] Of course, this exchange was more or less unidirectional. Some Chinese Buddhists felt that they had much to learn from the Tibetans, but there is no record of modern Tibetan Buddhists either feeling that their religious doctrine was inadequate or desiring to study doctrine unique to Chinese Buddhism. Despite his original focus on linking Buddhist doctrines, as Nationalist government funding increased Taixu adapted more of the politically charged rhetoric in his discussion of the school's goals. For instance, when Taixu welcomed the Tibetan scholar Sherap Gyatso to his Chongqing school in 1938, he explained that the work of the school was to link Chinese and Tibetan cultures and unite the two peoples, reflecting the more political goal of the school's funders.[24]

TAIXU'S RHETORIC. There is one aspect of Taixu's early treatment of the role of Buddhism that did foreshadow the military men's directives. In a 1934 lecture given at a Shanghai school Taixu argued that, in making preparations to open and develop Mongolia and Tibet, the first step was reliance on Buddhism.[25] Taixu's views on what should happen to Tibet in the event that China should gain control of it also emphasized the importance of Buddhism. As described earlier, Taixu believed that there were three classes of Buddhism in the world, and one of them (the esoteric tradition) was truly preserved only in Tibet. In order to protect this vital Buddhist system, Taixu suggested that the Chinese government make plans to consider Tibet a "special Buddhist region" relying on those who understood Buddhism and politics to direct a "self-government which relies on Buddhism."[26] Such hopes for Tibet's future may not have been in accord with the plans of the military leaders who presided over the school, but Taixu's suggestions would certainly have made it more likely that the leaders would succeed in achieving some kind of compromise with the Tibetan government.

The first resident Tibetan teacher, Tupten Gyatso, addressed these issues in his opening (Tibetan language) essay in the 1934 volume dedicated to the Sino-Tibetan Buddhist Institute.[27] Like Dai Jitao in his radio address the year before, this Tibetan teacher linked the development of unity between China and Tibet with the spread of Buddhist teachings, especially those of the founder of the Gelukpa tradition, Tsongkhapa.[28] These ideas were reiterated in Zhizang's 1934 article, where he suggested that while Chinese monks were spreading the Chinese government's intentions to the Tibetan people, the government should also invite Tibetan lamas to study in China. The hope was that this would make the Tibetans clearly understand the Chinese people's true feelings and willingness to resolve the Tibetan problem.[29] Within two years China's Nationalist government had embraced this idea and provided the funding to make it a reality. Thus the school influenced the government at the same time that government priorities influenced the school.

Nationalist Government Involvement

THE EXCHANGE PROGRAM.   The Nationalist government's first clear sign of embracing Chinese monks' suggestions for resolving the "problem" of Tibet's independence occurred when the Mongolian and Tibetan Affairs Commission inaugurated a program to subsidize the study abroad of Chinese and Tibetan monks in December 1936. Apparently the original plan was that each year two Chinese would be selected by the Chinese Buddhist Association to study in Tibet for five years, and two Tibetan monks would be selected by the Tibetan government to come to China to study. The first two Chinese monks (Mandu and Longguo) were sent to Tibet by the government in 1937.[30] The program was to last almost a decade, financing some twenty Chinese monks (with over ten more paying their own way). While only five of the twenty-one names listed in a 1945 government report on this program can be definitively linked with the Sino-Tibetan Buddhist Institute, the rhetoric of Taixu and Liu Xiang's original proposal is repeated with a slight, but significant, modification. The Mongolian and Tibetan Affairs Commission that directed the exchange shifted the discourse from an ethnic to a political relationship in which the cultures to be linked are those of "China Proper" (*neidi*) and Tibet (*Xizang*), rather than Chinese (*Han*) and Tibetan (*Zang*).[31]

This "exchange" program failed to attract much Tibetan participation, if indeed the invitation was even regularly proffered. Only a single instance of a

Photo 7.2 Dobi Geshé, Sherap Gyatso (1884–1968), photo shared by a disciple in 1997

Tibetan being invited and accepting the offer has been recorded. Li Dan, a member of the Guomindang Central Organization Department and the director of the Qinghai Tibetan Language Research Society (Zangwen yanjiu hui), led a group of twenty-one people from Xining to pay a "courtesy visit" to Tibet in 1935.[32] The group members split up and lived in the three central monasteries in and around Lhasa, visiting lamas and receiving teachings from them.[33] Yang Zhifu (Tib. Jampa Namgyel) studied in Drepung Monastery with the Amdo monk Sherap Gyatso (1884–1968), became his disciple, and later served as his translator.[34] From humble beginnings on the very fringe of Tibetan settlement in Amdo (Tib. Dobi, Ch. Xunhua) near Lanzhou, Sherap Gyatso had risen to the peak of Tibetan society. After he earned the highest *geshé* monastic degree in 1916, the thirteenth Dalai Lama asked him to assist in editing new editions of canonical Buddhist collections. Famous for his scholarly learning, Sherap Gyatso was also an extremely influential man in Central Tibetan social circles. A description of his power by another Amdo resident in Lhasa in the 1930s indicates that Sherap Gyatso's following was not limited to the monastic community: "Sherab Gyatso had many disciples. A lot of aristocrats were his disciples, and he controlled all the aristocrats. When Sherab Gyatso lived in Drepung, his courtyard was filled with aristocrats' horses. . . . Sherab Gyatso would go around Lhasa surrounded by a group of people and show off his power."[35]

However, after the Dalai Lama's death in 1933, Sherap Gyatso appears to have fallen out of favor with the conservatives who took power, no doubt precisely because he wielded so much power among the aristocracy.[36] Thus, when Li Dan relayed the invitation of the Chinese government's Lhasa representative to Sherap Gyatso offering him a return trip home with a stay in Nanjing, the monk accepted the offer.[37] The invitation was extended from the Education Department and the Mongolian and Tibetan Affairs Commission in the hope that Sherap Gyatso would come to China to give a series of lectures on Tibetan culture at China's top universities (Beijing, Qinghua, Zhongyang, Wuhan, and Zhongshan), which he did. In addition, they offered him the position of instructor in the field of Chinese and Tibetan culture as well as 1,000 *yuan* for traveling expenses. In late 1936 he left Tibet for China, stopping in India on his way.[38] When Sherap Gyatso arrived in China in the spring of 1937, he met with China's leaders and was rewarded with a religious title.[39] In a sense, for the Chinese, he filled the place left empty by the Panchen Lama's departure from China Proper, receiving from the Nationalist government the prestige, monetary awards, and even a permanent post at the Central University where the Panchen Lama had lectured just before he departed China Proper. Although Sherap Gyatso had less standing in the Tibetan religious hierarchy, he was the most prominent Tibetan intellectual to live in China after the death of the Panchen Lama.

As for the Chinese participation in this "exchange" program, the only specific report of the Chinese monks' activities in Tibet is that recorded by Welch, whose informants included a student of the Sino-Tibetan Buddhist Institute. After being at the school for three years, in 1936 this man was transferred to the Central Political Institute for cadre training. The next year he went to Tibet, where he stayed for thirteen years, living the dual life prescribed by his own interests and his sponsor's political needs. He succeeded in earning a *geshé* degree (probably the first Chinese to do so) from one of the great monasteries, which indicated the seriousness of his commitment to religious training. Meanwhile, he continued to work for the Mongolian and Tibetan Affairs Commission office in Tibet until the summer of 1949, when the Tibetans ejected all Nationalist officials and some three hundred other Chinese from Tibet for fear that the Communists had spies among them.[40]

The effectiveness of such men in the service of the Mongolian and Tibetan Affairs Council may have been part of what helped convince the Nationalist government to continue supporting the Sino-Tibetan Buddhist Institute after its longtime patron, Liu Xiang, died in 1938. From its inception, this school had received a subsidy from the provincial government's education office of between 5,000 and 7,200 *yuan* a year.[41] The other major source of funding was the contributions made by the trustees (about 3,700 *yuan* a year). Together with the incidental income from monastic land holdings, visitors, and so forth, the school operated on just over 10,000 *yuan* a year. It seems that no change in the regular provisions for the school was made when the Nationalist government retreated to make Chongqing its capital. For the school to continue to receive substantial funds in a period of such severe constraints on government spending, the school's mission must have been seen as very valuable indeed.

PUBLICATION SUPPORT. Moreover, the publishing program at the school greatly accelerated in 1938, when the Nationalist government's Ministry of Education established an editing and translating office at the school. The ministry's subsidy of 4,800 *yuan* a year was to finance the production of "bilingual Chinese and Tibetan textbooks" (*Han Zang hebi jiaokeshu*).[42] Prior to receiving central government support, Fazun had already developed a Tibetan grammar by 1935.[43] He had also just written the first and most interesting of his books on Tibet. *Contemporary Tibet* (*Xiandai Xizang*), published in 1937, clearly responded to Chinese concerns about the "Tibet problem." This work was quite frank both about the true nature of the situation in Tibet and about the depth of Chinese ignorance about Tibet—especially the relations between the Panchen and Dalai Lamas—despite a pretense of knowledge on the subject among some Chinese. He also detailed exactly why the Tibetans were not interested in closer relations with the Chinese. As he explained it, since the center (*zhongyang*, i.e., China) was unable to unite, it was too weak to help against other foreign powers or to concern itself with Tibet. In addition, the Tibetans felt that since China had Westernized it had become a Christian nation, and Buddhism had not survived.[44]

Even after the school received government funding to create bilingual texts, Fazun continued to spend most of his time translating religious works, such as the *Biography of Tsongkhapa (Zongkaba dashi zhuan)* in 1938 and Tsongkhapa's *Vast Treatise on the Graduated Esoteric Path* (Ch. *Mizong zidi guanglun*, Tib. *Sngags rim chen mo*) in 1939. By 1940 he had published a new book on Tibetan grammar (with a reader), revised his Tibetan language textbook, and published the voluminous *Political and Religious History of the Tibetan Race (Xizang minzu zhengjiao shi)*—probably the first Chinese language history of Tibet to rely largely on Tibetan language works.[45] Fazun specifically mentioned that the history text was written to fill the needs of his students. No doubt these materials dramatically improved the ability of the Chinese to learn about and understand Tibet from primary sources, both people and texts.[46] Despite the rhetoric of initiating a two-way exchange, however, these textbooks were all oriented toward teaching Chinese people about Tibet. The only work that was explicitly said to have been translated into Tibetan at this school was a Chinese Buddhist text that was absent in the Tibetan canon.[47] The Chongqing school eventually developed a Tibetan-Chinese dictionary as well, based on a translation of a Tibetan dictionary.[48]

Western Border Culture Institute

Work on the first Tibetan-Chinese dictionary to be developed in China also started in the 1930s at another Sichuan institute, the Western Border Culture Institute (Xichui wenhua yuan), without the support of the Chinese government.[49] Zhang Yisun, who founded this institute at the end of 1937, had been gathering materials for a Tibetan-Chinese dictionary since 1928. In 1934 he sought funds from the Nationalist government's Ministry of Education, but his request was denied. The first version of a Tibetan-Chinese "dictionary," really more of a glossary, was published by Zhang and the institute in Hong Kong in 1937.[50] In January 1938 the institute brought out a bilingual phrasebook treating different topics such as common phrases, food, weather, and so on.[51] In the following months the institute published two more texts: a Chinese-Tibetan glossary and a Chinese-Tibetan version of Sarat Chandra Das's compendium of letters in Tibetan.[52] A full-fledged Tibetan Chinese dictionary, entitled *Zang Han yiming da cihui*, was published by the institute in 1939.[53] In 1941 researchers at the Western Border Culture Institute in Chengdu took Jäschke's *Tibetan-English Dictionary* as their model and started translating the English entries into Chinese, producing by 1945 a ten-volume set of lexicographic materials. Later, under the Communist government, these materials would form the basis of the most comprehensive Tibetan dictionary in existence, soon to be available in English.[54]

Secular Educational Innovations

Shortly after the Panchen Lama's 1934 visit to Shanghai, the secular Mongolian and Tibetan College (Meng Zang xueyuan) was created, led by the director of the Shanghai Education Department.[55] Taixu's disciple, Fafang, argued that because Buddhism permeated Tibetan culture it was a mistake to have a Mongolian and Tibetan College that did not include the study of Buddhism. Fafang was attacking the secular versus religious division between Shanghai's Mongolian and Tibetan College and the Bodhi Society, which were founded at the same time.[56] One wonders whether financial considerations were also involved with this line of argument. Advocating Buddhist studies as essential to resolving the ethnic problems provided a justification for the continued tolerance and protection of Buddhism in general and a specific reason for funding Tibetan Buddhist studies among the Chinese. In any case, the Buddhists were successful in their bid for government funding, while the Mongolian and Tibetan College does not seem to have produced important intermediaries to help resolve the Sino-Tibetan conflict.

A more successful initiative was the government's effort to develop modern education in the Sino-Tibetan borderlands. In 1937, probably in anticipation of the Nationalist government retreat into China's ethnically diverse southwest, the Mongolian and Tibetan Department of the Ministry of Education was given charge of all border education. According to June Dreyer:

> A network of schools was set up to give primary-level instruction in "modern education, citizenship, Han language, and vocational skills and hygiene." Secondary schools were also to be founded, with emphasis on the development of technical abilities and "clear understanding of the Chinese race and nation." In official documents the variety of terms denoting barbarians was replaced by more neutral terms that reflected the influence of Western anthropology—for example, *chung-tsu* (ethnic group) and *jen-chung* (race).[57]

She also noted that, "while there was only one border school under the Ministry of Education before the war, 44 frontier schools of various grades were established or taken over by the Ministry after 1938."[58] A number of these were branch schools of the Nationalist government's Mongolian and Tibetan School sited in the borderlands (Meng-Zang xuexiao bianjiang fenxiao): at Jiuchuan in

Gansu, Xining in Qinghai, Kangding in Xikang, and Dali in Yunnan. Eventually, to embrace its broader mission, the name of the Mongolian and Tibetan School was changed to the Borderlands School (Bianjiang xuexiao).[59] In 1941 the Ministry of Education built another school at the important cultural center Derge in Kham, which had about one hundred students.[60]

This broadened mission yielded practical developments over the next several years. For example, in 1937 Qiang Jiyu, a councilor to Huang Musong's 1934 mission who remained in Tibet as a liaison, set up a primary school in Lhasa. The school was later taken over by the Lhasa branch of the Mongolian and Tibetan Affairs Commission, which created a second school in Gyantsé.[61] Aside from these developments in Central Tibet, in 1937 and 1938 Gu Jiegang conducted field research on the educational developments in Gansu, including the largest Tibetan monastery outside Central Tibet, Labrang Monastery.[62]

Shortly thereafter, the American-trained Chinese anthropologists Li Anzhe and his wife, Yu Shiyu, arrived in Labrang to conduct their own research.[63] Li noted that from 1938 to 1941 the Tibetan Cultural Association ran the Labrang Primary School with some one hundred students. The county government ran another primary school. An additional five short-courses (something less than a primary school education) were run by the county government in Getsho, Mewu, Khaja, Qingshui, and Qisuogou near Labrang. Each enrolled about twenty-five students, although the students were mostly Chinese. Finally, also starting in 1938, Labrang had a Vocational Middle School administered directly by the Ministry of Education. Its fifty students studied public health and animal husbandry. More short-lived efforts at encouraging borderland education were the ministry's traveling Education Team, which gave public lectures and showed movies, and the Education Institute sponsored by the Gansu Science Education Institute.

While in Labrang, Yu Shiyu started a long career in developing educational projects in Tibetan regions. From 1938 to 1945 she helped persuade the Tibetan Mrs. Huang Zhengqing to start the Labrang Tibetan girls' school. Mrs. Huang, wife of the local leader, was the principal, and the initial class of 80 students eventually grew to 130.[64] The education was at least partially very practical, as the girls helped to build the school by making bricks and also grew vegetables. Once Yu left in 1945 the school was run by the county government.[65] In later years Yu was again instrumental in running primary schools in Tibetan regions: in Chamdo from 1949 to 1951 and in Lhasa in 1952 (as vice principal).[66] No doubt educational projects similar to those in Labrang were being undertaken throughout the borderland regions.[67] Before examining the modern monastic educational institutions that were initiated near Labrang around the same time, I will examine the other secular institutions created to deal with the borderland peoples.

On the Communist front, the Nationalities Institute (Minzu xueyuan), a training school for non-Chinese Communist Party cadres, was founded in the fall of 1941 in Yan'an.[68] From 1941 the Nationalist government also sponsored research centers dedicated to examining issues related to China's borderlands. For example, when Li Anzhe came to Sichuan in 1941, he took a leadership role in the Western China Consolidated University (Huaxi xiehe daxue) and started the Western China Frontier Research Center (Huaxi bianjiang yanjiu suo). The center published an English language journal with funding from the American Viking Fund.[69] Also in 1941 Ouyang Wuwei returned from Lhasa to teach Tibetan at Chongqing's Central University (Zhongyang daxue).[70] From 1943 to 1946 the scholars of the Western China Frontier Research Center (Huaxi bianjiang yanjiu suo) conducted field research and published their findings. However, government funding ended in 1946 when the Nationalist government moved back east. That summer the Kham and Tibet Research Society (Kang Zang yanjiu she) was established to replace the Western China Frontier Research Center. For the next three years this society published the *Xikang Tibet Research Monthly (Kang Zang yanjiu yuekan)*.[71] Since national funding had been withdrawn, the chairman of Xikang Province, Liu Wenhui, contributed resources to keep it operating. Later, Sichuan provincial government funds and even a grant from the Nationalist government allowed the society to continue for a few years, until financial difficulties shut the organization down in September 1949.

Despite the weak financial support the Nationalist government granted to such institutions, the shift of government administration to the southwestern regions left some mark on the government, just as the Communist government was affected by its location in the northwestern borderlands. Although details on Tibetan Studies in Nanjing in the late 1940s are scarce, Ouyang wuwei taught Tibetan at Nanjing's National Defense and Border Affairs Research Center (Guofang bu bianwu yanjiusuo).[72] More significant for China's future, the Yan'an Nationalities Institute graduated its first class in 1944. The Khampa, Sanggyé Yeshé (best known by his Chinese name Tianbao), was among these early Communist cadres.[73] Shortly after the founding of the People's Republic of China, this school became the Central Institute for National Minorities (Zhongyang Minzu xueyuan, Tib. Mi rigs slob grwa chen po) and has continued to play an important role in linking Chinese and Tibetan cultures to this day.[74]

Tibetan Monastic Educational Innovations

Progressive Tibetan monks, most notably Sherap Gyatso, pioneered other innovations in borderland education. When he came to China in 1937 the Tibetan monastic scholar had been welcomed by China's leaders, including the

Examination Department chairman, Dai Jitao, the president of the Republican government, Lin Sen, and the real ruler of China, generalissimo Chiang Kai-shek.[75] Sherap Gyatso was the first Tibetan Buddhist to be granted a position in the modern university system in China: the post of lecturer on Tibetan culture at China's Central University in Nanjing (where he taught a weekly class on Tibetan culture).[76] This appointment was also made jointly at four other prominent universities: Beijing, Qinghua, Zhongshan, and Wuhan.[77] For this position Sherap Gyatso was given a salary of 1,000 *yuan* a month.[78]

In addition to lecturing at these universities, Sherap Gyatso was also closely associated with Chinese-run Tibetan Buddhist temples, lay associations, and schools, which united traditional Tibetan Buddhist education with modern Chinese education. His first opportunity to teach lay Chinese Buddhists was in Shanghai, at the Bodhi Society (Ch. Puti xuehui; Tib. Byang chub lam rim chen mo'i slob tshogs) in the spring of 1937.[79] The Panchen Lama, along with prominent Buddhist Chinese politicians and monks, had founded the society in 1934. An exchange of letters between the Panchen Lama and Sherap Gyatso in 1935 and 1936 attested to the friendly relations between these two Tibetan lamas.[80] No doubt the Panchen Lama and his associates had helped to arrange the three-week-long teachings Sherap Gyatso gave in Shanghai to more than three hundred students. In tune with the modern nature of the society, he taught a combination of traditional religious and historic topics: Tsongkhapa's life, *The Three Principles of the Path*, *The Graduated Path to Enlightenment*, the history of the Gelukpa school, and the history of Sino-Tibetan cultural exchange.[81]

In the next few years Sherap Gyatso was exposed to a range of such institutions, which combined modern educational techniques with traditional Tibetan Buddhist teachings. The most important of these were the schools of the two best-trained Chinese Tibetan Buddhists: Fazun and Nenghai. Nenghai had founded the first temple in China designed to teach Chinese Buddhists about Tibetan Buddhism. As early as the spring of 1939 Nenghai and Sherap Gyatso met in Chongqing, where officials had invited them to take part in a "dharma-assembly to avert disaster."[82] At this time, Nenghai, who had taught in a military academy before becoming a monk late in life, was in the process of repairing and opening his own monastic school. Sherap Gyatso was able to follow the progress of this venture when he was asked in 1940 to consecrate the image of Tsongkhapa at the temple.[83]

Around the same time he was invited to lecture on Buddhist scriptures at the Western Frontier Culture Institute.[84] He also visited and taught at the Sino-Tibetan Buddhist Institute in Chongqing.[85] There he could see the possibilities opened up by the resources made available by the Ministry of Education: the old monastery had been renovated and turned into a modern Buddhist Studies institute. But because the school was directed by Fazun, a monk, the students included monks and laymen, and the classes were a mix of religion and other general subjects, from geography and natural sciences to physical education and party ideology.[86] Although Sherap Gyatso had taught at the most prominent universities in China, he never fully embraced a secular modern style of education. The greater influence on him seems to have been these Chinese Tibetan Buddhist "hybrid institutions" which combined modern methods and topics with the Gelukpa Tibetan Buddhism in which Sherap Gyatso had been trained.

MOTIVATION FOR FOUNDING HIS OWN SCHOOL. These Chinese institutions may well have inspired his effort to bring modern education to the main monastery in his native area in Amdo (Qinghai). Even before he left Tibet, Sherap Gyatso had apparently thought in a general way about bringing the best that Tibet had to offer to his native region. After working for some fifteen years as an editor in the Dalai Lama's parklike summer residence, the Norbu Lingka, Sherap Gyatso said, "Later, when I return to my homeland, by all means I must make [something] like this."[87] However, Karma Khabum, one of the early students at the school, traced Sherap Gyatso's specific inspiration to create a school to his travels from Tibet through India to China: "Throughout the journey, the master focused on understanding changing societal developments as well as the conditions for running schools in India and Hong Kong and China's southern coastal areas. Recognizing the backward educational undertakings of his own people's culture, he resolved to set up several schools in Tibetan regions and rely on this to set in motion the development of the Tibetan regions."[88] Sherap Gyatso did specifically mention the advanced example of education in China Proper as a model in order to explain the importance of educational initiatives in his native area.[89] Of course, all these sources were published in China just at the time when the local Tibetans were seeking to revive the school in the 1990s, so it is not surprising that China's east coast would be touted as the model; nevertheless these ideas seem plausible. But Sherap Gyatso also realized that the conditions in Amdo were different from that of the seaboard areas he had been visiting. He knew that "while monasteries were plentiful, [the number of] public schools could not be compared to those in China Proper." For this reason, he planned to use "monastic education to lead Tibetans to keep up with the era's course of healthy development."[90] Karma Khabum explained the purpose of the school as "relying on improvement in borderland education to advance the Tibetan people's culture, publicizing the 'Three Principles of the People,' [and] explaining the policy of resisting [the Japanese] in order to build up the country."[91] The rhetoric of Sun Yat-sen's *Three Principles of the People,* with its Leninist influences on ethnic relations, provided an ideology that allowed the Tibetans and Chinese to pursue common goals, at least in theory. Sherap Gyatso's speech at the opening ceremony of the school espoused the sentiments that the monks should "become [accomplished] for the sake of the country and for the sake of their ethnicity having useful people of talent."[92] But he also said that he was building the school "as a means to support the people of Dobi and free them from suffering."[93]

FOUNDING AND FUNDING THE SCHOOL. On his return home in 1939 Sherap Gyatso spent some time discussing his plans for reestablishing his village's monastery, Dobi Monastic School (*dratsang*) Ganden Pelgyé Ling. As a first step in this direction, all the local monasteries of the Dobi region were consolidated into the single Dobi Monastic School to facilitate proper management. Apparently this arrangement also lessened the financial burdens of religious belief on the common people (presumably by reducing costs), although it is doubtful that this was Sherap Gyatso's intention at the time. Despite this efficiency, or perhaps because of it, his first effort at reforming monastic education seems to have met with some local resistance.

A short time later he was able to use his national connections to convince the local people of the advantages of such a school. When the provincial Muslim warlord tried to conscript young men from his village, Sherap Gyatso petitioned the national Ministry of Education to start a vocational school in his home village. Since students were exempt from conscription, Sherap Gyatso's ability to negotiate this national recognition allowed him to secure local support *and* national funding in a single stroke. In the fall of 1941 the Republican government's Ministry of Education approved Dobi Monastic School, and the school became known as the Qinghai Tibetan Buddhist and Chinese Language School.[94]

In February 1942 the school opened, with Sherap Gyatso presiding as director.[95] The Ministry of Education apparently gave start-up funding of 800 Mexican silver dollars (*bai yang yuan*),[96] and Sherap Gyatso took responsibility for constructing the administrative and class buildings.[97] To run the school, he added 1,000 *yuan* of his own funds to the monastery's rental income,[98] and "each month the Ministry of Education gave a subsidy of 3,000 *yuan* for operational funds."[99] This was a substantial sum at the time, demonstrating the seriousness of the government's commitment to the school.

FACULTY, STUDENTS, AND CLASSES. The Tibetan culture faculty were traditionally trained Tibetan monks (*geshés*), and the Chinese language teachers were Chinese or Tibetan laymen.[100] In keeping with the effort to modernize the school, the student body comprised a combination of monks and lay villagers who were distinguished by their different clothing and different courses. The monks wore robes, while the lay students wore clothes with the symbol of the school.[101] As the school had formerly been a monastery, the rules of the monastery were still observed and students had to take part in the ongoing religious activities. The students were divided into two classes based on age.[102] Those eight to twenty (about fifty students) were placed in the youth class, and those older than twenty (about forty students) were placed in the adult class.

The youth class studied Chinese, both written and spoken, Tibetan spelling and introduction to logic and epistemology (*bsdus grwa*). The adult class only studied spoken Chinese, along with Tibetan grammar, poetry, and synonyms. The monks must have made up the bulk of the older class, as the adults were said to have also studied the five sciences—logic, the perfections, madyamika, abidharma, and vinaya—and the main elements of Tibetan culture.[103] After the Communists took over, the school was converted into a regular lower school in 1951. Thus it was only for the first ten years of its existence that Sherap Gyatso had free rein to combine what he saw as the best of the traditional Tibetan monastic education with the modern methods and topics to which he had been exposed in China.

IMPACT OF THE SCHOOL. What were the results of Sherap Gyatso's innovative school? Did he have a lasting influence on Sino-Tibetan education? Unlike some other Tibetan lamas who taught the Chinese about Tibetan Buddhism, Sherap Gyatso did not ultimately play an important role in training Chinese Tibetologists. Instead, his contribution was local and focused on improving the basic education of Tibetans. Given the geographic location of his native area on the Chinese and Tibetan linguistic and cultural borders he took a realistic approach: integrating modern and bilingual education with Tibetan educational traditions.

Although detailed information on all the graduates of the school is not available, several of the teachers and students of Dobi Monastic School were able to turn this educational experience to their advantage in Communist China. One of the students, Karma Khabum, became an editor for the *Qinghai Peoples' Arts Magazine* (*Mtsho sngon mang tshogs sgyu rtsal*). The former manager of the school, Drakpa Gyatso, is a chief editor at the Qinghai Nationalities Publishing House (Mtsho sngon mi rigs dpe skrun khang). One of the former Chinese language teachers, Chöpel Gyatso, is deputy director of the Translation Bureau of the Qinghai Province People's Government (Mtsho sngon zhing chen mi dmangs srid gzhung). At the national level, one graduate, Püntsok Trashi, now works at the Chinese Tibetology Center (Ch. Zhonguo Zangxue yanjiu zhongxin, Tib. Krung go'i Bod kyi shes rig zhib 'jug lte gnas) in Beijing. Twenty-four others hold various positions in the provincial, prefectural, county, and village governments, while those who are especially knowledgeable about culture help maintain local Tibetan ethnic culture.[104] Whatever one's opinion of Tibetans working within the state institutions of Nationalist or Communist China, Sherap Gyatso's ability to foresee the future needs of his people was remarkable. For someone born in the nineteenth century and raised within the conservative Gelukpa scholastic culture, Sherap Gyatso showed great flexibility in adapting to the times. Ultimately his work had more practical progressive results than the work of his much acclaimed student Gendün Chömpel. The history of the school Sherap Gyatso started demonstrates the creative adaptations to modernity that one Tibetan monk pursued on the borderlands between Tibet and China. Although Sherap Gyatso has been accused of being a traitor to Tibet, he was certainly a strong advocate for his native region. Tibetans in Dobi are very proud of his success in establishing this school and are in the process of rebuilding it with Chinese (and Taiwanese) aid.

The Indigenization of Tibetan Buddhism Among the Chinese

After the death and departure of the leading Tibetan lamas of the 1930s, there was a final phase of renewed interest in Tibetan Buddhist and esoteric Buddhist activity in Republican China. As in the early 1930s this renewal took place again in Sichuan; thereafter it only faintly spread to eastern China after the Japanese were driven out. Yet this renaissance was marked by the distinction of being an indigenized one: modern Tibetan Buddhist temples under the direction of Chinese masters of Tibetan teachings grew up at this time. Meanwhile, inspired by the esoteric Tibetan Buddhist model, Chinese Buddhist politicians also sponsored dharma assemblies that joined exoteric and esoteric Buddhist practices to protect their country.

After the Tibetan lamas who had officially been designated protectors of the country left the domestic scene, the Chinese who had embraced Tibetan Buddhism took a more prominent role in leading protective ceremonies. The monk Nenghai and the politician Dai Jitao were the most important figures in this indigenization of Tibetan Buddhism among the Chinese. A handful of ethnically Tibetan and Mongol Tibetan Buddhists played minor roles in the last decade of Republican rule, but none had much of a following of their own. They merely lent authenticity to the rituals, rather than being central to them, as Tibetan lamas had been in the previous decades.

Buddhist Institutional Innovations

While the Chinese and Tibetan Buddhists worked with ideas and funding derived from various provincial and Nationalist government sources, the Chinese laity developed their own educational institutions. In north China, interest in Tibetan Buddhism continued in modest form throughout the Japanese occupation. The Esoteric Institute (Mizang yuan) was founded in

Beiping in 1934. Even after the Japanese occupied the city in 1937, this institute continued to host Tibetan lamas. To the west of Beiping, Hu Zihu, the original sponsor of Beijing's 1924 Tibetan language school, set up the Sino-Tibetan Institute (Han Zang xueyuan) in Xiantong Temple on Mount Wutai in 1939.[105] Two years later he established the Tibetan Language Research Team (Zangwen yanjiu ban) at the same location. That same year in Beiping, he founded the Institute for the Propagation of Mahayana Buddhist Teachings (Dasheng Fojiao honghua yuan) with more than one hundred monk-associates (*senglü*).[106] Whether by necessity or design, none of these northern schools took on any of the political roles that characterized similar institutions to the south.

Kham also saw the development of new Sino-Tibetan Buddhist institutions, one with government assistance. Liu Wenhui's efforts at starting a religious school in Kangding finally bore fruit in 1939. According to the Chinese Tibetologist Luo Rencang, from 1936 to 1939 the school had teachers and a principal but no students.[107] The first class of student-monks started in the spring of 1939 at the Five Sciences Institute (Wuming xueyuan); it was to remain active until 1944. This school opened in the very temple, Ngachö Gön, that had served as the home to Taixu's students in the 1920s and had been sent funds after the 1932 Sichuan dharma assembly.[108] Although Dorjé Chöpa was not mentioned in any of the literature on this school, his legacy was obviously important to this temple-school. Liu Wenhui's telegram to Ngakwang Khenpo (Awang kanbu) in Lhasa noted that there would be three hundred Kham monks, as well as an unspecified number of Chinese monks, at the school. To support the institute, Liu Wenhui promised annual funding of 50,000 *yuan*.[109]

Buddhist monks, both Chinese and Tibetan, also pursued new approaches to monastic education. Taixu's last innovation resembled Liu's in that it created a place where Chinese monks could study in a Tibetan context. In 1944 the Sino-Tibetan Buddhist Institute opened a branch Chinese Monastic Institute (Han seng yuan) in Litang. Taixu was the official head, and some Chinese monks used this as a staging ground for entering Tibet.[110] Lastly, in a development similar to Sherap Gyatso's new school, the religious leader of Labrang Monastery in Gansu, the fifth Jamyang Zhepa (1916–1947) added Chinese primary school material to the training of younger monks in 1945. He also studied Chinese with Huang Mingxin, a Chinese monk and his disciple.[111] In the coming years Labrang produced a number of bilingual Tibetans who served as intermediaries between Communist China and Tibet.

Nenghai's Monastic Educational Innovations

While Fazun served as director for the government's Buddhist school in Chongqing in the 1930s, Nenghai continued his religious practice and taught at monasteries at Mount Wutai. In 1936, at the invitation of a senior Chinese monk, Guanghui, he tried to incorporate Tibetan Buddhist teachings and practices within the context of a Chinese Buddhist temple dedicated to the protection of the country (Huguo Bishan shifang Pujisi, also known as Guangji maopeng).[112] Although he had the support of the Jasagh Lama, the head of the main temple at Mount Wutai (Pusading), the Tibetan esoteric practices were apparently unacceptable to the Chinese monks resident at the monastery.[113] In any case, the Japanese were advancing on north China, and Nenghai returned to Sichuan.

With the Japanese successes in late 1938, many in China were willing to entertain any alternatives to certain defeat, including esoteric Buddhism. In the spring of 1939, Nenghai trekked to the peak of the sacred Buddhist mountain, Mount Emei, southwest of Chengdu to perform a *homa* ritual. This is the first mention of a Chinese Buddhist practicing such a ritual in modern times. Shortly thereafter officials in the wartime capital of Chongqing asked Nenghai to lead a dharma-assembly to eliminate disaster (*xiaozai fahui*). Again, this occasion marked an innovation and an indigenization of what had become a regular Tibetan Buddhist practice in the Chinese cultural context. Sherap Gyatso was also invited to attend the assembly, but Nenghai—a Chinese schooled in Tibetan Buddhism—presided over such an assembly for the first time. Again the ceremony included a *homa* ritual as well as the recitation of scriptures. In the meantime, Nenghai had been rebuilding a Chinese temple, Jinci Monastery, on the outskirts of Chengdu, based on the pattern of a Tibetan monastic community. His biography called it the first Gelukpa esoteric temple in China Proper (*neidi shou chuang Huang mi genben taochang*). As such, it was honored with the title "Hall of the Vajra Way to Protect the Country" (Huguo jingang daochang) in 1939.[114] When Sherap Gyatso visited in 1940 he was so impressed with Nenghai's efforts to approximate Tibetan conditions that he exclaimed, "Coming here makes me feel like I am actually in a Tibetan monastery!"[115]

This school was a great success after Nenghai's failure at Mount Wutai. One of China's best-known contemporary Buddhist nuns started her education here and later started her own school for nuns nearby.[116] Probably the most significant development was the foundation of a translation center at the school.[117] For the first time since the eighteenth-century Qing imperial support for the translation of Tibetan scriptures into Mongol and Manchu, there was an institutional home to support the regular translation of important religious materials. But distinguishing this institution from those supported by the Qianlong emperor was its emphasis on translating texts into Chinese, which had not been undertaken on such an institutional basis since the times when Kumarajiva and Xuanzang translated scriptures into Chinese.

Photo 7.3 Jinci Monastery, partially rebuilt in 1999 (photo by the author)

Protective Buddhist Activity

Whereas Nenghai gained his reputation by studying in Tibet, Dai Jitao had confirmed his commitment to Tibetan Buddhism by studying with the Panchen Lama in China. As one of the lama's most prominent disciples, Dai assumed some of the responsibility for trying to protect the country after the Panchen Lama died in 1937. In September 1939 Dai held a Buddhist Ceremony to Protect the Country and Avert Disaster (*Huguo xiaozai fahui*) in Chengdu. The ceremony lasted forty-nine days, during which scriptures were recited.[118]In November he wrote verses praising the esoteric *Scripture for Humane Kings Who Wish to Protect Their States* (*Renwang huguo jing*), as he would do again two years later.[119] In 1942 President Lin Sen himself sponsored a dharma-assembly, putting Dai Jitao in charge.[120] Dai wrote a prayer for this forty-nine-day "Great Compassion Ceremony to Protect the Country and Eliminate Disaster" (*Huguo xiaozai da bei daochang*) but delegated the ritual duties to one of the most prominent Chinese Buddhists of the day, the monk Xuyun.[121] The biography of the Changja Qutughtu claimed that he had been invited to participate in both these rituals,[122] but Dai's contemporary writings do not confirm his presence.[123]

Once again, although the original model of this ceremony was carried over from the pattern established by the Tibetan lamas in China, the Chinese had taken charge of the rituals.

The final burst of Tibetan Buddhist activity in the Republican period occurred after the end of the Sino-Japanese War and lasted into the Communist period. Probably this last efflorescence reflected a concern over the civil war between the Nationalists and the Communists, and the hope that esoteric Buddhism could help. That Tibetan Buddhist practice, even without the presence of important lamas, was still valued at this late date demonstrates how much Tibetan Buddhism had become a part of the Chinese cultural world. In 1946 a Chinese monastery in Chengdu held a dharma-assembly for peace (*heping fahui*) and invited Nenghai to lecture on the scriptures for the event. Each day three thousand to four thousand people attended, roughly the same number of people associated with Dorjé Chöpa's 1931 assembly in Chengdu.[124] This event illustrated the remarkable change that had taken place in the intervening years. Not only had a Chinese mastered Tibetan Buddhism but the Chinese people also accepted one of their own as sufficiently skilled in Tibetan Buddhism to deserve the same attention as a "genuine" Tibetan. This may not seem a very remarkable point to those unfamiliar with Tibetan Buddhism in the West, but today in America no Western practitioner or student of Tibetan Buddhism can command nearly the same popularity as a recognized Tibetan lama.

Nenghai's Network of Buddhist Centers

Nenghai was also able to institutionalize his indigenized Tibetan Buddhism with the support of lay Buddhists in some of China's largest urban centers. First, in 1947 Chongqing Buddhists invited Nenghai to establish a Hall of the Vajra Way (Jingang daochang), which remained active until around 1956.[125] When he was in Beijing in 1948 Nenghai taught at established Buddhist study centers that had an ongoing interest in Tibetan Buddhism.[126] While living in Shanghai in 1949 Nenghai established a third Hall of the Vajra Way, which also remained active until the mid-fifties.[127] I suspect that these Chinese centers for Tibetan Buddhist practice were tolerated into the Communist era mainly to preserve appearances as the Communists consolidated their hold on Tibet. As tensions between Chinese and Tibetans culminated in 1958 in open rebellion in the Tibetan regions of Kham and Amdo (located mainly in Sichuan and Qinghai provinces), these halls vanish from the record. As one of the vice directors of the Chinese Buddhist Association, Nenghai no doubt had some advanced warning of where things were headed. Already by 1953 he had set up a fourth and final Hall of the Way in an isolated mountainside temple at Mount Wutai. This was his last refuge, where he would

Photo 7.4 Nenghai Lama teaching at his Hall of the Vajra Way at Jiexiang Temple, Mount Wutai, from the 1956 government publication *Buddhists in New China*

die in 1966, but a second generation of disciples continue to transmit Tibetan Buddhism to Chinese monks and laity there today.[128]

Organizational Linkage

The final innovative element linking Chinese and Tibetan Buddhist culture was the regular inclusion of Tibetan Buddhists in modern Chinese Buddhist organizations. The Changja Qutughtu had played a minor role in early Chinese Buddhist Associations but really became a key figure in the planning of such organizations dating from discussions he had had with Taixu in 1938 in Chengdu. Aside from minimal efforts at protecting Buddhist property, active official support for the nationwide organization of Buddhists was not forthcoming until 1945, when Taixu and the Changja Qutughtu were appointed to lead the Committee for the Reorganization of Chinese Buddhism. This committee founded the Nanjing-based Chinese Buddhist Association in May 1947. More than simply a shell organization to deal with passing threats to Buddhist property, as its predecessors of the same name had been, this association had government backing and branches down to the county level. When Taixu died that

March, the Changja Qutughtu was made the leader, "partly because of the importance the government then attached to consolidating relations with Tibet."[129] This was the first time since the Yuan dynasty that a Tibetan Buddhist had been actively in charge of a government office to oversee all Buddhists in China.[130] However, this was a short-lived phenomenon, which would be renewed under the Communists. In 1949 Liu Wenhui tried to persuade the Changja Qutughtu to stay in China, but he had thrown his lot in with the Nationalists and went to Taiwan. The reincarnation series seems to have nearly ended there with his death and has only been revived recently in India.[131]

In addition, Sherap Gyatso became a leader in various "borderland societies" such as the China Association for the Promotion of Border Culture and the Association for the Promotion of Tibetan Culture. Although he appears to have accepted titles from the Chinese government between 1947 and 1949, including the vice chairmanship of the Mongolian and Tibetan Affairs Commission, he apparently no longer had much enthusiasm for these offices.[132] In the end, Sherap Gyatso was less cooperative with the Republican government than the Panchen Lama had been. He was openly critical of the Nationalist government's frontier policies and explained that, "the main reason the Tibet problem cannot be completely resolved is because the center [*zhongyang*, referring to the Nationalist government] does not understand Tibet's internal conditions, but [mistakenly] thinks that it understands them very well."[133]

The Chinese effort to use, or rely on, Tibetan Buddhists as a means of influencing and trying to understand Tibet continued under the Communist regime. Sherap Gyatso played a prominent role in the invasion of Tibet, broadcasting the pending "liberation" on the radio and promising "religious freedom and respect for monasteries." The new Panchen Lama's entourage also quickly attached itself to the Communist government.[134] When the Central Tibetans were negotiating a settlement with the Communist authorities, they indicated the importance of maintaining relations through Buddhist intermediaries. One of their minimum requirements for agreeing that Tibet was part of China was that the "Chinese representative [to Tibet] must be Buddhist."[135] Based on an anonymous interview, Melvyn Goldstein has written that part of the effort to win over Tibetans includes the fact that Mao, in 1951, told a Chinese Communist Party official that, "when he arrived in Lhasa and met with the Dalai Lama he should prostrate before the Dalai Lama in accordance with Tibetan custom."[136] At the conclusion of the Seventeen-Point Agreement in 1951 many Tibetans were satisfied that their cultural and religious life had been safeguarded and therefore felt "that Communist China and Buddhist Tibet could co-exist peacefully."[137] The Communists were quite willing to agree to these conditions in order to secure Tibetan acquiescence to legally defining Tibet as part of China.

Moreover, by 1953, when the Communist Party decided to reconstitute the

Chinese Buddhist Association (the one formed in 1947 had followed the Nationalists to Taiwan), the importance of Tibetan Buddhists in the association had been embraced as party policy for two reasons. First, the association's stated goal, that all Buddhists in new China would serve the interests of the motherland, was again colored by Taixu's ideas: "to link up Buddhists from different parts of the country; and to exemplify the best traditions of Buddhism."[138] Second, the Tibetan presence in the association would give a good impression of the religious freedom in Tibet when the association's representatives traveled abroad or when visitors came to China. As the new association was a government-sponsored organization with no lower branches to supervise, one of its principle functions was to represent Chinese (now including Tibetan) Buddhism to the international community. In the Republic the Changja Qutughtu had been the only lama to play a major role in the Chinese Buddhist associations. When the association was reorganized under the Communists, Tibetans formed almost 30 percent of the ninety-three-person council. Both the Panchen and the Dalai Lamas were designated honorary presidents. Furthermore, when the Chinese president of the association died within four months of the inauguration in 1953, Sherap Gyatso was made the new president and remained in this position until 1964.[139] In this capacity he toured Buddhist countries in Southeast Asia in the 1950s and served as one of China's representatives at the international celebration of the twenty-five hundredth anniversary of the Buddha's death in 1956.[140] This Buddhist diplomacy was featured prominently in a bilingual (Chinese/English) pictorial publication issued in 1956, as well as in later releases of English language surveys of Buddhism in China produced with state support.[141]

At the same time the most prominent Chinese monks who had adopted Tibetan Buddhism, Nenghai and Fazun, also continued to play significant roles in Buddhist and political institutions. Nenghai had come to Beijing in 1950 to discuss with Sherap Gyatso the problem of "liberating" Tibet and was selected as the vice president of the Chinese Buddhist Association at its inauguration in 1953. While still in Sichuan, Nenghai had lectured on Tibet to the Southwest Army and his disciple Longguo served as a translator for this army.[142] Nenghai was also one of the only Chinese Buddhists selected as a representative to two National People's Congresses (in 1954 and 1955). Meanwhile, Fazun worked first in the People's Publishing House and, upon the founding of the Chinese Buddhist College in 1956, he was made vice principal of the school.[143] Although he was forced to do physical labor at the age of sixty-four during the Cultural Revolution, he survived this trial and was cleared of charges in 1972. However, he never recovered from this period and remained ill until his death. Nevertheless, when the Chinese Buddhist College was reopened in 1980, Fazun was made principal of the college. That same year he was also present at the opening of the fourth national conference of the Chinese Buddhist Association (the last one had been held in 1962). He died before the conference was over, in December 1980.[144]

Thus Tibetan Buddhists, whether ethnically Chinese or Tibetan, continued to play prominent roles in institutional Buddhism under the Communists. The first generation of Chinese monks to study and popularize Tibetan Buddhism has now vanished from the scene, but this generation's disciples, the books that were translated, as well as the direct contact these Chinese monks had with Tibetan Buddhist teachers have inspired a continued interest in Tibetan Buddhism among the Chinese. Although the work of Fazun and Nenghai in Sichuan and later in northern China may be responsible for much of this interest, the renewed prominence of Tibet in Chinese newspapers and a new freedom to travel within China have also led many monks and lay Buddhists from the stronghold of Chinese Buddhism in central eastern China to seek instruction from Tibetan monks, especially in Kham.[145] The growth of Chinese interest in and interaction with Tibetan Buddhists has been enormous in the past few years. Whether the authorities will permit this trend to continue remains to be seen. However, at least for now it is clear that once again this growing interest is of a personal and religious nature.

While the Chinese Communist government continues to be involved with the selection of suitable reincarnations for prominent lamas and the extensive propaganda war that has accompanied such affairs in recent years, there does not seem to be a conscious plan for using Buddhism to link Chinese and Tibetan cultures under the Communist regime. Possibly the Communists want to limit Chinese citizens' involvement with the Tibetan Buddhist religion only to those essential elements necessary for maintaining stability in Tibet—overseeing the selection of important incarnations, regulating the monasteries, and keeping the monks and nuns from becoming involved in anti-Chinese activities. In today's China it is possible that the government may be less concerned with the religious interactions of the different Buddhist communities in China precisely because of the successes the Communist government has had in truly linking Chinese and Tibetan cultures. In this respect the Nationalist government's gradual adoption of a policy of linking Tibetan and Chinese cultures marked the beginning of a new strategy in China's efforts at maintaining control of Tibet. Yet the lay sponsorship and activities that launched this interest in the 1920s is reflected in the revival of Chinese interest in Tibetan Buddhism that is observable in contemporary China. Although the Cultural Revolution dealt a severe blow to the Chinese and Tibetan monks who led the cross-cultural exchanges into the 1950s, their students and institutional influences have survived the Cultural Revolution and are again active today.

Postscript

I BELIEVE that this history is relevant to contemporary affairs. But, first, a caveat: I do not think that the history I have described here in any way justifies what has happened in Tibet since 1950. The current Chinese occupation of Tibet and the ongoing colonization cannot be justified on any basis I can see, with the exception that might makes right. And although the Chinese government may try to insert this study into a discourse that validates its control of Tibet, it would do so at the peril of revealing challenges to the tidy narrative it has presented thus far.

On the other hand, the version of Tibetan history that most Westerners know is also overly simplistic. In the early twentieth century certain Tibetans were not happy with affairs in Tibet and sought Chinese aid or assistance in changing them; others felt that union with China presented the best option for Tibet, or at least the part of Tibet with which they were most concerned, in the modern world. If we in the West, or Tibetans in exile in India, continue to deny this past, we will continue to be confused by those Tibetans still living in Tibet who work with the Chinese every day. Tibetans—despite the otherworldly image that some have of them—are people. As such, they are motivated by the same interests as other people around the world: ideological (religious or national or both) and economic (personal or local or both), to name the ones I address most directly. The Chinese people, despite often being seen by some sympathetic to the Tibetan cause as synonymous with the Chinese government—one which does not even represent them democratically—also have a wider variety of ideological and economic motivations than those for which they are often given credit. It has been my goal to shed light on some of these motivations and the impact they have had on Chinese and Tibetan interaction and relations.

I did not come to this topic as a historian seeking an interesting problem about which to write. Before I became a historian, I saw the problem through my experiences as an American exposed to both the Washington, D.C.–based public relations campaign about Tibet in the late 1980s and to the peculiarly insulated world of Chinese propaganda about Tibet in the early 1990s. I turned to history to try to explain the disjuncture in the rhetoric I encountered in these two worlds. My experiences convinced me that neither the Chinese nor the Tibetan versions of Chinese and Tibetan relations adequately reflected either the contemporary state of affairs or the history of these relations.

For this reason I hope that the audiences most exposed to the rival propaganda versions of this history read and reflect on the Chinese and Tibetan contact that I have recounted here, which is simply the tip of an iceberg of unmined historical interaction. If I had to label the audiences I most hope to reach, I would call one "the Tibetan sympathizers in the West" (including prominent personalities, politicians, Students for a Free Tibet, and even some Chinese dissidents). Another would be the Tibetans in exile, who often know as little about these historic relations as the Western sympathizers, because Tibetan agency in the events described here does not fit the image of victimization that is the hallmark of Tibetan nationalist accounts of Chinese aggression. I also hope to reach Chinese (both inside and outside China) who are so blinded by a nationalist version of history that they do not even recognize the Tibet issue as a problem worth addressing. I suggest that their ignoring China's occupation of Tibet, particularly the suppression of revolt in the late 1950s, is comparable to contemporary Japanese ignoring or denying the significance of the Japanese invasion of China, particularly the events in Nanjing. The scholarly audience for this work will, I hope, find this study interesting for its reflections on the role of race, nationalism, and religion in the modern world.

This history is also important because the issue of Tibet is linked intimately with the place of religion in modern China. The Chinese government, since the collapse of belief in Communist ideology after the Cultural Revolution, must deal with a return of interest in religious ideologies. Falungong is just the latest of these perceived threats. Deng Xiaoping's campaign against "Spiritual Pollution," although directed against secular Western "moral failings" such as hedonism in art and lifestyle, actually took place in the context of a renewed interest in religion in China in the early 1980s.

The beginnings of this phenomenon, which has grown dramatically since Deng's reforms in 1978, are well illustrated in *Red Dust,* the biographical account of the contemporary Chinese artist and writer Ma Jian. Ma Jian's interest in Buddhism was linked to a fascination with China's ethnic minorities and, in particular, with Tibet. For instance, Ma mentioned that he took Buddhist vows in Beijing before he started his cross-country journey both to escape arrest for being "spiritually polluted" and in search of religious liberation, especially through Tibetan Buddhism. When he reached Lhasa, he told a fellow Tibetophile

Chinese, "I came as a pilgrim. I was hoping for revelation." When he meets a "living buddha" he explains, "I became a Buddhist because I thought that the world was full of pain and the Buddha offered a path to freedom. I was rebelling against the Party and all it stood for."[1] Although at times his interests and those of his friends sound more like the American New Age interest in Native Americans, their desperate search for meaning in a world where Communism no longer holds to its ideals does accurately reflect the experience of many Chinese. And Ma Jian's story also reflects the enduring influence of the critical figures of the Republican period who survived into the Communist era. Ma's teacher in Beijing was Master Zhengguo (1913–1987), who studied and then taught at the Sino-Tibetan Buddhist Institute in Chongqing until it closed in 1949. In the early eighties, when Ma would have received his vows, the teacher was starting to address the needs of a new generation of Buddhist youth.[2]

A few anecdotes from my own experiences in contemporary China may also help to illustrate the return of interest in Tibetan Buddhism to a level not seen since the Republican period. My research on this topic started with examining the presence of Tibetan Buddhists in and around Beijing, including the Buddhist mountain, Mount Wutai. Travel to Beijing and Mount Wutai in 1993, 1997, and 1999 allowed me to observe a dramatic growth in the interest in Buddhism, and especially in institutions associated with Tibetan Buddhism. Third- and fourth-generation disciples of the Chinese lama Nenghai were active at Mount Wutai, using Fazun's translation of Gelukpa texts to practice and teach Tibetan Buddhism to a new generation. Most dramatic was the interest of well-educated youth, similar to Ma Jian, in becoming monks and nuns in the late 1990s. At the same time wealthy older Chinese were demonstrating a willingness to financially support Tibetan Buddhist learning and culture by drawing talented teachers, doctors, painters, and sculptors from Tibetan regions to China Proper.[3] Throughout China, but most surprisingly on the east coast of China, monasteries led by Nenghai's disciples were reviving to meet this Chinese interest in Tibetan Buddhist teaching and practice. Thus, when I traveled with a Tibetan Buddhist monk around China in 1997 and 1999, he would often be invited to stay in or, if unable, to return to a particular city to teach a lay or monastic community interested in Tibetan Buddhism. Similarly, on trains, many people—from college students to bank tellers—expressed an avid interest in learning some Buddhist teachings from my friend. This interest in Tibetan Buddhism, even among the mainstream Chinese Buddhists in Jiangnan, has been repeatedly confirmed by a leading scholar of Buddhism in modern China, Raoul Birnbaum, whose research trips regularly bring him into contact with the leading lights of these communities.[4]

What does all this interest mean? It is difficult to say for certain, as this is still a relatively new phenomenon. The Chinese government can look at this revival of interest in religion, and Tibetan Buddhism in particular, as a challenge or as an opportunity. One researcher at Beijing's Chinese Research Center for Tibetology (Zhongguo Zangxue yanjiu zhongxin) has spent the last few years studying Western interest in Tibetan Buddhism. Although there are obvious reasons that the Chinese government, which directs research at such institutes, would want this phenomenon in the West studied for international reasons, government officials may also be trying to understand what is happening domestically on the basis of this research. Perhaps the government will find that such interest in Tibetan Buddhism merely reflects one aspect of the diversity of interests in an open society (the so-called marketplace of religions) and that this is no threat to the state.

From the exiled Tibetan perspective, the willingness of some Tibetans to continue to teach Tibetan Buddhism to the Chinese may be looked at as evidence of collaboration. Already many young Tibetans educated at modern, secular schools both in exile and in China tend to blame Buddhism for having weakened Tibet to the point of allowing China to take over the country. These largely secular nationalists usually do not publicly criticize religion in the West and may even outwardly embrace some trappings of the religion. However, their interests and methods (especially the recommendation of violence as a solution) do not overlap with the religious leadership of either lamas still in Tibet or the Dalai Lama.

Contemporary Tibetans are in a bind. Buddhism concurrently is blamed for losing Tibet to China and yet is heralded as the hallmark of Tibetan nationalism that holds the people together, both in exile and in the face of Chinese colonial dominance and population transfer. Since the revival of religious freedom and the return of a popular nationalist movement in Tibet in the 1980s, many monks and nuns have strongly linked religion and nationalism. This is a dramatic shift from a century before, when the monks of Tengyeling sided with Qing forces and sheltered the Chinese in Lhasa. But rather than try to place blame, either on the past or present actors, I have tried to understand and communicate why and how Chinese and Tibetan Buddhists—monks, teachers, laypeople, and politicians—all engaged with the modern forces of race, religion, and nationalism to try to advance their various ideological and economic interests.

The Legacy of the Past

In human society the role of ideology as a binding force can hardly be exaggerated. For nation-states, compared to the empires that preceded them, ideology plays an even more visible and deliberate role. Benedict Anderson has argued that the basis of nationalism is the ability to imagine a community and that this is largely a modern phenomenon. Anthony Smith, rightly I think, emphasizes the importance of past ideas of identity, which are articulated and adapted in the modern circumstances of the nation-state. I see both of these theories of nationalism as valuable in assessing the history and recent developments in the relations between Chinese and Tibetans. With the fall of the Qing empire, its constituent parts had to be reconfigured. For most Tibetans and Mongolians, and even for some Chinese such as Zhang Binglin, this meant that the non-Chinese former dependencies of the empire should go their separate ways. However, as China Proper became united under one leadership that gradually resolved the internal problems of China, nationalist Chinese expressed the will to overcome what they saw as the humiliation of the imperialist partition of the former empire, now identified with modern China in their minds—never mind that the Qing empire had obviously been an imperialist power in its own right. Yet until the internal divisions in China were fully resolved, the weakened state was forced to rely more on ideological arguments and persuasion than military force to accomplish its goals on the former Qing frontiers. And as I have argued, the development of an ideology of pan-Asian Buddhism by the Republican Chinese government was eminently useful to the Communist state in its effort to exercise the military power they commanded after taking control of China.

Although ethnic Tibetan Buddhists figure prominently in my writing, this book is equally focused on China and the Chinese. How did the Chinese—especially government officials, Buddhist laymen, and monks—try to convince themselves, the international community, and the Tibetans that Tibet was a part of China? Three modern ideologies were deployed in this effort: racial unity, nationalism, and, finally, unity through a "global religion," Buddhism. The first two ideologies were successful only among the Chinese and had little resonance for the Tibetans, even the few who were directly exposed to these ideas through living in China. Instead, the ideas of racial unity and nationalism were most effective in convincing the Chinese leaders and educated (indoctrinated?) Chinese public that Tibet was indeed a part of China.

Ideas of racial unity were adopted by Yuan Shi-kai from the 1912 Qing dynastic abdication agreement and advocated through the first third of the twentieth century. And once the Manchus were displaced, Chinese revolutionaries such as Sun Yat-sen were willing to accept this idea. Sun was then ready to argue that all five races were part of the Yellow Race, which the Chinese would lead in the new era. Yet this idea of racial unity advocated by Chinese to keep the Qing imperial territories together was hardly communicated to the Tibetans at all. The earliest surviving translation of Sun Yat-sen's work into Tibetan dates from 1944, and even this was an abbreviated version, and the bearer of these political tracts was turned back at the Tibetan border.[5] Only Tibetans who came to China were exposed to this rhetoric. But to reach China they passed through war-torn regions, where Muslims, Chinese, and Tibetans were often slaughtering one another with incredible brutality, so such ideas were hardly convincing. The racial rhetoric of unity instead served only to assure the Chinese of their right to rule the far-flung regions of the former empire; they saw themselves as the overwhelming majority. Yet, in the face of ethnic conflict, this idea did nothing practical to hold the empire together. These days racial discourse used to link the ethnic groups within China is more likely to employ "science" than myth. For instance, according to one Chinese scientist, "estimations of genetic distance based on gene frequency are claimed to have established that the racial differences between population groups living within China—including Tibetans, Mongols, and Uighurs—are comparatively small."[6] In a world where the genetic difference between humans and chimpanzees is now recognized to be comparatively small (less than 2 percent) this statement means little. Yet these and other pseudo-scientific ideas are propounded to serve state interests.[7]

Similarly, nationalist ideology was more effective in convincing the Chinese that their new state included Tibet than it ever was in getting the Tibetans to join the Chinese Republic; that is, the real success of nationalism was to convince Chinese, through the media and through educational indoctrination, that Tibet—like the other dependencies of the former Qing empire—was a natural and necessary part of the Chinese nation-state. But nationalist ideology could not bind Tibetans to the Chinese, largely because the Chinese controlled neither media (there effectively was none) nor education in Tibet. At most, Tibetans trained in this modern ideology sought Chinese support for autonomy, much as Chinese (both Nationalists and Communists) sought Soviet aid in establishing the Chinese party-state. Yet the failure of the Chinese Nationalist Party to truly support Tibetan autonomy doomed even the few feeble attempts at Chinese Nationalist–i nspired plots that materialized on the frontiers of Tibet.

With the failure to unite Chinese and Tibetans through racial or nationalist ideologies, the only option left to the Chinese seeking to include Tibet as part of the modern Chinese nation was the idea of Buddhism as a shared religion between the Chinese and the Tibetans. But this approach would require overcoming the long tradition of differentiating Chinese from Tibetan Buddhism. Yet even before the state was prepared to grapple with the problem (as they saw it) of Tibetan independence, some Chinese Buddhists already had been reaching out to Tibetan Buddhists as co-religionists. This initiative grew out of the movement of global religious ideas, marked by the 1893 Parliament of World Religions in Chicago. The idea that Buddhism was a unified world religion, first put forth in academic circles and then adopted as a political expedient, gave the Chinese a new way to connect with Tibetans and try to encompass them in a unified imagined political community.

Dai Jitao was the first politician to argue, in the early 1930s, that Buddhism was the critical link between China and Tibet. Dai became a disciple of the Panchen Lama, through esoteric rituals. He successfully campaigned for three Tibetan Buddhist lamas to be recognized as "protectors of the country" and even as state officials, with stipends and offices. Moreover, Chiang Kai-shek presided over ceremonies that honored these lamas with officials posts. President Lin Sen, also a Buddhist, hosted rituals and teachings in the halls of government. Some Tibetan Buddhist events drew tens of thousands of Chinese, causing one magazine to joke that Tibetan Buddhism should be declared the national religion. Eventually these three lamas were made "propaganda envoys" for Chinese unity with Inner Asia.

Starting with the decisions of key politicians to participate in and support Tibetan Buddhism, a rhetoric of Buddhist unity with Tibet and the measures to demonstrate the reality of this rhetoric became official government policy. Once the thirteenth Dalai Lama, as the leader of an independent Tibet, died in 1933, the Chinese government sent a Buddhist general on a mission to Tibet to advocate for this religious unity. With the full financial support of the Chinese government, he was able to donate 400,000 silver dollars to Tibetan monasteries and leaders, and he promised that the political and religious system would not be altered if Tibet united with China. In 1937, as the Japanese pressed the Chinese seat of government into retreat near the frontier with Tibet, the national government funded a Tibetan Buddhist academy in Sichuan. This pre–Cold War, regional studies institute trained monks and cadres to cultivate Buddhist links with Tibet. Then, when the Japanese cut the Burma road for supplying war materials to the Chinese government, a Buddhist was sent as an envoy to Tibet to try to open a second road through Tibet. Chiang Kai-shek even treated the present Dalai Lama's brother like a son while he received a modern secular education in China.[8] This man still serves as middleman with the Chinese today. In other words, the Chinese government consistently made the case that Chinese and Tibetans were Buddhist co-religionists and that Buddhism was respected and supported by their government.

The Communists continued this strategy and picked up support from lamas in exile in China when the Nationalists fled to Taiwan. They worked closely with Tibetan Buddhists—both ethnic Tibetans and Chinese—to devise a successful strategy to incorporate Tibet into China and succeeded where the Nationalists had failed for decades. No doubt their military force was critical in this success, but Tibetan acquiescence to a negotiated agreement was also central in denying the United States a public opening to assist the Tibetans in resisting the Chinese

Communists. And this Tibetan acquiescence was at least partially influenced, however misguidedly, by both the rhetoric and the reality of a Buddhist connection with China that had been cultivated over the preceding several decades.

Thus the ideology of global religions, especially of Buddhism, was critical to shaping the international politics of the relations of China and Tibet. Yet ideology does not exist or develop in a vacuum. Historic agents and actors must create, adapt, and ultimately embrace or defeat an ideology to demonstrate its effect in the world. With the demise of the Qing empire at the beginning of the twentieth century, the Chinese tried, without success, to incorporate all the former empire's territory, including Tibet. At the same time the Tibetan Buddhist political elite had some success in their effort to establish Tibet as an independent modern nation-state. The creation of these modern nation-states led Chinese and Tibetans to actively engage in political and cultural relations with each other for the first time in recent history. When political relations between the elite leadership of these two nations broke down, interactions were still sustained through cultural connections. These interactions were dependent on two marginalized groups—Chinese Buddhists at odds with a secular Chinese state and Tibetan Buddhist leaders at odds with the centralizing religious Tibetan nation-state—both seeking to utilize their intermediary position between the two ethnic groups to retain their status in a changing world. Through their willingness to adapt to modern conditions, these individuals provided an important link between the Chinese and Tibetan political elite. Ultimately they assisted the Chinese government in its incorporation of Tibet, with Buddhist culture as the link where national and racial ideologies had failed.

The central thesis of this book is that Buddhism was the key factor in maintaining a tenuous link between China and Tibet during the Republican period (1912–1949), a link the Communists could exploit when exerting control over Tibet by force in the 1950s. For this reason I argue that Buddhist religious culture played an essential role in the formation of the modern Chinese nation-state. The majority of this book has been devoted to understanding the efforts of Buddhists and politicians to integrate Buddhist culture with modern Chinese politics. I have argued that the politicians did not merely "use" Buddhism to pursue their own goals but that the Buddhists themselves also sought to engage with contemporary political realities, to "use" politics to pursue *their* goals.

Echoes of Imperialism

A comparison between the strategies of the Qing empire and those of the modern Chinese nation in negotiating the relations with Tibetan Buddhists demonstrates a remarkable continuity between these periods. Yet there were also important innovations in the Republican era. Tibetan Buddhists actively participated in national politics through unprecedented methods, which included holding public religious rituals or lecture series, addressing the media, and taking secular political offices. At the same time Chinese politicians transformed the religious offices of the former Qing empire into modern political institutions such as diplomatic and propaganda offices staffed by Tibetan Buddhists. Chinese Buddhists—in an effort to prove themselves useful to the modern Chinese nation—assisted in this process by providing an important pool of religiously trained specialists who could link Tibetan and Chinese religious cultures. Thus the process of Buddhists attempting to adapt to modernity led them to an engagement with politics. This ultimately resulted in an incorporation of Tibetan Buddhist culture into the educational and political institutions of China.

My purpose in investigating this topic was to explore an early period in which some Tibetans and Chinese were willing to work together on cultural projects, some with obvious political implications, in the face of the political tensions that existed between the two nations. My research has yielded new knowledge about Chinese and Tibetan interaction, which occurred both with and without government sponsorship in the Republican period, particularly the process whereby the modernization of Sino-Tibetan relations led to Tibetan Buddhist education becoming institutionalized as part of the Chinese state. I argue that the new institutions developed by the Buddhist responses to modernity eventually made it possible for Tibetan Buddhist culture to be partially incorporated into the educational structure of the People's Republic of China. In addition, my work illuminates the origin of patterns that have continued to the present day in the institutions that now manage religious and educational exchanges between Chinese and Tibetans, such as Beijing's Central University for Nationalities as well as the Chinese Buddhist Association and its Tibetan affiliates.

Based on my research in early twentieth-century Chinese and Tibetan relations, I suggest that state support for Tibetan Buddhism has been and will continue to be the crucial factor in managing Chinese and Tibetan relations. With the exception of the Cultural Revolution, even the Chinese Communist government has recognized the continuing importance of Buddhism in maintaining Tibet as a viable part of the Chinese nation-state. In an effort to deflect international criticism of human rights and religious freedom violations in Tibet, the government has tried to demonstrate that Tibetan culture, essentially a Buddhist culture, is thriving under Chinese rule. Most recently the Chinese Communist Party—an avowedly atheistic regime—has been forced to try to build its legitimacy by authorizing children as reincarnated lamas.

Why is the atheistic government of China involving itself in the controversial issues of authorizing Tibetan Buddhist reincarnations fifty years after forcibly annexing Tibet? The Communists may have felt that raising a generation of Tibetans without religion during the Cultural Revolution would put an end to the need to work with and through the religious elite, but the revival of Buddhism in the period of reforms made it clear they were wrong. The Chinese Communists, like the Republic's Nationalists before them, have found that Tibet can only really be ruled through religion. The Public Security Bureau and the People's Liberation Army can control Tibet, but the religious authority of numerous lamas, such as the current Panchen Lama, is of desperate importance to the Communist Party. Contemporary Chinese government policies toward Tibet include not just the overt political processes, such as governmental recognition of certain lamas, but also the more subtle aspects of cultural interaction: the roles of Tibetan Buddhists in official Buddhist organizations of China, of Chinese monastic adherents of Tibetan Buddhism as leaders of Chinese Buddhist academies, and of Chinese and Tibetan scholars in promoting the state's efforts to integrate Tibetan religious culture within a more broadly defined Chinese culture.

Since the reform era that followed the end of the Cultural Revolution, the government has permitted certain Sino-Tibetan institutions to reopen. For instance, although Sherap Gyatso died as a result of abuse inflicted during the Cultural Revolution, in 1981 his school was rededicated by the tenth Panchen Lama, Chökyi Gyentsen (1938–1989).[9] Nevertheless, without direct government support, the school has never returned to its former stature (some two hundred students in the 1940s) and hovers around eighty students, who receive a rather inadequate education.[10] Similarly, Nenghai's efforts at encouraging modern Sino-Tibetan education have not been entirely dismantled, despite his death during the Cultural Revolution. Temples at Mount Wutai, including the site of his last school, continue to train Chinese monks in a combination of Chinese and Tibetan scriptures (in Chinese translation). Moreover, Nenghai's monastic school at Jinci Temple outside Chengdu is undergoing a kind of renewal under the direction of a Tibetan lama and his Chinese and Tibetan disciples. In the early 1980s one of Nenghai's best-known students, a nun named Longlian, started a modern school for nuns (Sichuan Nizhong Foxueyuan) just opposite Jinci Temple. The government, especially through the Chinese Buddhist Association, encouraged this school, the first of its kind for nuns' higher education in China.[11] Also in Sichuan in the early 1990s, the Tibetan Language University of Eastern Tibet moved south to Dartsedo (Kangding), the site of Republican-era modern Tibetan educational institutions.[12]

As for central government support for Buddhist education, Tibetan Buddhism has continued to be a top priority. The Chinese Buddhist College was reopened in 1980 with Fazun as its principal. In the fall of 1987 China's Tibetan Language division of the Higher Buddhist Studies Institute (Ch. Zhongguo Zangyu xi gaoji Foxue yuan, Tib. Krung go Bod brgyud mtho rim nang bstan slob gling) opened at Beijing's Xihuang si (Western Yellow Temple) with encouragement from the tenth Panchen Lama.[13] This monastic school is charged with training all the young Tibetan Buddhist incarnations born in China and, to this end, has compiled a series of introductory textbooks for all the Tibetan religious traditions.[14] According to Tsering Shakya, the Communist "authorities announced that the main task of the college was to produce 'patriotic lamas who would cherish the unity of the motherland.'"[15] Similar developments have taken place in the field of secular institutions for studying Tibet in China.

Most recently the Chinese government has articulated its intentions to utilize the academic study of Tibetan culture in China to try to influence world opinion about the situation in Tibet. This effort does not emphasize Buddhism as did many of the Republican Chinese cross-cultural schools, but Buddhism is, of course, an important topic of Tibetan studies, even in China. Once again, Sichuan Province is serving as an important middle ground for cultural exchange, this time under national (Communist) government direction: "In 2000 the China Institute for Tibetan Studies was established in Chengdu, Sichuan, to be jointly run by Sichuan and Tibet Universities and receiving an annual research grant of 300,000 *yuan* (U.S.$36,390) from the Chinese Ministry of Education."[16] When I attended the second international Tibetan Studies conference at Beijing's Chinese Research Center for Tibetology in 1999, I was able to directly observe efforts to influence and manipulate international scholarly opinion. The recent visits of Chinese Tibetologists to Harvard in the spring of 2002 were also apparently an outgrowth of this strategy.[17]

On other fronts some of the novel practical and rhetorical strategies for demonstrating the usefulness of Buddhism during the Republican period continue to be employed today. As before, the Buddhist interest in offering protection and assistance is equally deployed by lay and monastic communities as well as government-backed Buddhist leaders. For instance, Chinese and Tibetan Buddhists are still participating in efforts to relieve the people and the country of disasters. During the floods of 1998, which made international news because of their severity, "the Mount Wutai Buddhist circles held a great dharma-assembly to eliminate disasters and relieve the people scourged by natural disaster."[18] The monks and nuns collected more than 200,000 *yuan* (roughly U.S.$25,000) and 130 sets of clothing, while the attending peoples' donations totaled more than 350,000 *yuan* (U.S.$42,000). The officially approved Buddhist journal, *Fayin* (*Voice of the Dharma*), also reported that the child recognized by the Chinese authorities as the eleventh Panchen Lama, and kept under their strict control, donated money to disaster areas.[19] In fact, the very language of "Protecting the Country and Benefiting the People" (*Huguo limin*) that was carried over from imperial times to the Republican period has resurfaced in modern Tibetan art depicting the latest Panchen Lama incarnation.[20]

Reminiscent of Taixu's textual approach to linking Chinese and Tibetan cultures, the "*goutong*" rhetoric of "linking Han and Tibetan Buddhism" was recently resurrected in *Fayin*.[21] The journal's English translation of one article's title renders "*goutong*" as "communication." The Tibetan author, Samdrup Trashi, discussed the historical "communication" between Chinese and Tibetans with reference to the literary work of Mongol and Mongour Tibetan Buddhists in the Qing dynasty. At the same time he expressed an interest in making Chinese Buddhist history and scriptures available to Tibetans through translations and a Tibetan language history of Chinese Buddhism.[22] Some fifty years after Taixu's death a Tibetan was finally expressing a desire to fill in the gaps of Tibetan knowledge of Chinese Buddhism similar to that which Taixu and his Chinese monastic students had felt about expanding their knowledge of Tibetan Buddhism.

These elements of continuity with the Republican era are rarely covered in Western media, which has focused on the more aggressive development designs of the Chinese government. Reminiscent of the 1930s drive to open and develop Kham and Tibet (*kaifa Kang Zang*), the recent Western Development Program has generated resistance by Tibetans in Tibet and by their international supporters. As an alternative to pursuing grand new ventures such as railroads into Tibet and poorly planned World Bank–style development projects, the policy of respect and support for Tibetan Buddhism initiated in the Republican era and continued into the early Communist period, as well as elements of similar practices today, may point to a more successful policy that the Chinese could adopt in the current era. Some Tibetans have long hoped for the disintegration of the Chinese state, and America's Central Intelligence Agency supported their efforts to undermine Chinese authority in Tibet until 1969. The Chinese Communist authorities now view Tibetan expressions of discontent as necessarily linked to a separatist movement designed to "split Tibet from the motherland." Rather than hoping for or fearing such an unlikely division, both Tibetans and Chinese—as well as the international community—might instead seek to concentrate on the positive outcomes desired by all parties. Tibetans want genuine autonomy, especially in the realm of religion, and the Chinese want an end to the separatist threat. The positive cultural interactions between Chinese and Tibetans during the Republican and even early Communist periods demonstrate the potential benefits of returning to a policy of guaranteeing real religious freedom and respect for Tibetan Buddhist culture to help resolve the current conflict.

Appendix 1. Institutions Associated with Tibetan Buddhism in China

YEAR STARTED OR (FIRST REFERENCE)	PLACE	NAME	FOUNDER(S) OR TEACHER
1922	Wuchang	Buddhist Studies Institute (Wuchang Foxueyuan)	Taixu
1924	Beijing	Buddhist Institute for the Study of the Tibetan Language (Fojiao Zangwen xueyuan)	Dayong, Hu Zihu
1925	Beijing–Daqianlu	Team to Study the Dharma Abroad in Tibet (Liu Zang xuefa tuan)	Dayong, Hu Zihu
1926	Wuchang	Tantrayana Study Society (Micheng xuehui)	Dorjé Chöpa
(1927)	Shandong	Buddhist Mantra Association (Fojiao zhenyan hui)	Dorjé Chöpa (invited)
1928	Chongqing	Harmonious Association for World Buddhism (Shijie Fojiao Datong hui)	Norlha Qutughtu
1929	Daqianlu	Association of Students of the Beiping Buddhist Institute for the Study of the Tibetan Language's 1925 Team to Study the Dharma Abroad in Tibet (Beiping Fojiao Zangwen xueyuan yizhou liu Zang xuefa tuan zhu [Daqianlu tongxuehui])	Dagang
1929	Wuchang	Headquarters of the World Buddhist Institute (Shijie Foxueyuan)	Taixu
1931	Chongqing	Committee to Organize the World Buddhist Institute's Sino–Tibetan Buddhist Institute (Shijie Fojiao xueyuan Han–Zang jiaoli yuan)	Taixu, Liu Xiang

YEAR STARTED OR (FIRST REFERENCE)	PLACE	NAME	FOUNDER(S) OR TEACHER
1932	Chongqing	World Buddhist Institute's Sino–Tibetan Buddhist Institute (Ch. Shijie Foxueyuan Han Zang jiaoli yuan, Tib. 'Jig rten Sangs rgyas kyi chos grwa R.gya dang Bod pa'i bstan tshul bslab grwa khang)	Taixu, Liu Xiang
(1933)	Nanjing	Tantrayana Practice and Study Society (Micheng xiuxueshe)	Norlha Qutughtu (invited)
1934	Shanghai	Bodhi Society (Puti xuehui)	Duan Qirui, Panchen Lama
1934	Beiping	Esoteric Institute (Mizang yuan)	unknown
1936	Mount Wutai	Guangji maopeng, Huguo Bishan shifang Puji Temple	Nenghai
1937	Shanghai	Bodhi Society (Ch. Puti xuehui; Tib. Byang chub lam rim chen mo'i slob tshogs)	Sherap Gyatso (invited)
1939	Chengdu	Jinci Temple, Hall of the Vajra Way to Protect the Country (Huguo jingang daochang)	Nenghai
1939	Dobi	Dobi Monastic School (dratsang) Ganden Pelgyé Ling	Sherap Gyatso
1939	Kangding	Five Sciences Institute (Wuming xueyuan)	Liu Wenhui
1939	Mount Wutai, Xiantong Temple	Sino–Tibetan Institute (Han Zang xueyuan)	Hu Zihu
1941	Mount Wutai, Xiantong Temple	Tibetan Language Research Team (Zangwen yanjiu ban)	Hu Zihu

YEAR STARTED OR (FIRST REFERENCE)	PLACE	NAME	FOUNDER(S) OR TEACHER
1941	Beiping	Institute for the Propagation of Mahayana Buddhist Teachings (Dasheng Fojiao honghua yuan)	Hu Zihu
1942	Dobi	Qinghai Tibetan Buddhist and Chinese Language School (Tib. Mtsho sngon nang bstan gzhung lugs dang Rgya yig khrid sbyong khang, Ch. Qinghai Lama jiaoyi guowen jiangyisuo)	Sherab Gyatso
1944	Litang	Sino–Tibetan Buddhist Institute Branch, Chinese Monastic Institute (Han seng yuan)	Taixu
1945	Nanjing	Committee for the Reorganization of Chinese Buddhism (Zhongguo Fojiao zhengli weiyuanhui)	Taixu, Changja Qutughtu
1947	Nanjing	Chinese Buddhist Association (Zhongguo Fojiao Hui)	Taixu, Changja Qutughtu (under Nationalist Chinese government auspices)
1947	Chongqing	Hall of the Vajra Way (Jingang daochang)	Nenghai
(1948)	Beijing	North Sea Bodhi-study Association (Beihai Puti xuehui) and the Beijing Laypersons Group (Beijing Zhushilin)	Nenghai (invited)
1949	Shanghai	Hall of the Vajra Way (Jingang daochang)	Nenghai
1953	Mount Wutai, Jixiang Temple	Hall of the Vajra Way (Jingang daochang)	Nenghai

YEAR STARTED OR (FIRST REFERENCE)	PLACE	NAME	FOUNDER(S) OR TEACHER
1953	Beijing	Chinese Buddhist Association (Zhongguo Fojiao Hui)	Sherab Gyatso, Nenghai Lama (under Chinese Communist government auspices)
1956	Beijing	China's Buddhist Studies Institute (Zhongguo Foxueyuan)	Fazun
1980	Beijing	Chinese Buddhist College (Zhongguo Foxueyuan)	reopened by Fazun
1981	Dobi	Dobi Monastic School (dratsang) Ganden Pelgyé Ling	reopened by tenth Panchen Lama
1980s	Chengdu	Sichuan Nuns' Buddhist Studies Institute (Sichuan Nizhong Foxueyuan)	Longlian
1980s	Dartsedo (Kangding)	Tibetan Language University of Eastern Tibet	unknown
1987	Beijing	China's Tibetan Language division of the Higher Buddhist Studies Institute (Ch. Zhongguo Zangyu xi gaoji Foxueyuan, Tib. Krung go Bod brgyud mtho rim nang bstan slob gling)	tenth Panchen Lama

Appendix 2. Correct Tibetan Spellings

PHONETIC SPELLING	TIBETAN SPELLING
Amdo	A mdo
Amdo geshé	A mdo dge bshes
Amdo Geshé Jamröl Rölpé Dorjé Lodrö	A mdo dge bshes 'Jam rol rol pa'i blo gros
Amdowa	A mdo ba
Batang	'Ba' thang
Böpa	Bod pa
Chamdo	Chab mdo
Changja	Lcang skya
Changja Rölpé Dorjé	Lcang skya Rol pa'i rdo rje
Chökyi Gyentsen	Chos kyi rgyal mtshan
Chömpel Jikmé	Chos 'phel 'jigs med
Chöpel Gyatso	Chos dpal rgya mtsho
Dartsedo	Dar rtse mdo
Degé	Sde dge
densa sum	gdan sa gsum
Dobi	Rdo sbis
Dobi Dratsang Ganden Pelgyé Ling	Rdo sbis grwa tshang Dga' ldan 'phel rgyas gling
Dobi Geshé	Rdo sbis Dge bshes
Dorjé Chöpa	Rdo rje gcod pa
Dorjé Tseten	Rdo rje tshe brtan
Drakkar	Brag dkar
Drakkar Lama	Brag dkar Bla ma
Drakpa Gyatso	Grags pa rgya mtsho
Drepung	'Bras spungs

PHONETIC SPELLING	TIBETAN SPELLING
Ganden	Dga' ldan
Ganden Pelgyé Ling	Dga' ldan 'phel rgyas gling
Gara Lama	Mga ra bla ma
Gelukpa	Dge lugs pa
Gendün Chömpel	Dge 'dun chos 'phel
geshé	dge bshes
*Getok Trülku	*Dge thog sprul sku
Golok	Mgo lok
Gomang	Sgo mang
Gongkar Trashi	Gong dkar Bkra shis
Gönpo Kyap	Mgon po skyabs
Gurongtsang	Dgu rong tshang
Gya(l)rong	Rgya(l) rong
Gyantsé	Rgyal rtse
hashang	hwa shang
Jamchen Chöjé Shakya Yeshé	Byams chen Chos rje Sha kya ye shes
Jampa	Byams pa
Jampa Gegen	Byams pa dge rgan
Jampa Lama	Byams pa bla ma
Jampa Mönlam	Byams pa smon lam
Jampa Namgyel	Byams pa rnam rgyal
Jamyang Chöpel Rinpoché	'Jam dbyangs chos 'phel Rin po che
Jamyang Zhepa	'Jam dbyangs bzhad pa
Jangchup Lamrim Gön	Byang chub lam rim dgon
Kagyüpa	Bka' brgyud pa
Kardzé	Dkar mdzes
Karma Khabum	Skar ma mkha' 'bum
Karma Pakshi	Karma Pakshi
Karmapa	Kar ma pa
Kashak	Bka' shag
Kelzang Chönjor	Skal bzang chos 'byor
Kelzang Tsering	Skal bzang tshe ring
Kham	Khams
Khampa	Khams pa
Khangsar	Khang gsar
Khangsar Rinpoché	Khang gsar rin po che
Khangsar Rinpoché Ngakwang Yangchen Chökyi Wangchuk	Khang gsar rin po che Ngag dbang dbyang can chos kyi dbang phyug

PHONETIC SPELLING	TIBETAN SPELLING
Khangsartsang	Khang gsar tshang
khangtsen	khang mtshan
khenpo	mkhan po
Könchok Jungné	Dkon mchog 'byung gnas
Labrang	Bla brang
Lhamo Tseten	Lha mo tshe brtan
Lhasa	Lha sa
Litang	Li thang
Loselling	Blo gsal gling
Lozang Gyentsen	Blo bzang rgyal mtshan
Lozanq Penden Tenpé Drönmé	Blo bzang dpal ldan bstan pa'i sgron me
Lozang Püntsok	Blo bzang phun tshogs
Lozang Tenpa	Blo bzang bstan pa
Lozang Tenpel	Blo bzang bstan 'phel
Lozang Tupten Chökyi Nyima	Blo bzang thub bstan chos kyi nyi ma
Markham	Smar kham
Meru Samshak	Rme ru Bsam shag
Mipam Rinpoché	Mi pham rin po che
Ngachö Gön	Lnga mchod dgon
Ngakwang Khenpo	Ngag dbang mkhan po
Ngakwang Lozang	Ngag dbang blo bzang
Ngakwang Lozang Gyatso	Ngag dbang blo bzang rgya mtsho
Norbu Lingkha	Nor bu gling kha
Norlha	Nor lha
Nyingmapa	Rnying ma pa
Orgyen Jikdrel Chöying Dorjé	O rgyan 'jigs bral chos dbyings rdo rje
Pakpa	'Phags pa
Pakpa Lama Lodrö Gyentsen	'Phags pa Bla ma Blo gros rgyal mtshan
Penden Yeshé	Dpal ldan ye shes
Pomda	Spom mda'
Pomdatsang	Spom mda' tshang
Pomdatsang Rapga	Spom mda' tshang Rab dga'
Püntsok Trashi	Phun tshogs bkra shis
Püntsok Wanggyel	Phun tshogs dbang rgyal
Rapga	Rab dga'
Riwoché	Ri bo che
Rölpé Dorjé	Rol pa'i rdo rje
Sakya Dakchen Zangpopel	Sa skya Bdag chen Bzang po dpal

(continued)

PHONETIC SPELLING	TIBETAN SPELLING
Sakyapa	Sa skya pa
Samdrup Trashi	Bsam grub bkra shis
Sanggyé Yeshé	Sangs rgyas ye shes
Sera	Se ra
Sherab Gyatso	Shes rab rgya mtsho
Sok	Sog
Sönam Rapten	Bsod nams rab brtan
Sumchupa	Gsum bcu pa
Sumpa Khenpo Yeshé Penjor	Sum pa Mkhan po Ye shes dpal 'byor
Tendzin Gyatso	Bstan 'dzin rgya mtsho
Tengyeling	Bstan rgyas gling
Trashi Lhünpo	Bkra shis lhun po
Trinlé Gyatso	'Phrin las rgya mtsho
tsampa	rtsam pa
Tsang	Gtsang
Tsongkhapa Lozang Drakpa	Tsong kha pa Blo bzang grags pa
Tsongkhapa	Tsong kha pa
Tukwan Lozang Chökyi Nyima	Thu'u bkwan Blo bzang chos kyi nyi ma
Tupten Gyatso	Thub bstan rgya mtsho
Ü	Dbus
Wangdü Norbu	Dbang 'dus nor bu
Yeshé Geshé	Ye shes Dge bshes
Zhikatsé	Gzhis ka rtse

Notes

INTRODUCTION

1. John Kenneth Knaus, *Orphans of the Cold War: America and the Tibetan Struggle for Survival* (New York: Public Affairs, 1999), 78–96; Kenneth Conboy and James Morrison, *The CIA's Secret War in Tibet* (Lawrence: University Press of Kansas, 2002), 11–12. For further details of American involvement with Tibet, see Thomas Laird, *Into Tibet: The CIA's First Atomic Spy and His Secret Expedition to Lhasa* (New York: Grove, 2002); Roger E. McCarthy, *Tears of the Lotus: Accounts of Tibetan Resistance to the Chinese Invasion, 1950–1962* (Jefferson, N.C.: McFarland, 1997).

2. Knaus, *Orphans of the Cold War*, 96; Tsering Shakya, "The Genesis of the Sino-Tibetan Agreement of 1951," in *The History of Tibet*, ed. Alex McKay, Vol. 3, *The Modern Period: 1895–1959. The Encounter with Modernity*, 602–604 (London: RoutledgeCurzon, 2003).

3. The government of the People's Republic of China (PRC) considers citizens of all ethnicities to be Chinese (*Zhongguoren*). However, the ethnicity to which the English language refers as "Chinese" is designated "Han" by the PRC government. This book accords with the convention of equating the English language term for Chinese with the Chinese language term "Han," because the phrase "Han Chinese" seems redundant in the context of Chinese and Tibetan relations. Likewise I use the terms "Tibetan" to refer to all Tibetans regardless of their regional affiliation; that is, not all the people that anthropologists (Chinese and Western alike) designate as Tibetans would recognize themselves as Tibetan ("Böpa") as opposed to being Khampa, Amdowa, or even Golok. Nevertheless, because they share certain ethnic features, I use this general term.

4. For details on the recent Chinese efforts to increase security in Tibet and develop its mineral and hydropower potential, see Tibet Information Network, "Mining Tibet: Mineral Exploitation in Tibetan Areas of the PRC" (London: Tibet Information Network, 2002); and idem, "China's Great Leap West," (London: Tibet Information Network, 2000). For a historical perspective on China's security interests in Tibet, see Dawa Norbu, *China's Tibet Policy* (Richmond, UK: Curzon, 2001).

5. Benedict Anderson, *Imagined Communities: Reflections on the Origins and Spread of Nationalism*, rev. ed. (New York: Verso, 1996), 12–22.

6. For the use of this term in Qing China, see Donald Lopez, "'Lamaism' and the Disappearance of Tibet," in *Constructing Tibetan Culture: Contemporary Perspectives*, ed. Frank J. Korom (Quebec: World Heritage, 1997), 22.

7. For background on these topics, see Donald Lopez, ed., *Curators of the Buddha: The Study of Buddhism under Colonialism* (Chicago: University of Chicago Press, 1995); and idem, "Pandit's Revenge," *Journal of the American Academy of Religion* 68, no. 4 (2000): 831–835; the articles on the theme of "Religion and Empire" in the *Journal of the American Academy of Religion* 71, no. 1 (2003): 1–134; and Peter van der Veer and Hartmut Lehman, *Nation and Religion: Perspectives on Europe and Asia* (Princeton, N.J.: Princeton University Press, 1999), to name just part of the recent work in this field. I am grateful to Peter Hansen for bringing my attention to some of these sources.

8. Many thanks to Karl Gerth for suggestions about how to articulate the process described here.

9. Heather Stoddard, *Le mendiant de l'Amdo*, Recherches sur la Haute Asie, no. 9 (Paris: Société d'Ethnographie, 1985).

10. Ya Hanzhang, *Dalai Lama zhuan* (Beijing: Renmin chubanshe, 1984); idem, *Banchan E'erdeni zhuan* (Lhasa: Xizang renmin chubanshe, 1987); idem, *The Biographies of the Dalai Lamas*, trans. Wang Wenjiong (Beijing: Foreign Languages Press, 1991); idem, *Biographies of the Tibetan Spiritual Leaders Panchen Erdenis*, trans. Chen Guansheng and Li Peizhu (Beijing: Foreign Languages Press, 1994); Yâ Han krang (Ya Hanzhang), *PaN chen sku phreng rim byon gyi mdzad rnam* (*Biographies of the Panchen Lamas*), trans. Blo bzang phun tshogs and Rta mgrin 'Brug grags (Lhasa: Bod ljongs mi dmangs dpe skrun khang, 1992); Danzhu Angben, *Libei Dalai lama yu Banchan Erdeni nianpu* (*Chronicle of the Genealogy of the Dalai Lamas and Panchen Erdens*) (Beijing: Zhongyang minzu daxue chubanshe, 1998). I suspect that these materials, as well as the recently released copies of the Ninth Panchen Lama's biography, were the primary sources for the chronological account, Bod rang skyong ljongs srid gros lo rgyus rig gnas dpyad gzhi'i rgyu cha u yon lhan khang (Tibetan Cultural and Historical Materials Office), *PaN chen sku 'phreng dgu pa Blo bzang bstan chos kyi nyi ma gang gi dgung tshigs dang bstun pa'i mdzad rnam rags bsgrigs* (Rough Biography of the Ninth Panchen Lama), *Bod kyi lo rgyus rig gnas dpyad gzhi'i rgyu cha bdams bsgrigs* (*Materials on the Culture and History of Tibet*), vol. 22 (Beijing: Mi rigs dpe skrun khang, 2000). Unfortunately this book came into my hands too late to be examined in the present study.

11. This lama is variously referred to as the sixth and ninth Panchen Lama. The source of this discrepancy depends on how one counts the number of incarnations. One arrives at the number six if one counts from the first lama said to have received this title (Blo bzang chos kyi rgyal mtshan, 1570–1662) from the fifth Dalai Lama. However, Blo bzang chos kyi rgyal mtshan was later considered to be the third in a reincarnation series. Adding these additional three incarnations yields nine. The officials of the monastery associated with this lama, as well as the Chinese government, use the number nine, while in the past the Lhasa government, and now the Tibetan government-in-exile, has tended to use the number six to refer to this Panchen Lama; see Hisao Kimura (as told to Scott Berry), *Japanese Agent in Tibet: My Ten Years of Travel in Disguise* (London: Serindia, 1990), 63. However, both governments now refer to the recently deceased Panchen Lama (Chos kyi rgyal mtshan, 1938–1989) as the tenth Panchen Lama. See Doboom Tulku, "The Lineage of the Panchen Lamas: A Brief History and Biographical Notes," trans. Thupten T. Rikey, *Lungta* 1, no. 10 (1996): 6. For this reason, and for consistency with the numbering of the Dalai Lama, which also projects the incarnation series back beyond the awarding of the title Dalai Lama to the "third" Dalai Lama, I use the system that numbers both incarnations back beyond the people who were first given these respective titles.

12. Fabienne Jagou, "A Pilgrim's Progress: The Peregrinations of the 6th Panchen Lama," *Lungta* 1, no. 10 (1996): 12–23. Also published in Alex McKay, ed., *The History of Tibet*, Vol. 3, *The Modern Period*, 419–434. I have not yet been able to examine her recent work: *Le 9e Panchen Lama (1883–1937): Enjeu des relations sino-tibétaines* (Paris: École Française d'Extrême Orient, 2004).

13. Bod ljongs chab gros rig gnas lo rgyus dpyad gzhi'i rgyu cha zhib 'jug u yon lhan khang, *Bod kyi rig gnas lo rgyus dpyad gzhi'i rgyu cha bdams bsgrigs* (*Materials on the Culture and History of Tibet*), 22 vols. (Lhasa: Bod ljongs chab gros rig gnas lo rgyus dpyad gzhi'i rgyu cha zhib 'jug u yon lhan khang, 1982–2000); Xizang zizhizhou zhengxie wenshi ziliao yanjiu weiyuanhui, *Xizang wenshi ziliao xuanji* (*Selected Cultural and Historical Materials on Tibet*), 22 vols. (Beijing: Minzu chubanshe, 1982–2002). As officially supported memoirs, the reliability of these accounts is suspect and some of the authors have retracted statements made in this series.

14. One text that has not been cited for these modern studies of Tibet is Thub bstan nor bzang Tâ bla ma's *Gong sa bcu gsum pa'i srid phyogs mdzad rnam* (*Twentieth-century Political History*), 2 vols. (n.d.). This text was written in Tibetan cursive script and poorly mimeographed in India as part of the PL-480 program. Although I have not studied the text, it is clearly focused on the life of the thirteenth Dalai Lama and was written by someone who bore the Qing title of Da lama and thus may have served in some official capacity, before or even after the fall of the Qing.

15. Mei Jingshun, "Minguo yilai de Han Zang Fojiao guanxi (1912–1949): Yi Han Zang jiaoli yuan wei zhongxin de tantao" (Sino-Tibetan Relations during the Republican Period [1912–1949]: Probing into the Sino-Tibetan Buddhist Institute at the Center of Relations), *Zhonghua Foxue yanjiu* (*Chung-hwa Institute of Buddhist Studies,* Taipei) 2 (1998): 251–288; and "Minguo zaoqi xianmi Fojiao chongtu de tantao" (Probing into the Conflicts of Exoteric and Esoteric Buddhism in the Early Republic), *Zhonghua Foxue yanjiu* (*Chung-hwa Buddhist Studies*) 3 (1999): 251–270; Françoise Wang-Toutain, "Quand les maîtres chinois s'éveillent au bouddhisme tibétain: Fazun: le Xuanzang des temps moderns," *Bulletin de l'École Française d'Extrême-Orient* 87 (2000): 707–727; Ester Bianchi, *The Iron Statue Monastery "Tiexiangsi": A Buddhist Nunnery of Tibetan Tradition in Contemporary China* (Firenze: L. S. Olschki, 2001); and "The 'Chinese lama' Nenghai (1886–1967): Doctrinal Tradition and Teaching Strategies of a Gelukpa Master in Republican China," in *Buddhism between China and Tibet* (forthcoming); Monica Esposito, *The Image of Nineteenth- and Twentieth-Century Tibet* (Paris: École Française d'Extrême-Orient, forthcoming).

16. *Haichaoyin* was published starting in 1919. While researching this book, I had access to one of the most complete collection of this magazine at Harvard's Yen-ching Library, but the first decade of issues and several issues in later years were absent from the collection. In 2003 a nearly complete collection was reprinted, but I have not been able to incorporate these newly available resources.

17. Tsering Shakya, *The Dragon in the Land of Snows: A History of Modern Tibet since 1947* (London: Pimlico, 1999), xxvii; K. Dhondup, *The Water-bird and Other Years: A History of the Thirteenth Dalai Lama and After* (New Delhi: Rangwang, 1986), vi; see also Norbu, *China's Tibet Policy*, x.

18. John King Fairbank, *Trade and Diplomacy on the China Coast: The Opening of the Treaty Ports, 1842–1854*, 2 vols. (Cambridge, Mass.: Harvard University Press, 1953), 1:42. F. W. Mote makes much the same distinction regarding the role of the Manchus in bringing Inner Asia

under imperial control in his recent survey of imperial Chinese history; see his *Imperial China, 900–1800* (Cambridge, Mass.: Harvard University Press, 1999), 856–857. It is interesting to note that in Mote's work, as well as in Jonathan Spence's *Search for Modern China*, 1st ed. (New York: Norton, 1990), the maps of pre-Communist China never include Central Tibet, demonstrating these scholars' opinions, articulated by Mote (698–702, 876–879), that Central Tibet was not a part of China, despite having a special relationship with various imperial dynasties.

19. Evelyn Rawski, *The Last Emperors: A Social History of Qing Imperial Institutions* (Berkeley: University of California Press, 1998), 301.

20. Josef Kolmas, *The Ambans and Assistant Ambans of Tibet: A Chronological Study* (Praha: Oriental Institute, 1994). Several Chinese martial bannermen held this post and two Chinese civilian officers were appointed as assistant *ambans* after the late Qing reforms in 1905–1906.

21. Exceptions to this general rule are found in Stoddard, *Le mendiant de l'Amdo;* and Melvyn C. Goldstein, *The Demise of the Lamaist State: A History of Modern Tibet, 1913–1951* (New Delhi: Munshiram Manoharlal, 1989), 65.

22. Sun Yat-sen, *San min zhuyi* (Taipei: Zhongyang wenwu gongying she, 1985), 4–6; or *The Triple Demism of Sun Yat-sen*, trans. Paschal M. D'Elia (Wuchang: Franciscan Press, 1931), 67–69. The original text or any translation of the final version of Sun Yat-sen's *Sanmin zhuyi* (Three principles of the people) can be consulted. This passage occurs in the first lecture on *Minzu zhuyi* (usually translated as "nationalism" but should be understood to include an element of race, as the 1931 translation makes clear).

23. See chapter 19 of Dai's *Path for Youth* reproduced in Chen Tianxi, *Dai Jitao xiansheng de shengping* (*The Life of Dai Jitao*) (Taipei: Taiwan shangwu yinshuguan, 1968), 511–513; analyzed in detail in chapter 5 of this book.

24. In the late 1960s, as Holmes Welch was writing *The Buddhist Revival of China,* Harvard East Asian series, 33 (Cambridge, Mass.: Harvard University Press, 1968), he had the following reply from the Dalai Lama's office, in response to a draft chapter he had sent them, which described the tensions between the Tibetan government and some of the lamas who lived in exile in China: "Many of the Tibetan lamas in China 'persistently remained loyal to the Tibetan government and did many good services for their country (336 n. 42).'" With regard to these "good services," Welch had learned that among Tibetans, "there was hope that as Tantric Buddhism became popular in China and if enough Chinese officials and businessmen became disciples of Tibetan masters, it would create an influential body of opinion opposed to any invasion of Tibet" (178).

25. The Nationalist government refers to the government of the Nationalist Party that ruled China from 1927 to 1949. By China Proper, I mean those parts of China that were culturally and institutionally integrated into the Chinese state. These are opposed to frontier territories, which were at best loosely or nominally ruled by a central government and not characteristically dominated or surrounded by Chinese traditional culture. See, for instance, the turn-of-the-century geography, M. Kennelly, *L. Richard's Comprehensive Geography of the Chinese Empire and Dependencies*, trans. M. Kennelly (Shanghai: T'usewei Press, 1908), 7. Other easy-to-find reference points for what I mean by China Proper are maps of the Ming dynasty territory. For maps specific to the Qing period, see the maps from Rawski's *Last Emperors* and "Qing Colonialism," *International History Review* 20, no. 2 (1998).

I. IMPERIAL TRADITIONS

1. For details on the aristocratic families, see Luciano Petech *Aristocracy and Government in Tibet, 1728–1959*, vol. 45, *Serie Orientale Roma* (Rome: Instituto Italiano per il Medio ed Estremo Oriente, 1973). In twentieth-century Tibet some military and commercial families were raised to power by the thirteenth Dalai Lama as part of his effort at nationalist centralization of authority. Despite leaning toward a more secular approach to solving Tibet's problems, these families tended to see themselves as loyal to the Dalai Lama (and thereby, ultimately, to the Gelukpa tradition from which his authority derived). In any case, they were always overruled by the religious elites in decisions about Tibet's future. For details, see Stoddard, *Le mendiant de l'Amdo*; Knaus, *Orphans of the Cold War*, 57–59; Goldstein, *The Demise of the Lamaist State*, 179–185;

2. Anthony Smith, *National Identity* (Reno: University of Nevada Press, 1991), 53.

3. Smith, *National Identity*, 53. Note that although Tibetans and Mongols were aligned as Tibetan Buddhist commoners, it was very rare for Tibetans to venerate Mongol lamas in the way that it was typical for Mongols to venerate Tibetan lamas. The one prominent exception to this was the fourth Dalai Lama, who was born to a Mongol princely family. The Jebstundamba Qutughtu was certainly a prominent Tibetan Buddhist incarnation, but he was much more important to the Mongols than to the Tibetans. For instance, while it was common for Mongols from all regions to go to Tibet to study with Tibetan lamas, I have never heard of Tibetans leaving Tibet to study with Mongol lamas. For this reason, I treat the Tibetan elite as separate from the ethnically Mongol Tibetan Buddhists, even those that were lamas.

4. Smith, *National Identity*, 54.

5. Like nearly every other scholar who has discussed the Lifanyuan, I have used a new translation for this government agency but one that I think accurately reflects the Chinese name of the office. I believe that the common occurrence of the term "colonial" in the translation of this agency's name does not reflect how the agency was conceived or operated for most of its almost three-hundred-year existence, especially in Tibet.

6. Elliot Sperling, "Tangut Background to Mongol-Tibetan Relations," in *Tibetan Studies: Proceedings of the Sixth Seminar of the International Association for Tibetan Studies, Fagernes, 1992* (Oslo: Institute for Comparative Research in Human Culture, 1994), 801–824.

7. Christiaan Klieger, *Tibetan Nationalism: The Role of Patronage in the Accomplishment of a National Identity* (Berkeley: Folklore Institute, 1992), 20.

8. For a detailed presentation of this aspect of Tibetan society, see David S. Ruegg, *Ordre spirituel et ordre temporel dans la pensée Bouddhique de l'Inde et du Tibet, Publications de l'Institut de Civilisation Indienne* (Paris: Collège de France, 1995); and Dung dkar blo bzang phrin las, *The Merging of Religious and Secular Rule in Tibet*, trans. Chen Guansheng (Beijing: Foreign Languages Press, 1991).

9. Bstan 'dzin rgya mtsho, Dalai Lama XIV, *Freedom in Exile: The Autobiography of the Dalai Lama* (New York: HarperCollins, 1990), 202–203.

10. Elliot Sperling, "Notes on References to 'Bri-gung-pa—Mongol Contact in the Late Sixteenth and Early Seventeenth Centuries," in *Tibetan Studies: Proceedings of the Fifth Seminar of the International Association for Tibetan Studies, Narita 1989* (Narita-shi: Naritasan Shinshoji, 1992), 741–750; Elliot Sperling, "Early Ming Policy Toward Tibet: An Examination of the Proposition That the Early Ming Emperors Adopted a 'Divide and Rule' Policy toward Tibet" (Ph.D. dissertation, Indiana University, 1983).

11. A host of available sources, nearly all of Gelukpa provenance, assert that the Gelukpa tradition was oppressed at this time, for example, by having monasteries forcibly converted to the Kagyüpa school's affiliation. For one Sakyapa source and an overview of the situation, see Zahiruddin Ahmad, *Sino-Tibetan Relations in the Seventeenth Century*, vol. 40, *Serie Orientale Roma* (Rome: Instituto Italiano per il Medio ed Estremo Oriente, 1970), 100–120; Guiseppe Tucci, *Tibetan Painted Scrolls*, 2 vols. (Rome: Librera dello Stato, 1949), 54–57. The prominent Tibetologist R. A. Stein, not known for a Gelukpa bias, paints much the same picture in his authoritative *Tibetan Civilization* (trans. J. E. Stapleton Driver [Stanford: Stanford University Press, 1972], 81–82), although he, too, may have been using the same sources as Shakabpa. For a Tibetan perspective, see Zhwa sgab pa Dbang phyug bde ldan (Tsepon W. D. Shakabpa), *Bod kyi srid don rgyal rabs* (*An Advanced Political History of Tibet*), vol. 1 (Kalimpong: Shakabpa House, 1976), 365–410; or the English summary of the same text: W. D. Shakabpa, *Tibet: A Political History* (New York: Potala, 1988), 92–104.

12. For a list of these regents, see Luciano Petech. "The Dalai-Lama and Regents of Tibet: A Chronological Study," in *Selected Papers on Asian History*, Serie orientale Roma; vol. 60 (Rome: Istituto Italiano per il Medio ed Estremo Oriente, 1988), 125–149.

13. For further details on the history of this temple, see Naquin, *Peking*, 344; Ferdinand Lessing and Gösta Montell, *Yung-ho-kung, an Iconography of the Lamaist Cathedral in Peking: with Notes on Lamaist Mythology and Cult*, Sino-Swedish Expedition. Publication 18. Series no. VIII. Ethnography vol. 1 (Stockholm: Goteborg, 1942); and Patricia Berger, *Empire of Emptiness: Buddhist Art and Political Authority in Qing China* (Honolulu: University of Hawaii Press, 2003).

14. This is according to the biographer of the Tibetan Buddhist lama who founded this temple with the Qianlong emperor's support. See Thu'u bkwan Chos kyi nyi ma, *Lcang skya Rol pa'i rdo rje'i rnam thar* (*Biography of Lcang skya Rol pa'i rdo rje*) (Lanzhou: Kan su'i mi rigs dpe skrun khang, 1989 [1792–94], 220), or Tuguan (Tib. Thu'u bkwan), *Zhangjia Guoshi Ruobi duoji zhuan*, trans. Chen Qingying and Ma Lianlong (Beijing: Minzu chubanshe, 1988), 137.

15. The ethnicity of this figure's various incarnations is not always clear from the sources. A single contemporary reference designated the early twentieth-century incarnation as a Mongol (*Menggu*), see *Haichaoyin* 6, no. 4 (1925): 11. Moreover, the most famous of this incarnation series, Changja Rölpé Dorjé, was clearly ethnically Monguor (Tib. *Hor*) according to his biographies. For this reason I was tempted to use the Mongol form of this lama's name, Jangjia, because the incarnation series was often drawn from the Tibetanized Mongol remnants of Yuan garrisons in the Amdo/Qinghai area, called Monguors, and ministered to this community, as well as to Mongols in the area and at imperial centers around Beijing. However, one recent work listed the ethnic origins of the various incarnations of this series of lamas, unfortunately without reference to the original source of these ethnic designations (Nian Zhihai and Bai Gengdeng, eds., *Qinghai Zangchuan Fojiao siyuan ming jian* [*The Clear Mirror of Tibetan Buddhist Temples of Qinghai*] [Lanzhou: Gansu minzu chubanshe, 1993], 124). In this account the first and the sixth incarnations are the only ones listed as Monguors, while the second was designated as Chinese and the remainder as Tibetans. If we accept this list, the last incarnation (dealt with here) would have been ethnically Tibetan. And like the second and most famous incarnation of the series, the last was brought to the capital in Beijing at a young age (nine years old in the latter case) and raised in China Proper. According to Louis Schram, the name of this incarnation series derives from Chinese, the Zhang family (Ch. *Zhang jia*) into which the first reincarnation was born ("The Monguors of the Kansu-

Tibetan Border, II," *Transactions of the American Philosophical Society*, new ser., vol. 47, pt. 1 [1961], 29). According to Matthew Kapstein, based on Tibetan sources, "The name is not at all derived from Chinese, but from the Tibetan name of the Amdo village (Pale Willow) which was the native place of the half Chinese (father from Xi'an), half Tibetan yogin who later incarnated as the 'first' (actually therefore second) Lcang skya" (personal communication). My own perspective is that his name, although it has meaning in Tibetan, is clearly derived from the Chinese. This is based especially on my study of the local monasteries in Amdo/Qinghai, in which more than forty Tibetan Buddhist temples are named after a particular family (Ch. *jia*), based on that family's Chinese surname. The modern Tibetan spelling of these temple names (*kya, ca*) clearly reflects the Chinese phonetic (*jia*) in the local Tibetan pronunciation, just as would *skya* (from *Lcang skya*). Moreover, there are two temples in the area near where the early incarnations were born which share similar Chinese and Tibetan phonetic pronunciations and spellings with the incarnations title (Ch. *Zhangjia si*, Tib. *Lcang kya zi*, *Krang kya zi*). See Nian and Bai, *Qinghai Zangchuan Fojiao siyuan ming jian* (101, 118, and also 244) for details on these temples. For further information on this incarnation series, see E. Gene Smith, "The Life of Lcang skya Rol pa'i rdo rje," in *Among Tibetan Texts: History and Literature of the Himalayan Plateau,* ed. Kurtis R. Schaeffer, 133–146 (Boston: Wisdom, 2001); Karl-Heinz Everding, *Die Präexistenzen der Lcang skya Qutuqtus: Untersuchungen zur Konstruktion und historischen Entwicklung einer lamaistischen Existenzenlinie* (Wiesbaden: Harrassowitz, 1988); Ngag dbang chos ldan (Shes rab dar rgyas) and Klaus Sagaster, *Subud erike, "ein Rosenkranz aus Perlen": die Biographie des 1. Pekinger lCang skya Khutukhtu, Ngag dbang blo bzang chos ldan* (Wiesbaden: Harrassowitz, 1967); Hans-Rainer Kämpfe, *Die soziale Rolle des 2. Pekinger Lcang skya qutuqtu Rol pa'i rdo rje (1717–1786): Beitrage zu einer Analyse anhand tibetischer und mongolischer Biographien* (Bonn: Rheinische Friedrich-Wilhelms-Universität, 1974); and *Nyi ma'i 'od zer/ Naran-u gerel: Die Biographie des 2. Pekingger lCang skya Qutugtu Rol pa'i rdo rje (1717–1786)*, Monumenta Tibetca Historica, Abteilung II:Vitae, Band 1 (St. Augustin: VGH Wissenschaftsverlag, 1976); Wang Xiangyun. "Tibetan Buddhism at the Court of Qing: The Life and Work of lCang-skya Rol-pa'i-rdo-rje, 1717–86" (Ph. D. dissertation, Harvard University, 1995).

16. Chia Ning, "The Li-fan Yuan in the Early Ch'ing Dynasty" (Ph.D. dissertation, The Johns Hopkins University, 1992), 225.

17. *Neiwufu chudian cheng'an (Record of Imperial Household Ceremonies)*, Jindai zhongguo shiliao conggan xubian di liushisan ji, ed. Chen Yunlong.

18. Rawski, *The Last Emperors*, 271.

19. Susan Naquin, *Peking: Temples and City Life, 1400–1900* (Berkeley: University of California Press, 2000), 585.

20. I have not seen evidence that there were other monasteries that regularly hosted Tibetan monks. Although there were numerous imperially sponsored Tibetan Buddhist temples in and around the Qing court, even temples as important as the Xihuangsi (the Western Yellow Temple), built for the fifth Dalai Lama's visit in the mid-seventeenth century, was not kept in good repair, and thus presumably was not the regular home of monks from Tibet. For instance, for the irregular visits of the third Panchen Lama in the late eighteenth century and the thirteenth Dalai Lama in 1908 the temple had to be repaired. There is no indication in the Chinese records, discussed below, that even such important monasteries were regularly staffed by ethnic Tibetan lamas.

21. Yang Xuandi and Jin Feng, eds., *Lifanyuan zili*, drawn from *Guangxu Daqing huidian zeli* (*Lifanyuan xiu* 1891), (Neimenggu wenhua chubanshe, 1998), 416, 426.

22. For details, see my forthcoming article, "A Tibetan Buddhist Mission to the East: The Fifth Dalai Lama's Journey to Beijing, 1652–1653," in *Tibetan Society and Religion: The Seventeenth and Eighteenth Centuries*, ed. Bryan Cuevas and Kurtis Schaeffer (Leiden: Brill, forthcoming).

23. The Mongol term *jasagh* (Ch. *zhasa*, Tib. *dza sag*) refers to the official appointment of these lamas, "by law" (Kangxi chao, *Daqing huidian* zhong de Lifanyuan ziliao [Materials on the Court for Managing the Frontiers from the Kangxi Reign Period's *Collected Regulations of the Qing*], in *Qingdai Lifanyuan ziliao jilu* [*Compilation of Qing Dynasty Materials on the Court for Managing the Frontiers*] [Lanzhou: Quanguo guoshuguan wenxian souwei zhongxin, 1988], 17).

24. Yang and Jin, *Lifanyuan zili*, 404, 406–407, 424.

25. Wang Lu, "Wutaishan yu Xizang" (Mount Wutai and Tibet), *Wutaishan yanjiu* (*Mount Wutai Research*), no. 4 (1995): 23.

26. *Qingliang shan zhi* (1701), juan 7, 21b–24a. Cui Zhengsen and Wang Zhichao, *Wutaishan Beiwen xianzhu* (*Extant Stele Inscriptions of Mount Wutai*) (Taiyuan: Bei yueyi chubanshe, 1995), 347, from Kangxi stele, 1714. For details about his interaction with the Fifth Dalai Lama, see the Dalai Lama's autobiography: Ngag dbang blo bzang rgya mtsho, *Ngag dbang blo bzang rgya mtsho'i rnam thar* (*The Biography of [the Fifth Dalai Lama] Ngakawang Lozang Gyatso*) (Lhasa: Bod ljong mi dmangs dpe skrun khang, 1989 [1681]), 407; or its Chinese translation: Awang luosang jiacou, *Wushi Dalai lama zhuan*, trans. Chen Qingying and Ma Lianlong, *Zhongguo bianjiang shi di ziliao conggan-Xizang juan* (Beijing: Zhongguo Zangxue chubanshe, 1992), 338.

27. Preface preserved in 1755 reprint of Zhencheng's *Qiangliang shan zhi* (1596), 4.

28. For more details, see David Farquhar, "Emperor as Bodhisattva in the Governance of the Ch'ing Empire," *Harvard Journal of Asiatic Studies* 38, no. 1 (1978): 5–34.

29. Cui and Wang, *Wutaishan Beiwen xianzhu*, 347; Zhang Xixin, *Qing zhengfu yu lama jiao* (*The Qing Government and Lama Religion*). (Lhasa: Xizang renmin chubanshe, 1988), 205–506.

30. Cui and Wang, *Wutaishan Beiwen xianzhu*, 347; Zhang, *Qing zhengfu yu lama jiao*, 205–506. Text from a Kangxi stele dated 1714.

31. Cui and Wang, *Wutaishan Beiwen xianzhu*, 347

32. *Qingdai Lifanyuan ziliao jilu*, 406.

33. Wang Lu, "Wutaishan yu Xizang," 28.

34. Yang and Jin, *Lifanyuan zili*, 407.

35. Goldstein, *The Demise of the Lamaist State*, 214 n. 5.

36. Rawski, *The Last Emperors*, 271. See also Naquin, *Peking*, 353.

37. Naquin, *Peking*, 351–353.

38. *Neiwufu chudian cheng'an*, 156–157.

39. Naquin, *Peking*, 344.

40. For example, see Yang and Jin, *Lifanyuan zili*, 416.

41. Chia, "The Li-fan Yuan," 226.

42. *Meng Zang yuan tongji biao* (1916?), 271–313.

43. William Mayers and G.M.H. Playfair, *The Chinese Government: A Manual of Chinese Titles, Categorically Arranged and Explained, with an Appendix*, 3rd ed. rev. by G.M.H. Playfair (Taipei: Ch'eng-Wen, 1970 [1897]).

44. Yang and Jin, *Lifanyuan zili*.

45. Alastair Lamb, *British India and Tibet, 1766–1910* (London: Routledge and Kegan Paul, 1986 [1960]), 216–219.

46. Mongolian and Tibetan Affairs Bureau, 1912 (Meng Zang shiwuchu), Mongolian and Tibetan Affairs Court, 1914 (Meng Zang yuan), Mongolia and Tibetan Commission, 1927 (Meng Zang weiyuan hui).

47. *Meng Zang yuan tongji biao* (1916?), 271–313. For documents on the 1917–24 appointment of Tibetan monks to Beijing, see Zhongguo Zangxue yanjiu zhongxin, Zhongguo diyi lishi dang'an guan, Zhongguo di'er lishi dang'an guan, Xizang zizhichu dang'an guan, Sichuan sheng dang'an guan, 1994. *Yuan yi lai Xizang difang yu zhongyang zhengfu guanxi dang'an shiliao huibian (Assembled Archival Materials on Tibet's Relations with the Central Government since the Yuan),* 7 vols. (Beijing: Zhongguo Zangxue chubanshe, 1994), 7:3066–3087.

48. Edward Rhoads, *Manchus & Han: Ethnic Relations and Political Power in Late Qing and Early Republican China,* Studies on Ethnic Groups in China (Seattle: University of Washington Press, 2000), 247.

49. See, for instance, the forthcoming volume *Buddhism between China and Tibet,* edited by Matthew Kapstein.

50. Holmes Welch, *The Practice of Chinese Buddhism, 1900–1950* (Cambridge, Mass.: Harvard University Press, 1967); idem, *Buddhism under Mao* (Cambridge, Mass.: Harvard University Press, 1972); John Blofeld, *The Jewel in the Lotus: An Outline of Present Day Buddhism in China* (Westport, Conn.: Hyperion, 1975 [1948]); idem, *The Tantric Mysticism of Tibet* (Boston: Shambhala, 1987); idem, *Mantras: Sacred Words of Power* (London: Allen and Unwim, 1977); idem, *Compassion Yoga: The Mystical Cult of Kuan Yin* (London: Allen and Unwim, 1977); idem, *The Wheel of Life: The Autobiography of a Western Buddhist* (Boston: Shambhala, 1988).

51. Fafang, "Zhongguo Fojiao xianzhuang" (The Current State of Chinese Buddhism), *Haichao yin* 15, no. 10 (1934): 22–23. Fafang was later a lecturer on Mahayana Buddhism at the University of Ceylon in the 1940s; see Welch, *The Buddhist Revival of China,* 63, 181.

52. Zhou Guanren, "Goutong Han Zang wenhua" (Linking Chinese and Tibetan Culture), *Hai chao yin* 17, no. 6 (1936): 7. For details on this transmission to Japan, see Zhou Yi-liang, "Tantrism in China," *Harvard Journal of Asiatic Studies* 18, no. 3/4 (1945): 241–245.

53. See, for instance, Tsongkhapa, *The Great Treatise on the Stages of the Path to Enlightenment,* trans. Lamrim Chenmo Translation Committee, vol. 1 (Ithaca, N.Y.: Snow Lion, 2000), 112. Originally the Chinese monk had been called *Hwa shang* Mâhayâna, although Tsongkhapa did not use this full name. See also Leonard van der Kuijp, "On the Sources for Sa skya Pandita's Notes on the Bsam yas Debate," *Journal of the International Association of Buddhist Studies* 9, no. 2 (1986): 147. There were also exceptions to this attitude, especially among the Mongour Tibetan Buddhist lamas at the Qing court. For example, Lcang skya Rol pa'i rdo rje even had a throne set up for a Chinese monk to lecture to him on the *Huayanjing* after seeing this monk in a dream (Thu'u bkwan, *Lcang skya Rol pa'i rdo rje'i rnam thar,* 308; or Tuguan, *Zhangjia Guoshi Ruobi duoji zhuan,* 191). As Matthew Kapstein explains (in *The Tibetan Assimilation of Buddhism: Conversion, Contestation, and Memory* [Oxford: Oxford University Press, 2000], 78–82) Tsong-khapa, not to mention other Tibetan lamas, did not equally stigmatize all of Chinese Buddhism.

54. Patricia Berger, "Preserving the Nation: The Political Uses of Tantric Art in China," in *Latter Days of the Law: Images of Chinese Buddhism, 850–1850* (Lawrence, Ks.: Spencer Museum of Art, 1994), 107.

55. Luciano Petech, *China and Tibet in the Early Eighteenth Century: History of the Establishment of Chinese Protectorate in Tibet, T'oung pao;* Monographie 1 (Leiden: Brill, 1950), 241. For further details on this aversion, see a forthcoming article by Shen Weirong.

56. Naquin, *Peking*, 208.

57. Ibid., 209. Hoong Teik Toh has argued that "a 'Tibetan monk' or *lama* in the Ming period could refer to any Buddhist monk who practiced Tibetan Buddhism regardless of his ethnicity" ("Tibetan Buddhism in Ming China," Ph.D. dissertation, Harvard University, 2004). I tend to agree with his assessment; unfortunately this still leaves us fairly little concrete evidence of which lamas were ethnically Chinese prior to the twentieth century.

58. Ibid., 589.

59. Ngag dbang blo bzang rgya mtsho, *Ngag dbang blo bzang rgya mtsho'i rnam thar*, 403; Dan jun—Zaina panduo and Li Decheng, *Mingcha shuang huangsi: Qingdai Dalai he Panchan zai jing zhuyang di (The Famous Pair of Yellow Temples: The Qing Dynasty Residences of the Dalai and Panchen Lamas)* (Beijing: Zongjiao wenhua chubanshe, 1997), 244. For more details on the fifth Dalai Lama's time in Beijing, see Gray Tuttle, "A Tibetan Buddhist Mission to the East: The Fifth Dalai Lama's Journey to Beijing, 1652–1653."

60. Yang and Jin, *Lifanyuan zili*, 404–405. The statutes specify that one of the four jasagh lamas of Beijing should be drawn from a Mongol who knew the scriptures well, while another should be a Chinese who understood how to get things done (*Hanren da lama . . . mingbai neng shi zhe*). The same contrast is drawn in the case of Yonghegong staff, where two posts were to be filled by Chinese managers (*Hanren ni'erba*, the latter term from Tib. *gnyer ba*: steward, manager), while the other two positions were to be filled by Mongol lamas well versed in scripture.

61. Matthew Kapstein (personal communication, November 2004) has suggested that Chinese influence on material culture as well as astrology, divination, and medicine was enormous; however, the research to trace the exact nature and mechanism of this influence has not yet been sufficiently developed.

62. Rawski, *The Last Emperors*, 36–37.

63. Ahmad, *Sino-Tibetan Relations*, 157–158.

64. The Qing court may have had access to the Ming dynasty work *Xifanguan yiyu (Tibetan-Chinese vocabulary)*, but even this listed less than one thousand entries, including only thirty-two on Buddhism, so it hardly represented a comprehensive linguistic reference work for dealing with the Tibetans. See Tatsuo Nishida, *Xifanguan yiyu no kenkyu (A Study of the Tibetan-Chinese Vocabulary Hsi-fan-kuan i-yu: An Introduction to Tibetan Linguistics)* (Kyoto: Nakanishi, 1970), 81–121). This Japanese text has an English translation of the terms in the Ming period Tibetan-Chinese vocabulary that is the focus of the monograph.

65. Chia, "The Li-fan Yuan," 251–257.

66. The earliest Chinese bannermen (*Hanjun*, bound to the dynasty as hereditary servants) to serve as an assistant *amban* in Tibet was assigned to that post from 1833 to 1834. Thereafter two Chinese bannermen served as head *ambans*, while three Chinese bannermen and two Chinese civil officials (in the twentieth century) served as assistant *ambans* in Tibet. These men represent 8 out of 173 assignments to the two posts from 1727 to 1912. For more details, see Kolmas, *The Ambans and Assistant Ambans of Tibet*, 67–71.

67. W. Woodville Rockhill mentioned the handful of Chinese and Manchu clerks sent to Tibetan regions during the Qing dynasty (*Tibet: A Geographical, Ethnological, and Historical Sketch Derived from Chinese Sources* (1891), 238).

68. Zhen Canzhi, "The Autobiography of Ts'an-chih Chen," in *Tibetan Lives: Three Himalayan Biographies,* ed. Peter Richardus (Richmond, Surrey, UK: Curzon, 1998), 161–208.

69. Kolmas, *The Ambans and Assistant Ambans of Tibet*, 65–66.

70. Liu Manqing, *Kang-Zang zhaozheng* (*Expedition to Kham and Tibet*) (Shanghai: Shangwu yinshuguan, 1933).

71. Michel Foucault, *Power/Knowledge: Selected Interviews and Other Writings 1972–1977*, trans. Colin Gordon, Leo Marshal, John Mepham, and Kate Soper (New York: Pantheon, 1980), 124.

72. In this respect I take issue with the comparisons to colonialism made in "Manchu Colonialism," *The International History Review* 20, no. 2 (1998): 255–388.

73. D. R. Howland, *Borders of Chinese Civilization: Geography and History at Empire's End* (Durham, N.C.: Duke University Press, 1996).

74. Rockhill, *Tibet*, 2–4.

75. Rhoads, *Manchus & Han*, 76.

76. Thomas Heberer. *China and Its National Minorities: Autonomy or Assimilation* (Armonk, N.Y.: M. E. Sharpe, 1989), 18. According to Heberer: "When the People's Republic was founded in 1949, eleven written languages of ethnic minorities were in regular use, and seven others were used sporadically" ("Ethnic Minorities and Cultural Identity in the People's Republic of China, with Special Reference to the Yi Nationality," in *Ethnic Minorities in China*, ed. Thomas Heberer [Aachen: Rader Verlag, 1987], 16).

77. Pamela Crossley, "Thinking about Ethnicity in Early Modern China," *Late Imperial China* 11, no. 1 (1990b): 9 n. 12. See also idem, *A Translucent Mirror: History and Identity in Qing Imperial Ideology* (Berkeley: University of California Press, 1999).

78. James L. Hevia. *Cherishing Men from Afar: Qing Guest Ritual and the Macartney Embassy of 1793* (Durham, N.C.: Duke University Press, 1995), 48.

79. Farquhar, "Emperor as Bodhisattva," 5–34.

80. James A. Millward, *Beyond the Pass: Economy, Ethnicity, and Empire in Qing Central Asia, 1759–1864* (Stanford: Stanford University Press, 1998), 201–202.

81. Lamb, *British India and Tibet*, 217.

2. GLOBAL FORCES IN ASIA (1870s–1910s)

1. Anthony Smith, *Ethnic Origins* (Oxford: Blackwell, 1986), 165–166.

2. Francis Younghusband, *India and Tibet: A History of the Relations Which Have Subsisted between the Two Countries from the Time of Warren Hastings to 1910; with a Particular Account of the Mission to Lhasa of 1904* (Delhi: Book Faith India, 1998 [1910]), 1–3. See also Sir Clements R. Markham, ed., George Bogle, and Thomas Manning, *Narratives of the Mission of George Bogle to Tibet and of the Journey of Thomas Manning to Lhasa*, 3rd ed. (New Delhi: Cosmo, 1989); Alastair Lamb, *Bhutan and Tibet: The Travels of George Bogle and Alexander Hamilton, 1774–1777*, Vol. 1, *Letters, Journals, and Memoranda* (Hertingfordbury: Roxford, 2002).

3. Younghusband, *India and Tibet*, 6. Brackets in the original.

4. Ibid., 15–17, 25–27.

5. Lamb, *British India and Tibet,* 172.

6. At least until the eighteenth century Armenian traders were active in Tibet, entering from both the north (Xining) and the south (Calcutta, Patna); see Hugh Richardson, "Armenians in India and Tibet," in *High Peaks, Pure Earth: Collected Writings on Tibetan History and Culture,* ed. Micheal Aris (London: Serindia, 1998), 463–467. Their presence appears to have declined in the late seventeenth century, as that of Muslim merchants from Kashmir increased. For further details, see Abdul Wahid Radhu, *Islam in Tibet and Tibetan Caravans,* ed.

Henry Gray, 17–21 (Louisville: Fons Vitae, 1997); and Ghulam Muhammad, *Récit d'un voyageur musulman au Tibet,* ed. and trans. Marc Gaborieau (Paris: Klincksieck, 1973). For an account of the 1840–41 Kashmiri attempt to militarily capture the source of Tibet's finest wool, see Sarat Chandra Das, *Journey to Lhasa and Central Tibet,* ed. William Woodville Rockhill, 2nd rev. ed. (London: J. Murray, 1970 [1902]), 53.

7. A second mission in 1783–84 actually won concessions from the regent of the young seventh Panchen Lama for natives of India (not the British) to come to Tibet to trade. But as mentioned above, the Gurkha invasion of Tibet in 1792, and the untimely visit of a British agent in Nepal at this time, led to an abrogation of this early British and Tibetan agreement. In any case, the agreement only extended to the province of Tsang, where the Panchen Lama had some influence. See Younghusband, *India and Tibet,* 25–26.

8. Ibid., 12–14.

9. Ibid., 18.

10. Rockhill, *Tibet,* 35, 259. He notes that, in the late nineteenth century, porters were arranged in Daqianlu (Tib. Dartsedo) to carry the tea to Tibet.

11. Younghusband, *India and Tibet,* 38. See also Lamb, *British India and Tibet,* 159–161.

12. Alex McKay, *Tibet and the British Raj: The Frontier Cadre 1904–1947* (Richmond, Surrey: Curzon, 1997), 7.

13. Das, *Journey to Lhasa,* 50–55.

14. Younghusband, *India and Tibet,* 45–53.

15. Listed as an appendix to Alastair Lamb, *Britain and Chinese Central Asia: The Road to Lhasa, 1767–1905* (London: Routedge and Kegan Paul, 1960), 342–344.

16. Arash Bormanshinov, "A Secret Kalmyk Mission to Tibet in 1904," *Central Asiatic Journal* 36, no. 3–4 (1992): 161–187; "Kalmyk Pilgrims to Tibet and Mongolia," *Central Asiatic Journal* 42, no. 1 (1998): 1–23; "A Kalmyk Intelligence Mission to Tibet in 1904," *Central Asiatic Journal* 43, no. 2 (1999): 168–174. Alexandre Andreyev, *Soviet Russia and Tibet: The Debacle of Secret Diplomacy, 1918–1930s* (Leiden: Brill, 2003).

17. Kennelly, *L. Richard's Comprehensive Geography,* 548.

18. Lamb, *British India and Tibet,* 173.

19. Ibid., 183.

20. Marius B. Jansen, *The Making of Modern Japan* (Cambridge, Mass.: Harvard University Press, 2000), 428–444.

21. John Snelling, *Buddhism in Russia: The Story of Agvan Dorzhiev, Lhasa's Emissary to the Tsar* (Rockport, Mass.: Element, 1993), 53–65.

22. Quoted in Snelling, *Buddhism in Russia,* 74.

23. Snelling, *Buddhism in Russia,* 79, 83 n. 10, 283–284; Alexander Andreyev, "Russian Buddhists in Tibet, from the End of the Nineteenth Century–1930," *Journal of the Royal Asiatic Society* 11, no. 3 (2001): 349–362.

24. Snelling, *Buddhism in Russia,* 84, 104.

25. Younghusband, *India and Tibet,* 60–61.

26. For an example of such fund-raising trips, see Andreyev, "Russian Buddhists in Tibet," 359.

27. Younghusband, *India and Tibet,* 65.

28. Snelling, *Buddhism in Russia,* 105.

29. Younghusband, *India and Tibet,* 25.

30. The works of Alistair Lamb, Peter Hopkirk, Karl Meyers, and Alexandre Andreyev, too numerous to list here, detail many of these explorations. For details on the sojourn of a Japanese

resident in Tibet, see Ekai Kawaguchi, *Three Years in Tibet* (Delhi: Book Faith India, 1995); Scott Berry, *Monks, Spies, and a Soldier of Fortune* (London: Athlone, 1995); and idem, *A Stranger in Tibet: The Adventures of a Wandering Zen Monk* (New York: Kodansha International, 1989).

31. Turn-of-the-century Russia maps are the most detailed maps of central Tibet, although, because they are in Cyrillic, they have not been used by many Tibetologists. Personal communication, Merrick Lex Berman (March 2004). See the Web site of the China GIS (CHGIS), based at Harvard University.

32. Lamb, *British India and Tibet*, 185–195.

33. Jansen, *The Making of Modern Japan*, 433.

34. Lamb, *British India and Tibet*, 219.

35. Ibid.

36. Younghusband, *India and Tibet*, 66–69.

37. Snelling, *Buddhism in Russia*, 112–113. See also Dorjiev's own biography, which implies that the "mint" was created in preparation for flight from Tibet, in order to bring along supplies for the journey: Thupten J. Norbu and Dan Martin, "Dorjiev: Memoirs of a Tibetan Diplomat," *Hokke-Bunka Kenkyu (Journal of the Institute for the Comprehensive Study of the Lotus Sutra)*, no. 17 (1991): 31.

38. Younghusband, *India and Tibet*, 146, 300.

39. Ibid., 253–256. For an equally disparaging Tibetan Buddhist perspective on the knowledge Tibetans had of the outside world, see Norbu and Martin, *Dorjiev*, 30–31.

40. Younghusband, *India and Tibet*, 253–256.

41. Ibid., 285.

42. Kolmas, *The Ambans and Assistant Ambans of Tibet*, 66 n. 86.

43. Hugh Richardson, *High Peaks, Pure Earth*, 535–538.

44. Stein Tønneson and Hans Antlöv, eds., *Asian Forms of the Nation* (Richmond, Surrey: Curzon, 1996), 2.

45. Smith, *National Identity*, 69.

46. Michael C. van Walt, "Whose Game? Records of the Indian Office concerning Events Leading up to the Simla Conference." In *Soundings in Tibetan Civilization*, ed. International Association for Tibetan Studies Seminar, Barbara Nimri Aziz and Matthew Kapstein, 215–230 (New Delhi: Manohar, 1985).

47. Elliot Sperling, "The Chinese Venture in K'am, 1904–1911, and the Role of Chao Erhfeng," *Tibet Journal* 1, no. 2 (1976): 11–14.

48. Eric Teichman, *Travels of a Consular Officer in Eastern Tibet Together with a History of the Relations between China, Tibet and India* (Cambridge: Cambridge University Press, 1922), 6.

49. Sperling, "The Chinese Venture in K'am," 14.

50. Ibid., 14–15.

51. Carter J. Eckert et al., *Korea Old and New: A History* (Seoul: Korea Institute, Harvard University, 1990), 206–208.

52. Ibid., 214, 222–223.

53. Teichman, *Travels of a Consular Officer in Eastern Tibet*, 33.

54. Sperling, "The Chinese Venture in K'am," 18–24.

55. Younghusband, *India and Tibet*, 339.

56. Ibid., 361.

57. Snelling, *Buddhism in Russia*, 83.

58. Kimura, *Japanese Agent in Tibet*, 104.

59. Houghton Library, Harvard University, possesses William Woodville Rockhill's diary and reports on the Dalai Lama (to the United States president) as well as the many letters the Dalai Lama sent the minister over the years. Many thanks to Ken Knaus for making me aware of these materials and to Thomas Ford for having made microfilms of these delicate and important documents for researchers' use.

60. Ya, *The Biographies of the Dalai Lamas,* 258–159; W. D. Shakabpa, *Tibet: A Political History,* 221–222; Younghusband, *India and Tibet,* 356.

61. Shakabpa, *Tibet: A Political History,* 222; Sir Charles Arthur Bell, 1987 [1946], *Portrait of a Dalai Lama: The Life and Times of the Great Thirteenth* (London: Wisdom, 108).

62. Younghusband, *India and Tibet,* 360.

63. Snelling, *Buddhism in Russia,* 95–96.

64. Shakabpa, *Tibet: A Political History,* 222.

65. Younghusband, *India and Tibet,* 361–362.

66. Ibid., 363–365.

67. Bell, *Portrait of a Dalai Lama,* 105–108.

68. Younghusband, *India and Tibet,* 376.

69. Bell, *Portrait of a Dalai Lama,* 111.

70. Ibid., 119.

71. Ibid., 136.

72. Ibid., 120–121, 131–138.

73. Ibid., 114.

74. Ibid., 137.

75. Ibid., 136.

76. Ibid., 143.

77. Ibid., 160.

78. Snelling, *Buddhism in Russia,* 148–151. The validity or even existence of the Mongolia-Tibetan Treaty of January 11, 1913, has been challenged. See Alex McKay, *The History of Tibet,* vol. 3, *The Modern Period: 1895–1959, The Encounter with Modernity* (London: Routledge/Curzon, 2003), 171–190, which reproduced both the treaty and a critical examination of the treaty by Parshotma Mehra drawn from the *Journal of Asian History* 3, no. 1 (1969).

79. Warren W. Smith Jr., *Tibetan Nation: A History of Tibetan Nationalism and Sino-Tibetan Relations* (Boulder, Colo.: Westview, 1996), 183.

80. Dhondup, *The Water-bird and Other Years,* 54.

81. Michael C. van Walt van Praag, *The Status of Tibet: History, Rights, and Prospects in International Law* (London: Wisdom, 1987), 50.

82. Kimura, in *Japanese Agent in Tibet* (105), noted that one of the Japanese in Tibet after 1912 played a role in creating this national symbol. See also Patrick French, *Tibet, Tibet: A Personal History of a Lost Land* (New York: HarperCollins, 2003), 14, citing Berry, *Monks, Spies and a Soldier of Fortune.*

83. Shen Tsung-Lien and Liu Shen-chi, *Tibet and the Tibetans* (Stanford: Stanford University Press, 1953).

84. Melvyn C. Goldstein, Dawei Sherap, and William Siebenschuh, *A Tibetan Revolutionary: The Political Life and Times of Bapa Phüntso Wangye* (Berkeley: University of California Press, 2004), 71.

85. Stanley J. Tambiah, *World Conquerer and World Renouncer: A Study of Buddhism and Polity in Thailand Against a Historical Background* (London: Cambridge University Press, 1976),

101–131. My thanks to Matthew Kapstein for suggesting this model for describing the relations within the Tibetan cultural area.

86. Ibid., 112.

87. For details on the misgovernment of Kham by the Lhasa administration, see Kimura, *Japanese Agent in Tibet,* 168, 173–179, 210, 220.

88. John King Fairbank and Merle Goldman, *China: A New History,* enl. ed. (Cambridge: Belknap Press, Harvard University Press, 1998), 249.

89. See Goldstein, *The Demise of the Lamaist State,* 63–64. This monastery was the seat of one of the Tibetan incarnation series that had been honored and made wealthy by the Qing dynasty, so its residents were friendly to the Chinese in Tibet.

90. Dhondup, *The Water-bird and Other Years,* 50.

91. Fairbank and Goldman, *China: A New History,* 249.

92. Goldstein, *The Demise of the Lamaist State,* 112.

93. Dhondup, *The Water-bird and Other Years,* 40.

94. Tambiah, in *World Conqueror, World Renouncer* (126), describes this sort of effort citing Weber's model of patrimonial domination.

95. Geoffrey Samuel, *Civilized Shamans* (Washington, D.C.: Smithsonian Institute, 1993), 52.

96. Goldstein, *The Demise of the Lamaist State,* 112, 87.

97. Ya, *Biographies of the Tibetan Spiritual Leaders Panchen Erdenis,* 258–260. This is discussed in detail in the following chapters.

98. There is some disagreement in the sources over the year this lama was born. In the earliest known source on this lama, a short biography presumably based on information provided by the lama himself, his year of birth is given as 1865 (Jerome Cavanaugh, *Who's Who in China, 1918–1950, with an Index,* supplement to the 4th ed. [Hong Kong: Chinese Materials Center, 1982], 81; repeated in the 5th ed., 193). This was also the birth date given by his biographer, a Chinese disciple. See Han Dazai, *Kang-Zang Fojiao yu Xikang Nona Hutuketu yinghua shilüe (Brief Account of Kham-Tibetan Buddhism and the Manifestation of the Norlha Qutughtu of Kham)* 1937, 4r, 8v. Many thanks to Peng Wenbin and Lawrence Epstein for bringing this rare text to my attention. According to *Haichaoyin* (17:7, 82), Han Dazai was the lama's secretary. For a birth date of 1864, see Zhou Xilang, "Nona hutuketu," in *Sichuan jin xiandai renwu chuan (Biographies of Sichuan's Contemporary Figures),* vol. I, ed. Sichuan sheng difang zhi bianji weiyuanhui, Sheng zhi renwu zhi bianji, and Ren Yimin, Sichuan sheng difang zhi ziliao congshu (Chengdu: Sichuan sheng shehui kexue yuan chubanshe, 1985), 289. Dhondup (*The Water-bird and Other Years,* 55) mentioned one Gara lama (Tib. Mgar ra bla ma) who was imprisoned by Tibetans but later escaped to China; unfortunately he gives few details. Likewise Melvyn C. Goldstein, Dawei Sherap, and William Siebenschuh, in *A Tibetan Revolutionary: The Political Life and Times of Bapa Phüntso Wangye* (Berkeley: University of California Press, 2004), described a chronology of Gara Lama's life that matches that of the Norlha Qutughtu's major life events, although his birth date is not mentioned (15 n. 1). It does seem probable that these two different titles— Norlha Qutughtu and Gara Lama—describe a single individual. The only problem with this identification is that the birth date for the lama given by modern Tibetan scholars is more than a decade later (1876) than the birth date given for Norlha Qutughtu in Chinese sources. See Rje drung 'Jam dpal rgyal mtshan, "Ri bo che dgon pa dang Rje drung sprul sku Mgar ra bla ma bcas kyi lo rgyus rags bsdus" (A Brief History of Riwoché Monastery, the Jedrung Incarnation, and Gara Lama), in *Bod kyi rig gnas lo rgyus dpyad gzhi'i rgyu cha bdams bsgrigs, 'don*

thengs drug pa (*Materials on the Culture and History of Tibet, volume 6*) (Lhasa: Bod ljongs chab gros rig gnas lo rgyus dpyad gzhi'i rgyu cha zhib 'jug u yon lhan khang, 1985), 210. This birth date would have allowed for this figure to have been a rival candidate for recognition as the thirteenth Dalai Lama, as stated in Skal bzang bkra shis, "Mgar ra bla ma Lu'u jun dmag Khams khul 'byor skabs mnyam 'brel dang Go min tang skabs Bod Sog u yon lhan khang u yon sogs byas skor" (On Gara Lama and the Lu Army Corp in Kham and the Guomindang [Nationalist Party]'s Mongolian and Tibetan Affairs Commission), in *Bod kyi lo rgyus rig gnas dpyad gzhi'i rgyu cha bdams bsgrigs*, 10 (*Materials on the Culture and History of Tibet,* new ser., vol. 10), general ser. vol. 19 (Beijing: Mi rigs dpe skrun khang, 1996), 113. Of course, the birth date of 1865 given in his biographies, and by his own student, if correct, would have precluded him from consideration from this high status, as he would have been much too old to have been considered a reincarnation of the previous Dalai Lama. Oddly these Tibetan-language accounts scarcely mention the Norlha Qutughtu's time in China. The latter article covers some of his political involvement with the Sichuan warlords, Liu Xiang, said to have been his patron (in the priest-patron relationship, Tib. *mchod yon*), and Liu Wenhui, as well as Chiang Kai-shek in a few brief pages (119–122) but fails to mention his substantial Buddhist following or ritual activity in China. These articles are the only sources to identify Norlha Qutughtu and Gara Lama as the same person. In his article, Rje drung 'Jam dpal rgyal mtshan said that the lama in question changed his name to Nub bla (Western La[ma]), when he came to Nanjing and adds that he entered into a patron-priest relationship with Chiang Kai-shek (Ch. Jiang Jieshi, Tib. Cang Ce hre). The Chinese language "translation" of this article added an additional sentence, which said that Chiang awarded the lama with the title "Nula hutuketu"; see Jizhong—Jiangbai jianzan [Rje drung 'Jam dpal rgyal mtshan], "Leiwuqisi Jizhong houfo he Gere lama jianli" (Short History of Ri bo che Monastery's Rje drung Incarnation and Mga ra lama), in *Xizang zizhizhou zhengxie wenshi ziliao xuanji* (*Selected Materials on the Culture and History of Tibet*) 6:79–90 (Beijing: Minzu chubanshe, 1985), 89.

99. There is also some disagreement over how this lama's incarnation name, which I shall use throughout the book in lieu of his religious name, should be spelled in Tibetan. The earliest printed source I can find, the Panchen Lama's autobiography, used Nor lha (see Blo bzang thub bstan chos kyi nyi ma, Panchen Lama VI (IX), 1944, *Skyabs mgon thams cad mkhyen pa Blo bzang thub bstan chos kyi nyi ma dge legs rnam rgyal bzang po'i zhal snga nas kyi thun mong pa'i rnam bar thar pa rin chen dbang gi rgyal po'i 'phreng ba* (*The Autobiography of the Sixth [Ninth] Panchen Lama Blo bzang thub bstan chos kyi nyi ma*), reproduced from the Bkra shis lhun po blocks, 549). Likewise the memoirs of a Tibetan official in China used Nor lha (see Thub bstan sangs rgyas, *Rgya nag tu Bod kyi sku tshab don gcod skabs dang gnyis tshugs stangs skor gyi lo rgyus thabs bral zur lam* (*Experiences of a Former Tibetan Representative in China, 1930–1939*) (Dharamsala: Library of Tibetan Works and Archives, 1982), 44. Two much later and thirdhand sources—the first being Skal bzang bkra shis's article (120) and the second being Mi nyag Mgon po's 1997 biography (*'Bo Gangs dkar sprul sku'i rnam thar dad pa'i pad dkar* (*The White Lotus of Faith: A Biography of the 'Bo Gangs dkar Incarnation*) [Beijing, Mi rigs dpe skrun khang, 1997]) of his teacher, who was a disciple of the lama in question—both used Nor bla, although Skal bzang bkra shis's article also used Nor lha at least once (122). I favor the earlier accounts, but either may be correct. I have also seen another religious name given for this lama: Trinlé Gyatso.

100. Two conflicting dates are given in Han (*Kang-Zang Fojiao*) for his arrival in Beijing: March 15, 1924 (4v) and October 15, 1925 (8v). Other sources, including Welch, *The Buddhist Revival in China*, 175, indicate that he was present in Beijing in 1924, so I have accepted this date.

101.Ya, *Biographies of the Tibetan Spiritual Leaders Panchen Erdenis,* 262.

102. Han, *Kang-Zang Fojiao,* 4v.

103.Wu Fengpei, ed., "Zhongyin *Shi Zang jicheng, Xizang jiyao* yu (Preface to the Reprint of *Record of the Journey of an Envoy to Tibet, Summary of Tibet*), in *Shi Zang jicheng, Xizang jiyao, Lasa jianwen ji (Record of the Journey of an Envoy to Tibet, Summary of Tibet, Record of What I Heard and Saw in Tibet*), Xizang xue Hanwen wenxian congshu, di'er ji (Collection of Chinese Language Documents for the Study of Central Tibet, 2) (Beijing: Quanguo guoshuguan wenxian suowei xiazhi zhongxin, 1991), 4. Gurongtsang is the name of an incarnation lineage. This particular individual's name was Orgyen Jikdrel Chöying Dorjé (ca. 1875–1932). He was an Amdo disciple of the celebrated Mipam Rinpoché (1846–1912) and was effectively made head of the Nyingma order in Qinghai by the Chinese authorities in about 1918. Many thanks to Matthew Kapstein for clarification about the identification of this individual and for informing me about the existence of his biography: Bstan 'dzin, *Dgu rong sku phreng snga phyi'i rnam thar* (The Biographies of the Earlier and Later Incarnations in the Gurong Series of Incarnations) (Lanzhou: Kan su'u mi rigs dpe skrun khang, 1994). According to Tashi Tsering of Dharamsala's Amyne Machin Institute, after this failed attempt at establishing relations between Tibet and China, the lama returned to Nanjing and was given a prominent government position (personal communication, November 9, 2003).

104. Sir Charles Arthur Bell, *Tibet, Past and Present* (Delhi: Motilal Banarsidass, 2000 [1924]), 211.

105. Ibid., 219. Bell described the chief articles of trade: "Food, dress, utensils, and ornaments are all imported from China in large quantities. . . . A considerable portion of the wealth of Tibet is spent on dress. But the chief import from China is tea. . . . The chief exports from Tibet to China are wool, hides, musk, [and] medicinal herbs." In 1945 additional items being transported to Tibet from Qinghai ("a year's supply of liquor, soy sauce, vinegar, raisins, silver coins and silver ingots . . . horses and mules") or for sale in Lhasa ("goods imported from India: cotton and woolen textiles, blankets, shoes, hats, soap . . . matches, dyes, cups, mirrors, sunglasses, cigarettes, white and brown sugar and ivory bracelets") were observed by a Japanese passing through Central Tibet; see Kimura, *A Japanese Agent in Tibet,* 103, 119.

106. For the most thorough introduction to what race meant to modern Chinese, see Frank Dikötter, *The Discourse of Race in Modern China* (Stanford: Stanford University Press, 1992). See also his edited volume *The Construction of Racial Identities in China and Japan: Historical and Contemporary Perspectives* (Honolulu: University of Hawaii Press, 1997).

107. John Fitzgerald, "The Nationless State: The Search for a Nation in Modern Chinese Nationalism," *Australian Journal of Chinese Affairs,* no. 33 (January 1995): 85–86.

108. Michael Weiner, "The Invention of Identity: 'Self' and 'Other' in Pre-war Japan," in idem, ed., *Japan's Minorities: The Illusion of Homogeneity* (London: Routledge, 1997), 2.

109. Diköttter, *The Discourse of Race in Modern China,* 108.

110. Rhoads, *Manchus & Han,* 45, 64–65, 101.

111. Crossley, *A Translucent Mirror,* 360.

112. Fitzgerald, "The Nationless State," 87.

113. Dikötter, *The Discourse of Race in Modern China,* 86.

114. Pamela Crossley, *Orphan Warriors: Three Manchu Generations and the End of the Qing World* (Princeton, N.J.: Princeton University Press, 1990), 186.

115. Kai-wing Chow, "Imagining Boundaries of Blood: Zhang Binglin and the Invention of the Han 'Race' in Modern China," in Dikötter, *The Construction of Racial Identities,* 37.

116. Crossley, *A Translucent Mirror,* 351.

117. Crossley, *Orphan Warriors,* 186. Zhang is cited as saying, "Chinese and barbarians could not and should not be amalgamated, and the empire should be broken up in order to accommodate the separate destinies of its peoples" (355).

118. Rhoads, *Manchus & Han,* 294.

119. Ibid., 114–116. Hengjun may have been the first person to insist that "members of all five races were 'Chinese.' Whatever their ethnic differences, they were all 'citizens' of China."

120. Chow, "Imagining Boundaries of Blood," 39.

121. Rhoads, *Manchus & Han,* 127.

122. Ibid., 137; see also 267. Once the Chinese were in control of China, these numbers would change. The 1912 plans for the legislature (of 862 members) included 54 seats for Mongolia and 20 for Tibet, but these were not reserved for ethnic representatives. They were merely geographical divisions, usually filled by Chinese who had an interest in a region. No seats were reserved for the Manchus, as they had no province or territory in which they were a majority.

123. Rhoads, *Manchus & Han,* 207.

124. Ibid., 221.

125. Ibid., 223.

126. Ibid., 226.

127. Ibid., 238. He would later reconstitute the Republic of China as the "Empire of China" (Zhonghua Diguo) in early 1916. Hengjun, one of the architects of the "*wuzu gonghe*" rhetoric, was among the imperial clansmen who were central to this short-lived revival.

128. Ibid., 223–224.

129. Zhangjia dashi yuanqi dianli weiyuanhui, *Huguo jingjue fujiao dashi Zhangjia hutuketu shiji ce (Historical Traces of the Changja Qutughtu, the State-Protecting, Completely Enlightened Master Who Assists with Teaching)* (Taipei: Zhangjia dashi yuanqi dianli weiyuanhui, 1957), 32. This book is also one source of this lama's name (27): Luosang bandian danbi rongmei (Blo bzang dpal ldan bstan pa'i sgron me) and lists him as the nineteenth incarnation, or the seventh since the first lama to be confirmed in this title by the Kangxi emperor. For a shorter version of the lama's name in Tibetan script see: Blo bzang thub bstan chos kyi nyi na, *Skyabs ngon thams cad mkhyen pa,* 103.

130. Zhangjia dashi yuanqi dianli weiyuanhui, *Huguo jingjue fujiao dashi,* 33.

131. Rhoads, *Manchus & Han,* 264.

132. Translation of the Presidential Order enclosed in a letter from Britain's Chinese minister, cited in Michael C. van Walt, "Whose Game?" in *Soundings in Tibetan Civilization,* ed. Barbara Nimri Aziz and Matthew Kapstein, (New Delhi: Manohar, 1985), 219.

133. Goldstein, *The Demise of the Lamaist State,* 65–67.

134. Rhoads, *Manchus & Han,* 265.

135. Teichman, *Travels of a Consular Officer in Eastern Tibet,* 17–18, cited in Goldstein, *The Demise of the Lamaist State,* 59.

136. Bell, *Tibet, Past and Present,* 135. One Chinese source is said to contain these telegrams: Shih Ch'ing-yang's *Zangshi jiyao* (fascicle 1, 9b), an unpublished manuscript written while its author was the chairman of the Mongolian and Tibetan Affairs Commission, cited in Li Tieh-tseng, *The Historical Status of Tibet* (New York: King's Crown, 1956), 291, as including the exchange of telegrams between Yuan Shikai and the Dalai Lama in 1912. Presumably the Tibetan government would also have preserved such an important document, tantamount to

a declaration of independence if we are to believe Bell. Yet no such document has ever been made available to the interested public. That this exchange of documents has never been published suggests that neither Tibetan nor Chinese nationalists would benefit from the content of these letters becoming available. Tibetan assertions of independence from 1913 are contained in two documents cited secondhand only, but the originals also have never been made available to the public as far as I know. The first document is the January 8, 1913, proclamation of the thirteenth Dalai Lama to his officials and subjects, which stated that Tibet is an independent (lit. autonomous) country (Tib. *Rgyal khab rang dbang*), reproduced in Zhwa sgab pa, *Bod kyi srid don rgyal rabs*, 2:222; translation in Shakabpa, *Tibet: A Political History*, 248; and Goldstein, *The Demise of the Lamaist State*, 59–62. The other document cited to demonstrate Tibetans' articulation of their independence is the Mongolia-Tibetan Treaty of January 11, 1913; however, doubt about the validity of this treaty has been raised. See Alex McKay, *The History of Tibet*, 3:171–190, which also reproduced the Dalai Lama's proclamation and Parshotma Mehra's article, "The Mongolia-Tibet Treaty of January 11, 1913," published originally in the *Journal of Asian History* 3, no. 1 (1969).

137. The term contained the idea of ethnicity as well, but it seems anachronistic to translate it as nationality at this early date.

138. Chow, "Imaging Boundaries of Blood," 50.

139. Frank Dikötter, "Racial Discourse in China: Continuities and Permutations," in idem, *The Construction of Racial Identities*, 22.

140. Crossely, *Orphan Warriors*, 186.

141. Mark Elliot, *The Manchu Way: The Eight Banners and Ethnic Identity in Late Imperial China* (Stanford: Stanford University Press, 2001), 359. See also Rhoads, *Manchus & Han*, 293–294.

142. Fitzgerald, "The Nationless State," 89 n. 30.

143. Julie Lee Wei, Raymond H. Myers, and Donald G. Gillin, *Prescriptions for Saving China: Selected Writings of Sun Yat-sen*, trans. Julie Lee Wei, E-su Zen, and Linda Chao (Stanford: Hoover Institution Press, 1994), 89 (emphasis added).

144. Sun Yat-sen, *Memoirs of a Chinese Revolutionary* (Great Britain [Taipei]: [Sino-American Publishing], 1918 [1953]), 180–181 (emphasis added).

145. Ibid., 180–181 (emphasis added).

146. Chiang Kai-shek, *China's Destiny and Chinese Economic Theory*, trans. Philip Jaffee (New York: Roy, 1947), 77.

3. BUDDHISM AS A PAN-ASIAN RELIGION (1890s–1928)

1. Derek R. Peterson and Daren R. Walhof, *The Invention of Religion: Rethinking Belief in Politics and History* (New Brunswick, N.J.: Rutgers University Press, 2002), 1.

2. Ibid., 7.

3. There are hints in the historical record that some Chinese Buddhists from as far back as the Yuan dynasty had had an active interest in Tibetan Buddhist practices, but this was not a mainstream perspective. See Christopher Beckwith, "A Hitherto Unnoticed Yüan-period Collection Attributed to 'Phagspa," in *Tibetan and Buddhist Studies Commemorating the 200th Anniversary of the Birth of Alexander Csoma de Körös*, Bibliotheca orientalis Hungarica, vol. 29 (Budapest: Akademiai Kiado, 1984), 9–15.

4. Peterson and Walhof, *The Invention of Religion*, 6.

5. I am grateful to Elliot Sperling, who raised the important point that many Chinese had a very different view of the Tibetans, namely, as cruel "barbarians." For one presentation of this perspective, see Thomas Heberer, "Old Tibet a Hell on Earth? The myth of Tibet and Tibetans in Chinese Art and Propaganda," in *Imagining Tibet: Perceptions, Projections and Fantasies,* ed. Thierry Dodin and Heinz Räther (Somerville:Wisdom, 2001), 111–150. However, this idea was never raised in the materials I saw. Far from trying to defend Tibetans from such criticism, the most that Chinese supporters did to explain Tibetan culture was to justify the differences between Chinese and Tibetan Buddhism: vegetarian versus omnivorous diets, strict monasticism versus married lamas, and so forth. Even the critics of Tibetan lamas did not dwell on the "barbaric" features of the Tibetan people that were generally characteristic of Chinese perceptions of non-Chinese peoples.

6. Other terms such as *nang pa* and *sang gyas pa* were shared by the Bon po religious tradition, which was especially strong in Kham. There was also a small minority of Muslim Tibetans. However, in Tibet these other religious traditions did not hold the cultural or political power that the Buddhists did.

7. Matthew Kapstein has suggested that "Tibetans did have, and at times expressed, a concept of 'Buddhism' (*Sangs rgyas kyi bstan pa/—chos*) that included Chinese Buddhism. This is clear in a whole variety of eighteenth-century works (by Thu'u bkwan, Mgon po skyabs, Lcang skya, Sum pa, Kah thog Rig 'dzin, etc.). Occasionally it comes up in earlier writings as well (going back at least to the Yuan).The question is not so much whether the concept existed but rather when and how it was deployed" (personal communication, November 2004). In this context I would suggest that the recognition that "the teachings/dharma of the Buddha" (the literal translation of *Sangs rgyas kyi bstan pa/ chos*) is conceptually related across languages is different from the modern concept of ethnic variants of a single unified "Buddhism." In other words, I would not translate the Tibetan phrase "*Sangs rgyas kyi bstan pa/ chos*" as "Buddhism," at least not before the second half of the twentieth century. The modern term "Buddhism" is not limited to Buddhist teachings or doctrine (*bstan pa/ chos*) but is generally understood to include the entirety of the Buddhist religion (not just doctrine or teachings, but also institutions, historic origins, etc.), which is not included in the Tibetan terms in question. I would also note that the Yuan dynasty and Qing dynasty were periods of exceptionally close relations with Tibetans, and, in the latter period, Tibetanized Monguors and Mongols from the frontier between China and Tibet were more likely to view Chinese and Tibetan "Buddhisms" as linked than were ethnic Tibetans. For the modern period, the main point is that ethnic Tibetans did not turn to Chinese Buddhists for the study of Buddhism.

8. Blo bzang thub bstan chos kyi nyi ma, *Skyabs mgon thams cad mkhyen pa,* 640–641, 649, 115.

9. For example, see the 1933 and 1934 volumes of *Haichaoyin* in which critics of Tibetan Buddhism still use the somewhat pejorative and misleading "Lamaism," while Chinese monks educated in Tibetan Buddhism use the newer phrase.

10. Three of China's most prominent monasteries (Jinshan, Gaomin, and Tianning), as well as the leading ordination center (at Paomashan), were located east of Nanjing near the Yangtze River; see Welch, *The Buddhist Revival of China,* 103, 114, 250–251. The three leading Gelukpa Tibetan monasteries (*densa sum*), Ganden, Drepung, and Sera, were all in the vicinity of Lhasa; see Goldstein, *The Demise of the Lamaist State,* 24–31.

11. Welch, *The Buddhist Revival of China,* 176.

12. For Tsongkhapa's critique, see Tsongkhapa, *The Great Treatise on the Stages of the Path to Enlightenment,* 1:112.

13. For an examination of the influence of Chan Buddhism in Tibet, see Kapstein, *The Tibetan Assimilation of Buddhism*, chap. 5.

14. Dan Martin noted that the latter lama even "translated from Chinese into Tibetan a summarized account of the Indian travels of Xuanzang/Hsüan-tsang (Thang-zing/Thang-zang-gtsang) with the title *Thang-gur Dus-kyi Rgya-gar Zhing-gi Bkod-pa'i Dkar-chag,* known to us from citations, and published in facsimile edition by Sh. Bira" (*Tibetan Histories: A Bibliography of Tibetan-Language Historical Works* [London: Serindia, 1997], 125).

15. Welch, *The Buddhist Revival of China*, 176.

16. Dai Jitao, *Banchan dashi shuo liuzi daming jenyan fa yao* (*Essentials of the Panchen Lama's Teachings on the Six-Syllable Mantra*), vol. 3, *Dai Jitao xiansheng wencun* (Taipei: Zhongguo guomindang zhongyang weiyuanhui, 1959 [1931]), 1173.

17. Jonathan S. Walters, *Finding Buddhists in Global History: Essays on Global and Comparative History* (Washington, D.C.: American Historical Association, 1998).

18. For further details on this figure, see Gabrielle Goldfuss, *Vers un Bouddhisme du XXe siècle. Yang Wenhui (1837–1911), réformateur, laïque et imprimeur,* Mémoires de l'institut des hautes études Chinoises, 38 (Paris: Collége de France, Institut des hautes études Chinoises, 2001).

19. Goldfuss, *Yang Wenhui*, 78.

20. Welch, *The Buddhist Revival of China*, 4–5. Goldfuss, *Yang Wenhui*, 82, 113.

21. Goldfuss, *Yang Wenhui,* 74.

22. Ibid., 108–109.

23. Welch, *The Buddhist Revival of China,* 8–9. Goldfuss, *Yang Wenhui*, 111.

24. Welch, *The Buddhist Revival of China,* 198 (emphasis added).

25. John Calthorpe Blofeld, "Lamaism and Its Influence on Chinese Buddhism," *T'ien Hsia monthly* (September 1938): 157–160; Wing-tsit Chan, *Religious Trends in Modern China: Lectures on the History of Religions,* new ser., no. 3, The Haskell Lectures at the University of Chicago, 1950 (New York: Columbia University Press, 1953,) 74; Huang Hao, "Sanshi niandai Zhongguo Zangmi yanjiu—*Zangmi xiufa midian* ping jie" (Chinese Research on Tibetan Esoterica in the 1930s—Critique and Introduction to *Secret Scriptures of the Tibetan Esoteric Dharma Practices*), *Minzu yanjiu hui xun* (*Newsletter on Ethnic Studies*) 17, no. 3 (1997): 53. See also Welch, *The Buddhist Revival of China,* 179, 337 n. 45.

26. Welch, *The Buddhist Revival of China,* 26–27.

27. Ibid., 174.

28. For more details on the Monguors, see Louis Schram, "The Monguors of the Kansu-Tibetan Frontier, I," *Transactions of the American Philosophical Society,* new ser., vol. 44, pt. 1 (1954); "The Monguors of the Kansu-Tibetan Border, II," *Transactions of the American Philosophical Society,* new ser., vol. 47, pt. 1 (1957); "The Monguors of the Kansu-Tibetan Frontier, III," *Transactions of the American Philosophical Society,* new ser., vol. 51, pt. 3 (1961), soon to be reissued in a single volume, with new introductory materials.

29. Naquin, *Peking,* 585, cf. Rawski, *The Last Emperors,* 252.

30. Naquin, *Peking,* 69–70.

31. Ibid., 591.

32. Smith, *Tibetan Nation,* 183, 205. Ya, *The Biographies of the Dalai Lamas,* 314, 322.

33. Welch, *The Buddhist Revival of China,* 39. Despite this government order, this organization seems to have continued to exist in some capacity, as the Panchen Lama lectured to this group when in Beijing in 1932. See Blo bzang thub bstan chos kyi nyi ma, Panchen Lama VI (IX), *PaN chen thams cad mkhyen pa rje btsun Blo bzang thub bstan chos kyi nyi ma dge legs rnam*

rgyal bzang po'i gsung 'bum (*The Collected Works of the Sixth [Ninth] Panchen Lama Blo bzang thub bstan chos kyi nyi ma*) (New Delhi: Reproduced from the Bkra shis lhun po blocks, 1973 [1944]), 1:583.

34. Beckwith, "A Hitherto Unnoticed Yüan-period Collection," 9–15. I do not readily accept the idea that this Tibetan collection entered and continuously remained "a basic teaching text of the esoteric school in China" after the Yuan dynasty, as Beckwith seems to do. Instead, in the absence of other evidence, I suspect that this text was only recently rediscovered in the modern period: see a recent reprint of this collection (Pakpa was listed as Yuan dynasty *guoshi*, translator and editor of the collection) found in the 1930s in Beijing by Chen Jiamin *shangshi* (*bla ma*), who later revised the collection; see Puosiba [Pakpa], *Sajia taoguo xinbian,* vol. Zangmi xilie 6801, Huihai congshu (Taizhong: Huihai shuzhai, 1992).

35. Mei Jingshun, "Minguo zaoqi xianmi Fojiao chongtu de tantao" (Probing into the Conflicts of Exoteric and Esoteric Buddhism in the Early Republic), *Zhonghua Foxue yanjiu (Chung-hwa Buddhist Studies)* 3 (1999): 251–270. 255–257.

36. Weihuan, "Buddhism in Modern China," *T'ien Hsia monthly* (September 1939): 140–155.

37. Wing-tsit Chan, *Religious Trends in Modern China,* 75, 77.

38. Blofeld, "Lamaism and Its Influence on Chinese Buddhism," 159.

39. Shi Dongchu, *Zhongguo Fojiao jindai shi* (*Modern History of Chinese Buddhism*), 2 vols. (Taipei shi: Zhonghua Fojiao wenhua guan, 1974), 1:437. Bai Puren was also known as Bai lama. Bai, in Chinese, means "white," and this lama's Mongolian name was probably Chaghan (Mong. white). An important incarnation series during the Qing dynasty, the Chaghan lamas might have been linked to this twentieth-century figure, but the lines of affiliation are not clear.

40. Sanskrit title: *Suvarnaprabhasottamasutra.* Full name: *Jin guang ming zuisheng wang jing,* ed. Ci Yi, *Foguang da cidian,* 7 vols. (Beijing: Beijing tushuguan chubanshe, 1989), 4:3524; originally translated into Chinese by Yijing. For further details, see Johan Nobel, *Suvarnaprabhasottamasutra. Das Goldglanz-Sutra: ein Sankrittext des Mahayana-Buddhismus: I-Tsing's chinesische Version und ihre tibetische Übersetung* (Leiden: E. J. Brill, 1958). For an English translation, see R. E. Emmerick, *The Sutra of Golden Light: Being a Translation of the Suvarnabhasottamasutra* (London: Luzac, 1970).

41. Sanskrit: *devaraja.* Ch. *si tian wang.* Ci Yi, *Foguang da cidian,* 4:3524.

42. On the role of Tibetan Buddhism at Chengde in the Qing period, see Anne Chayet, *Les temples de Jehol et leurs modèles tibétains,* Synthèse, no. 19 (Paris: Editions Recherche sur les civilisations, 1985); Philippee Forêt, *Mapping Chengde: The Qing Landscape Enterprise* (Honolulu: University of Hawaii, 2000); and the collection of essays from a conference on Chengde organized by Donald Lopez at the University of Michigan: James Millward, Ruth Dunnell, Mark Elliot, and Phillippe Forêt, *New Qing Imperial History: The Making of Inner Asian Empire at Qing Chengde* (London: Routledge/Curzon, 2004).

43. In 1923 the Commission to Rearrange Beijing's Lama Temples (Beiping Lama simiao zhengli weiyuanhui) was initiated by the Republican government's Mongolian and Tibetan Affairs Commission (Meng-Zang weiyuanhui) at Yonghegong. The Xihuangsi (Western Yellow Temple), renovated in 1908 for the thirteenth Dalai Lama's visit, was also involved. See Dan jun—Zaina panduo and Li, *Mingcha shuang huangsi,* 251.

44. Shi Dongchu, *Zhongguo Fojiao jindai shi,* 1:437.

45. Karl Ludvig Reichelt, *Truth and Tradition in Chinese Buddhism: A Study of Chinese Mahayana Buddhism,* trans. Katrina Van Wagenen Bugge (New Delhi: Munshiram Manoharalal, 2001 [1928]), 309–310.

46. Mei Jingshun, "Minguo yilai de Han Zang Fojiao guanxi (1912–1949):Yi Han Zang jiaoli yuan wei zhongxin de tantao" (Sino-Tibetan Relations during the Republican Period (1912–1949): Probing into the Sino-Tibetan Buddhist Institute at the Center of Relations), *Zhonghua Foxue yanjiu* (Chung-hwa Institute of Buddhist Studies,Taipei) 2 (1998): 257.

47. Mei, "Minguo yilai de Han Zang Fojiao guanxi," 257; Fazun, "Zhuzhe ru Zang de jing-guo" (The Author's Experiences upon Entering Tibet), in *Xiandai Xizang* (*Contemporary Tibet*) (Chengdu: Dongfang shushe, 1943), 126.

48. Wang-Toutain, "Fazun: le Xuanzang des temps moderns," 713.

49. Welch, *The Buddhist Revival of China,* 197.

50. Shi Dongchu, *Zhongguo Fojiao jindai shi,* 511. For more details on this scripture, see Charles Orzech, *Politics and Transcendent Wisdom: The Scripture for Humane Kings in the Creation of Chinese Buddhism* (University Park, Pa.: Pennsylvania State University Press, 1998). Along with the *Fahua jing* and the *Jin guang ming jing,* the *Renwang jing* was of the three quasi-esoteric texts popular in China that promised protection to the country in which it was recited (Ci Yi, *Foguang da cidian,* 4:3524).

51. Mei, "Minguo yilai de Han Zang Fojiao guanxi," 271.

52. Welch's spelling of the lama's name, Dorje Tsripa Gegen, was based on the Chinese (Duojie jiuba gegen) (1968, 369). Wang-Toutain ("Fazun: le Xuanzang des temps moderns," 712–713) gave the unlikely transcription Rdo rje rtis/rtsis pa dge dgen [*sic:* rgan] but did not cite the source for this transcription. The correct Tibetan spelling, Rdo rje gcod pa, was pro-vided by Alak Zenkar Rinpoché Tudeng Nima to Robert Barnett (personal communication). Shi Dongchu (*Zhongguo Fojiao jindai shi,* 437) relates another story about this lama's arrival in Beijing. He claims that Duan Qirui wanted Dorjé Chöpa to practice the dharma in order to avert disaster. However, to avoid the stigma of superstition, Duan had a representative ask the lama on his behalf. In reward for the lama's assistance, he gave him the title Nomin han (Mong. *Nom-un khan;* Tib. *Chos rje*).As this event is not recorded in other sources, it seems not to have been well publicized, if indeed it happened at all. His biography indicated that he served as a translator for the thirteenth Dalai Lama at Wutaishan and Beijing in 1907–8 (Chengdu Xi'nan heping fahui banshichu, *Chengdu Xi'nan heping fahui tekan* [Chengdu: Chengdu Xi'nan heping fahui banshichu, 1932], 25). If this was accurate, Dorjé Chöpa may have been translating Chinese for him, because the Dalai Lama was said to already be fluent in Mongolian; see Dundul Namgyal Tsarong, *In the Service of His Country: The Biography of Dasang Damdul Tsarong, Commander General of Tibet* (Ithaca, N.Y.: Snow Lion, 2000), 19. Robert Barnett graciously shared with me the following information based on his discussion with Tudeng Nima: "His closest friend was a close friend of DC [Dorjé Chöpa] and told him many stories about him, and of course they are from the same area. He doubts that DC had very good Chinese or that he could have translated for the thirteenth [Dalai Lama] at Wutaishan, because he suspects that he would have only known Kangding Chinese, and probably only a basic level at that" (per-sonal communication).

53. Shi Dongchu, *Zhongguo Fojiao jindai shi,* I:437–438.

54. As this town truly straddled the Sino-Tibetan cultural frontier, it was well known by both names, so I will vary the Chinese or Tibetan name according to circumstance (e.g., how the name appears in the materials I am consulting) throughout this book.

55. Special thanks to Yudruk Tsomu for locating the correct Tibetan spelling of this tem-ple's name. This temple was designated as one of the so-called Eight *Dalama* temples (*ba Dalama si*) recognized by the Qing court; see Cihai, "Can bai Dayong fashi daochang ji"

(Record of Attending the [Memorial] Ceremony for Master Dayong), *Haichaoyin* 11, no. 1 (1930): 3. For more details on the "Eight *Dalama*s," see He Juefei, *Xikang jishi shiben shizhu (Annotated Poems Recording the Events of Xikang)*, Xizangxue Hanwen wenxian congshu (Chinese-language Tibetological Literature Series) 2 (Lhasa: Xizang renmin chubanshe, 1988), 149–151. This status may help to explain both the presence of Tibetan monks who could speak Chinese and the ability of the Chinese monks to gain admittance there. The long-standing connections with Beijing were probably still partially intact at this time. This temple was the site of Dayong's memorial ceremony, attended by the two hundred Tibetan resident monks and some thirty Chinese monks studying in Kham. According to Gyurme Dorje's *Tibet Handbook* (Lincolnwood [Chicago]: Passport Books, 1996, 503–504), the monastery, once home to more than one hundred monks, was "founded by Minyakpa Tenpel nyima in the 17th century as a branch of Drepung Losaling College" and hosted the fourteenth Dalai Lama on his way to Beijing in 1954. For an overview of the temple's continuing importance, see Sichuan sheng Kangding xianzhi bianji weiyuanhui, *Kangding xianzhi (Kangding County Gazetteer)* (Chengdu: Sichuan chubanshe, 1995), 442. Later, in 1937, the temple would host a ceremony, attended by Dai Jitao, memorializing the ninth Panchen Lama. During the period in which Kangding served as the capital of the Xikang Provincial Government, a Tibetan Buddhist school called the Wuming xueyuan (see chapter 7) operated here. At present, the monastery is home to the prefecture and county Buddhist associations.

    56. Shi, *Zhongguo Fojiao jindai shi*, 437–438.

    57. Some of these translations may be included in the reprint of the lama's 1930 bilingual work, which I did not discover in time to examine carefully: Duojue jueda [sic:ba], *Micheng fahai (Dharma Ocean of the Esoteric Vehicle)* (Taipei: Xinwen feng chubanshe gongci, 1987 [1930]).

    58. "Bai Lama lixiang qingxing," *Haichaoyin* 7, no. 2 (1926): 8. Cited in Mei, "Minguo zaoqi xianmi Fojiao chongtu," 260–261 n. 28.

    59. Jerome Cavanaugh and Chinese Materials Center, *Who's Who in China, 1918–1950: With an Index,* 4th ed. (Hong Kong: Chinese Materials Center, 1982), 446; supplement to the 4th ed., 37. Zhao had switched his allegiance to the Beijing government during the Northern Punitive Expedition that same year

    60. Fafang, "Zhongguo Fojiao xianzhuang," 24; Mei, "Minguo yilai de Han Zang Fojiao guanxi," 275 n. 20.

    61. Chengdu Xi'nan heping fahui banshichu, *Chengdu Xi'nan heping fahui tekan,* 29–30.

    62. I have not attempted to document exhaustively every lama who visited China. For a list of some of these figures, see Welch, *Buddhist Revival,* 335 n. 37.

    63. Ya, *Biographies of the Tibetan Spiritual Leaders Panchen Erdenis,* 261.

    64. Jagou, "A Pilgrim's Progress," 14.

    65. Welch, *The Buddhist Revival of China,* 157.

    66. Danzhu Angben, *Libei Dalai Lama yu Banchan Erdeni nianpu,* 636.

    67. Similarly, two of the most prominent American scholars of Tibetan Buddhism (Robert Thurman and Jeffrey Hopkins) studied in an ethnically Mongol Tibetan Buddhist monastery in New Jersey (Rick Fields, *How the Swans Came to the Lake: A Narrative History of Buddhism in America* [Boulder: Shambhala, 1981], 291–293). For more details on Chinese Tibetologists, see my article "Modern Tibetan Historiography in China," *Papers on Chinese History* (1998): 85–108.

    68. Welch, *The Buddhist Revival of China,* 197. See *Haichaoyin* 6, no. 4 (1925): 11.

69. Welch, *The Buddhist Revival of China,* 251.

70. This temple had a history of association with Tibetan Buddhism from the time of the Mongol empire in China when Sakya Dakchen Zangpopel resided there.

71. My identification of this last bodhisattva is tentative. Ci Yi, in *Foguang da cidian,* 2:1117, indicates that there are five vajra bodhisattvas, but many variants are listed in volume 4. I suspect that this refers to Vajrapani, because these three bodhisattvas are traditionally associated with one another in Tibetan Buddhism. In any case, it is clear that this bodhisattva is associated with the esoteric tradition because of the Chinese term *jingang.*

72. Danzhu Angben, *Libei Dalai Lama yu Banchan Erdeni nianpu,* 637.

73. Welch, *The Buddhist Revival of China,* 239.

74. Hoong Teik Toh has argued that the "Indian" and "Western" monks encountered by Chinese on this island in the late Yuan dynasty (1276–1368) and Ming dynasty (1368–1644) were actually Tibetan Buddhists ("Tibetan Buddhism in Ming China," 115–118).

75. Welch, *The Buddhist Revival of China,* 5.

76. These were probably Mexican silver dollars, which were one of the only reliable forms of currency in the unstable political and economic situation in China at this time.

77. That Chinese studied Tibetan Buddhism in the Yuan, Ming, and Qing periods is by and large agreed on, but specific evidence of this idea is generally scarce. See, for instance, Christopher Beckwith, "A Hitherto Unnoticed Yüan-period Collection Attributed to 'Phagspa,'" for the Yuan; Patricia Berger, "Preserving the Nation," and Heather Karmay, *Early Sino-Tibetan Art* (Warminster: Aris and Phillips, 1975), for the Ming; and Berger, *Empire of Emptiness,* and Wang, "Tibetan Buddhism at the Court of Qing," for the Qing.

78. Danzhu Angben, *Libei Dalai Lama yu Banchan Erdeni nianpu,* 637.

79. In fact, he was so comfortable in these surroundings that he treated his Chinese escort with contempt, basically ignoring their sovereignty over this territory. See Bell, *Portrait of a Dalai Lama,* 81–82.

80. Danzhu Angben, *Libei Dalai Lama yu Banchan Erdeni nianpu,* 637.

81. For photos of Qing examples of a golden certificate and of a golden seal, see *A Collection of the Historical Archives of Tibet,* ed. Archives of the Tibet Autonomous Region (Beijing: Wenwu chubanshe, 1995), entries 74 and 71, respectively.

82. Ya, *The Biographies of the Dalai Lamas,* 263.

83. Ya, *Biographies of the Tibetan Spiritual Leaders Panchen Erdenis,* 264; Danzhu Angben, *Libei Dalai Lama yu Banchan Erdeni nianpu,* 637–638.

84. What exactly occurred is left to the reader's imagination, as no concrete details are provided.

85. Han, *Kang-Zang Fojiao,* 4v.

86. Ibid., 8v.

87. Howard L. Boorman and Richard C. Howard, eds., *Biographical Dictionary of Republican China,* 3 vols. (1970), 3:335.

88. The link between these two men was one bureau chief Li (which bureau is not specified), a native of Sichuan Province, who was in Beijing on government business when he met the Norlha Qutughtu at the Panchen Lama's residence there (Han, *Kang-Zang Fojiao,* 4v, 8v–9r). See also Skal bzang bkra shis, "Mgar ra bla ma," 119, which confirms that this lama was invited to Sichuan by Li Gongdu, Liu Xiang's secretary, who met him in Beijing. On Li Gongdu, see "Xinwen" (News) *Haichaoyin* 15, no. 4 (1934): 112/524.

89. Personal communication with descendants, August 1999.

90. Robert Kapp, *Szechuan and the Chinese Republic, 1911–1938* (New Haven:Yale University Press, 1973), 93, 32.

91. Shi Dongchu, *Zhongguo Fojiao jindai shi,* 398.

92. Han, *Kang-Zang Fojiao,* 4v.

93. Gan Wenfeng, "Zangchuan Fojiao zai Chongqing" (Tibetan Buddhism in Chongqing), in *Chongqing wenshi ziliao (Chongqing Cultural and Historical Materials),* no. 41, ed. Zhongguo renmin zhengzhi xieshang huiyi and Chongqing shi weiyuanhui wenshi ziliao weiyuanhui, 172.

94. Han, *Kang-Zang Fojiao,* 9r.

95. Ibid., 4v.

96. Cavanaugh and Chinese Materials Center, *Who's Who in China, 1918–1950,* supplement to the 4th ed., 82.

97. Han, *Kang-Zang Fojiao,* 4v.

98. Prasenjit Duara, *Rescuing History from the Nation* (Chicago: University of Chicago Press, 1995), 157.

99. Writing in the People's Republic of China, Yu Lingbo ("Goutong Han-Zang wenhua de Shi Fazun (1902–1980)" ["Master Fazun's Linking Chinese and Tibetan Culture (1902–1980)"], in *Zhongguo jinxiandai Fojiao renwu zhi [Records of Chinese Contemporary Buddhist Figures]* [Beijing: Zongjiao wenhua chubanshe, 1995], 264) called it the "Fu Zang xue fa tuan." Shi Dongchu (*Zhongguo Fojiao jindai shi,* 448), writing in Taiwan, called it "Liu Zang xuefa tuan." Although the distinction between "going" (*fu*) and "going abroad" (*liu*) to study is subtle, it deserves notice. Contemporary PRC publications might be expected to edit out the suggestion that Chinese were "going abroad" when traveling to Tibet, although this did slip past the censors' eyes in some internal (*neibu*) biographical publications. See also the Taiwanese reprint of Fazun, "Wo ru Zang de jingguo" (My Experiences upon Entering Tibet), in *Fazun wenji (Collected Works of Fazun),* ed. Hong Jisong and Huang Jilin, Dangdai Zhongguo Fojiao dashi wenji, no. 9 (Taipei: Wenshu chubanshe: Menshi bu Wenshu Fojiao wenhua zhongxin, 1988), 267, which used the abbreviated phrase "*liuxue tuan.*" In the 1930s even studying in Kham was considered to be "studying abroad," as demonstrated by a lecture given by Taixu and Hengyan recorded in an article in *Haichaoyin* (11, no. 9 [1930]: 4) entitled "Liuxue Xikang Fojiao tuan jinguang" (The Present Condition of the Buddhist Team Studying Abroad in Kham).

100. Fazun, "Zhuzhe ru Zang de jingguo," 129.

101. Dingzhi, *Nenghai shangshi zhuan (Biography of Guru Nenghai),* Nenghai shangshi chuanji, Vol. 6 (Taipei: Fangguang wenhua shiye youxian gongci, 1995), 15.

102. Dingzhi, *Nenghai shangshi zhuan,* 17.

4. OVERCOMING BARRIERS BETWEEN CHINA AND TIBET (1929–1931)

1. Mei, "Minguo yilai de Han Zang Fojiao guanxi," 8.

2. Fazun, "Wo ru Zang de jingguo," 272.

3. Mei, "Minguo yilai de Han Zang Fojiao guanxi," 8.

4. Chengdu Xi'nan heping fahui banshichu, *Chengdu Xi'nan heping fahui tekan,* 69–70. See, especially, letters to Nenghai and Dagang.

5. Dingzhi, *Nenghai shangshi zhuan,* 17–18.

6. Fazun, "Fazun zhi Hu Zihu jushi shu" (Letter from Fazun to Layman Hu Zihu), in *Fazun wenji (Collected Writings of Fazun),* ed. Hong Jisong and Huang Jilin, Dangdai Zhongguo Fojiao

dashi wenji, no. 9 (Taibei: Wenshu chubanshe: Menshi bu Wenshu fojiao wenhua zhongxin), 1988 [1931], 258: *"dayang liang bai yuan."*

7. Ibid., 260, 259.

8. Fazun, "Zhuzhe ru Zang de jingguo," 129.

9. Dingzhi, *Nenghai shangshi zhuan,* 21.

10. Dayong sought to hire the old imperial court's language instructor, still present in Beijing and residing in Yonghegong, but to no avail (Chengdu Xi'nan heping fahui banshichu, *Chengdu Xi'nan heping fahui tekan,* 29).

11. Fazun, "Fazun fashi zishu" (Autobiography of Master Fazun), in Hong and Huang, *Fazun wenji,* 245.

12. Yu Daoquan, *Love Songs of the Sixth Dalai Lama Tshangs dbyangs rgya mtsho,* trans. Yu Daoquan, National Research Institute of History and Philology Monographs, series A, no. 5 (Beijing: Academica Sinica, 1930), v.

13. Fu Chongju, *Chengdu tonglan* (*Comprehensive Guide to Chengdu*) (Chengdu: Bashu shushe, 1987 [1909]), 55. My thanks to Kristin Stapelton for pointing out this information to me. For details, see Ganzi zhou zhi bianji weiyuanhui, *Ganzi zhou zhi* (*Ganzi Prefectural Gazetteer*) (Chengdu: Sichuan minzu chubanshe, 1998), vol. 3 (education section): The school was founded in 1906 (by the Zhao brothers, no doubt).

14. Fazun, "Fazun fashi zishu," 245. These were entitled *Siti hebi fanyi mingyi ji* (for Buddhist terms) and simply *Siti hebi* (for secular terminology). Perhaps this was based on the short Ming period vocabulary, mentioned above, studied by Tatsuo Nishida.

15. The famed quintalingual glossary of the Qianlong period was organized for the benefit of Manchus and was scarcely accessible to Chinese commoners, even in the early Republican period.

16. See Rockhill, *Tibet.*

17. Fazun, "Wo ru Zang de jingguo," 268.

18. Gyurme Dorje, *Tibet Handbook,* 503–506.

19. See Zongkaba, *Puti dao zidi guanglun* (*The Great Treatise on the Graduated Path to Enlightenment*), trans. Fazun (Shanghai: Shanghai Foxue shuju, 1935 [reprint, n.d.]), 610.

20. Dingzhi, *Nenghai shangshi zhuan,* 16.

21. *Han Zang jiaoli yuan li'an wenjian huibian* (*Compilation of Registered Documents of the Sino-Tibetan Buddhist Institute*), Chongqing 1936 (hereafter, *HZJLY* 1936), 14.

22. For an eighteenth-century Chinese perspective on these differences, see Rockhill, *Tibet,* 221–234.

23. In the eighteenth century there had been six military posts, a single Chinese inn, and a scattering of Chinese temples along the route to Tibet, but these were doubtless defunct after the bitter fighting between Chinese and Tibetans in the first two decades of the twentieth century (see Rockhill, *Tibet,* 35, 259).

24. Fazun, "Wo ru Zang de jingguo," 268: *"chuangzuo putong sengren jin Zang."* Although this could simply mean dressed as ordinary (Chinese) monks, I assume it means that they were pretending to be Tibetan monks so as not to attract notice. As such, they would have had to travel at high altitude at a pace to which they were not accustomed. In his 1943 account Fazun explained that they were too exhausted to continue past Kardzé. See also Fazun, "Fazun zhi Hu Zihu jushi shu," 254. Fazun's autobiography ("Fazun fashi zishu," 246), written some fifty years after the events, indicated that they could not have gone any farther because of a Tibetan government decree. Possibly both factors played a role.

25. See Dingzhi, *Nenghai shangshi zhuan*, 16: Nenghai was said to have had some twenty laymen studying with him while in Litang in 1926–27. These would almost certainly have been Chinese. Also, a military encampment apparently helped Nenghai and his group cross a line of control into Tibetan-controlled territory (18). Again, I assume that this was a Chinese military encampment.

26. Fazun, "Wo chuguo de Xizang," 269.

27. Ibid., 272.

28. Dingzhi, *Nenghai shangshi zhuan*, 19.

29. Fazun, "Wo chuguo de Xizang," 267.

30. Yu Lingbo, *Zhongguo jinxiandai Fojiao renwu zhi*, 265. Fazun indicated that thirty people started out ("Wo chuguo de Xizang," 267).

31. Dingzhi, *Nenghai shangshi zhuan*, 16.

32. Fazun, "Fazun fashi zishu," 255 (emphasis added). The use of the term *Zhongguo* (for China) is a tacit but clear recognition that Chamdo was not part of China at this time.

33. Fazun, "Wo chuguo de Xizang," 267.

34. For one contemporary description of the Chinese loss of position in this region, see Fazun, "Fazun zhi Hu Zihu jushi shu," 254. For an account of this region just after these Chinese monks passed through, see Goldstein, Sherap, and Siebenschuh, *A Tibetan Revolutionary*, chaps. 1, 2.

35. Rockhill, *Tibet*, 112.

36. Yu Lingbo, *Zhongguo jinxiandai Fojiao renwu zhi*, 264. See also Dingzhi (*Nenghai shangshi zhuan*, 16) in which an official with a Chinese name (though possibly an ethnic Tibetan) was suspicious of Nenghai and gave him the choice of turning back or pushing forward but would not allow him to remain within the territory under his jurisdiction.

37. Fazun, "Wo chuguo de Xizang," 269; idem, "Fazun zhi Hu Zihu jushi shu," 254

38. Fazun, "Wo chuguo de Xizang," 272.

39. Although some Chinese monks apparently traveled relatively quickly to Tibet once they had reached Chamdo, these men disappear from the historical record. See Fazun, "Wo chuguo de Xizang," 271. Masters Liangchan and Fangguang proceeded immediately to Lhasa and made it, but apparently without proper connections they accomplished little. See also Fazun, "Fazun zhi Hu Zihu jushi shu," 255.

40. Fazun, "Wo chuguo de Xizang," 269: Ch. Zhajia si, Zhajia fashi; Fazun, "Fazun fashi zishu," 254: Zhage si.

41. Fazun's translation of Tsongkhapa's *Lam rim chen mo* (*Puti dao zidi guanglun*, 610) gave the Tibetan of Andong geshe as Amdo geshé. For further references to this figure, see Wang-Toutain, "Fazun: le Xuanzang des temps moderns," 716.

42. Dingzhi, *Nenghai shangshi zhuan*, 17.

43. Ibid. The basis for this biographic information is drawn from the memoirs of the Lhasa noblewomam Dorje Yudon Yuthok, *House of the Turquoise Roof* (Ithaca, N.Y.: Snow Lion, 1990), 127–128, and a Chinese language biography included in Nenghai's disciple Qingding's *Qingding shangshi kaishi lu* (*Record of Guru Qingding's Teaching*) (Chengdu: Chengdushi xinwen chubanchu, 1999), 47–57. To my eye, the two photographs in these accounts seem to depict the same figure, and the year of birth is only off by two years, while both agree that the lama died in 1941. If my identification is correct, the lama's full name is Ngakwang Yangchen Chökyi Wangchuk, as given in Yuthok. Ester Bianchi's forthcoming work on Nenghai ("The Movement of 'Tantric Rebirth' in Modern China: Rethinking and Re-vivifying Esoteric

Buddhism according to the Japanese and Chinese Traditions," in *Buddhism between China and Tibet,* ed. Matthew Kapstein) includes a translation of the Chinese language biography of Khangsar Rinpoché that attributes his name to his place of birth (Kham) and the Tibetan word for place (*sa*), but this smacks of a folk etemology. Although Tibetan lamas are frequently given names based on the locality they are from, this combination of a well-known place name such as Kham with *sa* is not an attested way of naming a locality as far as I can discover. On the other hand, Khangsar (meaning "new house," in this case drawn from a house he inhabited at Drepung monastery; see Yuthok, *House of the Turquoise Roof,* 127) was the name both of a prominent Tibetan lama in Lhasa in the early twentieth century and the name of a family and their territory in Kham: the Khangsartsang (lineage) in Kardzé.

44. Yuthok, *House of the Turquoise Roof,* 128.

45. Goldstein, *The Demise of the Lamaist State,* 26–31.

46. Dingzhi, *Nenghai shangshi zhuan,* 20. Gumu zhacang, Waxu micun. Micun (Tib. *mi mtshan*) is a subunit of a *khangtsen.*

47. Mongol monks came from as far away as the Volga, Lake Baikal, and Urga. Although the Tibetan government was aware of the nationality of these monks, this feature was not a matter that would prevent them from entering the monasteries.

48. Kimura, *Japanese Agent in Tibet,* 121. Kimura's fellow agent Nishikawa was genuinely interested in Buddhism and was allowed to study in Drepung (*Japanese Agent in Tibet,* 142, 148, 162–163).

49. Chengdu Xi'nan heping fahui banshichu, *Chengdu Xi'nan heping fahui tekan,* 29–30.

50. Ibid., 34.

51. Gan Wenfeng, "Zangchuan Fojiao zai Chongqing," 170–171. Possibly the rivalry between Liu Wenhui (the uncle) and Liu Xiang (the nephew) was played out even in the support of Dorjé Chöpa in Sichuan. This Communist-era source did not even mention Liu Xiang, but association with warlords is not something typically celebrated in the "Cultural and Historical Materials" series in which the article is found. Until more sources are available it is a safe assumption that Liu Xiang at least approved of such a large expenditure in his territorial capital, even if he did not contribute to building the stupa.

52. Chengdu Xi'nan heping fahui banshichu, *Chengdu Xi'nan heping fahui tekan,* 35, 71.

53. Ibid., 43.

54. Ibid., 41

55. Ibid., 39–40.

56. Ibid., 59–60, 34.

57. Ibid., 40

58. Goldstein, Sherap, and Siebenschuh, *A Tibetan Revolutionary,* 25, 29.

59. Chengdu Xi'nan heping fahui banshichu, *Chengdu Xi'nan heping fahui tekan,* 148. The various forms of exchange were converted into the most valuable unit, Mexican silver dollars.

60. Ibid., 104–105.

61. Ibid., 88.

62. Ibid., 130–131.

63. Ibid., 79.

64. Typical of the Chinese misunderstanding of Tibetan Buddhism, all the monks were called lamas, a title that should have been reserved for Dorjé Chöpa alone.

65. Chengdu Xi'nan heping fahui banshichu, *Chengdu Xi'nan heping fahui tekan,* 69–70; see, especially, letters to Nenghai and Dagang.

66. Ibid., 149. Possibly these monks were following Nenghai to Tibet.

67. The Tang emperors had supported a Central Asian monk by the name of Amoghavajra (Ch. *Bukong Jingang,* 705–774) to initiate them into esoteric Buddhism and to set up altars "for *homa* used for 'averting disasters, increase, subjugation, and joy.'" See Orzech, *Politics and Transcendent Wisdom,* 142.

68. Don A. Pittman, *Toward a Modern Chinese Buddhism* (Honolulu: University of Hawaii Press, 2001). Taixu also figures prominently in Goldfuss, *Yang Wenhui,* as well as in Gotelind Müller, *Buddhismus und Moderne: Ouyang, Taixu und das Ringen um ein zeitgemässes Selbstverständnis im Chinesischen Buddhismus des frühen 20. Jahrhunderts,* Münchener Ostasiatische Studien, 63 (Stuttgart:Verlag, 1993).

69. Reichelt, *Truth and Tradition,* 301–302.

70. Welch, *The Buddhist Revival of China,* 157. See also Hoh Chih-hsiang's 1933 preface to Cavanaugh, *Who's Who in China, 1918–1950,* supplement to the 4th ed. (i), which noted: "As a special feature, the book contains the first Chinese Buddhist monk and one Tibetan religious leader from Hsikang in Inner Tibet [Norlha Qutughtu]."

71. Welch, *The Buddhist Revival of China,* 58.

72. Pittman, *Toward a Modern Chinese Buddhism,* 99; and Welch, *The Buddhist Revival of China.*

73. Welch, *The Buddhist Revival of China,* 198.

74. The mantra from this scripture was reputed to have been responsible for saving the Japanese from the Mongol incursions in the thirteenth century.This esoteric practice may have eventually been dropped because of the irony of its historical antecedent and its inability to protect China from Japan (Welch, *The Buddhist Revival of China,* 179).

75. Charles Orzech, "Buddhism's Assimilation to Tang Political Culture," in *Sources of Chinese Tradition,* ed.William de Bary and Irene Bloom (New York: Columbia University Press, 1999), 477–480.

76. Orzech, *Politics and Transcendent Wisdom,* 90, 121.

77. See Fitzgerald, *Awakening China.*

78. Orzech, *Politics and Transcendent Wisdom,* 68, 4.

79. Ibid., 8.

80. Fori, "Jinjin mizong re zhi fansi" (Thoughts on the Zeal of Esoteric Buddhism in Recent Times), *Fayin (Voice of the Dharma),* no. 137 (1996): 32. As described by Fori, the goal was "to deeply enter eastern [Japanese] esoterica and Tibetan esoterica and fuse them with Chinese esoterica [*shen ru Dongmi Zangmi er zhiwei Zhongmi*]."

81. Hu Ruyan, "Jianli Dayong fashi daochang muhua yuan qi" (Collecting Funds for Dayong's Memorial Ceremony), *Haichaoyin* 21, no. 1 (1930): 4. This issue also included a photo of Dayong, with the caption, "The honored image of Dayong Asheli (Sanskrit, *Ācârya*)." This monk was also called Dayong hutuketu by Dai Jitao, in *Dai Jitao xiansheng wencun,* 3:1251.

82. Mei, "Minguo yilai de Han Zang Fojiao guanxi," 255–256, 276 n. 27.

83. Ibid., 255–256, 276 n. 28, reported in *Weiyin* (January 1930), which gave the reason for the opposition.

84. Ibid., 255–256, 276 n. 26, reported in *Weiyin* (January 1930). Elsewhere (259) Mei implied that Liu Xiang had already sent monks in 1929, but the September 1930 *Weiyin* article is the only contemporary source on such activities.

85. Manzhi, "Shijie Fojiao xuefan Han Zang jiaoli yuan zhi shiming" (The Mission of the

World Buddhist Institute's Sino-Tibetan Buddhist Institute), *Haichaoyin* 13, no. 1 (1932): 1. Mei says that the two men met in November ("Minguo yilai de Han Zang Fojiao guanxi," 259), whereas Shi Weixian reported that they met in August ("Han Zang jiaoliyuan yu Taixu fashi" [The Sino-Tibetan Buddhist Institute and Master Taixu], in *Weixian fashi shi wenji* [*Master Weixian's Collected Poems and Writings*] [Chengdu: Chengdu shi xinwen chubanju, 1995], 2). In both cases the original idea to send monks to Tibet was credited to Liu Xiang.

86. Shortly after his rival Liu Wenhui was recognized as governor in 1931 by the Nanjing government, Liu Xiang started a civil war in Sichuan. Having driven Liu Wenhui into retreat in the Tibetan regions of western Sichuan, Liu Xiang was made the new chairman of Sichuan by the Nationalist government. In the end, Liu Wenhui would remain in the Tibetan portions of Sichuan until the Communists came to power in 1949 (Kapp, *Szechuan and the Chinese Republic,* 82–90).

87. Shi Weixian, "Han Zang jiaoliyuan yu Taixu fashi," 2.

88. Yang Ming and Niu Ruifang, "Chongqing Han Zang jiaoli yuan shi wei" (Chongqing's Sino-Tibetan Buddhist Institute from Start to Finish), in *Ba-Yu wenhua* (*Ba [xian] and Chongqing Culture*) (Chongqing: Chongqing chubanshe, 1991), 383.

89. Taixu, "Lüeshu Xizang Fojiao yu" (Preface to a Brief Account of Tibetan Buddhism), *Haichaoyin* 11, no. 7 (1930): 1–2.

90. Taixu, "Zhi Liu Fucheng zhunzhang ji Chuandong ge xin Fozhe shu" (Letter to General Liu Fucheng [Liu Xiang] and the Buddhist Faithful of Eastern Sichuan), in *Taixu dashi quanshu,* 62 vols. (*Complete Works of the Venerable Taixu*) (Taipei: Haichaoyin she, 1953 [1930]), 51:225–226.

91. Fazun, "Fazun zhi Hu Zihu jushi shu."

92. Taixu, "Yu Fazun shu" (Letters Given to Fazun), in idem, *Taixu dashi quanshu,* 51:56.

93. Published in Manzhi, "Shijie Fojiao xuefan Han Zang jiaoli yuan zhi shiming." I saw a copy of a pamphlet of the same name at the Chongqing municipal historical library archives. When I expressed interest in copying this archival source, the book suddenly disappeared, ostensibly for conservation, although I saw it tucked away in the change drawer when paying for other copies made at the archives. Evidently once a foreigner expressed interest in this pamphlet, the staff found it too sensitive to allow access. The largest section of the pamphlet was Manzhi's article completed in January 1932 in Shanghai. Also included were articles by Taixu (dated December 1931) and Liu Xiang (dated March 1931).

94. Orzech, "Buddhism's Assimilation to Tang Political Culture," 477.

95. Manzhi, "Shijie Fojiao xuefan Han Zang jiaoli yuan zhi shiming," 2.

96. Liu Xiang, "Zhiling zhengzi di erbasisan hao (Administrative order #2843)," (Chongqing: Goumin gemingzhun di ershiyi zhun silingbu [Headquarters of the Twenty-first Nationalist Revolutionary Army]), March 26, 1931), in "Shijie Foxueyuan Han Zang jin zhan" (Progress of the World Buddhist Institute, Sino-Tibetan [Branch]), *Haichaoyin* 13, no. 8 (1932): 53. More than one dozen similar army orders and numerous letters from Sichuan Buddhist institutions were preserved in the Chongqing archives' partially bilingual volume: *Shijie Foxue fan Han Zang jiaoli yuan kaixue jinian tekan / 'Jigs rten sangs rgyas kyi chos grwa rgya dang bod pa'i bstan tshul bslab grwa khang da ltar bkod pa'i bslab grwa shin tu rnyed dka' ba'i pad* [sic; *dpe*] *cha* (*Special Memorial Issue at the Start of Classes at the World Buddhist Institute's Sino-Tibetan Buddhist Institute*), (Chongqing: Han Zang Jiaoli Yuan, 1932) (hereafter, *HZJLY* 1932).

97. Yang and Niu, "Chongqing Han Zang jiaoli yuan shi wei," 384.

5. THE FAILURE OF RACIAL AND NATIONALIST IDEOLOGIES (1928–1932)

1. An excellent example of both the Tibetan resistance to new ideologies and Chinese efforts to overcome them through educating Tibetan youth can be seen in Goldstein, Dawei Sherap, and Siebenschuh, *A Tibetan Revolutionary*, 51–55.

2. Ya gave the name of the temple in which this first office was set up as Fuyou Temple (*Banchan E'erdeni zhuan*, 264).

3. Danzhu Angben, *Libei Dalai Lama yu Banchan Erdeni nianpu*, 638.

4. Li Pengnian and Wan Renyuan, eds., *Jiushi Banchan neidi huodong ji fanzang shouxian dang'an xuanbian* (*Selections from the Archives Concerning the Ninth Panchen's Activities in China and the Restrictions on His Return to Tibet*) (Beijing: Zhongguo Zangxue chubanshe, 1992), 10.

5. The text of the petition is found in the Panchen Lama's biography in Shi Miaozhou, *Meng Zang Fojiao shi* (*Mongol-Tibetan Buddhist History*), Xizangxue Hanwen wenxian congshu (Collection of Chinese Language Documents for the Study of Central Tibet), 2 (Beijing: Quanguo tushuguan wenxian zhongxin, 1993 [1934]) 175–179.

6. Li and Wan, *Jiushi Banchan neidi huodong*.

7. Jensine Andresen, "Kâlacakra: Textual and Ritual Perspective" (Ph.D. dissertation, Harvard University, 1997), 17. For details on Tibetan Buddhists conferring this initiation on the Mongol emperors of the Yuan dynasty, see also the article by Leonard van der Kuijp, "The Kâlachakra and the Patronage of Tibetan Buddhism by the Mongol Imperial Family" (Bloomington: Department of Central Eurasia Studies, Indiana University, 2004). This article was printed as a booklet in the Central Eurasia Studies Lectures, no. 4, and will appear with revisions in Kapstein, *Buddhism Between China and Tibet*.

8. Wu Fengpei, "Zhongyin *Shi Zang jicheng, Xizang jiyao* yu," 2–3.

9. The official Tibetan title, if there was one, is not known. A representative of the Dalai Lama's office in China called this institution simply the Panchen's Representative Office (Tib. *PaN chen don gcod khang*), see Thub bstan sangs rgyas, *Rgya nag tu Bod kyi sku tshab,* 26.

10. Danzhu Angben, *Libei Dalai Lama yu Banchan Erdeni nianpu,* 639. Administrative changes in the Xining (Qinghai) branch are described in a document dated May 1929 (Li and Fang, *Jiushi Banchan neidi huodong,* 10–11).

11. Jagou, "A Pilgrim's Progress," 15–16.

12. In May 1929 and April 1930, respectively; see Danzhu Angben, *Libei Dalai Lama yu Banchan Erdeni nianpu,* 640.

13. Jagou, "A Pilgrim's Progress," 16.

14. Han, *Kang-Zang Fojiao,* 4v.

15. Ibid., 5r, 9r; Sichuan sheng difang zhi bianji weiyuanhui, Sheng zhi renwu zhi bianji, and Ren Yimin, eds., *Sichuan jin xiandai renwu zhuan* (*Biographies of Sichuan's Contemporary Figures*), 6 vols. (Chengdu: Sichuan sheng shehui kexue yuan chubanshe, 1985), 1:291.

16. Cavanaugh and Chinese Materials Center, *Who's Who in China, 1918–1950*, supplement to the 4th ed., 81.

17. Wu asserted that the Dalai Lama's representative Könchog Jungné worked jointly with the Mongolian and Tibetan Affairs Commission but gave no specific details to back up this claim ("Zhongyin *Shi Zang jicheng, Xizang jiyao* yu," 2). Huang Hao does the same, adding that Könchog Jungné had been in the capital since 1924 as the representative of the Dalai Lama and Kashak (*Zai Beijing de Zangzu wenwu* [Beijing: Minzu chubanshe, 1993], 59).

18. Ya, *Biographies of the Tibetan Spiritual Leaders Panchen Erdenis,* 281. Huang, *Zai Beijing de Zangzu wenwu,* 59.

19. Ya, *The Biographies of the Dalai Lamas,* 341.

20. Goldstein, *The Demise of the Lamaist State,* 539. Goldstein gave the earth-serpent year as 1927, although this Tibetan year corresponds to 1929.

21. Huang, *Zai Beijing de Zangzu wenwu,* 57. On page 59 Huang said that the office was established in 1930.

22. Thupten Sangay, *Rgya nag tu Bod kyi sku tshab,* 13, 29–30. Huang referred to a Central [Government] Mongolian and Tibetan Conference (Zhongyang Meng Zang huiyi) to which the Yonghegong Jasagh Lama and resident *khenpo* at the capital (*jing,* here presumably still referring to Beijing, although this is unclear), Zhouni Luozangwa (Tib. Co ne Blo bzang ba), served as the attending representative of Tibet (*Zai Beijing de Zangzu wenwu,* 59).

23. Ya, *The Biographies of the Dalai Lamas,* 342, 345–346; Goldstein, *The Demise of the Lamaist State,* 214, 219; Shi Dongchu, *Zhongguo Fojiao jindai shi,* 376. After the Nationalist government's 1937 retreat to Chongqing, the Dalai Lama's office was, like the Panchen Lama's, transferred there. See Goldstein, Dawei Sherap, and Siebenschuh, *A Tibetan Revolutionary,* 33.

24. Shi Dongchu, *Zhongguo Fojiao jindai shi,* 357.

25. Stoddard, *Le mendiant de l'Amdo,* 83. The recent work by Goldstein, Dawei Sherap, and Siebenschuh (*A Tibetan Revolutionary*) described how some young Tibetan students in China were also exposed to and inspired by Soviet Communist literature (especially works by Stalin and Lenin) on nationality policy. As these works were officially banned by the Nationalist government, Sun Yat-sen's ideology continued to set the standard in China, but it, too, was no doubt influenced by Lenin's ideas.

26. Elmer T. Clark, *The Chiangs of China* (Nashville: Abingdon-Cokesbury, 1943), 73, 76. Some of the Amdo Tibetans I met in 1997 were convinced that Chiang Kai-shek had remained a dedicated Buddhist throughout his life.

27. Under the Qing in 1907 a school was built by the Chinese in Batang, which produced a number of important Tibetans who would later serve as intermediaries in twentieth-century Sino-Tibetan relations. See Goldstein, Dawei Sherap, and Siebenschuh, *A Tibetan Revolutionary,* 8. As early as 1913 the Beijing government had created a Mongolian and Tibetan Academy at the insistence of the Mongol Prince Gung, but, according to Sechin Jagchid, "this center did not influence the Tibetans to any significant degree" (*The Last Mongol Prince: The Life and Times of Demchugdondrob, 1902–1966,* Studies on East Asia, 21 [Bellingham: Western Washington University, 1999], 15). This institution was apparently continued under the Nanjing government, at least in name, but still did not graduate any Tibetan students as far as I can tell; see June Teufel Dreyer, *China's Forty Millions: Minority Nationalities and National Integration in the People's Republic of China,* Harvard East Asia series, 87 (Cambridge, Mass.: Harvard University Press, 1976), 18.

28. Marie-Claire Bergère, *Sun Yat-sen,* trans. Janet Lloyd (Stanford: Stanford University Press, 1998), 403. Given in Japan on November 28, 1924.

29. Gu Jiegang, *The Autobiography of a Chinese Historian, Being the Preface to a Symposium on Ancient Chinese History (Ku shih pien),* trans. Arthur W. Hummel (Leyden: Brill, 1931), 167–168; cited in Laurence Schneider, *Ku Chieh-kang and China's New History: Nationalism and the Quest for Alternative Traditions* (Berkeley: University of California Press, 1971), 267.

30. Chapter 19 of Dai's *Path for Youth* was reproduced in Chen Tianxi, *Dai Jitao xiansheng de shengping,* 511–513. Cited hereafter as Dai, *Path for Youth.*

31. Dai, *Path for Youth*, 512.

32. Ibid.

33. Schneider, *Ku Chieh-kang and China's New History*, 259 (citing *Gushi bian*. II [1926]: 5).

34. This was no doubt what Peter Hopkirk called the University of the Toilers of the East, set up in Moscow in 1922 (*Setting the East Ablaze: Lenin's Dream of an Empire in Asia* [London: Murray, 1984], 138–139, 161–163, 177–178). On Tibetan students in Soviet schools, starting in 1925, see Andreyev, *Soviet Russia and Tibet*, 208–212.

35. Dai, *Path for Youth*, 513.

36. Ibid.

37. Chen Tianxi, *Dai Jitao xiansheng de shengping*, 514.

38. Ibid.

39. Wu noted that the Mongolian and Tibetan School fell under the jurisdiction of the Mongolian and Tibetan Affairs Commission's Tibetan Affairs Office ("Zhongyin *Shi Zang jicheng, Xizang jiyao* yu," 6). On the other hand, Dreyer noted that in 1930 a Mongolian and Tibetan department was established under the Ministry of Education (*China's Forty Millions*, 18). Further research will be necessary to determine the administrative place of this school.

40. Chen Tianxi, *Dai Jitao xiansheng de shengping*, 515.

41. Most of the young Tibetans who attended Chinese Nationalist schools were drawn from such areas (Batang, Labrang, Dartsedo) where Chinese, and often foreign missionary, presence was strong. See Goldstein, Dawei Sherap, and Siebenschuh, *A Tibetan Revolutionary*, 30–33, passim.

42. Wu mentioned this mission ("Zhongyin *Shi Zang jicheng, Xizang jiyao* yu," 4).

43. Here, I am discussing those Tibetan lamas who had shown some interest in learning about China. For the most part Tibetans were as or possibly more ignorant of their powerful neighbor than Chinese were about Tibet. Like the Chinese, the Tibetans had produced no bilingual dictionaries of their respective languages.

44. Shi Dongchu, *Zhongguo Fojiao jindai shi*, 381.

45. Li and Wan, *Jiushi Banchan neidi huodong*, 10.

46. For a different perspective on this problem, see Lydia Liu, "The Question of Meaning-Value in the Political Economy of the Sign," in *Tokens of Exchange: The Problem of Translation in Global Circulations*, ed. Lydia Liu, Post-Contemporary Interventions (Durham: Duke University Press, 1999), 34–37. Liu's work suggests that linguistic equivalents do not necessarily exist between languages. She examines the power relations of the colonial encounters and translation in this context. Her insights might explain why certain terms central to Sino-Tibetan relations only in appear in Chinese and not Tibetan.

47. A 1930 article in *Haichaoyin* suggests that there was another important figure who might have served as a representative for the Panchen Lama. This article, written by Lozang Gyentsen, indicates that this man's own teacher, Zerenqun (Tib. Tshe ring ?), was the Panchen Lama's secretary and was involved with traveling on behalf of the Panchen Lama's Nanjing office to the capital (*Haichaoyin* 11 [1930]: 8, 19).

48. The Panchen Lama's autobiography mentioned this event but not the letters or speech. In the first instance the meeting is called *Krung go'i rgyal khab kyi legs tshogs spel thabs zhing chen khag gi 'thus mi tshogs 'du* and was associated with Duan, in his capacity as ruler (Ch. *zhizheng*) of China (Tib. *Tön khri kring*) (Blo bzang thub bstan chos kyi nyi ma, *Skyabs mgon thams cad mkhyen pa*, 101). In the second instance the Tibetan transliteration of the conference is given

as *Hrang ha'u hud,* which is translated as *Rgyal khabs kyi chab srid skor zhing chen khag sogs kyi tshogs 'du* (125–126).

49. Li and Wan, *Jiushi Banchan neidi huodong,* 3.

50. Paul Kocot Nietupski, *Labrang: A Tibetan Buddhist Monastery at the Crossroads of Four Civilizations (Photos from the Griebnow Archives, 1921–1949)* (Ithaca, N.Y.: Snow Lion, 1999), 87; citing Jonathan N. Lipman, "The Border World of Gansu, 1895–1935" (Ph.D. dissertation, Stanford University, 1981).

51. Li and Wan, *Jiushi Banchan neidi huodong,* 4.

52. Danzhu Angben, *Libei Dalai Lama yu Banchan Erdeni nianpu,* 638.

53. Li Tieh-tseng said that there "was talk of a Pan-Moslem movement against Buddhist Tibet" (*The Historical Status of Tibet* [New York: King's Crown, 1956], 161).

54. Blo bzang thub bstan chos kyi nyi ma, *Skyabs mgon thams cad mkhyen pa,* 575, 638, 643, 650, 675, 683.

55. Ibid., 575, 638.

56. Ibid., 157, at Wutaishan.

57. Another, nearly contemporary text in which this term frequently appears is Sun Krung hran (Sun Zhongshan = Sun Yat-sen), *San min kru'u yi'i bsdus don (Sanmin zhuyi yaoyi = Essentials of the Three Principles of the People),* trans. Yang Kri hphu (Yang Zhifu) and Gomindwang krung dbyangs rtsa 'dzugs las khungs gyi mthas mtshams skad yig rtsom sgyur lhan khang (The Guomindang's Central Organizing Office's Committee for Translating and Editing Border Languages), bilingual ed. (Taipei: Meng-Zang weiyuanhui, 1971 [1943]). Many thanks to Elliot Sperling for sharing this invaluable resource with me. For details on this text, see my forthcoming article. According to 1990s interviews of Bapa Phüntso Wangye conducted by Melvyn Goldstein et al., the terms *Bod rigs* (Tibetan) and *mi rigs* (nationality) were used as early as 1939 in the name of the newly formed Tibetan Communist Revolutionary Group and in letters to Stalin and Mao Zedong. Of course, these early examples were kept secret to protect the group (Goldstein, Dawei Sherap, and Siebenschuh, *A Tibetan Revolutionary,* 32–33). Songs from the 1940s expressed these terms more openly (75, 87).

58. Blo bzang thub bstan chos kyi nyi ma, *Skyabs mgon thams cad mkhyen pa,* 121.

59. Blo bzang thub bstan chos kyi nyi ma, *PaN chen thams cad mkhyen pa,* 388.

60. In light of Lydia Liu's work on translation, I hesitate to use terms such as *direct* or *literal* translation or the idea of equivalence. However, the fact remains that within a decade of the printing of this biography the Chinese Communists had developed more or less fixed equivalents of certain Chinese terms in order to be able to communicate their ideology to the Tibetans. Thus these early instances of a Tibetan grappling with these same terms is of particular interest in the study of modern Sino-Tibetan relations.

61. Blo bzang thub bstan chos kyi nyi ma, *Skyabs mgon thams cad mkhyen pa,* 138.

62. Ibid., 642.

63. Ibid., 548.

64. Bapa Phüntso Wangye also encountered people we would call Tibetans who did not identify as such (a feature which still persists to this day, at least in Amdo): "He liked to talk about us being Khampas, not Tibetans, or *pöpa* as we called them. He saw the two as different nationalities, or ethnic groups" (Goldstein, Sherap, and Siebenschuh, *A Tibetan Revolutionary,* 54).

65. Blo bzang thub bstan chos kyi nyi ma, *Skyabs mgon thams cad mkhyen pa,* 138, 548.

66. Ibid., 130.

67. For example, the Panchen Lama referred to male and female Chinese and Mongols (*Rgya Sog pho mo*) (ibid., 125).

68. Li and Wan, *Jiushi Banchan neidi huodong*, 20–21. In 1929 the Panchen Lama's Qinghai representatives (10) had included the phrase "the amalgamation of the five races" (*wuzu tonghua*) in the context of discussing the liberation and unification of the Tibetan and Mongolian peoples without even mentioning the Chinese (*Han* or *Zhonghua minzu*).

69. Lydia Liu, "The Question of Meaning-Value in the Political Economy of the Sign," 13–41.

70. Li and Wan, *Jiushi Banchan neidi huodong,* 5–6.

71. Ibid., 8, 10.

72. Ibid., 12.

73. Ibid., 18.

74. Wu cited references to the Dalai Lama or his representatives uncritically using the "*wuzu*" racial rhetoric ("Zhongyin *Shi Zang jicheng, Xizang jiyao* yu," 8, 19). Given the Panchen Lama's reticence, I find it hard to believe that the Dalai Lama would have embraced this racial rhetoric so wholeheartedly. Until the original documents in their entirety are made available, it will remain unclear how the Central Tibetan government understood and responded to these ideas.

75. For detailed information on Kham history in the twentieth century, see Carol McGranahan, "Between Empire and Exile: A Khampa History of Twentieth Century Tibet" (Ph.D. dissertation, University of Michigan, 2001).

76. Bilingual personnel were so rare that the Mongolian and Tibetan Affairs Commission even hired a half-Tibetan, half-Chinese Muslim woman named Liu Manqing as an interpreter in 1928. Shortly thereafter she volunteered for a semi-official mission to Tibet to tell the Dalai Lama and Tibetans about "the doctrine of the Kuomintang and the Government's plan for national construction and development." She spent the first half of 1930 in Lhasa on this mission. See Li, *The Historical Status of Tibet,* 151.

77. Goldstein et al's recent work adds some detail to this story and differs on one key point, noted below. See Goldstein, Sherap, and Siebenschuh, *A Tibetan Revolutionary,* 10–13.

78. Dikötter, *The Discourse of Race in Modern China,* 123.

79. Cynthia Bell, *Ritual Theory, Ritual Practice* (New York: Oxford University Press, 1992), 191; cited in Martin Mills, *Identity, Ritual and State in Tibetan Buddhism: The Foundations of Authority in Gelukpa Monasticism* (London: Routledge/Curzon, 2003), 302.

80. According to Stoddard, Kelzang Tsering had also attended this school (*Le mendiant de l'Amdo,* 83).

81. Opinions are divided as to whether Kelzang Tsering was acting under orders in these actions. Li suggested that he exceeded his orders by setting up the autonomous region (*The Historical Status of Tibet*, 278, n. 137; citing Hong Dizhen, *Xizang shi di dagang* [*An Outline of the History and Geography of Tibet*] [Shanghai: Zhengzhong shuju, 1936], 255–257). The modern Communist gazetteer for the region (Ganzi zhou zhi bianji weiyuanhui, *Ganzi zhou zhi* [Kardzé Prefectural Gazetter], 1:113) made the unlikely assertion that the Nationalist government supported him in calling for Kham autonomy. Hugh Richardson may come closest to the truth in speculating that Kelzang Tsering pretended to act on Chiang Kai-shek's authority (*A Short History of Tibet* [New York: Dutton, 1962], 131; cited in Stoddard, *Le mendiant de l'Amdo,* 92).

82. Ganzi zhou zhi bianji weiyuanhui, *Ganzi zhou zhi,* 1:113; Li, *The Historical Status of Tibet,* 161.

83. Kapp, *Szechuan and the Chinese Republic,* 21.

84. Hong, *Xizang shi di dagang,* 256. Goldstein et al.'s Tibetan informant for their recent work did not mention this aspect of Kelzang Tsering's activities. Given that Kelzang Tsering was welcomed back into Nationalist government circles, it may be that the account I relied on exaggerated the extent of his move toward complete independence. Yet Goldstein et al.'s informant also stated that Kelzang Tsering "had his own agenda, which included . . . returning governance of Kham and Batang to Tibetans," so possibly this is all a matter of the degree of independence sought (Goldstein, Dawei Sherap, and Siebenschuh, *A Tibetan Revolutionary,* 10, 28, 44).

85. Hong, *Xizang shi di dagang,* 263. In fact, Central Tibetan resistance to the idea of an autonomous Kham created with the support of the Chinese Nationalist government led to a surprise attack on Kelzang Tsering's troops by the Central Tibetan army. This was a crippling blow to Kelzang Tsering's efforts and gave Liu Wenhui time to respond to this threat. See Goldstein, Dawei Sherap, and Siebenschuh, *A Tibetan Revolutionary,* 12–13.

86. Chinese transliteration of Tibetan: Gesang qunjue.

87. According to Michel Peissel, from 1933 to 1949 "the large towns of Khams, with the exception of Chamdo (under Lhasa) and Kanting [*sic*] (under Chinese control) continued to assert their autonomy in a turmoil of medieval intrigues involving the local princes of Derge, the rulers of Batang, the great abbots of Litang and, all these in turn, with their unruly vassals, the nomad princes, heads of the country's numerous tribes" (*Cavaliers of Kham: The Secret War in Tibet* [London: Heinemann, 1972], 13). Goldstein et al. also mentioned a 1935 attempted coup in Batang, again by a Tibetan educated in China (*A Tibetan Revolutionary,* 15–20).

88. Ganzi zhou zhi bianji weiyuanhui, *Ganzi zhou zhi,* 3:2095.

89. For one exceptional Khampa who helps illustrate this point, see Goldstein, Dawei Sherap, and Siebenschuh, *A Tibetan Revolutionary,* 54–55.

90. Wilhelm Filchner, *A Scientist in Tartary: From the Hoang-ho to the Indus,* trans. E. O. Lorimer (London: Faber and Faber, 1939), 47.

91. From Stoddard's account, this military academy seems to be synonymous with the Central Political Institute (*Le mendiant de l'Amdo,* 82). This man may have served as the director of the Panchen Lama Qinghai office in 1929; the Chinese transliteration of the director's name was Wangdui nuobu (Li and Fang, *Jiushi Banchan neidi huodong,* 10–11).

92. Pomdatsang, meaning "the house of Pomda," is a family name. For more information on this family, see McGranahan, "Between Empire and Exile: A Khampa History of Twentieth Century Tibet."

93. Stoddard, from whom I draw these spellings, was uncertain of the spelling of Meru Samshak (*Le mendiant de l'Amdo,* 363).

94. Ibid., 300 n. 91. Unfortunately neither the names and histories of those who attended nor references for this information are provided. For detailed information of the numbers and individual Tibetans who attended one of these schools, see Goldstein, Dawei Sherap, and Siebenschuh, *A Tibetan Revolutionary,* 24, 31, passim.

95. Goldstein, Dawei Sherap, and Siebenschuh, *A Tibetan Revolutionary,* 15–20.

96. Stoddard, *Le mendiant de l'Amdo,* 83. See also Kimura, *Japanese Agent in Tibet,* 190–195: Another nephew of Jiang Xinxi, Phun tshogs dbang rgyal (Phuntsok Wangyel), studied at the

Chinese Nationalist Party's Central Political College but was recruited by Communist Party agents and embraced Communism while there. In 1945 he planned another abortive attempt at achieving autonomy in part of Khams, Bde chen (in Yunnan), on behalf of the Eastern Tibet People's Autonomous Alliance. This man is the subject of Goldstein et al.'s *A Tibetan Revolutionary*, and this event is described in chapter 8 of that book.

97. For more details on this revolt, see Goldstein, Dawei Sherap, and Siebenschuh, *A Tibetan Revolutionary*, 15 n. 1. Goldstein et al. glosses the *Sanmin zhuyi* as "Three Rights of the People" (Tib. *Don gsum ring lugs*) (*The Demise of the Lamaist State*, 450 n. 83).

98. Stoddard, *Le mendiant de l'Amdo*, 81, 97.

99. Goldstein, *The Demise of the Lamaist State*, 463.

100. Goldstein, Dawei Sherap, and Siebenschuh, *A Tibetan Revolutionary*, 76–78, 87–89.

101. Stoddard, *Le mendiant de l'Amdo*, 105.

102. In fact, the documents also indicate what the present government of Communist China, represented by the editors of the collected government archives, chose to share with the rest of the world through open publication.

103. Schneider, *Ku Chieh-kang and China's New History*, 260–261.

104. Ibid., 260.

105. Dikötter, *The Construction of Racial Identities*, 9.

106. Ibid., 8.

107. Schneider, *Ku Chieh-kang and China's New History*, 14.

108. Han Tze-ki, "Ethnic and Cultural Pluralism: Gu Jiegang's Vision of a New China in His Studies of Ancient History," *Modern China* 22, no. 3 (1996): 315–339.

109. Barry Sautman, "Myths of Descent, Racial Nationalism and Ethnic Minorities in the People's Republic of China," in *The Construction of Racial Identities in China and Japan: Historical and Contemporary Perspectives*, ed. Frank Dikötter (Honolulu: University of Hawaii Press, 1997), 83.

6. THE MERGING OF SECULAR AND RELIGIOUS SYSTEMS (1931–1935)

1. Duara, *Rescuing History from the Nation*, 109.

2. Peterson and Walhof, *The Invention of Religion*, 8.

3. Duara, *Rescuing History from the Nation*, 109–110.

4. Fafang, "Zhongguo Fojiao xianzhuang," *Haichaoyin* 15, no. 10 (1934): 24; cited in Mei, "Minguo yilai de Han Zang Fojiao guanxi," 275–276 n. 23, which said that this was a lecture given at India's Mahabodhi Society.

5. Robert Weller, *Resistance, Chaos, and Control in China: Taiping Rebels, Taiwanese Ghosts, and Tiananmen* (Seattle: University of Washington Press, 1994), 22.

6. Duara, *Rescuing History from the Nation*, 95–110.

7. Lin Yutang, *My Country and My People* (New York: John Day, 1935), 123–124.

8. For Chinese language records of this British invitation, see Wu Fengpei, *Banchan fu Yin jilüe* (*Brief Record of the Panchen Lama's Going to India*), Qingdai Xizang shiliao conggan (Collected Materials on Qing Dynasty Tibet), 2 (Chongqing: Wenhai chubanshe, 1937). The Norlha Qutughtu was not so prominent a figure in Tibet, being but one of many local lamas in Kham, and was not especially popular because of his association with Zhao Erfang, the Qing

Chinese Bannerman known as "the Butcher" for his role in brutally enforcing Qing rule in Kham in the first decade of the twentieth century. Nevertheless, his contacts and knowledge of affairs in Kham may have been of some benefit to the Chinese Nationalists, especially in their campaign against the Communists on the Long March.

9. Franz Michael, *Rule by Incarnation: Tibetan Buddhism and Its Role in Society and State* (Boulder: Westview, 1982), 40–50.

10. Li and Wan, *Jiushi Banchan neidi huodong,* 15–17. See also, Zhongguo Zangzu yanjiu zhongxin et al., *Yuan yi lai Xizang difang yu zhongyang zhengfu guanxiu,* 6:2513–2523.

11. Ya, *Biographies of the Tibetan Spiritual Leaders Panchen Erdenis,* 269–270. Ya summarized the government position as conditioning assistance to the Panchen Lama on his announcement that "all Tibetan foreign and military affairs shall be administered by the central government."

12. Herman William Mast III, "An Intellectual Biography of Tai Chi-t'ao from 1891 to 1928" (Ph.D. dissertation, University of Illinois, 1970), 171.

13. Boorman and Howard, *Biographical Dictionary of Republican China,* 3:204. Other sources that indicate the depth of Dai's faith in Buddhism can be found in a memorial volume dedicated to Dai on the tenth anniversary of his death: Lin Jing, "Bukong jushi yu Fojiao" (Layman Bukong [Dai] and Buddhism), in *Dai xiansheng shishi shi zhounian jinian tekan (Special Issue Memorial on the Tenth Anniversary of the Death of Dai)* (1959), 39–44; Zhou Tiyou, "Jitao xiansheng yu bianjiang" ([Dai] Jitao and the Borderlands), in *Dai Jitao xiansheng shishi shi zhounian jinian tekan,* 35–37.

14. Dai Jitao, "Huguo xuanhua guanghui yuanjue dashi song" (Praise for the Master [the Panchen Lama] Who Protects the Country, Propagates Transformation, and Radiates Wisdom), in *Dai Jitao xiansheng wencun (Extant Writings of Dai Jitao),* 4 vols. (Taipei: Zhongguo guomindang zhongyang weiyuanhui, 1959 [1938]), 3:1142.

15. Shi Dongchu, *Zhongguo Fojiao jindai shi,* 356.

16. Zhongguo Zangxue yanjiu zhongxin et al., *Yuan yi lai Xizang difang yu zhongyang zhengfu guanxi,* vols. 6–7.

17. Ya, *Biographies of the Tibetan Spiritual Leaders Panchen Erdenis,* 271–272; Danzhu Angben, *Libei Dalai Lama yu Banchan Erdeni nianpu,* 641; Blo bzang thub bstan chos kyi nyi ma, *Skyabs mgon thams cad mkhyen pa,* 543.

18. Li and Wan, *Jiushi Banchan neidi huodong,* 22.

19. The Panchen Lama visited Sun Yat-sen's tomb around this time (Blo bzang thub bstan chos kyi nyi ma, *Skyabs mgon thams cad mkhyen pa,* 549). The Panchen Lama's autobiography does not record the text of these speeches (555–556).

20. The Panchen Lama's 1924 "History of the Last Thirty Years in Tibet" (*Xizang jin sanshi nian lishi*) was also published in 1931 in *Haichaoyin* 12 (7): 86; cited in Shi Dongchu, *Zhongguo Fojiao jindai shi,* 367.

21. Li and Wan, *Jiushi Banchan neidi huodong,* 3.

22. Ya, *Biographies of the Tibetan Spiritual Leaders Panchen Erdenis,* 272.

23. Gou Qing, "A Brief Account of the 9th Panchen Erdeni," *Tibet Studies,* no. 1 (1989): 70–82.

24. Li and Wan, *Jiushi Banchan neidi huodong,* 4.

25. For a fuller extract of the text, see Danzhu Angben, *Libei Dalai Lama yu Banchan Erdeni nianpu,* 641. Cf. Ya, *Biographies of the Tibetan Spiritual Leaders Panchen Erdenis,* 269–270.

26. Typically translated "kingdom," *guo* traditionally referred primarily to the ruling dynasty

as synecdoche for the entire empire. Toward the end of the Qing period this term took on the more modern sense of country or state.

27. Dai, "Banchan dashi shuo liuzi daming jenyan fa yao," 3:1173–1174.

28. Shi Dongchu, *Zhongguo Fojiao jindai shi*, 484. He gave Dai's wife a Tibetan name, Padma (Lianhua), meaning "lotus."

29. Berger, "Preserving the Nation," 92. For the details of Amoghavarjra's translation, see Orzech, *Politics and Transcendent Wisdom*.

30. Berger, "Preserving the Nation," 93.

31. Blo bzang thub bstan chos kyi nyi ma, *Skyabs mgon thams cad mkhyen pa*, 550.

32. Li and Wan, *Jiushi Banchan neidi huodong*, 28. Cf. Blo bzang thub bstan chos kyi nyi ma, *Skyabs mgon thams cad mkhyen pa*, 556: the Tibet transliteration was *Hus sgo shan ha'o kung hud tâ ze;* the Tibetan translation is not exact but preserved the phrase "protector of the country": *Rgyal khab skyong pa'i dge rgan chen po bstan srid yongs kyi bdag po thams cad mkhyen pa.* The Chinese government's official journal *Chinese Affairs* (December 31, 1933) apparently gave the English translation of this title as "The Great Wise Priest Who Guards the Nation and Spreads Culture." See E. T. Williams, "Tibet and Her Neighbors," *Bureau of International Relations* 3, no. 2 (1937): 134.

33. Li and Wan, *Jiushi Banchan neidi huodong*, 28.

34. Ibid., 26.

35. Ibid., 26–27. Danzhu Angben, *Libei Dalai Lama yu Banchan Erdeni nianpu*, 642; Jagou, "A Pilgrim's Progress," 16.

36. Li and Wan, *Jiushi Banchan neidi huodong*, 30–33.

37. Jagchid, *The Last Mongol Prince*, 46.

38. Ya, *Biographies of the Tibetan Spiritual Leaders Panchen Erdenis*, 273.

39. Welch, *The Buddhist Revival of China*, 176: "Wise, Enlightened Teacher, Protector of the Nation." It is remarkable that the Norlha Qutughtu's biography did not mention the conferral of such a title (see Han, *Kang-Zang Fojiao*).

40. Sichuan sheng difang zhi bianji weiyuanhui, *Sheng zhi renwu zhi bianji*, and Ren Yimin, *Sichuan jinxiandai renwu zhuan* 1985, 291.

41. For more details on this event, see Huang Hao, "Sanshi niandai Zhongguo Zangmi yan-jiu—*Zangmi xiufa midian* ping jie," 53.

42. Han, *Kang-Zang Fojiao*, 6v–7r.

43. Welch, *The Buddhist Revival of China*, 143. I give Welch's spelling. This Tibetan might have been the Panchen Lama's representative to Nanjing, Blo bzang rgyal mtshan (Lozang Gyentsen, currently transliterated into Chinese as *Luoseng Jianzan*); see Ya, *Dalai Lama zhuan*, 290. Welch noted that other sources give Taixu credit for advancing this proposal (*The Buddhist Revival of China*, 326 n. 34).

44. Welch, *The Buddhist Revival of China*, 143, 327 n. 34.

45. See, especially, Berger's *Empire of Emptiness*.

46. Dai Jitao, "Zhi Henan Li zhuxi dian" (Telegram to Henan's Chairman Li), in *Dai Jitao xiansheng wencun*, 3:1293.

47. Dai Jitao, "Zhi Meng Zang Qing Kang ge di tongbao shu" (Letter to Compatriots in Mongolia, Tibet, Qinghai, and Kham), in *Dai Jitao xiansheng wencun*, 3:1257–1261.

48. Mei, "Minguo yilai de Han Zang Fojiao guanxi," 282 n. 135.

49. Dai Jitao, "Renwang huguo fahui fayuan wen" (Vows for the Humane King Who Wishes to Protect His State Dharma-Assembly), in *Dai Jitao xiansheng wencun*, 3:1176–1177.

50. Dai Jitao, "Gaige siyuan sengjia zhidu zhi yijian" (Ideas on Reforming the Monastic System), in *Dai Jitao xiansheng wencun*, 3:1306.

51. Ibid., 3:1309.

52. Ibid., 3:1311.

53. This is an old idea in China, applied especially to the Mongols. Dai does not seem to have asked himself why, if their martial spirit had been quelled, the Tibetans were so successfully defending their borders from the Chinese once they had access to British arms in the twentieth century.

54. Changxing, "Shilun fahui quan faqi wen" (Exhortation to Sponsor the Kâlacakra Assembly), *Haichaoyin* 12, no. 12 (1931): 2–4. Although I generally translate *guo* as "country," the term *state* is used in the conventional translation of this title.

55. Gösta Montell, "Sven Hedin and the Panchen Lama," in *Saviours of Mankind,* Series no. VIII, Ethnography, vol. 9–10; The Sino-Swedish Expedition, 45–46; Reports from the Scientific Expedition to the Northwestern Provinces of China under the Leadership of Dr. Sven Hedin (Stockholm: Sven Hedin Foundation, 1961), 103.

56. "Beiping Shilun jingang fahui" (Beiping's Kâlacakra Vajra Dharma-Assembly), *Haichaoyin* 12, no. 8 (1932): 47–50.

57. Lin Yutang's English language publication cited above was an exception. Danzhu Angben, *Libei Dalai Lama yu Banchan Erdeni nianpu*, 644; Ya, *Biographies of the Tibetan Spiritual Leaders Panchen Erdenis*, 274. The Panchen Lama's own record of the teaching specifically listed his main students as Kru'u cang cun (Ch. Zhu Jiangzhun: General Zhu), Wam cungkrang (Ch. Wang zhunzhang, Army Commander Wang [Zanxu?]), and Gya'o cunkrang (Ch. Jiao zhunzhang, Army Commander Jiao) (Blo bzang thub bstan chos kyi nyi ma, *PaN chen thams cad mkhyen pa'i gsung 'bum,* 533). His biography also mentioned Duan Qirui (Tib. *Ton cu rus*) in association with General Zhu and the Beijing Kalacakra (Blo bzang thub bstan chos kyi nyi ma, *Skyabs mgon thams cad mkhyen pa,* 638). Dai, in his capacity as director (*yuanzhang*) of the examination branch of the government (Tib. *Tas yon krang* = Ch. *Dai yuanzhang*) also made a donation to this event (640).

58. "Beiping Shilun jingang fahui," *Haichaoyin* 12, no. 8 (1932): 47.

59. Ibid.

60. Ibid., 48–49.

61. Similarly the Panchen Lama demonstrated his ability to see Chinese Buddhists not merely as "others" but also as co-religionists. He addressed his teachings to the "[Chinese] Buddhist [lay] community [and] monks" (Tib. *Bu ja'o ste chos pa rnams*). This contrasted with the more typical transliterated reference to Chinese monks as *hwa shang* (Tib.) = *heshang* (Ch.).

62. Changxing, "Shilun fahui quan faqi wen," 4.

63. Blo bzang thub bstan chos kyi nyi ma, *PaN chen thams cad mkhyen pa'i gsung 'bum,* 534.

64. Danzhu Angben, *Libei Dalai Lama yu Banchan Erdeni nianpu*, 645. In October 1932 he again received newspaper reporters to present a talk entitled "Thoughts on the Past, Present, and Future."

65. Li, *The Historical Status of Tibet,* 162; cited in Smith, *Tibetan Nation,* 224.

66. Li, *The Historical Status of Tibet,* 163–164.

67. Sun Yat-sen, *San min zhuyi,* 3.

68. Li, *The Historical Status of Tibet,* 159.

69. Dai Jitao, "Zhi Dalai dashi shu" (Letter to the Dalai Lama), in *Dai Jitao xiansheng wen-*

cun (Taipei: Zhongguo guomindang zhongyang weiyuanhui, 1959 [1932]), 3:1212 (letter dated May 28, 1932).

70. Ibid., 3:1213 (letter dated May 28, 1932).

71. Ibid., 3:1214 (letter dated June 21, 1932).

72. Ibid.

73. Ibid., 3:1217 (letter dated August 20, 1932); 3:1218 (letter dated September 1932).

74. Ibid., 3:1221 (letter dated October 28, 1932).

75. Blo bzang thub bstan chos kyi nyi ma, *Skyabs mgon thams cad mkhyen pa,* 647: The full Tibetan transliteration reads *Shis bru'i sho he hre PaN kran ho phu;* the full Tibetan translation reads *Nub phyogs bde ldan la 'gyur med brtan par gnas pa'i mdzad pa PaN chen sang rgyas mngon sum.*

76. Ya, *Biographies of the Tibetan Spiritual Leaders Panchen Erdenis,* 274–275 (emphasis added).

77. Jagchid, *The Last Mongol Prince,* 53.

78. The Chinese version reads "*tuanjie wuzu*" (Ya, *Banchan E'erdeni zhuan,* 253). Interestingly the Tibetan translation of Ya's Chinese original does not preserve this phrase, replacing the number "five," as in five races or nationalities, with the word "various" (Tib. *khag*) (Yâ Han krang [Ya Hanzhang], *PaN chen sku phreng rim byon gyi mdzad rnam* (*Biographies of the Panchen Lamas*), trans. Blo bzang phun tshogs, 'Brug grags [Lhasa: Bod ljongs mi dmangs dpe skrun khang, 1992], 568). The concept of five races appears to have even less resonance now among Tibetans than it did in the Panchen Lama's time. The English translation of Ya's Chinese original used the official Communist translation of "*zu*," which is now understood as "nationality" rather than "race" (Ya, *Biographies of the Tibetan Spiritual Leaders Panchen Erdenis,* 275).

79. Shi Dongchu, *Zhongguo Fojiao jindai shi,* 381, citing *Haichaoyin* 14, no. 1 (1933).

80. Ibid.: *Banchan sui bu an Hanwen, ran shu nian qian you yiben yanjiu Sanmin Zhuyi, zhi ci zhuyi que ke jiu guo.*

81. The Chinese translation of the Tibetan letter was printed in Taixu's magazine: Luoseng nianzha, Jiangba yundan, Yixi bandian, Dunzhu, "Xizang biqiu seng jinggao neidi zhu da jushi xuelei shu" (Letter from Tibetan Bhiksu Monks Respectfully Reporting Their Suffering to All the Great Laity of China Proper), *Haichaoyin* 13, no. 12 (1932): 109–112.

82. Taixu, "Du Xizang biqiu xue shu gao Zhongyang zhengfu ji guomin" (Having Read the Letter of Tibetan Monks' Suffering, Telling the Chinese Government and the Country's People), *Haichaoyin* 13, no. 12 (1932): 108–109.

83. Manzhi, "Shijie Fojiao xuefan Han Zang jiaoli yuan zhi shiming," 18.

84. Taixu, "Shijie Foxue fan Han Zang jiaoli yuan yuanqi" (Origin of the World Buddhist Institute's Sino-Tibetan Buddhist Institute), in *Taixu dashi quanshu* (*Complete Works of the Venerable Taixu*) (Hong Kong, 1953 [1932]), 1033–1035.

85. Kapstein's *The Tibetan Assimilation of Buddhism* provides a text-based analysis of some of the connections between Chinese and Tibetan cultures in this period.

86. Taixu, "Shijie Foxue fan Han Zang jiaoli yuan yuanqi," 1033–1035.

87. Shi Dongchu, *Zhongguo Fojiao jindai shi,* 381. Shi noted that Lin Sen discussed the five races and unity at this meeting.

88. Ya, *Biographies of the Tibetan Spiritual Leaders Panchen Erdenis,* 275. This event is also recorded in Blo bzang thub bstan chos kyi nyi ma, *Skyabs mgon thams cad mkhyen pa,* 648–649.

89. Dai Jitao, "Yaoshi qi Fo fahui fayuan wen" (Religious Vows for the Seven Medicine Buddhas Dharma Assembly), in *Dai Jitao xiansheng wencun* (Taipei: Zhongguo guomindang zhongyang weiyuanhui, 1959 [1933]), 3:1178.

90. For the most detailed study of the Medicine Buddha in English, see Raoul Birnbaum, *The Healing Buddha* (Boston: Shambhala, 1989).

91. Dai, *Dai Jitao xiansheng wencun*, 1142.

92. Dai, "Yaoshi qi Fo fahui fayuan wen," 1180.

93. Ibid., 1179.

94. Dai, "Renwang huguo fahui fayuan wen," 1176–1177.

95. Li and Wan, *Jiushi Banchan neidi huodong*, 56. Moreover, although the Panchen Lama mentioned that the Qianlong emperor protected Tibet by sending troops and high commissioners, he did not trace the origins of the five races concept to this time as have many recent works on Qing history (55).

96. Jagchid, *The Last Mongol Prince*, 53.

97. Ibid., 66.

98. Jagou, "A Pilgrim's Progress," 16.

99. Jagchid, *The Last Mongol Prince*, 70.

100. During the summer before the conference, the Panchen Lama's representative in Beiping had sent a telegram to the head of the Mongolian and Tibetan Affairs Commission which used the phrase "the unity of the five races" (*tuanjie wuzu*) (Li and Wan, *Jiushi Banchan neidi huodong*, 64).

101. Dai Jitao, "Zhi Banchan dashi dian (Telegram to the Panchen Lama)," in *Dai Jitao xiansheng wencun*, 1:292 (telegram sent from Nanjing, October 8, 1933).

102. Li and Fang, *Jiushi Banchan neidi huodong*, 72. Document dated October 25, 1933.

103. Jagou, "A Pilgrim's Progress," 17.

104. Williams, "Tibet and Her Neighbors," 133–134.

105. Han, *Kang Zang Fojiao*, 5v–6r.

106. Ibid., 5v.

107. Ibid., 9r.

108. Nuona Hutuketu (Norlha Qutughtu), *Mizong Lianhuasheng dashi mifa* (*The Esoteric Teachings of the Esoteric School's Master Padmasambhava*) (Taipei: Wulin, 1985 [1930–36]), 147.

109. Welch, *The Buddhist Revival of China*, 175. Although no gender ratio can be determined, the Norlha Qutughtu's biography, unlike those of other figures in China at that time, does mention that he had women disciples and a long-standing interest in improving the status of women in Kham (Han, *Kang-Zang Fojiao*, 3r, 6v).

110. One notable exception, nowadays at least, can be seen in a 1994 *Time* magazine article, cited by June Campbell, that listed the worldwide assests of one of the Tibetan Buddhist traditions as totalling more than U.S.$1.2 billion with 428 meditation centers (*Traveller in Space: In Search of Female Identity in Tibetan Buddhism* [London: Athlone, 1996] 193 n. 2). However, Robert Barnett, a leading scholar of modern Tibet, suggested that the research for the article in *Time* was flawed (personal communication, March 2004).

111. Alexander Berzin, *Relating to a Spiritual Teacher* (Ithaca, N.Y.: Snow Lion, 2000), 16.

112. Dai Jitao, "Zhongguo zhi zongjiao gaige yu jiuguo shiye" (China's Religious Reforms and the Enterprise of Saving the Nation), in *Dai xiansheng Foxue lunji* (*Dai Jitao's Collected Buddhist Studies Essays*) (Taipei: Zhonghua Fojiao wenhua guan, 1972 [1933]), 17–20. The text of the broadcast was also reprinted in *Haichaoyin* 14, no. 5 (1933). In January 1933 he also published a text entitled "Chenxing Zhongguo yu chenxing Fojiao" (The Flourishing of China and the Flourishing of Buddhism), *Haichaoyin* 14, no. 1 (1933): 11–13.

113. Dai, "Zhongguo zhi zongjiao gaige yu jiuguo shiye," 17–20.

114. Dai, "Zhi Banchan dashi dian," 293.

115. Ya, *Biographies of the Tibetan Spiritual Leaders Panchen Erdenis,* 283; Li and Fang, *Jiushi Banchan neidi huodong,* 74.

116. Ya, *Biographies of the Tibetan Spiritual Leaders Panchen Erdenis,* 282, 280.

117. Hangzhou had been associated with Tibetan Buddhists as early as the Yuan dynasty (Su Bai, "Yuandai Hangzhou Zangchuan mijiao ji qi you guan guiji" [On the Tibetan Buddhism of the Yuan Dynasty's Hangzhou and Some Remains Concerned], in *Zangchuan Fojiao siyuan kaogu* [*Archaeological Studies on Monasteries of Tibetan Buddhism*] [Beijing: Wenwu chubanshe, 1996], 365–387).

118. For a comparison of the Panchen Lama in exile in China and the Dalai Lama in exile, see Gray Tuttle, "Uniting Religion and Politics in a Bid for Autonomy: Lamas in Exile in China (1924–1937) and America (1979–1991)" in *Buddhist Missionaries in the Era of Globalization*, ed. Linda Learman (Honolulu: University of Hawaii Press, 2004).

119. Shi, *Zhongguo Fojiao jindai shi,* 382

120. Zhang Zhungu, *Duan Qirui zhuan (Biography of Duan Qirui)*, 2 vols. (Taipei: Zhongwai tushu chubanshe, 1973), 1:13.

121. Ya, *Biographies of the Tibetan Spiritual Leaders Panchen Erdenis,* 284.

122. Dai, "Huguo xuanhua guanghui yuanjue dashi song," 3:1142.

123. Blo bzang thub bstan chos kyi nyi ma, *Skyabs mgon thams cad mkhyen pa,* 680–681: Tib. Hong mu pung [sung] = Ch. Huang Musong; Tib. Dâ zhiu' bâ ze = Ch. Taixu fashi.

124. Blo bzang thub bstan chos kyi nyi ma, *PaN chen thams cad mkhyen pa,* 388–389. The three instances in the Panchen Lama's biography in which Sun's name is explicitly mentioned prior to 1935 do not deal with his ideology. The first reference to Sun was occasioned by the Panchen Lama's visit to his tomb and memorial outside Nanjing. The second mention of Sun Yat-sen occurred in reference to the May 1931 memorial for Sun which the Panchen Lama attended. Similarly the third mention is made in relation to a Sun Yat-sen conference at which the Panchen Lama gave talks late in 1932. The contents of the talks are not mentioned (Blo bzang thub bstan chos kyi nyi ma, *Skyabs mgon thams cad mkhyen pa,* 549, 555–556, 645–646).

125. Zhizang, "Du *Xizang wenti zhi jianlun* hou de ganqing" (Sentiments after Reading *Self-criticism on the Tibet Problem*), *Haichaoyin* 15, no. 10 (1934): 109.

126. Lao She, "Jiuguo nan ge" (Song of Saving the Country from Difficulties), in *Lunyu wen xuan yi ji (Selections from Humor)* (Shanghai: Shidai shuju, 1949), 75–79.

127. Kaiyang, "Zun Lamajiao wei guojia jiao yi" (A Proposal to Make the Lama Religion Our National Religion), *Lunyu (Humor)* 1, no. 4 (1932): 114. I want to thank Kristen Stapleton for bringing this article to my attention, which also led me to Lao She's piece.

128. Da Gongbao, "The Whole Story of Tibet's Political and Religious [System] (*Xizang zhengjiao zhi shiwei*)," *Haichaoyin* 15, no. 4 (1934): 110. It is interesting to note that the Chinese and Tibetan versions of this phrase reverse the order of the two elements (religion and politics), with the unsurprising result that religion takes precedence in the Tibetan version, and politics in the Chinese version.

129. Williams, "Tibet and Her Neighbors," 135.

130. Ya, *Biographies of the Tibetan Spiritual Leaders Panchen Erdenis,* 284.

131. Guo Qing, "A brief account of the 9th Panchen Erdeni," *Tibet Studies,* no. 1 (1989): 77; Dai Jitao made a similar argument sometime later: "Without a doubt, the essence of my belief in the Three Principles of the People and the essence of my having taken refuge in the

Three Jewels is completely identical. . . . I believe that the Three Principles of the People and the Three Jewels—the Buddha, the Dharma, and the monastic community—are not different" ("Zhong Yin liang guo guomin de jiushi qingshen" [The Spirit of China and India's Peoples Saving the World], in *Dai Jitao xiansheng wencun* [Taipei: Zhongguo guomindang zhongyang weiyuanhui, 1959 (1942)], 3:1333).

132. Danzhu Angben, *Libei Dalai Lama yu Banchan Erdeni nianpu*, 652: March 27, 1934, in Hangzhou, "Buddhism and My View of Director [Sun]'s Noble Doctrine of Equality" (*Fojiao yu Zongli guijiao de pingdeng jian*); April 16, 1934 in Shanghai: "Tibet and China" (*Xizang yu Zhongguo*).

133. Blo bzang thub bstan chos kyi nyi ma, *Skyabs mgon thams cad mkhyen pa*, 688–689.

134. Ibid., 689–690.

135. Ibid., 690.

136. Dai Jitao, "Cheng Zhongyang zhengzhi huiyi wen" (Text Presented to the Central Political Conference), in *Dai Jitao xiansheng wencun* (Taipei: Zhongguo guomindang zhongyang weiyuanhui, 1959 [1934]), 1:298.

137. In this context it should be noted that, even once China had the military force and wealth to effectively incorporate Tibet, the Chinese Communist Party still allowed for a special relationship with Tibet. The Chinese government signed what was effectively a treaty, called the Seventeen-Point Agreement, the only such document to be designed to bring any of the former frontier dependencies of the Qing empire into the modern Chinese nation-state.

138. Spencer Chapman, *Lhasa: The Holy City* (Freeport, N.Y.: Books for Libraries Press, 1972 [1940]).

139. Williams, "Tibet and Her Neighbors," 136.

140. Jagou, "A Pilgrim's Progress," 18, 20; citing Chen Wenjian, *Banchan dashi dong lai shiwu nian dashiji* (*Important Notes Taken for Fifteen Years after the Great Master Panchen Came to the East*) (Chongqing, 1943), 44, 64. Welch credits the Minister of the Interior, Qu Yingguang, as the moving force behind the formation of this society (*The Buddhist Revival in China,* 337 n. 45).

141. "Puti xuehui cheng Junweihui baohu fawu" (The Bodhi Society Presents the National Military Council's [Order of] Protection for Buddhist Property), *Haichaoyin* 18, no. 4 (1937): 93.

142. Welch, *The Buddhist Revival of China,* 329 n. 47.

143. Zhizang, "Du *Xizang wenti zhi jiantao* hou de ganqing," 109.

144. Zhongguo di'er lishi dang'anguan and Zhongguo Zangxue yanjiu zhongxin, eds., *Huang Musong, Wu Zhongxin, Zhao Shouyu, Dai Chuanxian: Feng shi banli Zangshi baogao shu* (*Huang Musong, Wu Zhongxin, Zhao Shouyu, Dai Chuanxian: Reports of Envoys Sent to Handle Tibetan Affairs*) (Beijing: Zhongguo Zangxue chubanshe, 1993), see photos on pages i, xv.

145. See Cavanaugh and Chinese Materials Center, *Who's Who in China, 1918–1950,* supplement to the fourth edition [1933], 53, and fifth edition [1936], 113. For an excellent study of Chinese self-consciousness about the nature and meaning of clothing in the Republican period, see Karl Gerth, *China Made: Consumer Culture and the Creation of the Nation* (Cambridge, Mass.: Harvard University Asia Center, 2003), chap. 2.

146. Ya, *Biographies of the Tibetan Spiritual Leaders Panchen Erdenis,* 275, 286; Goldstein (*The Demise of the Lamaist State,* 224), citing Khung chin tshun, "Hong mu'o sung Bod du bskyod pa'i gnas tshul dngos bkod pa" (Account of Huang Musong's Mission to Tibet in 1934 by a

Member of That Mission), in *Bod kyi rig gnas lo rgyus rgyu cha bdam bsgrigs, 'don thengs lnga ba* (*Materials on the Cultural History of Tibet, no. 5*) (Lhasa: Bod rang skyong ljongs chab srid gros tshogs rig gnas lo rgyus rgyu cha u yon lhan khang, 1985), 109–161. The original Chinese language sources for describing this mission have only recently begun to be discussed in Western scholarly literature. See Hsiao-Ting Lin, "The 1934 Chinese Mission to Tibet: A Re-examination," *Journal of the Royal Asiatic Society* 12, no. 3 (2002). The major primary sources for this mission include Huang Musong, *Shi Zang jicheng* (*Record of the Journey of an Envoy to Tibet*), in *Shi Zang jicheng, Xizang jiyao, Lasa jianwen ji* (*Record of the Journey of an Envoy to Tibet, Summary of Tibet, Record of What I Saw and Heard in Lhasa*), ed. Laba pingcuo and Chen Jiajin (Beijing: Quanguo guoshuguan wenxian suowei xiazhi zhongxin, 1991); "Huang Musong fengshi ru Zang cefeng bing zhicha Dalai dashi baogao shu" (Report on Huang Musong's Entering Tibet under Orders to Confer Titles and Mourn the Thirteen Dalai Lama), in *Huang Musong, Wu Zhongxin, Zhao Shouyu, Dai Chuanxian: Feng shi banli Zangshi baogao shu* (*Huang Musong, Wu Zhongxin, Zhao Shouyu, Dai Chuanxian: Reports of Envoys Sent to Handle Tibetan Affairs*), ed. Zhongguo di'er lishi dang'anguan and Zhongguo Zangxue yanjiu zhongxin (Beijing: Zhongguo Zangxue chubanshe, 1993), 1–120. The deputy official, Gao Zhangzhu, on this 1934 mission recorded his experience in *Bianjiang wenti lunwen ji* (Collected Essays on Borderland Problems) (Zhengzhong shu ju, 1948).

147. Surely Huang's threat of an invasion force led by the Panchen Lama only served to make the Tibetan government more suspicious of China's plans (Goldstein, *The Demise of the Lamaist State*, 234).

148. Jagou, "A Pilgrim's Progress," 19.

149. Ibid., 20.

150. Williams, "Tibet and Her Neighbors," 136.

151. Jizhong—Jiangbai jianzan, "Leiwuqisi Jizhong houfo he Gere lama jianli," 89; Rje drung 'Jam dpal rgyal mtshan, "Ri bo che dgon pa dang Rje drung sprul sku Mgar ra bla ma," 231–233.

152. Han, *Kang Zang Fojiao*, 9r. See also Shi Dongchu, *Zhongguo Fojiao jindai shi*, 439.

153. Ganzi zhou zhi weiyuanhui, *Ganzi zhou zhi*, 1:114: *Sanmin zhuyi gongxiao*.

154. Dai Jitao, "Dai Chuanxian fengming qianwang Ganzi ji Banchan jingguo baogao ji Kang xing erji" (Report on Dai Chuanxian's Visit to Ganzi under Orders to Mourn the Panchen Lama and Diaries of His Visit to Kham), in *Huang Musong, Wu Zhongxin, Zhao Shouyu, Dai Chuanxian: Feng shi banli Zangshi baogao shu* (*Huang Musong, Wu Zhongxin, Zhao Shouyu, Dai Chuanxian: Reports of Envoys Sent to Handle Tibetan Affairs*), ed. Zhongguo di'er lishi dang'anguan and Zhongguo Zangxue yanjiu zhongxin (Beijing: Zhongguo Zangxue chuban-she, 1993), 481–554.

7. LINKING CHINESE AND TIBETAN CULTURES (1934–1950S)

1. "Shijie Foxue yuan Han Zang jin zhan" (Progress of the World Buddhist Institute, Sino-Tibetan [Branch]), *Haichaoyin* 13, no. 8 (1932): 6. The full name of the school was given as Shijie Foxue yuan Han Zang Focheng jiaoli yuan, Tib. 'Jig rten Sangs rgyas kyi chos grwa Rgya dang Bod pa'i bstan tshul bslab grwa khang (World Buddhist Institute's Sino-Tibetan Buddhayana Philosophy Institute).

2. Pittman, *Toward a Modern Chinese Buddhism*, 98–99.

3. Similarly, at Shanghai's Mongolian and Tibetan School, only one ethnic Tibetan

(Luosang jinpi, Blo bzang sbyin pa?) is listed among the teachers (Fafang, "Meng Zang xueyuan yu Puti xuehui" (The Mongolian and Tibetan College and the Bodhi Society), *Haichaoyin* 15, no. 9 [1934]: 2).

4. He taught at the school from 1932 to 1934 and then did not reappear on the roster until 1944, when he was again listed as a manager (*HZJLY* 1932, 77). See also *Shijie Foxue yuan Han Zang jiaoli yuan kaixue jinian tekan* (*Special Memorial Issue at the Start of Classes at the World Buddhist Institute's Sino-Tibetan Buddhist Institute*) (Tibetan title: *Rgya Bod lung rigs bslab grwa'i khyad dpe*) (Chongqing, hereafter *HZJLY* 1944, 16).Yu Lingbo, *Zhongguo jinxiandai Fojiao renwu zhi*, 187.

5. *HZJLY* 1932, 77; for a sample of his orthographic abilities, see page 4 of this document. Another Tibetan, Blo gros 'jam dbyang [*sic*; dbyangs] (Ch. Luozhu jiangyang) had similar difficulty spelling correctly, even his own name. For a more sustained sampler of a bilingual text, see pages 110–120, a translation of verses by Tsongkhapa.

6. He was again listed as the Tibetan language teacher in 1944 (*HZJLY* 1944, 16) after some of the other teachers had left.

7. Fazun, *Fazun wenji* (*Collected Works of Fazun*), ed. Hong Jisong and Huang Jilin, Dangdai Zhongguo Fojiao dashi wenji, 9 (Taipei: Wenshu chubanshe: Menshi bu Wenshu Fojiao wenhua zhongxin, 1988), 273–276.

8. Fazun, *Fazun wenji*, 247–248, 279–282. His teacher, known by the title Amdo *geshé*, died just before he returned to China.

9. *HZJLY* 1936, 26–27.

10. "Fojiao xinwen" (Buddhist News), *Haichaoyin* 21, no. 10 (1940): 20; *HZJLY* 44, 16. Dongben Dalama died shortly after arriving in China. I am not certain what the Chinese transcription of his name might represent in Tibetan. It is interesting to note that one of the first, if not the first, Tibetan Buddhists to teach Tibetan in a Western university was the Mongol Chaghan incarnation, Rnam rgyal rdo rje Dalama. Both these men shared this originally Qing imperial title of *dalama,* as did the Gurongtsang incarnation sent to Tibet by the Gansu provincial government in 1919. Rnam rgyal rdo rje had been invited to the United States by the Kalmyck Mongols of Philadelphia and came to teach Tibetan language at the University of California, Berkeley, with the assistance of Professor James Bosson (personal communication, February 2004) in the early sixties. Like Dongben, this lama had to produce his own teaching materials, as there was such of dearth of materials at the time.

11. Shi Weixian, "Han Zang jiaoliyuan yu Taixu fashi," 2.

12. Cavanaugh, *Who's Who in China, 1918–1950*, 6th ed., 82; supplement to the 5th ed., 49.

13. Shi Weixian, "Han Zang jiaoliyuan yu Taixu fashi," 2, 4. He Beiheng, who had taken refuge with (that is, become a Buddhist disciple of) Taixu just before Liu Xiang had given him responsibility for making preparation for the school in 1930, became the guardian (*yuan hu*) of the school when it opened in 1932.

14. Shi Weixian, "Han Zang jiaoliyuan yu Taixu fashi," 9. These are also the dates that Shi gives for the zenith of the school's flourishing, which was negatively effected by the departure of the Nationalist government in 1945.

15. Ibid., 3.

16. I suspect that one of the last references to this five race theory occurred in an undated essay (although it probably dates from around this time) by Fazun which opened with the phrase: "The Tibetan race (*minzu*) is one of China's (*Zhonghua*) five great races (*minzu*)." One of the reasons I suspect that this is a late source is that it was unusual in pairing the fivefold

division of ethnic groups not merely with "lineage" (*zu*) but with the more complicated newer term "race/nation/ethnic group" (*minzu*) (Fazun, "Yuan Ming jian yu Zhongguo you guan zhi Xizang Fojiao" (Tibetan Buddhism in the Yuan and Ming Dynasties and Its Connection with China), in *Han Zang Fojiao yanjiu huibian* (*Compilation of Sino-Tibetan Buddhist Research*), ed. Xizangxue congshu pian weihui, 101–111 (Taipei: Wenshu chubanshe, 1976), 101.

17. Zhou Guanren, "Goutong Han Zang wenhua," 4–8.

18. Cavanaugh and Chinese Materials Center, *Who's Who in China, 1918–1950,* 5th ed., 81.

19. Zhou Guanren, "Goutong Han Zang wenhua," 4–8.

20. Shi Weixian, "Han Zang jiaoliyuan yu Taixu fashi," 3, 5, 9–10. History, geography, law, agriculture, ethics, and hygiene are topics mentioned in this account of the school's history. There were also visiting lecturers such as the writers Jia Laoshe and Guo Muorou and the economist Ma Yinqu (10). Only four Tibetan monks are mentioned as having taught at the school, and, of these, one (Sherap Gyatso) was only a visiting lecturer after 1937. The others were discussed above. See "Fojiao xinwen" (Buddhist News), *Haichaoyin* 21, no. 10 (1940): 20.

21. Shi Weixian, "Han Zang jiaoliyuan yu Taixu fashi," 6. Taixu was also involved with conducting defensive training in which all the students (including the monks) dressed in army uniforms. He encouraged the students to be as patriotic and protective of religion as they were energetic in practicing the bodhisattva and vajra deeds (their religious practices). In 1942, and again in 1943, Taixu agreed to send students (some twenty in all, at least fourteen of whom were monks) to attend summer training camps and Three Principles of the People Youth Teams for high school and college students (8, 26).

22. Ibid. Although Tibetan geography is essential to understanding Tibetan Buddhist history, the level of training these students received would also have prepared them well for aiding in administrative and intelligence-gathering positions. For a sample of the kind of Chinese language materials available on Tibetan geography at this time, see Ren Naiqiang's work.

23. *Taixu wenji* (*Collected Writings of Taixu*), ed. Hung Jisung and Huang Jilin, Dangdai Zhongguo Fojiao dashi wenji, 2 (Taipei: Wenshu chubanshe, 1987), 215, 220–221.

24. Taixu, "Cong goutong Han Zang wenhua shuo dao ronghe Han Zang minzu" (From Linking Chinese and Tibetan Cultures to Merging the Chinese and Tibetan Peoples), in *Taixu dashi quanshu* (*Complete Works of the Venerable Taixu*) 62 vols. (Hong Kong: Taixu dashi quanshu chuban weiyuanhui, 1953 [1938]), 15:182.

25. Ibid., 55:416–417. The lecture from which this information was drawn was almost certainly given at the Mongolian and Tibetan School discussed in Fafang's article, "Meng Zang xueyuan yu Puti xuehui," 1–3.

26. Zhou Guanren, "Goutong Han Zang wenhua," 7.

27. *HZJLY* 1934, 1–10.

28. Ibid., 6–7.

29. Zhizang, "Du *Xizang wenti zhi jianlun* hou de ganqing," 109.

30. Luo Rencang, "Hangzhan qijian Sichuan Zangxue yanjiu gaishu" (A General Account of Tibetological Research in Sichuan Province during the Period of Resistance Against Japanese Aggression), *Zhongguo Zangxue* (*China Tibetology*), no. 3 (1996): 15.

31. Zhongguo Zangxue yanjiu zhongxin et al., *Yuan yi lai Xizang difang yu zhongyang zhengfu guanxi,* 7:2980; Shi Weixian, "Han Zang jiaoliyuan yu Taixu fashi," 10. Shi Weixian says that more than ten people from the school went to study abroad in Tibet but lists the names of only nine of these men. To judge by the five individuals for whom Shi lists their date of departure, this program only affected the school's students starting in 1938 and was busiest in

1943. Moreover, this number was only a very small proportion of the entering (450) or graduating (130) classes. Once again, this disparity between the original plan and the actual practice gave the advantage to the Chinese Buddhists whose study was financed by the government.

32. "Xiandai Fojiao shiliao: Guonei Fojiao: Xizang Xirao geshe li jing jiangxue" (Contemporary Buddhist Historic Materials: Domestic Buddhism: Tibet's Geshé Sherap Gyatso Arrives at the Capital and Gives Lectures at the University) *Haichaoyin* 18, no. 4 (1937): 91.

33. One member of the group, Ouyang Wuwei (b. 1913, Tib. Chömpel Jikmé) stayed at Drepung monastery for seven years before returning to teach in universities in China. He started studying Tibetan in 1933 at the Qinghai Teacher's College, Xining. That same year he had organized the Tibetan Language Research Society with friends; see "Yidai Zangxue dashi Zhunbi jimei lama (Ouyang Wuwei jiaoshou) chuanlüe" (A Brief Biography of the First-generation of Tibetan Studies Master Chömpel Jikmé [Professor Ouyang Wuwei]), *Faguang* (Dharma Light Monthly), November 10, 1991, 2. My thanks to Liu Kuo-wei for this reference.

34. Yang Xiaoping, "Xirao jiacuo dashi shengping shilüe" (The Brief Life Story of Master Sherap Gyatso), in *Wenshi ziliao xuanji* (*Selected Cultural and Historic Materials*), ed. Zhongguo renmin zhengzhi xieshang huiyi quanguo weiyuanhui and Wenshi ziliao yanjiu weiyuan hui (Beijing: Wenshi ziliao chubanshe, 1984), 151. His Tibetan name was given in Sun Krung hran, *San min kru'u yi'i bsdus don*, 111.

35. A mdo Byams pa, video recording made by Enrico dell'Angelo, viewed at Latse Contemporary Tibetan Cultural Library, New York City, November 9, 2003. Typescript extract translated by Pema Bhum.

36. Heather Stoddard, "The Long Life of rDo-sbis dGe-bshes Shes-rab rGya-mcho," in *4th Seminar of the International Association of Tibetan Studies*, ed. Helga Uebach and Jampa L. Panglung (Munich: Kommission für zentralasiatische Studien, 1988), 466.

37. For a firsthand account, see Dgon gsar Thub bstan 'jigs bral, "Dge ba'i bshes gnyen chen po Shes rab rgya mtsho rin po che mes rgyal nang sar phebs kyi gras tshul rjes dran byas pa" (Remembrance of the Situation When Great Geshé Sherap Gyatso Rinpoché Went Inland to the Motherland [China Proper]), in *Dge ba'i bshes gnyen chen po Shes rab rgya mtsho (The Great Geshé Sherap Gyatso)*, (Xining, 1997), 227–228. Gongbasa—Tudeng jizha, "Xirao jiacuo dashi: Fanhui neidi shikuang zhuiji" (Master Sherap Gyatso: Remembering the Actual Circumstances of Returning to China Proper), in *Xirao jiacuo dashi (Master Sherap Gyatso)*, ed. Zhengxie Qinghai sheng weiyuanhui wenshi ziliao weiyuanhui (Xining, 1997), 112.

38. Quhua (Chos dpal [rgya mtsho]), "Xirao jiacuo dashi shengping jilüe" (The Brief Life Story of Master Sherap Gyatso) in *Xirao jiacuo dashi (Master Sherab Gyatso)*, ed. Zhengxie Qinghai sheng weiyuanhui wenshi ziliao weiyuanhui, (Xining, 1997), 159–197, 169.

39. Yang Xiaoping, "Xirao jiacuo dashi shengping shilüe," 145–161,151; Zeng Guojing and Guo Weibing, *Lidai Zangzu mingren chuan (Biographies of Famous Tibetans of Past Dynasties)* (Lhasa: Xizang renmin chubanshe, 1996), 348; "Xiandai fojiao shiliao: Guonei Fojiao: Xizang Xirao geshe li jing jiangxue," 91–92. 'Phrin las and Grags pa, eds., *Rje btsun Shes rab rgya mtsho 'jam dpal dgyes pa'i blo gros kyi gsung rtsom (The Collected Works of the Venerable Shes rab rgya ntsho)*, Vol.3 (Xining: Mtsho sngon mi rigs dpe skrun khang, 1984), 629–630.

40. Welch, *The Buddhist Revival of China*, 178–179; Goldstein, *The Demise of the Lamaist State*, 614.

41. Taixu, *Taixu dashi quanshu*, 55:415. In his 1934 lecture in Shanghai, Taixu said that the provincial educational office allocated the school 600 *yuan* a month (7,200 *yuan* a year). The

figure of 5,000 *yuan* a year is drawn from Shi Weixian's history of the school (5) and may reflect an average over a longer period of time.

42. Shi Weixian, "Han Zang jiaoliyuan yu Taixu fashi," 5.

43. Fazun, *Zangwen wenfa (Tibetan Grammar)*, 2 vols., Xizangxue wenxian zongshu bieji (Beijing: Zhongguo Zangxue chubanshe, 1995 [1935 (1940)]). This text was in use in 1936, see *HZJLY* 1936, 13.

44. Fazun, *Xiandai Xizang*, 21, 112–15.

45. Fazun, with Sherap Gyatso named as consultant, Chen Mingshu, ed., *Zangwen duben chugao (First Draft of Tibetan Language Reader)*, woodblock print ed., 8 vols. (Chongqing: Han Zang jiaoliyuan, 1940).

46. Fazun, *Fazun wenji*, 324–325.

47. Wang Yao, "Zangxue ling mo" (Gaoxiong: Foguang chubanshe, 1992), 280.

48. Chos kyi grags pa, *Dge bshes Chos kyi grags pas btsams pa'i brda dag ming tshig gsal ba/ Gexi Quzha Zangwen cidian: Zang, Han duizhao* (Beijing: Mi rigs dpe skrun khang/ Minzu chubanshe, 1995 [1957]). The Tibetan dictionary was compiled by a Mongol *geshé* in 1946. The block edition was completed in 1949, and Fazun and others translated the definitions into Chinese before its publication. The handwritten draft of this translation is preserved in the Chongqing municipal archives.

49. For the history of the institute and dictionary, see Huang Xianming, "Xichui wenhua yuan" (Western Border Culture Institute), *Xizang yanjiu*, no. 2 (1990): 162; and "Xichui wen-hua yuan" (Western Border Culture Institute), in *Chengdu wenshi ziliao xuanji* (Chengdu: Chengdu chubanshe, 1989), 168–171.

50. Zhang Xu [= Zhang Yisun], *Zang Han jilun cihui (Tibetan-Chinese Vocabulary, Gathered and Arranged)* (Hong Kong: Xichui wenhua yuan, 1937).

51. Zhang Xu [= Zhang Yisun], *Zang Han yu duikan (Tibetan and Chinese Language Bilingual Phrasebook)* (Hong Kong: Xichui wenhua yuan, 1938).

52. Zhang Xu [= Zhang Yisun], *Han Zang yuhui (Chinese-Tibetan Vocabulary)* (Chengdu: Xichui wenhua yuan, 1938); and *Zangwen shudu guifan (Models of Tibetan Language Correspondence)* (Chengdu: Xichui wenhua yuan, 1938), based on Sarat Chandra Das, *Yig kur nam shag: Being a Collection of Letters, Both Official and Private, and Illustrating the Different Forms of Correspondance Used in Tibet* (Calcutta: Bengal Secretariat Press, 1901).

53. *Zang Han yiming da cihui (The Great Tibetan-Chinese Vocabulary)* ([Chengdu]: Xichui wenhua yuan, 1939). I was fortunate to be able to purchase originals of these now rare texts from Professor James Bosson when he retired.

54. Zhang Yisun, *Bod Rgya tshig mdzod chen mo/ Zang Han da cidian* (Beijing: Mi rigs dpe skrun khang/ Minzu chubanshe, 1998 [1993]).

55. Fafang. "Meng Zang xueyuan yu Puti xuehui," 2. This article described its organization and listed the founders.

56. Ibid., 1–3.

57. Dreyer, *China's Forty Millions*, 18. Citing *China Handbook, 1937–1945* (New York: Macmillan, 1947), 74.

58. Dreyer, *China's Forty Millions*, 32.

59. Chen Tianxi, *Dai Jitao xiansheng de shengping*, 514–515.

60. See Goldstein, Sherap, and Siebenschuh, *A Tibetan Revolutionary*, 48, 51.

61. Li Tieh-tseng, *The Historical Status of Tibet*, 287 n. 268.

62. Li An-che, *Labrang: A Study in the Field*, The Documentation Center for Asian Studies,

Special series 5 (Tokyo: Institute of Oriental Culture, 1982), 116. For further details, see Gu's record of his trip, *Xibei kaocha riji (Diary of Investigations in the Northwest)*.

63. Li Anzhe, "Xizang xi Fojiao seng jiaoyu zhidu" (Tibet's Buddhist Monastic Educational System), *Haichaoyin* 21, nos. 5–6 (1940): 95–99. See also Zhang Qinyou, "Ji Zhongguo Zangxue xianbei—Li Anzhe, Yu Shiyu jiaoshou zai Labuleng de suiyue" (Remembering the Elder Generation of China's Tibetology—Professors Li Anzhe and Li Shiyu's Years at Labrang [Monastery]) *Xizang yanjiu (Tibetan Studies)*, no. 1 (1989): 140–143.

64. Luo Rencang, "Hangzhan qijian Sichuan Zangxue yanjiu gaishu," 20 n. 8. For rich insights into the situation in Labrang at this time, see Paul Kocot Nietupski, *Labrang: A Tibetan Buddhist Monastery at the Crossroads of Four Civilizations (Photos from the Griebnow Archives, 1921–1949)* (Ithaca, N.Y.: Snow Lion, 1999).

65. Li An-che, *Labrang*, 116.

66. Wang Yao and Chen Qingying, eds., *Xizang lishi wenhua cidian (Dictionary of Tibetan History and Culture)* (Hangzhou: Xizang renmin chubanshe, Zhejiang renmin chubanshe, 1998), 150.

67. For example, in 1939 Shen Guoan (Tib. Tsogpa Dorje) started a school in his Kangding home. He used Western methods, which he picked up in Kalimpong when studying English after having been being driven from Tibet with the other Chinese in 1913. He taught Tibetan to two prominent Chinese Tibetologists: Liu Liquan, who married his daughter, and Ren Naiqiang. In addition, Li Anzhe and R. A. Stein also benefited from his knowledge of Tibetan culture (personal communication with Ren Xinjian, Ren Naiqiang's son, summer of 1999).

68. Dreyer, *China's Forty Millions*, 75.

69. Luo Rencang, *Zhongguo Zangxue*, 18.

70. "Yidai Zangxue dashi Zhunbi jimei lama," 2.

71. Ren Xinjian, "Kang Zang yanjiu she jieshao" (A Brief Introduction to the Research Institute of Kham and Tibet), *Zhongguo Zangxue (China Tibetology)*, no. 3 (1996): 21–23; for a detailed analysis of the journal and its contributors (including the Tibetan Luozhu qingzuo), see 26–29. See also Josef Kolmas, "Index to Articles in the *K'ang-Tsang Yen-Chiu Yüeh-K'an (A Contribution to the Bibliography of Tibet)*," *Journal of the Tibet Society* 1 (1982): 15–40; *Chinese Studies on Tibetan Culture: A Facsimile Reproduction of the K'ang-Tsang Yen-Chiu Yüeh-K'an (Hsik'ang-Tibet research monthly)*, vol. 332, Sata-Pitaka series: Indo-Asian Literatures (New Delhi: International Academy of Indian Culture, 1983 [1946–1949]).

72. "Yidai Zangxue dashi Zhunbi jimei lama," 2.

73. Dreyer, *China's Forty Millions*, 69.

74. The Tibetan name of this school is found in Grags pa and 'Phrin las, eds., *Rje btsun Shes rab rgya mtsho*, 3:639. For further details on this institution, see Gray Tuttle, "Modern Tibetan Historiography in China," *Papers on Chinese History* 7 (1998): 88–93.

75. Dgon gsar, "Dge ba'i bshes gnyen chen po Shes rab rgya mtsho," 229. Gongbasa, "Xirao jiacuo dashi," 113. Cf. *Fojiao banyue kan* 7.8: 16–17. "Xiandai Fojiao shiliao: Guonei Fojiao: Xizang Xirao geshe li jing jiangxue," *Haichaoyin* 18, no. 4 (1937): 91–92.

76. Dgon gsar, "Dge ba'i bshes gnyen chen po Shes rab rgya mtsho," 228. Gongbasa, "Xirao jiacuo dashi," 113.

77. "Xiandai Fojiao shiliao," 91–92. Yang Xiaoping, "Xirao jiacuo dashi shengping shilüe," 151.

78. Dgon gsar, "Dge ba'i bshes gnyen chen po Shes rab rgya mtsho," 229. Gongbasa, "Xirao jiacuo dashi," 112: *Yin yuan.*

79. Grags pa and 'Phrin las, *Rje btsun Shes rab rgya mtsho*, 630. This society seems to have been translated a number of different ways into Tibetan. Phun tshogs gave the name Jangchup Lamrim Gön (*Dge bshes Shes rab rgya mtsho dang Rdo sbis grwa tshang* [Beijing: Mi rigs dpe skrun khang, 1998], 221). Gongbasa just called it a Buddhist monastery ("Xirao jiacuo dashi," 113).

80. Phun tshogs, *Dge bshes Shes rab rgya mtsho*, 22–23.

81. Dgon gsar, "Dge ba'i bshes gnyen chen po Shes rab rgya mtsho," 229. Gongbasa, "Xirao jiacuo dashi," 112; 'Phrin las and Grags pa, *Rje btsun Shes rab rgya mtsho*, 630.

82. Dingzhi, *Nenghai shangshi zhuan*, 31.

83. Ibid., 49

84. Huang Xianming, "Xichui wenhua yuan," 162.

85. 'Phrin las and Grags pa, *Rje btsun Shes rab rgya mtsho*, 629–630.

86. Shi Weixian, "Han Zang jiaoliyuan yu Taixu fashi," 6.

87. Phun tshogs, *Dge bshes Shes rab rgya mtsho*, 39.

88. Skar ma mkha' 'bum, "Dge bshes Shes rab rgya mtsho Mtsho sngon Bod rgyud nang bstan gyi bstan don dang Rgya yig khrid sbyong 'dzin grwa gsar btsugs pa" (The Establishment of the New Mtsho sngon Classes for the Study of the Meaning of the Teachings of the Tibetan Tradition of Buddhist Teachings and Chinese Writing), in *Dge ba'i bshes gnyen chen po Shes rab rgya mtsho* (*The Great Geshé Sherap Gyatso*), ed. Mtsho sngon zhing chen srid gros kyi rig gnas lo rgyus kyi dpyad gzhi'i yig cha'i u yon lhan tshogs (Xining, 1997), 288; Gama kanben, "Dashi chuangban Qinghai Lama jiaoyi guowen jiangxisuo" (The Master Establishes the Qinghai Institute for Lectures and Studies of Lama Religious Doctrine [and] National Written Language), in *Xirao jiacuo dashi* (*Master Sherab Gyatso*), ed. Zhengxie Qinghai sheng weiyuanhui wenshi ziliao weiyuanhui, (Xining, 1997), 138.

89. Pengcuo (Phun tshogs), "Zao fu seng zi yi dashi" (Recollecting the Master's Bringing Benefit to His Native Place), in *Xirao jiacuo dashi* (*Master Sherab Gyatso*), ed. Zhengxie Qinghai sheng weiyuanhui wenshi ziliao weiyuanhui (Xining, 1997), 150; Gus 'bangs Phun tshogs, "Pha yul bde skyid kyi dpal la 'god pa'i ston zla'i bsil sbyin mkhan po'i rang gzugs" (The Cooling Autumn Moon's Own Form Abides: A Record of the Splendor of the Fatherland's Happiness), in *Dge ba'i bshes gnyen chen po Shes rab rgya mtsho* (*The Great Geshé Sherap Gyatso*) (Xining, 1997), 311.

90. Skar ma mkha' 'bum, "Dge bshes Shes rab rgya mtsho," 287; Gama kanben, "Dashi chuangban Qinghai lama," 138–139.

91. Skar ma mkha' 'bum, "Dge bshes Shes rab rgya mtsho," 288; Gama kanben, "Dashi chuangban Qinghai lama," 139.

92. Gama kanben, "Dashi chuangban Qinghai lama," 139.

93. Phun tshogs, *Dge bshes Shes rab rgya mtsho*, 65.

94. Li Cunfu gave the name of this school as Qinghai Lama jiaoyi guowen jiangyisuo (Qinghai Institute for Lectures and Studies of Lama Religious Doctrine [and] National Written Language) ("Xirao jiacuo dashi nianbiao" [Chronology of Master Sherap Gyatso's Life], in *Xirao jiacuo dashi* [*Master Sherab Gyatso*], ed. Zhengxie Qinghai sheng weiyuanhui wenshi ziliao weiyuanhui, (Xining, 1997), 246). The Tibetan version with interesting variations on the terms for Tibetan Buddhism and the "national" language—Mtsho sngon Bod brgyud nang bstan gyi bstan don dang Rgya yig slob sbyong 'dzin grwa (Mtsho sngon Class for the Study of the Meaning of Teachings of the Tibetan Tradition of Buddhist Teachings and Chinese Writing)—is given in Lis Tshun hphu'u, "Dge bshes Shes rab rgya mtsho'i mdzad 'phrin lo tshigs (1884–1968)" (Chronology of Important Events of Geshé Sherab Gyatso's Life), in *Dge*

ba'i bshes gnyen chen po Shes rab rgya mtsho (The Great Geshé Sherap Gyatso) (Xining, 1997), 502. For the other versions of the name of the school, see Phun tshogs, *Dge bshes Shes rab rgya mtsho*, 62: Mtsho sngon nang bstan gzhung lugs dang rgya yig khrid sbyong khang. Skar ma mkha' 'bum, "Dge bshes Shes rab rgya mtsho," 139: Mtsho sngon Bod rgyud nang bstan gyi bstan don dang rgya yig khrid sbyong 'dzin grwa; Gama kanben, "Dashi chuangban Qinghai lama," 288: Qinghai Lama jiaoyi guowen jiangyisuo.

95. Li Cunfu, "Xirao jiacuo dashi nianbiao," 246–247; Skar ma mkha' 'bum, "Dge bshes Shes rab rgya mtsho," 288; Gama kanben, "Dashi chuangban Qinghai lama," 139.

96. Chen Xianfu, "Ji yu Xirao jiacuo da shi de yi ci tanhua," in *Xirao jiacuo dashi*, ed. Zhengxie Qinghai sheng weiyuanhui wenshi ziliao weiyuanhui, (Xining, 1997), 137.

97. Phun tshogs, *Dge bshes Shes rab rgya mtsho*, 64.

98. From its ten *mu* of land (about one and a half acres).

99. Skar ma mkha' 'bum, "Dge bshes Shes rab rgya mtsho," 288; Gama kanben, "Dashi chuangban Qinghai lama," 139.

100. According to Skar ma mkha' 'bum, the second Chinese language teacher, Lhamo Tseten, was a nomad Tibetan layman whose younger brother is now famous for his role in advocating modern Tibetan education, Dorjé Tseten (former director of the Chinese Tibetology Center in Beijing) ("Dge bshes Shes rab rgya mtsho," 290).

101. Skar ma mkha' 'bum, who attended the school, said that all the students were monks ("Dge bshes Shes rab rgya mtsho," 290). A less reliable source indicates that the students were of many different ethnic backgrounds, including Tibetan, Han, Salar, and Hui ethnicities (Chen Xianfu, "Ji yu Xirao jiacuo," 137).

102. For possible origins of this class division in the Chinese universities system, see Pengcuo, "Zao fu seng zi yi dashi," 146. All the students were male. This was a monastic school, and the one local nunnery was not included in the consolidation efforts.

103. On this last subject of study the Chinese version (Gama kanben, "Dashi chuangban Qinghai lama," 140) differs from the Tibetan version (Skar ma mkha' 'bum, "Dge bshes Shes rab rgya mtsho," 290). The Chinese version says that, of five sciences offered for study, students chose one. The five sciences are *bsdus grwa (tshad ma), phar phyin, dbu ma, mngon pa*, and *'dul ba*. In any case, the training for the older students more closely resembled a traditional Tibetan education.

104. Phun tshogs, *Dge bshes Shes rab rgya mtsho*, 65–66.

105. Yu Lingbo, *Zhongguo jinxiandai Fojiao renwu zhi*, 452.

106. Fori, "Jinjin mizong re zhi fansi" (Thoughts on the zeal of Esoteric Buddhism in recent times), *Fayin* (Voice of the Dharma), no. 137 (1996): 26.

107. Personal communication, 1999. At the time Luo was researching an article to be called "The Nationality and Religious Policy of Liu Wenhui's Tenure in Khams" (*Liu Wenhui zhu Kang de minzu zongjiao zhengci*).

108. He Juefei named Anjue si (Ngachö Gön) as the location for this school (*Xikang jishi shiben shizhu*, 50). He also listed the five sciences studied, including logic and medicine. See also Sichuan sheng Kangding xianzhi biajiweiyuan hui, *Kangding xianzhi (Kangding County Gazetteer)*, 442; "Kangding Muyaxiang Wuming xueyuan zhuxing kaixue dianli" (Opening ceremony for Kangding Muya village's Five Sciences Institute), *Haichaoyin* 20, nos. 4–6 (1939): 61. This latter notice said that the school opened in Sengzha si, possibly another name for the same temple.

109. He Juefei, *Xikang jishi shiben shizhu*, 50–51.

110. Luo Rencang, *Zhongguo Zangxue*, 15.

111. Li An-che, *Labrang*, 24.

112. Dingzhi, *Nenghai shangshi zhuan*, 27.

113. Ibid.

114. Ibid., 30–32. In 1941 Nenghai would add a *homa* altar to this temple as well.

115. Shi Shiliang, "Jindai hongyang Gelupai de liang wei Hanzu dade ji qi yi, zhujian jie" (A Brief Account of the Great Virtue of Two Chinese Men Who Propagated the Dge lugs Sect and Their Translations), *Xizang yanjiu* 2, no. 47 (1993): 51. In recent years the monastery has reopened under the direction of a Khampa lama and his students.

116. Ester Bianchi, 2001. "The Iron Statue Monastery 'Tiexiangsi': A Buddhist Nunnery of Tibetan Tradition in Contemporary China" (Firenze: L. S. Olschki, 2001); Qiu Shanshan, *Dangdai diyi bixiuni: Longlian fashi zhuan* (The number one contemporary bhiksuni: The biography of Master Longlian) (Fuzhou: Fujian meishu chubanshe, 1997).

117. Nenghai's works have been reprinted in a seven-volume set in Taiwan and a three-volume set in China, with numerous local reprints of particular texts in places like Mount Wutai and Chengdu.

118. Dai Jitao, "Chengdu xiujian huguo xiaozai fahui fayuan wen" (Religious Vows for the Chengdu Dharma-Assembly Held to Protect the Country and Avert Disaster), in *Dai Jitao xiansheng wencun* (*Extant Writings of Dai Jitao*) (Taipei: Zhongguo guomindang zhongyang weiyuanhui, 1959 [1939]), 3:1182.

119. Dai Jitao, *Dai Jitao xiansheng wencun*, 3:1136–1137, 1323–1324.

120. Shi Dongchu, *Zhongguo Fojiao jindai shi*, 465.

121. Dai Jitao, "Huguo xiaozai hui qiyuan wen" (Prayers for the assembly to protect the country and avert disaster), in idem, *Dai Jitao xiansheng wencun*, 3:1184–1186. It is said of Xuyun that he went to Tibet in the nineteenth century.

122. Zhangjia dashi yuanqi dianli weiyuanhui, *Huguo jingjue fujiao dashi*, 34.

123. Dai Jitao, "Huguo xiaozi hui qiyuan wen," 3:1184–1186.

124. Dingzhi, *Nenghai shangshi zhuan*, 52.

125. Ibid., 58. Even afterward the monk that Nenghai had appointed to lead this hall managed to maintain the Tibetan Buddhist tradition among the Chinese in Sichuan well into the 1990s. See Qingding, *Qingding shangshi kaishi lu* (*Record of Qingding Lama's Teaching*) (Chengdu: Chengdushi xinwen chubanchu, 1999).

126. Dingzhi, *Nenghai shangshi zhuan*, 53. He taught at the North Sea Bodhi-study Association (Beihai Poti xuehui) and at the Beijing Laypersons Group (Beijing Jushilin), which still prints Tibetan scriptures in Chinese translations.

127. Ibid., 54, 56–58.

128. Bei Fu, "Hongyang Zangmi de Qinghai fashi," *Wutaishan yanjiu* 50, no. 1 (1997): 35–39; Gray Tuttle, "Tibetan Buddhism at a Chinese Buddhist Sacred Mountain in Modern Times," *Journal of the International Association for Tibetan Studies*, forthcoming (2004).

129. Welch, *The Buddhist Revival of China*, 47.

130. In 1408 the fifth Karmapa lama was apparently granted this position of authority, although he seems not to have accepted or acted on it. See Karmay, *Early Sino-Tibetan Art*, 79.

131. Zhangjia dashi yuanqi dianli weiyuanhui, *Huguo jingjue fujiao dashi*, 34–35. Isabelle Charleux noted that "the Dalai Lama recently recognized the reincarnation of the Lcang skya [Changja] qutughtu, who lives in India" ("Buddhist Monasteries in Southern Mongolia," in

The Buddhist Monastery [Paris: École française d'Extrême Orient, 2003], 361). As there was clearly a delay of some decades in this recognition, one can speculate numerous reasons for the near cessation of this series. From a Buddhist perspective, possibly the lama felt that he had completed his mission, especially since he was separated from the Monguor population in which the series arose. In this respect it is interesting to note that, in recent times, the reincarnations of lamas in exile have been recognized in Western children. From an economic perspective, the separation from the lama's extensive corporate estate, at Wutaishan, Dolon nor, Beijing, and Qinghai, may explain why no administrative body located a successor. From a political perspective, the incarnation series had not proved very useful to the Nationalist government, which had supported the lama for the past several decades, so there was little political incentive in continuing to recognize the lama.

132. Dingzhi, *Nenghai shangshi zhuan*, 31, 49; Stoddard, "The Long Life of rDo-sbis dGe-bshes Shes-rab rGya-mcho," 469.

133. Yang Xiaoping, "Xirao jiacuo dashi shengping shilüe," 153. He was even more critical of the Communist policies; see Robert Barnett, *A Poisoned Arrow: The Secret Report of the 10th Panchen Lama* (London: Tibet Information Network, 1997), xvii.

134. Goldstein, *The Demise of the Lamaist State*, 683.

135. Tsering Shakya, *The Dragon in the Land of Snows*, 65.

136. In the end, the official did not prostrate himself, although "he paid his respects by giving the Dalai Lama a Tibetan scarf." See Melvyn Goldstein, "On Modern Tibetan History: Moving beyond Stereotypes," in *Tibet and Her Neighbours, a History* (London: Edition Hansjörg Mayer, 2003), 221–222.

137. Tsering Shakya, *The Dragon in the Land of Snows*, 90.

138. Holmes Welch, *Buddhism under Mao* (Cambridge, Mass.: Harvard University Press, 1972), 20.

139. Ibid., 19. For the official Chinese pronouncements on the foundation of this association, see Chao Pu-chu, *Buddhism in China*, rev. ed. (Peking: Buddhist Association of China, 1960 [1957]), 39–40. For a critical view of the government's motives, see Yang I-fan, *Buddhism in China* (Hong Kong: Union Press, 1956), 87–95. In 1966 the Chinese Buddhist Association shut down because of the Cultural Revolution (Welch, 25). Sherap Gyatso died during the Cultural Revolution, in 1968, after being subjected to violent struggle sessions (Stoddard, "The Long Life of rDo-sbis dGe-bshes Shes-rab rGya-mcho," 470).

140. 'Phrin las and Grags pa, *Rje btsun Shes rab rgya mtsho*, 656–660. He even traveled to Europe.

141. Chinese Buddhist Association, *Buddhists in New China*, bilingual ed. (Chinese/English) (Beijing: Nationalities Publishing House, 1956); see also Chao Pu-chu, *Buddhism in China*.

142. Shi Shiliang. "Jindai yinyang Gelupai," 51. Xie Guoan (Paul Sherab) of the Kham and Tibetan Research Society in Chengdu also followed the army into Tibet to serve as a Tibetan language instructor (Ren Xinjian, "Kang Zang yanjiu she jieshao," 26).

143. Shi Shiliang, "Jindai yinyang Gelupai," 48.

144. Fazun, *Fazun wenji*, 250–251.

145. Raoul Birnbaum, personal communication, 1997. In 2001 the government banned Chinese Buddhists from studying at particular Tibetan teaching centers, citing unsanitary conditions as their justification. See International Campaign for Tibet, "Thousands of Monks and Nuns Ordered to Leave Remote Encampments," *Tibet Press Watch* 9, no. 4 (2001): 1, 13; "New

Details on Crackdown in Larung Gar," *Tibet Press Watch* 9, no. 6 (2001): 6–7; "U.S. Concerned at Crackdown on Tibetan Buddhist Institute," *Tibet Press Watch* 9, no. 5 (2001): 2, 12.

POSTSCRIPT

1. Ma Jian, *Red Dust*, trans. Flora Drew (New York: Anchor, 2001), 296, 316–317.

2. Zhengguo fashi yuanji shizhou nian jinianji weiyuanhui, "Zhengguo fashi nianbiao shilüe," in *Mianhuai Zhengguo fashi* (*Recollections of Master Zhengguo*) (Beijing: Guangjisi, 1997), 121, 128. When Zhengguo died in 1987, he was deputy director of the Chinese Buddhist Association and had just played a role in the founding of China's Buddhist Culture Research Institute (Zhongguo Fojiao wenhua yanjiu suo) at the Guangji Temple in Beijing.

3. For further details, see my "Tibetan Buddism at a Chinese Buddhist Sacred Mountain in Modern Times."

4. For his latest examination of modern Chinese Buddhism, see Raoul Birnbaum, "Buddhist China at Century's Turn," *China Quarterly*, no. 174 (special issue: *Religion in China Today*) (2003): 428–450.

5. Stoddard, *Le Mendiant de l'Amdo*, 223.

6. Dikötter, "Racial Discourse in China," 29.

7. Sautman, *Myths of Descent*, 92–93

8. Knaus, *Orphans of the Cold War*, 22.

9. Pengcuo, "Zao fu seng zi yi dashi," 149; Gus 'bangs Phun tshogs, "Pha yul bde skyid," 310.

10. Personal observation in 1997.

11. Li Yuchuan, "Danjin Zhongguo diyi ni—Longlian fashi" (China's Number One Nun Today—Master Longlian), in *Minzu zongjiao huaqiao,* ed. Sichuan sheng zhengxie wenshi ziliao weiyuanhui, Sichuan wenshi ziliao jicui, 5 (Chengdu: Sichuan renmin chubanshe, 1996), 561. Tibetan Buddhism is not part of the current curriculum (personal communication with a recent graduate, 1999).

12. Gyurme Dorje, *Tibet Handbook*, 505

13. "Dan jun—Zaina panduo and Li," *Mingcha shuang huangsi*, 252.

14. For instance, Zhing bza' Skal bzang chos kyi rgyal mtshan, *Bod Sog chos 'byung* (*Zang Meng Fojiao shi, Tibeto-Mongol Buddhist History*), Gangs can rig brgya'i sgo 'byed lde mig (Zangwen wenxian), 18 (Beijing: Mi rigs dpe skrun khang, 1992).

15. Tsering Shakya, *The Dragon in the Land of Snows*, 446.

16. Reported in *Xinhua,* November 10, 2000; cited in "Propaganda and the West: China's Struggle to Sway International Opinion on the 'Tibet issue,'" Tibet Information Network Special Report, July 16, 2001, 1–10.

17. In January 2002 a closed-door meeting was organized under the auspices of the Fairbank Center for East Asian Research at Harvard to promote dialogue between Tibetans-in-exile, American and Chinese Tibetologists, and Tibetan policy makers.

18. "Wutaishan Fomen juxing xiaozai zhenzai dafahui (The Mount Wutai Buddhist Circles Held a Great Dharma-Assembly to Eliminate Disasters and Relieve the People Scourged by Natural Disaster)," *Fayin* (*Voice of the Dharma*), no. 169 (1998): 34. The full title of the ceremony was "Wutaishan qidao Guotai min'an xiaozai miannan sunzi zhenzai dafahui."

19. "Shi yi shi Banchan xiang zaiqu juanhuan" (The Eleventh Panchen Lama Donates Money to Disaster Areas), *Fayin* (*Voice of the Dharma*), no. 169 (1998): 15.

20. Robert Barnett, talk given at Harvard University, March 3, 2004; a painting by Nyima Tsering, who sees himself as the unofficial "personal painter of the Panchen Lama" included this text (in the form of an imperial inscription typically bestowed on a temple) as part of his montage depicting the recognition of the new Panchen Lama. This artistic rendering was apparently inspired by the presentation of a large-format calligraphic message (*Huguo limin*) from Jiang Zemin to the eleventh Panchen Lama in December 1995. It is interesting that the artist too recognized the echo of the imperial tradition (reflected in his visual transformation of the media) of such a "gift," which can also be seen as a forceful directive. For a photo of this calligraphy, see International Campaign for Tibet and Kate Saunders, *When the Sky Fell to Earth: The New Crackdown on Buddhism in Tibet* (Washington, D.C.: International Campaign for Tibet, 2004).

21. Sangzhou zhaxi (Bsam grub bkra shis), "Tantan Han Zang Fojiao de goutong" (Discussions on the Communications between Chinese and Tibetan Buddhism), *Fayin* (*Voice of the Dharma*), no. 167 (1998): 37–38.

22. Sangzhou zhaxi, "Tantan Han Zang Fojiao," 37.

Bibliography

Bracketed years after publication dates indicate original (first) printings of the texts.

CHONGQING CITY ARCHIVAL SOURCES

HZJLY 1932 = 1932. *[Shijie Foxue yuan] Han Zang jiaoli yuan kaixue jinian tekan* (*Special Memorial Issue at the Start of Classes at the World Buddhist Institute's Sino-Tibetan Buddhist Institute*). (Tibetan title: *'Jigs rten sangs rgyas kyi chos grwa Rgya dang Bod pa'i bstan tshul bslab grwa khang da ltar bkod pa'i bslab grwa shin tu rnyed dka' ba'i pad [sic; dpe] cha*). Chongqing.

HZJLY 1934 = 1934. *Shijie Foxue yuan Han Zang jiaoli yuan tekan di yi qi* (*Special Issue of the World Buddhist Institute's Sino-Tibetan Buddhist Institute*) (Tibetan title: *'Jigs rten sangs rgyas gyis [sic] bstan tshul Rgya Bod bslab grwa khang lo dang po ba'i dpe cha*). Chongqing: Han Zang Jiaoli Yuan (Sino-Tibetan Buddhist Institute).

HZJLY 1936 = 1936. *Han Zang jiaoli yuan li'an wenjian huibian* (*Compilation of Registered Documents of the Sino-Tibetan Buddhist Institute*). Chongqing.

HZJLY 1944 = 1944. *Shijie Foxue yuan Han Zang jiaoli yuan kaixue jinian tekan* (*Special Memorial Issue at the Start of Classes at the World Buddhist Institute's Sino-Tibetan Buddhist Institute*) (Tibetan title: *Rgya Bod lung rigs bslab grwa'i khyad dpe*). Chongqing.

CHINESE SOURCES

Awang luosang jiacou. *Wushi Dalai lama zhuan* (Biography of the Fifth Dalai Lama). Translated by Chen Qingying and Ma Lianlong. Zhongguo bianjiang shi di ziliao conggan-Xizang juan (Collected materials on China's borderlands—Tibet). Beijing: Zhongguo Zangxue chubanshe, 1992.

Bei Fu. "Hongyang Zangmi de Qinghai fashi" (Master Qinghai's Propagation of Tibetan Esoterica). *Wutaishan yanjiu* 50, no. 1 (1997): 35–39.

"Beiping Shilun jingang fahui" (Beiping's Kâlacakra Varja Dharma-Assembly). *Haichaoyin* 12, no. 8 (1932): 47–50.

Changxing. "Shilun fahui quan faqi wen" (Exhortation to Sponsor the Kâlacakra Assembly). *Haichaoyin* 12, no. 12 (1931): 2–4.

Chen Tianxi. *Dai Jitao xiansheng de shengping* (*The Life of Dai Jitao*). Taipei: Taiwan shangwu yin-shuguan, 1968.

Chen Wenjian. *Banchan dashi dong lai shiwu nian dashiji* (*Important Notes Taken for Fifteen Years after the Great Master Panchen Came to the East*). Chongqing, 1943.

Chen Xianfu. "Ji yu Xirao jiacuo da shi de yi ci tanhua" (Remembering One Conversation with Master Sherap Gyatso). In *Xirao jiacuo dashi* (*Master Sherap Gyatso*), 136–137 (Xining, 1997).

Chengdu Xi'nan heping fahui banshichu. *Chengdu Xi'nan heping fahui tekan* (*Special Issue of Chengdu's Southwestern Dharma-Assembly for Peace*). Chengdu: Chengdu Xi'nan heping fahui banshichu, 1932.

Ci Yi, ed. *Foguang da cidian* (*Buddha's Radiance Great Dictionary*). Beijing: Beijing tushuguan chubanshe, 1989.

Cui Zhengsen and Wang Zhichao. *Wutaishan Beiwen xianzhu* (*Extant Stele Inscriptions of Mount Wutai*). Taiyuan: Bei yueyi chubanshe, 1995.

"*Dagong bao*: Xizang zhengjiao zhi shiwei" (The Whole Story of Tibet's Political and Religious [System] as reported in *Dagong bao*). *Haichaoyin* 15, no. 4 (1934): 110–111.

Dai Jitao. "Banchan dashi shuo liuzi daming jenyan fa yao" (Essentials of the Panchen Lama's Teachings on the Six Syllable Mantra). In Dai Jitao, *Dai Jitao xiansheng wencun* (*Extant Writings of Dai Jitao*), 4 vols., 3:1173–1174. Taipei: Zhongguo guomindang zhongyang weiyuanhui, 1959 [1931]. Dated June 7, 1931.

——. "Cheng Zhongyang zhengzhi huiyi wen" (Text Presented to the Central Political Conference). In *Dai Jitao xiansheng wencun* (*Extant Writings of Dai Jitao*), 4 vols., 1:297–300. Taipei: Zhongguo guomindang zhongyang weiyuanhui, 1959 [1934]. Dated May 24, 1934.

——. "Chengdu xiujian huguo xiaozai fahui fayuan wen" (Religious Vows for the Chengdu Dharma-Assembly Held to Protect the Country and Avert Disaster). In *Dai Jitao xiansheng wencun* (*Extant Writings of Dai Jitao*), 4 vols., 3:1182–1184. Taipei: Zhongguo guomindang zhongyang weiyuanhui, 1959 [1939]. Dated September 1939.

——. "Chenxing Zhongguo yu chenxing Fojiao" (The Flourishing of China and the Flourishing of Buddhism). *Haichaoyin* 14, no. 1 (1933): 11–13.

——. "Dai Chuanxian fengming qianwang Ganzi ji Banchan jingguo baogao ji Kang xing erji" (Report on Dai Chuanxian's Visit to Ganzi under Orders to Mourn the Panchen Lama and Diaries of His Visit to Kham). In *Huang Musong, Wu Zhongxin, Zhao Shouyu, Dai Chuanxian: Feng shi banli Zangshi baogao shu* (*Huang Musong, Wu Zhongxin, Zhao Shouyu, Dai Chuanxian: Reports of Envoys Sent to Handle Tibetan Affairs*), ed. Zhongguo di'er lishi dang'anguan and Zhongguo Zangxue yanjiu zhongxin, 481–548. Beijing: Zhongguo Zangxue chubanshe, 1993.

——. *Dai Jitao xiansheng Foxue lunji* (*Dai Jitao's Collected Buddhist Studies Essays*). Taipei: Zhonghua Fojiao wenhua guan, 1972.

——. *Dai Jitao xiansheng wencun* (*Extant writings of Dai Jitao*). 4 vols. Taipei: Zhongguo guomindang zhongyang weiyuanhui, 1959.

——. "Gaige siyuan sengjia zhidu zhi yijian" (Ideas on Reforming the Monastic System). In *Dai Jitao xiansheng wencun* (*Extant Writings of Dai Jitao*), 4 vols., 3:1306–1313. Taipei: Zhongguo guomindang zhongyang weiyuanhui, 1959 [1931].

——. "Huguo xiaozai hui qiyuan wen" (Prayers for the Assembly to Protect the Country and Avert Disaster). In *Dai Jitao xiansheng wencun* (*Extant Writings of Dai Jitao*), 4 vols., 3:1184–1186; see also 3:1335–1336. Taipei: Zhongguo guomindang zhongyang weiyuanhui, 1959 [1942].

———. "Huguo xuanhua guanghui yuanjue dashi song" (Praise for the Master [the Panchen Lama] Who Protects the Country, Propogates Transformation, and Radiates Wisdom). In *Dai Jitao xiansheng wencun* (*Extant Writings of Dai Jitao*), 4 vols., 3:1141–1143. Taipei: Zhongguo guomindang zhongyang weiyuanhui, 1959 [1938]. Dated August 1938.

———. (= Dai Chuanxian). "Ji Banchan dashi wen" (Text from the Memorial Ceremony for the Master, the Panchen Lama). In *Huang Musong, Wu Zhongxin, Zhao Shouyu, Dai Chuanxian: Feng shi banli Zangshi baogao shu* (*Huang Musong, Wu Zhongxin, Zhao Shouyu, Dai Chuanxian: Reports of Envoys Sent to Handle Tibetan Affairs*), ed. Zhongguo di'er lishi dang'anguan and Zhongguo Zangxue yanjiu zhongxin, 485. Beijing: Zhongguo Zangxue chubanshe, 1993 [1937].

———. "Meng Zang zhuangkuang yu" (Preface to *The Situation in Mongolia and Tibet*). In *Dai Jitao xiansheng wencun* (*Extant Writings of Dai Jitao*), 4 vols., 1:286–287. Taipei: Zhongguo guomindang zhongyang weiyuanhui, 1959 [1931].

———. *Qingnian zhi lu* (*Path for Youth*). In Chen Tianxi, *Dai Jitao xiansheng de shengping* (*The Life of Dai Jitao*), 511–513. Taipei: Taiwan shangwu yinshuguan, 1968 [1927].

———. "Renwang huguo fahui fayuan wen" (Vows for the Humane King Who Wishes to Protect His State Dharma-Assembly). In *Dai Jitao xiansheng wencun* (*Extant Writings of Dai Jitao*), 4 vols., 3:1176–1177. Taipei: Zhongguo guomindang zhongyang weiyuanhui, 1959 [1931]. Dated November 16, 1931.

———. "Yaoshi qi Fo fahui fayuan wen" (Religious Vows for the Seven Medicine Buddhas Assembly). In *Dai Jitao xiansheng wencun* (*Extant Writings of Dai Jitao*), 4 vols., 3: 1178–1182. Taipei: Zhongguo guomindang zhongyang weiyuanhui, 1959 [1933]. Dated January 1933.

———. "Zhi Banchan dashi dian" (Telegram to the Panchen Lama). In *Dai Jitao xiansheng wencun* (*Extant Writings of Dai Jitao*), 4 vols. Taipei: Zhongguo guomindang zhongyang weiyuanhui, 1959 [1933], 1:292 (telegram sent from Nanjing, October 8, 1933); 1:293 (telegram sent from Nanjing, December 20, 1933).

———. "Zhi Banchan dashi shu" (Letter to the Panchen Lama). In *Dai Jitao xiansheng wencun* (*Extant Writings of Dai Jitao*), 4 vols., 3:1222. Taipei: Zhongguo guomindang zhongyang weiyuanhui, 1959 [1934]. Letter dated January 18, 1934.

———. "Zhi Dalai dashi shu" (Letter to the Dalai Lama). In *Dai Jitao xiansheng wencun* (*Extant Writings of Dai Jitao*), 4 vols. Taipei: Zhongguo guomindang zhongyang weiyuanhui, 1959 [1932]: 3:1211–1213 (letter dated May 28, 1932); 3:1213–1216 (letter dated June 21, 1932); 3:1216–1218 (letter dated August 20, 1932); 3:1218 (letter dated September 1932); 3:1219–1220 (letter dated October 3, 1932); 3:1221 (letter dated October 28, 1932); 4:1485 (letter dated October 29, 1932); 3:1221 (letter dated December 8, 1932).

———. "Zhi Henan Li zhuxi dian" (Telegram to Henan's Chairman Li). In *Dai Jitao xiansheng wencun* (*Extant Writings of Dai Jitao*), 4 vols., 3:1293. Taipei: Zhongguo guomindang zhongyang weiyuanhui, 1959 [1942]. Letter dated March 4, 1942.

———. "Zhi Luoseng jianzan shu" (Letter to the Blo bzang rgyal mtshan). In *Dai Jitao xiansheng wencun* (*Extant Writings of Dai Jitao*), 4 vols., 4:1517–1518. Taipei: Zhongguo guomindang zhongyang weiyuanhui, 1959 [1934]. Letter dated January 19, 1934.

———. "Zhi Meng Zang Qing Kang ge di tongbao shu" (Letter to Compatriots in Mongolia, Tibet, Qinghai, and Kham). In *Dai Jitao xiansheng wencun* (*Extant Writings of Dai Jitao*), 4 vols., 3:1257–1261. Taipei: Zhongguo guomindang zhongyang weiyuanhui, 1959 [1931]. Dated June, 1931.

———. "Zhong Yin liang guo guomin de jiushi qingshen" (The Spirit of China and India's Peoples Saving the World). In *Dai Jitao xiansheng wencun (Extant Writings of Dai Jitao)*, 4 vols., 3:1333. Taipei: Zhongguo guomindang zhongyang weiyuanhui, 1959 [1942]. Dated March 27, 1942.

———. "Zhongguo zhi zongjiao gaige yu jiuguo shiye" (China's Religious Reforms and the Enterprise of Saving the Nation). In *Dai Jitao xiansheng Foxue lunji (Dai Jitao's Collected Buddhist Studies Essays)*, 17–20. Taipei: Zhonghua Fojiao wenhua guan, 1972 [1933].

Dan jun—Zaina panduo, and Li Decheng. *Mingcha shuang huangsi: Qingdai Dalai he Banchan zai jing zhuyang di (The Famous Pair of Yellow Temples: The Qing Dynasty Residences of the Dalai and Panchen Lamas)*. Beijing: Zongjiao wenhua chubanshe, 1997.

Danzhu Angben (Don grub dbang 'bum), ed. *Libei Dalai Lama yu Banchan erdeni nianpu (Chronicle of the Genealogy of the Dalai Lama and Panchen Erdeni)*. Beijing: Zhongyang minzu daxue chubanshe, 1998.

Dingzhi. *Nenghai shangshi zhuan (Biography of Guru Nenghai)*. Vol. 6, Nenghai shangshi quanji (The Complete Writings of Guru Nenghai), 7 vols. Taipei: Fangguang wenhua shiye you-xian gongci, 1995.

Duojue jue da [sic: ba]. *Micheng Fahai (Dharma Ocean of the Esoteric Vehicle)*. Taipei: Xinwen feng chubanshe gongci, 1987 [1930].

Fafang. "Huanyin Fazun shangren zhu Shijie Foxue fan Han Zang jiaoli yuan shi" (Welcoming Venerable Fazun's Management of the Sino-Tibetan Buddhist Institute's Affairs). *Haichaoyin* 15, no. 6 (1934): 4–7.

———. "Meng Zang xueyuan yu Puti xuehui" (The Mongolian and Tibetan College and the Bodhi Society). *Haichaoyin* 15, no. 9 (1934): 1–3.

———. "Zhongguo Fojiao xianzhuang" (The Current State of Chinese Buddhism). *Haichaoyin* 15, no. 10 (1934): 21–31.

Fazun. "Fazun fashi zishu" (Autobiography of Master Fazun). In *Fazun wenji (Collected Works of Fazun)*, ed. Hong Jisong and Huang Jilin, 243–252. Taipei: Wenshu chubanshe: Wenshu Fojiao wenhua zhongxin, 1988.

———. *Fazun wenji (Collected Works of Fazun)*. Ed. Hong Jisong and Huang Jilin. Taibei: Wenshu chubanshe: Wenshu Fojiao wenhua zhongxin, 1988.

———. "Fazun zhi Hu Zihu jushi shu" (Letter from Fazun to Layman Hu Zihu). In *Fazun wenji*, ed. Hong Jisong and Huang Jilin, 253–260. Taibei: Wenshu chubanshe: Wenshu Fojiao wen-hua zhongxin, 1988 [1931].

———. "Fazun zhi Hu Zihu jushi shu" (Letter from Fazun to Layman Hu Zihu). In *Zhongguo jinxiandai Fojiao renwu zhi (Records of Chinese Contemporary Buddhist Figures)*, 266–269. Beijing: Zongjiao wenhua chubanshe, 1995 [1931].

———. "Wo chuguo de Xizang" (Tibet as It Was When I Visited). In *Xiandai Xizang (Contemporary Tibet)*, 147–189. Chengdu: Dongfang shushe, 1943.

———. "Wo chuguo de Xizang" (Tibet as It Was When I Visited). In *Fazun wenji (Collected Works of Fazun)*, ed. Hong Jisong and Huang Jilin, 282–322. Taipei: Wenshu chubanshe: Wenshu fojiao wenhua zhongxin, 1988.

———. "Wo ru Zang de jingguo" (My Experiences upon Entering Tibet). In *Fazun wenji (Collected Works of Fazun)*, ed. Hong Jisong and Huang Jilin, 261–282. Taipei: Wenshu chubanshe: Wenshu Fojiao wenhua zhongxin, 1988.

———. *Xiandai Xizang (Contemporary Tibet)*. Chengdu: Dongfang shushe, 1943 [1937].

——. *Xizang minzu zhengjiao shi* (*The Political and Religious History of the Tibetan People*). 4 vols. Xizangxue wenxian congshu (Tibetological Literature Series). Beijing: Quanguo tushuguan wenxian suowei fuzhi zhongxin (National Library Center for Reduction and Duplication of Documents), 1991 [1940].

——. "Yuan Ming jian yu Zhongguo you guan zhi Xizang Fojiao" (Tibetan Buddhism in the Yuan and Ming Dynasties and Its Connection with China). In *Han Zang Fojiao yanjiu huibian* (*Compilation of Sino-Tibetan Buddhist Research*), ed. Xizangxue congshu pian weihui, 101–111. Taipei: Wenshu chubanshe, 1976.

——. *Zangwen wenfa* (*Tibetan Grammar*). 2 vols. Xizangxue wenxian congshu (Tibetological Literature Series). Beijing: Zhongguo Zangxue chubanshe, 1995 [1935].

——. "Zhuzhe ru Zang de jingguo" (The Author's Experiences upon Entering Tibet). In *Xiandai Xizang* (*Contemporary Tibet*), 123–146. Chengdu: Dongfang shushe, 1943.

——, with Sherap Gyatso. *Zangwen duben chugao* (*First Draft of a Tibetan Language Reader*). Edited by Chen Mingshu. Woodblock. 8 vols. Chongqing: Han Zang jiaoliyuan, 1940.

"Fojiao xinwen" (Buddhist News). *Haichaoyin* 21, no. 10 (1940): 20.

Fori. "Jinjin mizong re zhi fansi" (Thoughts on the Zeal of Esoteric Buddhism in Recent Times). *Fayin* (*Voice of the Dharma*) 137 (1996): 24–32.

Gama kanben [Skar ma mkha' 'bum]. "Dashi chuangban Qinghai lama jiaoyi guowen jiangxisuo" (The Master Establishes the Qinghai Institute for Lectures and Studies of Lama Religious Doctrine [and] National Written Language). In *Xirao jiacuo dashi* (*Master Sherap Gyatso*). Xining, 1997.

Gan Wenfeng. "Zangchuan Fojiao zai Chongqing" (Tibetan Buddhism in Chongqing). In *Chongqing wenshi ziliao* (*Chongqing Cultural and Historical Materials*), ed. Zhongguo renmin zhengzhi xieshang huiyi and Chongqing shi weiyuanhui wenshi ziliao weiyuanhui, 41:169–172. Xinan shifan daxue chubanshe, n.d.

Ganzi zhou zhi bianji weiyuanhui. *Ganzi zhou zhi* (*Ganzi Prefectural Gazetteer*). 2 vols. Chengdu: Sichuan minzu chubanshe, 1998.

Gao Zhangzhu. *Bianjiang wenti lunwen ji* (*Collected Essays on Borderland Problems*). Zhengzhong shu ju, 1948.

Gongbasa—Tudeng jizha [Dgon gsar Thub bstan 'jigs bral]. "Xirao jiacuo dashi: Fanhui neidi shikuang zhuiji" (Master Sherap Gyatso: Remembering the Actual Circumstances of Returning to China Proper). In *Xirao jiacuo dashi* (*Master Sherap Gyatso*). Xining, 1997.

Gongka laoren. *Baiyunjian de zhuanji—Gongka laoren xueshan xiuxing ji* (*Biography among the White Clouds—Record of Elder Gongka's Practice in the Snow Mountains*). Taipei: Zhengfayan chubanshe, 1994.

Han Dazai. *Kang Zang Fojiao yu Xikang Nuona hutuketu yinghua shilüe* (*Brief Account of Kham-Tibetan Buddhism and the Manifestation of Norlha Qutughtu of Kham*). 1937.

He Juefei. *Xikang jishi shiben shizhu* (*Annotated Poems on Recording the Events of Xikang*). Xizangxue Hanwen wenxian congshu (Chinese-language Tibetological Literature Series), 2. Lhasa: Xizang renmin chubanshe, 1988.

Hong Dizhen. *Xizang shi di dagang* (An Outline of the History and Geography of Tibet). Shanghai: Zhengzhang shuju, 1936.

Hua Qiyun. *Xizang wenti* (*The Tibet Problem*). Shanghai: Dadong shuju, 1930.

Huang Hao. *Zai Beijing de Zangzu wenwu* (*Tibetan Cultural Relics in Beijing*). Beijing: Minzu chubanshe, 1993.

———. "Sanshi niandai Zhongguo Zangmi yanjiu—*Zangmi xiufa midian* ping jie" (Chinese Research on Tibetan Esoterica in the 1930s—Critique and Introduction to *Secret Scriptures of the Tibetan Esoteric Dharma Practices*). *Minzu yanjiu hui xun* (*Newsletter on Ethnic Studies*) 17, no. 3 (1997): 52–56.

Huang Musong. *Shi Zang jicheng* (*Record of the Journey of an Envoy to Tibet*). In *Shi Zang jicheng, Xizang jiyao, Lasa jianwen ji* (*Record of the Journey of an Envoy to Tibet, Summary of Tibet, Record of What I Saw and Heard in Lhasa*), ed. Laba pingcuo and Chen Jiajin. Beijing: Quanguo guoshuguan wenxian suowei xiazhi zhongxin, 1991.

———. "Huang Musong fengshi ru Zang cefeng bing zhicha Dalai dashi baogao shu" (Report on Huang Musong's Entering Tibet under Orders to Confer Titles and Mourn the Thirteen Dalai Lama). In *Huang Musong, Wu Zhongxin, Zhao Shouyu, Dai Chuanxian: Feng shi banli Zangshi baogao shu* (*Huang Musong, Wu Zhongxin, Zhao Shouyu, Dai Chuanxian: Reports of Envoys Sent to Handle Tibetan Affairs*), ed. Zhongguo di'er lishi dang'anguan and Zhongguo Zangxue yanjiu zhongxin, 1–120. Beijing: Zhongguo Zangxue chubanshe, 1993.

Huang Xianming. "Xichui wenhua yuan" (Western Border Culture Institute). In *Chengdu wenshi ziliao xuanji* (*Selected Cultural and Historical Materials on Chengdu*). Chengdu: Chengdu chubanshe, 1989.

———. "Xichui wenhua yuan" (Western Border Culture Institute). *Xizang yanjiu* (*Tibetan Studies*) 2 (1990): 161–163.

Jiang Zandeng. *Taixu dashi jianzhuan (1890–1947)* (A Brief Biography of Master Taixu [1890–1947]). Xiandai Zhongguo Fojiao sixiang lunji (Collected Theses on Contemporary Chinese Buddhist Philosophy), 2. Taibei: Xinwen feng chuban gongsi, 1993.

Jizhong—Jiangbai jianzan [Rje drung 'Jam dpal rgyal mtshan]. "Leiwuqisi Jizhong houfo he Gere lama jianli" (Short History of Riwoché Monastery's Jedrung Incarnation and the Gara Lama). In *Xizang wenshi ziliao xuanji* (*Selected Cultural and Historical Materials on Tibet*), 6:79–90. Beijing: Minzu chubanshe, 1985.

Kaiyang. "Zun Lamajiao wei guojia jiao yi" (A proposal to make the Lama religion our national religion). *Lunyu* (*Humor*) 1, no. 4 (1932): 114.

Kangxi chao *Daqing huidian* zhong de Lifanyuan ziliao (Materials on the Court for Managing the Frontiers from the Kangxi Reign Period's *Collected Regulations of the Qing*). In *Qingdai Lifanyuan ziliao jilu* (*Compilation of Qing Dynasty Materials on the Court for Managing the Frontiers*). Lanzhou: Quanguo guoshuguan wenxian souwei zhongxin, 1988.

Lao She. "Jiuguo nan ge" (Song of Saving the Country from Difficulties). In Lunyu *wen xuan yi ji* (*Selections from* Humor). Shanghai: Shidai shuju, 1949.

Li Anzhe. "Xizang xi Fojiao seng jiaoyu zhidu" (Tibet's Buddhist Monastic Education System). *Haichaoyin* 21, nos. 5–6 (1940): 95–99.

Li Cunfu. "Xirao jiacuo dashi nianbiao" (Chronology of Master Sherap Gyatso's Life). In *Xirao jiacuo dashi* (Master Sherap Gyatso). Xining, 1997.

Li Pengnian and Wan Renyuan, eds. *Jiushi Banchan neidi huodong ji fanzang shouxian dang'an xuanbian* (*Selections from the Archives concerning the Ninth Panchen Lama's Activities in China and the Restrictions on His Return to Tibet*). Edited by Zhongguo dier lishi dang'an guan and Zhongguo Xizang yanjiu zhongxin. Beijing: Zhongguo Zangxue chubanshe, 1992.

Li Yuchuan. "Dangjin Zhongguo diyi ni—Longlian fashi" (China's Number One Nun Today—Master Longlian). In *Minzu zongjiao huaqiao,* ed. Sichuan sheng zhengxie wenshi ziliao weiyuanhui, Sichuan wenshi ziliao jicui, 5. Chengdu: Sichuan renmin chubanshe, 1996.

Lin Jing. "Bukong jushi yu Fojiao (Layman Bukong [Dai Jitao] and Buddhism)." In *Dai Jitao xiansheng shishi shi zhounian jinian tekan* (*Special Issue Memorial on the Tenth Anniversary of the Death of Dai Jitao*). 1959.

Liu Manqing. *Kang-Zang zhaozheng* (*Expedition to Kham and Tibet*). Shanghai: Shangwu yin-shuguan, 1933.

Liu Xiang. "Zhiling zhengzi di erbasisan hao" (Administrative order #2843). Chongqing: Guomin gemingzhun di ershiyi zhun silingbu (Headquarters of the Twenty-first Nationalist Revolutionary Army), March 26, 1931. In "Shijie Foxue yuan Han Zang jin zhan" (Progress of the World Buddhist Institute, Sino-Tibetan [Branch]). *Haichaoyin* 13, no. 8 (1932): 53.

Luo Rencang. "Hangzhan qijian Sichuan Zangxue yanjiu gaishu" (A General Account of Tibetological Research in Sichuan Province during the Period of Resistance against Japanese Aggression). *Zhongguo Zangxue* (*China Tibetology*) 3 (1996): 11–21.

Luoseng nianzha, Jiangba yundan, Yixi bandian, and Dunzhu. "Xizang biqiu seng jinggao neidi zhu da jushi xuelei shu" (Letter from Tibetan Bhiksu Monks Respectfully Reporting Their Suffering to All the Great Laity of China Proper). *Haichaoyin* 13, no. 12 (1932): 109–112.

Manzhi. "Shijie Fojiao xuefan Han Zang jiaoli yuan zhi shiming" (The Mission of the World Buddhist Institute's Sino-Tibetan Buddhist Academy). *Haichaoyin* 13, no. 1 (1932): 1–19.

Mei Jingshun. "Minguo yilai de Han Zang Fojiao guanxi (1912–1949): Yi Han Zang jiaoli yuan wei zhongxin de tantao" (Sino-Tibetan Relations during the Republican Period (1912–1949): Probing into the Sino-Tibetan Buddhist Institute at the Center of Relations). *Zhonghua Foxue yanjiu* (*Chung-hwa Buddhist Studies*) 2 (1998): 251–288.

——. "Minguo zaoqi xianmi Fojiao chongtu de tantao" (Probing into the conflicts of exoteric and esoteric Buddhism in the early Republic). *Zhonghua Foxue yanjiu* (*Chung-hwa Buddhist Studies*) 3 (1999): 251–270.

Meng Zang weiyuanhui. "Xizang yu neidi de Fojiao yinyuan" (The Buddhist Connections of Tibet and China Proper). *Haichaoyin* 4 (1940): 17.

Meng Zang yuan tongji biao (*Statistical Tables of the Mongolian and Tibetan Bureau*). (n.d. [1916?]).

Neiwufu qingdian cheng'an (*Record of Imperial Household Ceremonies*). Jindai Zhongguo shiliao congkan xubian di liushisan ji (Sequel to the Collection of Modern Chinese History Materials, 63). Taibei: Wenhai chubanshe, 1979 [ca. 1790].

Nian Zhihai and Bai Gengdeng, eds. *Qinghai Zangchuan Fojiao siyuan ming jian* (*The Clear Mirror of Tibetan Buddhist Temples of Qinghai*). Lanzhou: Gansu minzu chubanshe, 1993.

Nuona Hutuketu (Nor lha Qutughtu). *Mizong Lianhuasheng dashi mifa* (*The Esoteric Teachings of the Esoteric School's Master Padmasambhava*). Taipei: Wulin, 1985.

"Nuona lama zai Ganzi yuanji" (Death of Norlha Lama in Ganzi). *Haichaoyin* 17, no. 7 (1936): 82.

Pengcuo ([Gus 'bangs] Phun tshogs). "Zao fu sangzi yi dashi" (Recollecting the Master's Bringing Benefit to His Native Place). In *Xirao jiacuo dashi* (*Master Sharap Gyatso*), 144–153. Xining, 1997.

Puosiba ('Phags pa). *Sajia taoguo xinbian* (*New Edition of the Sakya Path and Fruit [Teachings]*). Huihai congshu (Ocean of Wisdom Collection) Zangmi xilie 6801 (Tibetan Esoterica 6801). Taizhong: Huihai shuzhai, 1992.

"Puti xuehui cheng Junweihui baohu fawu" (The Bodhi Society Presents the National Military Council's [Order of] Protection for Buddhist Property). *Haichaoyin* 18, no. 4 (1937): 93.

Qingdai Lifanyuan ziliao jilu (*Compilation of Qing Dynasty Materials on the Court for Managing the Frontiers*). Lanzhou: Quanguo guoshuguan wenxian souwei zhongxin, 1988.

Qingding. *Qingding shangshi kaishi lu* (*Record of Qingding Lama's Teaching*). Chengdu: Chengdushi xinwen chubanju, 1999.

Qingliang shan xinzhi (*New Gazetteer of Mount Qingliang [Wutai]*). Held at Gest Library, Princeton University, 1701 edition.

Qiu Shanshan. *Dangdai diyi bixiuni: Longlian fashi zhuan* (*The Number One Contemporary Bhiksuni: The Biography of Master Longlian*). Fujian meishu chubanshe: Fuzhou, 1997.

Quhua (Chos dpal [rgya mtsho]). "Xirao jiacuo dashi shengping jilüe" (The Brief Life Story of Master Sherap Gyatso). In *Xirao jiacuo dashi* (*Master Sherap Gyatso*). Xining, 1997.

Ren Xinjian. "Kang Zang yanjiu she jieshao" (A Brief Introduction to the Research Institute of Kham and Tibet). *Zhongguo Zangxue* (*China Tibetology*) 3 (1996): 21–29.

Sangzhou zhaxi (Bsam grub bkra shis). "Tantan Han Zang Fojiao de goutong" (Discussions on the Communications between Chinese and Tibetan Buddhism). *Fayin* (*Voice of the Dharma*) 167 (1998): 34–39.

Shi Dongchu. *Zhongguo Fojiao jindai shi* (*Modern History of Chinese Buddhism*). 2 vols. Taipei: Zhonghua Fojiao wenhua guan, 1974.

Shi Miaozhou. *Meng Zang Fojiao shi* (*Mongol-Tibetan Buddhist History*). Xizangxue Hanwen wenxian congshu (Chinese-language Tibetological Literature Series), 2. Beijing: Quanguo tushuguan wenxian zhongxin, 1993 [1934].

Shi Shiliang. "Jindai hongyang Gelupai de liang wei Hanzu dade ji qi yi, zhujian jie" (A Brief Account of the Great Virtue of Two Chinese Men Who Propagated the Geluk Sect and Their Translations). *Xizang yanjiu* (*Tibetan Studies*) 2, no. 47 (1993): 47–55.

Shi Weixian. *Han Zang jiaoliyuan yu Taixu fashi* (*The Sino-Tibetan Buddhist Institute and Master Taixu*). Chongqing: Chongqingshi Fojiao shehui, 1988.

——. "Han Zang jiaoliyuan yu Taixu fashi" (The Sino-Tibetan Buddhist Institute and Master Taixu). In *Weixian fashi shi wenji* (*Master Weixian's Collected Poems and Writings*), 1:1–32. Chengdu: Chengdu shi xinwen chubanju, 1995.

"Shi yi shi Banchan xiang zaiqu juanhuan" (The Eleventh Panchen Lama Donates Money to Disaster Areas). *Fayin* (*Voice of the Dharma*) 169 (1998): 15.

Sichuan sheng difang zhi bianji weiyuanhui, Sheng zhi renwu zhi bianji and Ren Yimin, eds. *Sichuan jinxiandai renwu zhuan* (*Biographies of Sichuan's Contemporary Figures*). 6 vols. Sichuan sheng difang zhi ziliao congshu. Chengdu: Sichuan sheng shehui kexue yuan chubanshe, 1985.

Sichuan sheng Kangding xianzhi bianji weiyuanhui. *Kangding xianzhi* (*Kangding County Gazetteer*). Chengdu: Sichuan chubanshe, 1995.

"Shijie Foxue yuan Han Zang jin zhan" (Progress of the World Buddhist Institute, Sino-Tibetan [branch]). *Haichaoyin* 13, no. 8 (1932): 52–55.

Su Bai. "Yuandai Hangzhou Zangchuan mijiao ji qi you guan guiji" (On the Tibetan Buddhism of the Yuan Dynasty's Hangzhou and Some Associated Remains). In *Zangchuan Fojiao siyuan kaogu* (*Archaeological Studies on Monasteries of Tibetan Buddhism*), 365–387. Beijing: Wenwu chubanshe, 1996.

Sun Yat-sen. *San min zhuyi*. Taipei: Zhongyang wenwu gongying she, 1985 [1924].

——. *The Triple Demism of Sun Yat-sen*. Translated by Paschal M. D'Elia. Wuchang: Franciscan Press, 1931.

Taixu. "Cong goutong Han Zang wenhua shuo dao ronghe Han Zang minzu" (From Linking Chinese and Tibetan Cultures to Merging the Chinese and Tibetan Peoples). In *Taixu dashi quanshu* (*Complete works of the Venerable Taixu*), 62 vols., 15:182–184. Hong Kong: Taixu dashi quanshu chuban weiyuanhui, 1953 [1938].

——. "Lueshu Xizang Fojiao yu" (Preface to a Brief Account of Tibetan Buddhism). *Haichaoyin* 11, no. 7 (1930): 1–2.

——. "Shijie Foxue fan Han Zang jiaoli yuan yuanqi" (Origin of the World Buddhist Institute's Sino-Tibetan Buddhist Institute). In *Taixu dashi quanshu* (*Complete works of the Venerable Taixu*), 62 vols., 61:1033–1035. Hong Kong: Taixu dashi quanshu chuban weiyuanhui, 1953 [1932].

——. *Taixu dashi quanshu* (*Complete Works of the Venerable Taixu*). 62 vols. Hong Kong: Taixu dashi quanshu chuban weiyuanhui, 1953.

——. *Taixu wenji* (*Collected Writings of Taixu*). Edited by Hung Jisung and Huang Jilin. Dangdai Zhongguo Fojiao dashi wenji, 2. Taipei: Wenshu chubanshe, 1987.

——. "Yu Fazun shu" (Letters Given to Fazun). In *Taixu dashi quanshu* (*Complete Works of the Venerable Taixu*), 62 vols., 51:56–84. Hong Kong: Taixu dashi quanshu chuban weiyuanhui, 1953 [1932].

——. "Zhi Liu Fucheng zhunzhang ji quandong ge xin Fozhe shu" (Letter to General Liu Fucheng [Liu Xiang] and the Buddhist Faithful of Eastern Sichuan). In *Taixu dashi quanshu* (*Complete Works of the Venerable Taixu*), 62 vols., 51:225–226. Hong Kong: Taixu dashi quanshu chuban weiyuanhui, 1953 [1932].

Tuguan (Thu'u bkwan [III] Blo bzang chos kyi nyi ma). *Zhangjia Guoshi Ruobi duoji zhuan*. Translated by Chen Qingying and Ma Lianlong. Beijing: Minzu chubanshe, 1994 [1788].

Wang Lu. "Wutaishan yu Xizang" (Mount Wutai and Tibet). *Wutaishan yanjiu* (*Mount Wutai Research*), no. 4 (1995): 22–29.

Wang Yao. *Zangxue ling mo*. Gaoxiong: Foguang Chubanshe, 1992.

Wang Yao and Chen Qingying, eds. *Xizang lishi wenhua cidian* (*Dictionary of Tibetan History and Culture*). Hangzhou: Xizang renmin chubanshe, 1998.

Wu Fengpei. *Banchan fu Yin jilüe* (*Brief Record of the Panchan Lama's Going to India*). Qingdai Xizang shiliao conggan (Collected Materials on Qing Dynasty Tibet), 2. Chongqing: Wenhai chubanshe, 1937.

——. "Zhongyin *Shi Zang jicheng*, *Xizang jiyao* yu" (Preface to the Reprint of *Record of the Journey of an Envoy to Tibet* and *Summary of Tibet*). In *Shi Zang jicheng, Xizang jiyao, Lasa jianwen ji* (*Record of the Journey of an Envoy to Tibet, Summary of Tibet, and Record of What I Saw and Heard in Lhasa*), ed. Laba pingcuo and Chen Jiajin, 1–20. Beijing: Quanguo guoshuguan wenxian suowei xiazhi zhongxin, 1991.

"Wutaishan Fomen juxing xiaozai zhenzai dafahui" (The Wutaishan Buddhists Hold a Great Dharma-Assembly to Eliminate Disasters and Relieve the People Scourged by Natural Disaster). *Fayin* (*Voice of the Dharma*) 169 (1998): 34.

"Wutaishan Guangji maopeng zhi guochu yu xianzai" (The Past and Present of Mount Wutai's Guangji Maopeng). *Haichaoyin* 17, no. 7 (1936): 79–82.

"Xiandai Fojiao shiliao: Guonei Fojiao: Xizang Xirao geshe li jing jiangxue" (Contemporary Buddhist Historic Materials: Domestic Buddhism: Tibet's Geshé Sherap Gyatso Arrives at the Capital and Gives Lectures at the University). *Haichaoyin* 18, no. 4 (1937): 91–92.

Xiangbian jiacuo. *Banchan dashi* (*The Panchen Lama*). Beijing: Dongfang chubanshe, 1989.

"Xizang Andong gexi ruji" (Obituary of Tibet's Amdo Geshé). *Haichaoyin* 17, no. 4 (1936): 174.

Xizang zizhizhou zhengxie wenshi ziliao yanjiu weiyuanhui, ed. *Xizang wenshi ziliao xuanji (Selected Materials on the Culture and History of Tibet)*. 22 vols. Beijing: Minzu chubanshe, 1982–2002.

Ya Hanzhang. *Dalai Lama zhuan (Biographies of the Dalai Lamas)*. Beijing: Renmin chubanshe, 1984.

——. *Banchan E'erdeni zhuan (Biographies of the Panchen Lamas)*. Lhasa: Xizang renmin chubanshe, 1987.

Yang Ming and Niu Ruifang. "Chongqing Han Zang jiaoli yuan shi wei" (Chongqing's Sino-Tibetan Buddhist Institute from Start to Finish). In *Ba-Yu wenhua (Ba[xian] and Chongqing Culture)*. Chongqing: Chongqing chubanshe, 1991.

Yang Xiaoping. "Xirao jiacuo dashi shengping shilüe" (The Brief Life Story of Master Sherap Gyatso). In *Wenshi ziliao xuanji (Selected Cultural and Historic Materials)*, ed. Zhongguo renmin zhengzhi xieshang huiyi quanguo weiyuanhui and Wenshi ziliao yanjiu weiyuan hui. Beijing: Wenshi ziliao chubanshe, 1984.

Yang Xuandi and Jin Feng, eds. *Lifanyuan zeli (Regulations and Precedents of the Court for Managing the Frontiers)*. [Huhhot]: Neimenggu wenhua chubanshe, 1998 [1891].

"Yidai Zangxue dashi Zhunbi jimei lama (Ouyang Wuwei jiaoshou) zhuanlüe" (A Brief Biography of the First Generation of Tibetan Studies Master Chömpel Jikmé [Professor Ouyang Wuwei]), *Faguang (Dharma Light Monthly)*, November 10, 1991, 2.

Yinshun, ed. *Taixu fashi nianpu (Chronology of Master Taixu's Life)*. Beijing: Zongjiao wenhua chubanshe, 1995.

Yu Lingbo. *Zhongguo jinxiandai Fojiao renwu zhi (Records of Chinese Contemporary Buddhist Figures)*. Beijing: Zongjiao wenhua chubanshe, 1995.

——. "Goutong Han-Zang wenhua de Shi Fazun (1902–1980)" (Shi Fazun, Linking Chinese and Tibetan Culture [1902–1980]). In *Zhongguo jinxiandai Fojiao renwu zhi (Records of Chinese Contemporary Buddhist Figures)*. Beijing: Zongjiao wenhua chubanshe, 1995.

Zeng Guojing and Guo Weibing. *Lidai Zangzu mingren zhuan (Biographies of Famous Tibetans of Past Dynasties)*. Lhasa: Xizang renmin chubanshe, 1996.

Zhang Qinyou. "Ji Zhongguo Zangxue xianbei—Li Anzhe, Yu Shiyu jiaoshou zai Labuleng de suiyue" (Remembering the Elder Generation of China's Tibetology—Professors Li Anzhe and Li Shiyu's Years at Labrang [Monastery]). *Xizang yanjiu (Tibetan Studies)* 1 (1989): 140–143.

Zhang Xixin, ed. "Qingdai lama jiao beike lu" (Records of Carved Stele of Qing Dynasty Lama Religion). In *Qing zhengfu yu lama jiao (The Qing Government and Lama Religion)*. Lhasa: Xizang renmin chubanshe, 1988.

Zhang Xu [= Zhang Yisun]. *Zang Han jilun cihui (Tibetan-Chinese Vocabulary, Gathered and Arranged)*. Hong Kong: Xichui wenhua yuan, 1937.

——. *Zang Han yu duikan (Tibetan and Chinese Language Bilingual Phrasebook)*. Hong Kong: Xichui wenhua yuan, 1938.

——. *Zangwen shudu guifan (Models of Tibetan Language Correspondence)*. Chengdu: Xichui wenhua yuan, 1938.

——. *Han Zang yuhui (Chinese-Tibetan Vocabulary)*. Chengdu: Xichui wenhua yuan, 1938.

——. *Zang Han yiming da cihui (The Great Tibetan-Chinese Vocabulary)*. [Chengdu]: Xichui wenhua yuan, 1939.

Zhang Yisun. *Bod Rgya tshig mdzod chen mo/ Zang Han da cidian (The Great Tibetan-Chinese Dictionary)*. Beijing: Mi rigs dpe skrun khang/ Minzu chubanshe, 1998 [1993].

Zhang Zhungu. *Duan Qirui zhuan (Biography of Duan Qirui)*. 2 vols. Vol. 1. Taipei: Zhongwai tushu chubanshe, 1973.

Zhangjia dashi yuanqi dianli weiyuanhui. *Huguo jingjue fujiao dashi Zhangjia hutuketu shiji ce (Historical Traces of the Changja Qutughtu, the State-Protecting, Completely Enlightened Master Who Assists with Teaching)*. Taipei: Zhangjia dashi yuanqi dianli weiyuanhui, 1957.

Zhencheng. *Qingliang shan zhi (Gazetteer of Mount Qingliang [Wutai])* (1596). Held at Yen-ching Library, Harvard University, 1755 edition.

Zhengguo fashi yuanji shizhou nian jinianji weiyuanhui. "Zhengguo fashi nianbiao shilüe" (Brief Chronological Table of Master Zhengguo's Life). In *Mianhuai Zhengguo fashi (Recollections of Master Zhengguo)*, 121–128. Beijing: Guangjisi, 1997.

Zhengxie Qinghai sheng weiyuanhui wenshi ziliao weiyuanhui, ed. *Xirao jiacuo dashi* (Master Sherap Gyatso). Xining, 1997.

Zhizang. "Du *Xizang wenti zhi jiantao* hou de ganqing" (Sentiments after Reading *Self-criticism on the Tibet Problem*), *Haichaoyin* 15, no. 10 (1934): 107–110.

Zhongguo Zangxue yanjiu zhongxin, Zhongguo diyi lishi dang'an guan, Zhongguo di'er lishi dang'an guan, Xizang zizhichu dang'an guan, Sichuan sheng dang'an guan. *Yuan yi lai Xizang difang yu zhongyang zhengfu guanxi dang'an shiliao huibian (Assembled Archival Materials on Tibet's Relations with the Central Government since the Yuan)*. 7 vols. Beijing: Zhongguo Zangxue chubanshe, 1994.

Zhou Guanren. "Goutong Han Zang wenhua" (Linking Chinese and Tibetan Culture). *Haichaoyin* 17, no. 6 (1936): 4–8.

Zhou Tiyou. "Jitao xiansheng yu bianjiang" ([Dai] Jitao and the Borderlands). In *Dai Jitao xiansheng shishi shi zhounian jinian tekan (Special Issue Memorial on the Tenth Anniversary of the Death of Dai Jitao)*, 27–37. 1959.

Zhou Xilang. "Nona hutuketu" (Norlha Qutughtu). In *Sichuan jin xiandai renwu chuan (Biographies of Sichuan's Contemporary Figures)*, vol. 1, ed. Sichuan sheng difang zhi bianji weiyuanhui, Sheng zhi renwu zhi bianji, and Ren Yimin. Chengdu: Sichuan sheng shehui kexue yuan chubanshe, 1985.

Zongkaba (Tsong kha pa). *Puti dao zidi guanglun (The Great Treatise on the Graduated Path to Enlightenment)*. Translated by Fazun. Shanghai: Shanghai Foxue shuju, reprint, n.d. [1935].

TIBETAN LANGUAGE SOURCES

Blo bzang thub bstan chos kyi nyi ma, Panchen Lama VI [IX]. *Skyabs mgon thams cad mkhyen pa Blo bzang thub bstan chos kyi nyi ma dge legs rnam rgyal bzang po'i zhal snga nas kyi thun mong pa'i rnam bar thar pa rin chen dbang gi rgyal po'i 'phreng ba (The Autobiography of the Sixth [Ninth] Panchen Lama Blo bzang thub bstan chos kyi nyi ma)*. Reproduced from the Bkra shis lhun po blocks, 1944.

Blo bzang thub bstan chos kyi nyi ma, Panchen Lama VI [IX]. *PaN chen thams cad mkhyen pa rje btsun Blo bzang thub bstan chos kyi nyi ma dge legs rnam rgyal bzang po'i gsung 'bum (The Collected Works of the Sixth [Ninth] Panchen Lama Blo bzang thub bstan chos kyi nyi ma)*. Vol. 1. New Delhi: Reproduced from the Bkra shis lhun po blocks, 1973 [1944].

Bod ljongs chab gros rig gnas lo rgyus dpyad gzhi'i rgyu cha zhib 'jug u yon lhan khang. *Bod kyi rig gnas lo rgyus dpyad gzhi'i rgyu cha bdams bsgrigs (Materials on the Culture and History of Tibet)*. 22 vols. Lhasa: Bod ljongs chab gros rig gnas lo rgyus dpyad gzhi'i rgyu cha zhib 'jug u yon lhan khang, 1982–2000.

Bod rang skyong ljongs srid gros lo rgyus rig gnas dpyad gzhi'i rgyu cha u yon lhan khang. *PaN chen sku 'phreng dgu pa Blo bzang bstan chos kyi nyi ma gang gi dgung tshigs dang bstun pa'i mdzad rnam rags bsgrigs* (Rough Biography of the Ninth Panchen Lama). *Bod kyi lo rgyus rig gnas dpyad gzhi'i rgyu cha bdams bsgrigs (Materials on the Culture and History of Tibet)*, vol. 22. Beijing: Mi rigs dpe skrun khang, 2000.

Bstan 'dzin. *Dgu rong sku phreng snga phyi'i rnam thar* (The Biographies of the Earlier and Later Incarnations in the Gurong Series of Incarnations). Lanzhou: Kan su'u mi rigs dpe skrun khang, 1994.

Chos dpal [rgya mtsho]. "Dge ba'i bshes gnyen chen po rje btsun Shes rab rgya mtsho mchog gi rnam thar mdo tsam brjod pa" (Brief Biography of the Great Geshé Sherab Gyatso). In *Dge ba'i bshes gnyen chen po Shes rab rgya mtsho (The Great Geshé Sherap Gyatso)*, ed. Mtsho sngon zhing chen srid gros kyi rig gnas lo rgyus kyi dpyad gzhi'i yig cha'i u yon lhan tshogs, 329–412. Xining, 1997.

Chos kyi grags pa. *Dge bshes Chos kyi grags pas btsams pa'i brda dag ming tshig gsal ba / Gexi Quzha Zangwen cidian: Zang, Han duizhao (Geshé Chödrak's Tibetan-Chinese Dictionary)*. Beijing: Mi rigs dpe skrun khang / Minzu chubanshe, 1995 [1957].

Dgon gsar Thub bstan 'jigs bral. "Dge ba'i bshes gnyen chen po Shes rab rgya mtsho rin po che mes rgyal nang sar phebs kyi gnas tshul rjes dran byas pa" (Remembering When the Great Geshé Sherap Gyatso Rinpoché Went Inland to the Motherland [China Proper]). In *Dge ba'i bshes gnyen chen po Shes rab rgya mtsho (The Great Geshé Sherap Gyatso)*, ed. Mtsho ngon zhing chen srid gros kyi rig gnas lo rgyus kyi dpyad gzhi'i yig cha'i u yon lhan tshogs, 227–231. Xining, 1997.

Grags pa, ed. *Rje btsun Shes rab rgya mtsho 'jam dpal dgyes pa'i blo gros kyi gsung rtsom (The Collected Works of the Venerable Shes rab rgya mtsho)*. Vols. 1–2. Xining: Mtsho sngon mi rigs dpe skrun khang, 1982.

Gus 'bangs Phun tshogs. "Pha yul bde skyid kyi dpal la 'god pa'i ston zla'i bsil sbyin mkhan po'i rang gzugs zhugs so" (The Cooling Autumn Moon's Own Form Abides: A Record of the Splendor of the Fatherland's Happiness). In *Dge ba'i bshes gnyen chen po Shes rab rgya mtsho (The Great Geshé Sherap Gyatso)*, ed. Mtsho sngon zhing chen srid gros kyi rig gnas lo rgyus kyi dpyad gzhi'i yig cha'i u yon lhan tshogs, 297–318. Xining, 1997.

'Jam dpal rgya mtsho. *Slob dpon chen po PaN chen rin po che (The Great Master Panchen Rinpoché)*. Bod gnas nyams zhis deb phreng gnyis pa. Dharamsala: Sherig Parkhang (Tibetan Cultural Printing Press), 1997.

Khung chin tshun (Kong Qingzong). "Hong mu'o sung Bod du bskyod pa'i gnas tshul dngos bkod pa" (Account of Huang Musong's Mission to Tibet in 1934 by a Member of That Mission). In *Bod kyi rig gnas lo rgyus rgyu cha bdam bsgrigs, 'don thengs lnga ba (Materials on the Cultural History of Tibet, no. 5)*, 109–161. Lhasa: Bod rang skyong ljongs chab srid gros tshogs rig gnas lo rgyus rgyu cha u yon lhan khang, 1985.

Lis Tshun hphu'u (Li Cunfu). "Dge bshes Shes rab rgya mtsho'i mdzad 'phrin lo tshigs (1884–1968)" (Chronology of Important Events of Geshé Sherap Gyatso's Life). In *Dge ba'i bshes gnyen chen po Shes rab rgya mtsho (The Great Geshé Sherap Gyatso)*, 501–509. Xining, 1997.

Mi nyag Mgon po.'*Bo Gangs dkar sprul sku'i rnam thar dad pa'i pad dkar* (*The White Lotus of Faith: A Biography of the 'Bo Gangs dkar Incarnation*). Beijing: Mi rigs dpe skrun khang, 1997.

Mtsho sngon zhing chen srid gros kyi rig gnas lo rgyus kyi dpyad gzhi'i yig cha'i u yon lhan tshogs, ed. *Dge ba'i bshes gnyen chen po Shes rab rgya mtsho* (*The Great Geshé Sherap Gyatso*). Xining, 1997.

Ngag dbang blo bzang rgya mtsho. *Ngag dbang blo bzang rgya mtsho'i rnam thar* (*The Biography of [the Fifth Dalai Lama] Ngakwang Lozang Gyatso*). Lhasa: Bod ljong mi dmangs dpe skrun khang, 1989 [1681].

'Phrin las and Grags pa, eds. *Rje btsun Shes rab rgya mtsho 'jam dpal dgyes pa'i blo gros kyi gsung rtsom* (*The Collected Works of the Venerable Shes rab rgya mtsho*). Vol. 3. Xining: Mtsho sngon mi rigs dpe skrun khang, 1984.

Phun tshogs. *Dge bshes Shes rab rgya mtsho dang Rdo sbis grwa tshang* (*Geshé Sherap Gyatso and the Dobi Monastic School*). Beijing: Mi rigs dpe skrun khang, 1998.

Rje drung 'Jam dpal rgyal mtshan. "Ri bo che dgon pa dang Rje drung sprul sku Mgar ra bla ma bcas kyi lo rgyus rags bsdus" (A Brief History of Riwoché Monastery, the Jedrung Incarnation, and the Gara Lama). In *Bod kyi rig gnas lo rgyus dpyad gzhi'i rgyu cha bdams bsgrigs, 'don thengs drug pa* (*Materials on the Culture and History of Tibet*), 6:207–233. Lhasa: Bod ljongs chab gros rig gnas lo rgyus dpyad gzhi'i rgyu cha zhib 'jug u yon lhan khang (Cultural and Historical Materials Office), 1985.

Skal bzang bkra shis. "Mgar ra bla ma Lu'u Jun dmag Khams khul 'byor skabs mnyam 'brel dang Go min tang skabs Bod Sog u yon lhan khang u yon sogs byas skor" (On Gara Lama and the Lu Army Corp in Kham and the Guomindang (Nationalist Party) Mongolian and Tibetan Affairs Commission). In *Bod kyi lo rgyus rig gnas dpyad gzhi'i rgyu cha bdams bsgrigs* (*Materials on the Culture and History of Tibet*), 10:113–122 (New series). General series, vol. 19. Beijing: Mi rigs dpe skrun khang, 1996.

Skal bzang rgya mtsho. "Rje btsun dam pa pra dzanyâ sa ra'i rnam par thar pa phun tshogs legs lam gyi rtse mo" (Biography of Sherap Gyatso). In *Rje btsun Shes rab rgya mtsho 'jam dpal dgyes pa'i blo gros kyi gsung rtsom* (*The Collected Works of the Venerable Sherap Gyatso*), ed. Grags pa and 'Phrin las. Vol. 3, 609–674. Xining: Mtsho sngon mi rigs dpe skrun khang, 1984.

Skar ma mkha' 'bum. "Dge bshes Shes rab rgya mtsho Mtsho sngon Bod rgyud nang bstan gyi bstan don dang Rgya yig khrid sbyong 'dzin grwa gsar du btsugs pa" (The Establishment of the New Mtsho sngon Classes for the Study of the Meanings of the Teachings of the Tibetan Tradition of Buddhist Teachings and Chinese Writing). In *Dge ba'i bshes gnyen chen po Shes rab rgya mtsho* (*The Great Geshé Sherap Gyatso*), ed. Mtsho sngon zhing chen srid gros kyi rig gnas lo rgyus kyi dpyad gzhi'i yig cha'i u yon lhan tshogs, 286–292. Xining, 1997.

Sun Krung hran (Sun Zhongshan = Sun Yat-sen). *San min kru'u yi'i bsdus don (Sanmin zhuyi yaoyi = Essentials of the Three Principles of the People*). Translated by Yang Kri hphu (Yang Zhifu) and Gomindwang krung dbyangs rtsa 'dzugs las khungs gyi mthas mtshams skad yig rtsom sgyur lhan khang (The Guomindang's Central Organizing Office's Committee for Translating and Editing Border Languages). Bilingual ed. Taipei: Meng-Zang weiyuanhui, 1971 [1943].

Thub bstan nor bzang Tâ bla ma. *Gong sa bcu gsum pa'i srid phyogs mdzad rnam* (*Twentieth-Century Political History of the Thirteenth Dalai Lama*). N.p., n.d.

Thub bstan sangs rgyas [Thupten Sangay]. *Rgya nag tu Bod kyi sku tshab don gcod skabs dang gnyis tshugs stangs skor gyi lo rgyus thabs bral zur lam (Experiences of a Former Tibetan Representative in China, 1930–1939)*. Dharamsala: Library of Tibetan Works and Archives, 1982.

Thu'u bkwan (III) Blo bzang chos kyi nyi ma. *Lcang skya Rol pa'i rdo rje'i rnam thar (Biography of Lcang skya Rol pa'i rdo rje)*. Lanzhou: Gansu'u mi rigs dpe skrun khang, 1989 [1792–1794].

Yâ Han krang (Ya Hanzhang). *PaN chen sku phreng rim byon gyi mdzad rnam (Biographies of the Panchen Lamas)*. Translated by Blo bzang phun tshogs and 'Brug grags. Lhasa: Bod ljongs mi dmangs dpe skrun khang, 1992.

Zhing bza' Skal bzang chos kyi rgyal mtshan. *Bod Sog chos 'byung (Zang Meng Fojiao shi; Tibeto-Mongol Buddhist History), Gangs can rig brgya'i sgo 'byed lde mig (Zangwen wenxian)*. Vol. 18. Beijing: Mi rigs dpe skrun khang, 1992.

Zhwa sgab pa Dbang phyug bde ldan (Tsepon W. D. Shakabpa). *Bod kyi srid don rgyal rabs (An advanced political history of Tibet)*. 2 vols. Kalimpong: Shakabpa House, 1976.

WESTERN LANGUAGE SOURCES

Abdul Wahid Radhu. *Islam in Tibet and Tibetan Caravans*. Edited by Henry Gray. Louisville: Fons Vitae, 1997.

Ahmad, Zahiruddin. *Sino-Tibetan Relations in the Seventeenth Century*. Serie Orientale Roma, vol. 40. Rome: Instituto Italiano per il Medio ed Estremo Oriente, 1970.

A mdo Byams pa. "Video Recording Made by Enrico dell'Angelo." New York: (viewed at) Latse Contemporary Tibetan Cultural Library, 2003. Extract translated by Pema Bhum.

Anderson, Benedict. *Imagined Communities: Reflections on the Origins and Spread of Nationalism*. Rev. ed. New York: Verso, 1996.

Andresen, Jensine. "Kâlacakra: Textual and Ritual Perspectives." Ph.D. dissertation, Committee on the Study of Religion, Harvard University, Cambridge, Mass, 1997.

Andreyev, Alexander. "Russian Buddhists in Tibet, from the End of the Nineteenth Century–1930." *Journal of the Royal Asiatic Society* 11, no. 3 (2001): 349–362.

——. *Soviet Russia and Tibet: The Debacle of Secret Diplomacy, 1918–1930s*. Leiden: Brill, 2003.

Archives of the Tibet Autonomous Region, ed. *A Collection of the Historical Archives of Tibet*. Beijing: Wenwu chubanshe, 1995.

Barnett, Robert. *A Poisoned Arrow: The Secret Report of the 10th Panchen Lama*. London: Tibet Information Network, 1997.

Beckwith, Christopher. "A Hitherto Unnoticed Yüan-period Collection Attributed to 'Phagspa." In *Tibetan and Buddhist Studies Commemorating the 200th Anniversary of the Birth of Alexander Csoma de Körös*. Budapest: Akademiai Kiado, 1984.

Bell, Sir Charles Arthur. *Portrait of a Dalai Lama: The Life and Times of the Great Thirteenth*. London: Wisdom, 1987 [1946].

——. *Tibet, Past and Present*. Delhi: Motilal Banarsidass, 2000 [1924].

Berger, Patricia. "Preserving the Nation: The Political Uses of Tantric Art in China." In *Latter Days of the Law: Images of Chinese Buddhism, 850–1850*, 89–124. Lawrence, Ks.: Spencer Museum of Art, 1994.

——. *Empire of Emptiness: Buddhist Art and Political Authority in Qing China*. Honolulu: University of Hawaii Press, 2003.

Bergère, Marie-Claire. *Sun Yat-sen.* Translated by Janet Lloyd. Stanford: Stanford University Press, 1998.

Berry, Scott. *Monks, Spies, and a Soldier of Fortune.* London: Athlone, 1995.

——. *A Stranger in Tibet: The Adventures of a Wandering Zen Monk.* New York: Kodansha International, 1989.

Berzin, Alexander. *Relating to a Spiritual Teacher.* Ithaca, N.Y.: Snow Lion, 2000.

Bianchi, Ester. *The Iron Statue Monastery "Tiexiangsi": A Buddhist Nunnery of Tibetan Tradition in Contemporary China.* Firenze: Olschki, 2001.

——. "The Movement of 'Tantric Rebirth' in Modern China: Rethinking and Re-vivifying Esoteric Buddhism according to the Japanese and Chinese Traditions." In *Buddhism between China and Tibet,* ed. Matthew Kapstein. Forthcoming.

Birnbaum, Raoul. *The Healing Buddha.* Boston: Shambhala, 1989.

——. "Buddhist China at Century's Turn." *The China Quarterly (Religion in China Today)* 174 (2003): 428–450.

Blofeld, John Calthorpe. *Compassion Yoga: The Mystical Cult of Kuan Yin.* London: Allen & Unwim, 1977.

——. *The Jewel in the Lotus: An Outline of Present-Day Buddhism in China.* Westport, Conn.: Hyperion, 1975 [1948].

——. "Lamaism and Its Influence on Chinese Buddhism." *T'ien Hsia Monthly* (September 1938): 51–160.

——. *Mantras: Sacred Words of Power.* London: Allen & Unwim, 1977.

——. *The Tantric Mysticism of Tibet.* Boston: Shambhala, 1987.

——. *The Wheel of Life: The Autobiography of a Western Buddhist.* Boston: Shambhala, 1988.

Boorman, Howard L., and Richard C. Howard, eds. *Biographical Dictionary of Republican China.* 3 vols. New York: Columbia University Press, 1968–1970.

Bormanshinov, Arash. "A Secret Kalmyk Mission to Tibet in 1904." *Central Asiatic Journal* 36, nos. 3–4 (1992): 161–187.

——. "Kalmyk Pilgrims to Tibet and Mongolia." *Central Asiatic Journal* 42, no. 1 (1998): 1–23.

——. "A Kalmyk Intelligence Mission to Tibet in 1904." *Central Asiatic Journal* 43, no. 2 (1999): 168–174.

Bstan 'dzin rgya mtsho, Dalai Lama XIV. *Freedom in Exile: The Autobiography of the Dalai Lama.* New York: HarperCollins, 1990.

Cadonna, Alfredo, and Ester Bianchi, eds. *Facets of Tibetan Religious Tradition and Contacts with Neighbouring Cultural Areas.* Firenze: Olschki, 2002.

Campbell, June. *Traveller in Space: In Search of Female Identity in Tibetan Buddhism.* London: Athlone, 1996.

Cavanaugh, Jerome and Chinese Materials Center. *Who's Who in China, 1918–1950, with an Index.* Hong Kong: Chinese Materials Center, 1982.

Chan, Wing-tsit. *Religious Trends in Modern China: Lectures on the History of Religions.* The Haskell Lectures at the University of Chicago, 1950. New series, No. 3. New York: Columbia University Press, 1953.

Chao Pu-chu. *Buddhism in China.* Rev. ed. Peking: Buddhist Association of China, 1960 (1957).

Chapman, F. Spencer. *Lhasa: The Holy City.* Freeport, N.Y.: Books for Libraries Press, 1972 (1940).

Charleux, Isabelle. "Buddhist Monasteries in Southern Mongolia." In *The Buddhist Monastery.* Paris: École Française d'Extrême Orient, 2003, 351–390.

Chayet, Anne. *Les temples de Jehol et leurs modèles tibétains.* Synthèse, no. 19. Paris: Editions Recherche sur les civilisations, 1985.

Chia, Ning. "The Li-fan Yuan in the Early Ch'ing Dynasty." Ph.D. dissertation, The John Hopkins University, 1992.

Chiang Kai-shek. *China's Destiny and Chinese Economic Theory.* Translated by Philip Jaffee. New York: Roy, 1947.

Chinese Buddhist Association, ed. *Buddhists in New China.* Bilingual ed. Beijing: Nationalities Publishing House, 1956.

Chow, Kai-wing. "Imagining Boundaries of Blood: Zhang Binglin and the Invention of the Han 'Race' in Modern China." In *The Construction of Racial Identities in China and Japan: Historical and Contemporary Perspectives,* 34–52. Honolulu: University of Hawaii Press, 1997.

Clark, Elmer T. *The Chiangs of China.* Nashville: Abingdon-Cokesbury, 1943.

Conboy, Kenneth, and James Morrison. *The CIA's Secret War in Tibet.* Lawrence: University Press of Kansas, 2002.

Craig, Mary. *Kundun: A Biography of the Family of the Dalai Lama.* Washington, D.C.: Counterpoint, 1997.

Crossley, Pamela. *Orphan Warriors: Three Manchu Generations and the End of the Qing World.* Princeton, N.J.: Princeton University Press, 1990.

——. "Thinking about Ethnicity in Early Modern China." *Late Imperial China* 11, no. 1 (1990): 1–35.

——. *A Translucent Mirror: History and Identity in Qing Imperial Ideology.* Berkeley: University of California Press, 1999.

Das, Sarat Chandra. *Yig kur nam shag: Being a Collection of Letters, Both Official and Private, and Illustrating the Different Forms of Correspondance Used in Tibet.* Calcutta: Bengal Secretariat Press, 1901.

——. *Journey to Lhasa and Central Tibet.* 2nd. rev. ed. London: J. Murray, 1970 [1902].

Dawa Norbu. *China's Tibet Policy.* Richmond, UK: Curzon, 2001.

Dhondup, K. *The Water-bird and Other Years: A History of the Thirteenth Dalai Lama and After.* New Delhi: Rangwang, 1986.

Dikötter, Frank. *The Discourse of Race in Modern China.* Stanford: Stanford University Press, 1992.

——. "Racial Discourse in China: Continuities and Permutations." In *The Construction of Racial Identities in China and Japan: Historical and Contemporary Perspectives,* 12–33. Honolulu: University of Hawaii Press, 1997.

——, ed. *The Construction of Racial Identities in China and Japan: Historical and Contemporary Perspectives.* Honolulu: University of Hawaii Press, 1997.

Doboom Tulku. "The Lineage of the Panchen Lamas: A Brief History and Biographical Notes." Translated by Thupten T. Rikey. *Lungta* 1, no. 10 (1996): 5–9.

Dreyer, June Teufel. *China's Forty Millions: Minority Nationalities and National Integration in the People's Republic of China.* Harvard East Asia series, 87. Cambridge, Mass.: Harvard University Press, 1976.

Duara, Prasenjit. *Rescuing History from the Nation: Questioning Narratives of Modern China.* Chicago: University of Chicago Press, 1995.

Dung dkar Blo bzang 'phrim [*sic:* 'phrin] las. *The Merging of Religious and Secular Rule in Tibet.* Translated by Chen Guansheng. Beijing: Foreign Languages Press, 1991.

Eckert, Carter J., Ki-baik Lee, Young Ick Lew, Michael Robinson, and Edward W. Wagner. *Korea Old and New: A History.* Seoul: Korea Institute, Harvard University, 1990.

Elliot, Mark. *The Manchu Way: The Eight Banners and Ethnic Identity in Late Imperial China.* Stanford: Stanford University Press, 2001.

Emmerick, R. E. *The Sutra of Golden Light: Being a Translation of the Suvarnabhasottamasutra.* London: Luzac, 1970.

Esposito, Monica, ed. *The Image of 19th–20th Century Tibet.* Paris: École Française d'Etrême-Orient, forthcoming.

Everding, Karl-Heinz. *Die Präexistenzen der Lcang skya Qutuqtus: Untersuchungen zur Konstruktion und historischen Entwicklung einer lamaistischen Existenzenlinie,* Asiatische Forschungen, Band 104. Wiesbaden: O. Harrassowitz, 1988.

Fairbank, John King. *Trade and Diplomacy on the China Coast: The Opening of the Treaty Ports, 1842–1854.* 2 vols. Cambridge, Mass.: Harvard University Press, 1953.

Fairbank, John King, and Merle Goldman. *China: A New History.* Enlarged ed. Cambridge, Mass.: Belknap Press of Harvard University Press, 1998.

Farquhar, David. "Emperor as Bodhisattva in the Governance of the Ch'ing Empire." *Harvard Journal of Asiatic Studies* 38, no. 1 (1978): 5–34.

Fields, Rick. *How the Swans Came to the Lake: A Narrative History of Buddhism in America.* Boulder: Shambhala, 1981.

Filchner, Wilhelm. *A Scientist in Tartary: From the Hoang-ho to the Indus.* Translated by E. O. Lorimer. London: Faber and Faber, 1939.

Fitzgerald, John. "The Nationless State: The Search for a Nation in Modern Chinese Nationalism." *Australian Journal of Chinese Affairs* 33 (January 1995): 75–104.

——. *Awakening China: Politics, Culture, and Class on the Nationalist Revolution.* Stanford: Stanford University Press, 1996.

Forêt, Philippe. *Mapping Chengde: The Qing Landscape Enterprise.* Honolulu: University of Hawaii Press, 2000.

Foucault, Michel. *Power/Knowledge: Selected Interviews and Other Writings, 1972–1977.* Translated by Colin Gordon, Leo Marshal, John Mepham, and Kate Soper. New York: Pantheon, 1980.

Franke, Herbert. "The Role of the State as a Structural Element in Polyethnic Societies." In *Foundations and Limits of State Power in China.* London: School of Oriental and African Studies, 1987.

French, Patrick. *Tibet, Tibet: A Personal History of a Lost Land.* New York: HarperCollins, 2003.

Gerth, Karl. *China Made: Consumer Culture and the Creation of the Nation.* Cambridge, Mass.: Harvard University Asia Center, 2003.

Ghulam Muhammad. *Récit d'un voyageur musulman au Tibet.* Edited and translated by Marc Gaborieau. Paris: Klincksieck, 1973.

Goldfuss, Gabrielle. *Vers un Bouddhisme du XXe siècle. Yang Wenhui (1837–1911), réformateur, laïque et imprimeur,* Mémoires de l'institut des hautes études Chinoises, XXXVIII. Paris: Collège de France, Institut des hautes études Chinoises, 2001.

Goldstein, Melvyn C. *The Demise of the Lamaist State: A History of Modern Tibet, 1913–1951.* New Delhi: Munshiram Manoharlal, 1989.

——. "On Modern Tibetan History: Moving beyond Stereotypes." In *Tibet and Her Neigbours, a History,* 219–206. London: Edition Hansjörg Mayer, 2003.

Goldstein, Melvyn C., Dawei Sherap, and William Siebenschuh. *A Tibetan Revolutionary: The Poltical Life and Times of Bapa Phüntso Wangye.* Berkeley: University of California Press, 2004.

Grunfeld, A. Tom. *The Making of Modern Tibet.* Rev. ed. Armonk, N.Y.: M. E. Sharpe, 1996 [1987].

Gu Jiegang. *The Autobiography of a Chinese Historian, Being the Preface to a Symposium on Ancient Chinese History (Ku shih pien).* Translated by Arthur W. Hummel. Leyden: Brill, 1931.

Guo Qing. "A Brief Account of the 9th Panchen Erdeni." *Tibet Studies* 1 (1989): 70–82.

Gyurme Dorje. *Tibet Handbook: with Bhutan.* Lincolnwood, Ill.: Passport, 1996.

Han Tze-ki. "Ethnic and Cultural Pluralism: Gu Jiegang's Vision of a New China in His Studies of Ancient History." *Modern China* 22, no. 3 (1996): 315–339.

Hartley, Lauran. "Contextually Speaking: Tibetan Literary Discourse and Social Change in the People's Republic of China (1980–2000)." Ph.D. dissertation, Indiana University, 2003.

Heberer, Thomas. "Ethnic Minorities and Cultural Identity in the People's Republic of China, with Special Reference to the Yi Nationality." In *Ethnic Minorities in China,* 3–24. Aachen: Rader Verlag, 1987.

——. *China and Its National Minorities: Autonomy or Assimilation.* Armonk, N.Y.: M. E. Sharpe, 1989.

——. "Old Tibet a Hell on Earth? The Myth of Tibet and Tibetans in Chinese Art and Propaganda." In *Imagining Tibet: Perceptions, Projections, and Fantasies,* ed. Thierry Dodin and Heinz Räther, 111–150. Somerville: Wisdom, 2001.

Hevia, James L. *Cherishing Men from Afar: Qing Guest Ritual and the Macartney Embassy of 1793.* Durham, N.C.: Duke University Press, 1995.

Hicks, Roger, and Ngakapa Chogyam. *Great Ocean: An Authorized Biography of the Buddhist Monk Tenzin Gyatso His Holiness the Fourteenth Dalai Lama.* New York: Penguin, 1990 [1984].

Hoong Teik Toh. "Tibetan Buddhism in Ming China." Ph.D. dissertation, Harvard University, 2004.

Hopkirk, Peter. *Setting the East Ablaze: Lenin's Dream of an Empire in Asia.* London: J. Murray, 1984.

Howland, D. R. *Borders of Chinese Civilization: Geography and History at Empire's End.* Durham, N.C.: Duke University Press, 1996.

International Campaign for Tibet. "New Details on Crackdown in Larung Gar." *Tibet Press Watch* 9, no. 6 (2001): 6–7.

——. "Thousands of Monks and Nuns Ordered to Leave Remote Encampments." *Tibet Press Watch* 9, no. 4 (2001): 1, 13.

——. "U.S. Concerned at Crackdown on Tibetan Buddhist Institute." *Tibet Press Watch* 9, no. 5 (2001): 2, 12.

—— and Kate Saunders. *When the Sky Fell to Earth: The New Crackdown on Buddhism in Tibet.* Washington, D.C.: International Campaign for Tibet, 2004.

Jagchid, Sechin. *The Last Mongol Prince: The Life and Times of Demchugdondrob, 1902–1966.* Studies on East Asia, 21. Bellingham: Western Washington University Press, 1999.

Jagou, Fabienne. "A Pilgrim's Progress: The Peregrinations of the 6th Panchen Lama." *Lungta* 1, no. 10 (1996): 12–23. Reprinted in *The History of Tibet,* ed. Alex Mckay. London: RoutledgeCurzon, 2003. Vol. 3, *The Modern Period, 1895–1959: The Encounter with Modernity,* 419–434.

——. *Le 9e Panchen Lama (1883–1937): Enjeu des relations sino-tibétaines.* Paris: École Française d'Extrême Orient, 2004.

Jansen, Marius B. *The Making of Modern Japan.* Cambridge, Mass.: Harvard University Press, 2000.

Kämpfe, Hans-Rainer. *Die soziale Rolle des 2. Pekinger Lcang skya-qutuqtu Rol pa'i rdo rje (1717–1786): Beitrage zu einer Analyse anhand tibetischer und mongolischer Biographien.* Bonn: Rheinische Friedrich-Wilhelms-Universität, 1974.

Kämpfe, Hans-Rainer, and Chu bzang Ngag dbang thub bstan dbang phyug (18th century). *Nyi ma'i 'od zer/ Naran-u gerel: Die Biographie des 2. Pekingger lCang skya Qutughtu Rol pa'i rdo rje (1717–1786),* Monumenta Tibetca Historica, Abteilung II: Vitae, Band 1. St. Augustin: VGH Wissenschaftsverlag, 1976.

Kapp, Robert. *Szechuan and the Chinese Republic, 1911–1938.* New Haven: Yale University Press, 1973.

Kapstein, Matthew. *The Tibetan Assimilation of Buddhism: Conversion, Contestation, and Memory.* Oxford: Oxford University Press, 2000.

Karmay [Stoddard], Heather. *Early Sino-Tibetan Art.* Warminster: Aris and Phillips, 1975.

Kawaguchi, Ekai. *Three Years in Tibet.* Delhi: Book Faith India, 1995.

Kennelly, M. L. *Richard's Comprehensive Geography of the Chinese Empire and Dependencies.* Translated and enlarged by M. Kennelly. Shanghai: T'usewei Press, 1908.

Kimura, Hisao (as told to Scott Berry). *Japanese Agent in Tibet: My Ten Years of Travel in Disguise.* London: Serindia, 1990.

Klieger, P. Christiaan. *Tibetan Nationalism: The Role of Patronage in the Accomplishment of a National Identity.* Berkeley: Folklore Institute, 1992.

Knaus, John Kenneth. *Orphans of the Cold War: America and the Tibetan Struggle for Survival.* New York: Public Affairs, 1999.

Kolmaš, Josef. "Index to Articles in the *K'ang-Tsang Yen-Chiu Yüeh-K'an*" (A contribution to the bibliography of Tibet). *Journal of the Tibet Society* 1 (1982): 15–40.

——. *Chinese Studies on Tibetan Culture: A Facsimile Reproduction of the K'ang-Tsang Yen-Chiu Yüeh-K'an (Hsik'ang-Tibet Research Monthly).* Sata-Pitika series, 332: Indo-Asian Literatures. New Delhi: International Academy of Indian Culture, 1983 [1946–1949].

——. *The Ambans and Assistant Ambans of Tibet: A Chronological Study.* Praha: Oriental Institute, 1994.

Laird, Thomas. *Into Tibet: The CIA's First Atomic Spy and His Secret Expedition to Lhasa.* New York: Grove, 2002.

Lamb, Alastair. *Britain and Chinese Central Asia: The Road to Lhasa, 1767–1905.* London: Routedge and Kegan Paul, 1960.

——. *British India and Tibet, 1766–1910.* 2nd rev. ed. London: Routedge and Kegan Paul, 1986 [1960].

——. *Tibet, China, and India, 1914–1950: A History of Imperial Diplomacy.* Hertingfordbury: Roxford, 1989.

——. *Bhutan and Tibet: The Travels of George Bogle and Alexander Hamilton, 1774–1777.* Vol. 1, *Letters, Journals, and Memoranda.* Hertingfordbury: Roxford, 2002.

Lessing, Ferdinand, and Gösta Montell. *Yung-ho-kung: An Iconography of the Lamaist Cathedral in Peking, with Notes on Lamaist Mythology and Cult.* Sino-Swedish Expedition, Publication 18. Series no. VIII, Ethnography, vol. 1. Stockholm: Goteborg. 1942.

Lopez, Donald. *Curators of the Buddha: The Study of Buddhism under Colonialism.* Chicago: University of Chicago Press, 1995.

——. "'Lamaism' and the Disappearance of Tibet." In *Constructing Tibetan Culture: Contemporary Perspectives,* ed. Frank J. Korom, 19–46. Quebec: World Heritage Press, 1997.

——. "Pandit's Revenge." *Journal of the American Academy of Religion* 68, no. 4 (2000): 831–835.

Li An-che. *Labrang: A Study in the Field.* Documentation Center for Asian Studies, Special series 5. Tokyo: Institute of Oriental Culture, 1982.

Li Tieh-tseng. *The Historical Status of Tibet.* New York: King's Crown, 1956.

Lin Yutang. *My Country and My People.* New York: John Day, 1935.

Liu, Lydia. "The Question of Meaning-Value in the Political Economy of the Sign." In *Tokens of Exchange: The Problem of Translation in Global Circulations,* ed. Lydia Liu, 13–41. Durham, N.C.: Duke University Press, 1999.

Ma Jian. *Red Dust.* Translated by Flora Drew. New York: Anchor, 2001.

Manchu Colonialism. *The International History Review* 20, no. 2 (1998): 255–388.

Markham, Clements R. Sir, ed.; George Bogle, and Thomas Manning. *Narratives of the Mission of George Bogle to Tibet and of the Journey of Thomas Manning to Lhasa.* 3rd ed. New Delhi: Cosmo, 1989.

Martin, Dan. *Tibetan Histories: A Bibliography of Tibetan-Language Historical Works.* London: Serindia, 1997.

Mast, III, Herman William. "An Intellectual Biography of Tai Chi-t'ao from 1891 to 1928." Ph.D. dissertation, University of Illinois, 1970.

Mayers, William, and G.M.H. Playfair. *The Chinese Government: A Manual of Chinese Titles, Categorically Arranged and Explained, with an Appendix.* 3d rev. ed. Taipei: Ch'eng-Wen, 1970 [1897].

McCarthy, Roger E. *Tears of the Lotus: Accounts of Tibetan Resistance to the Chinese Invasion, 1950–1962.* Jefferson, N.C.: McFarland, 1997.

McGranahan, Carol. "Between Empire and Exile: A Khampa History of Twentieth Century Tibet." Ph.D. dissertation, University of Michigan, 2001.

McKay, Alex. *Tibet and the British Raj: The Frontier Cadre, 1904–1947.* Richmond, Surrey, UK: Curzon, 1997.

——. *The History of Tibet.* Vol. 3, *The Modern Period, 1895–1959: The Encounter with Modernity.* London: RoutledgeCurzon, 2003.

Mehra, Parshotam. *Tibetan Polity, 1904–1937: The Conflict between the 13th Dalai Lama and the 9th Panchen: A Case Study,* Asiatische Forschungen: monographienreihe zur Geschichte, Kultur und Sprache der Völker Ost- und Zentralasiens, Band 49. Wiesbaden: O. Harrassowitz, 1976.

Michael, Franz. *Rule by Incarnation: Tibetan Buddhism and Its Role in Society and State.* Boulder, Colo.: Westview, 1982.

Millward, James A. *Beyond the Pass: Economy, Ethnicity, and Empire in Qing Central Asia, 1759–1864.* Stanford: Stanford University Press, 1998.

Millward, James, Ruth Dunnell, Mark Elliot, and Phillippe Forêt. *New Qing Imperial History: The Making of Inner Asian Empire at Qing Chengde.* London: Routledge/Curzon, 2004.

Montell, Gösta. "Sven Hedin and the Panchen Lama." In *Saviours of Mankind.* The Sino-Swedish Expedition, Publication 45–46. Series no. VIII, Ethnography, vols. 9–10. Stockholm: Sven Hedin Foundation, 1961.

Müller, Gotelind. *Buddhismus und Moderne: Ouyang, Taixu und das Ringen um ein zeitgemässes Selbstverständnis im Chinesischen Buddhismus des frühen 20. Jahrhunderts,* Münchener Ostasiatische Studien, 63. Stuttgart: Franz Steiner Verlag, 1993.

Mullin, Glenn H., and Cox Christine. *Path of the Bodhisattva Warrior: The Life and Teachings of the Thirteenth Dalai Lama*. Translated by Glenn H. Mullin and Cox Christine. Ithaca, N.Y.: Snow Lion, 1988.

Naquin, Susan. *Peking: Temples and City Life, 1400–1900*. Berkeley: University of California Press, 2000.

Nedostup, Rebecca. "Religion, Superstition, and Governing Society in Nationalist China." Ph. D. dissertation, Columbia University, 2001.

Ngag dbang chos ldan (Shes rab dar rgyas) and Klaus Sagaster. *Subud erike, "ein Rosenkranz aus Perlen": die Biographie des 1. Pekinger lCang skya Khutukhtu, Ngag dbang blo bzang chos ldan*. Asiatische Forschungen: monographienreihe zur Geschichte, Kultur und Sprache der Völker Ost- und Zentralasiens, Band 20. Wiesbaden: Harrassowitz, 1967.

Nietupski, Paul Kocot. *Labrang: A Tibetan Buddhist Monastery at the Crossroads of Four Civilizations (Photos from the Griebnow Archives, 1921–1949)*. Ithaca, N.Y.: Snow Lion, 1999.

Nobel, Johan. *Suvarnaprabhasottamasutra. Das Goldglanz-Sutra: ein Sankrittext des Mahayana-Buddhismus: I-Tsing's chinesische Version und ihre tibetische Ubersetung*. Leiden: Brill, 1958.

Orzech, Charles. *Politics and Transcendent Wisdom: The Scripture for Humane Kings in the Creation of Chinese Buddhism*. University Park: Pennsylvania State University Press, 1998.

——. "Buddhism's Assimilation to Tang Political Culture." In *Sources of Chinese Tradition*, ed. William Theodore de Bary and Irene Bloom. New York: Columbia University Press, 1999.

Peissel, Michel. *Cavaliers of Kham: The Secret War in Tibet*. London: Heinemann, 1972.

Petech, Luciano. *China and Tibet in the Early Eighteenth Century; History of the Establishment of Chinese Protectorate in Tibet*. T'oung pao; archives concernant l'histoire, les langues, la geographie, l'ethnographie et les arts de l'Asie orientale. Monographie 1. Leiden: Brill, 1950.

——. *Aristocracy and Government in Tibet, 1728–1959*. Serie Orientale Roma. Vol. 45. Rome: Instituto Italiano per il Medio ed Estremo Oriente, 1973.

——. *Selected Papers on Asian History*. Serie orientale Roma. Vol. 60. Roma: Instituto Italiano per il Medio ed Estremo Oriente, 1988.

Peterson, Derek R., and Daren R. Walhof, eds. *The Invention of Religion: Rethinking Belief in Politics and History*. New Brunswick, N.J.: Rutgers University Press, 2002.

Pittman, Don A. *Toward a Modern Chinese Buddhism*. Honolulu: University of Hawaii Press, 2001.

Rawski, Eveyln. *The Last Emperors: A Social History of Qing Imperial Institutions*. Berkeley: University of California Press, 1998.

Reichelt, Karl Ludvig. *Truth and Tradition in Chinese Buddhism: A Study of Chinese Mahayana Buddhism*. Translated by Katrina Van Wagenen Bugge. New Delhi: Munshiram Manoharalal, 2001 [1928].

"Religion and Empire." *Journal of the American Academy of Religion* 71, no. 1 (2003): 1–134.

Rhoads, Edward. *Manchus & Han: Ethnic Relations and Political Power in Late Qing and Early Republican China*, Studies on Ethnic Groups in China. Seattle: University of Washington Press, 2000.

Richardson, Hugh. "Armenians in India and Tibet." In *High Peaks, Pure Earth: Collected Writings on Tibetan History and Culture*, ed. Micheal Aris, 463–467. London: Serindia, 1998.

——. *A Short History of Tibet*. New York: Dutton, 1962.

Rockhill, W. Woodville. *Tibet: A Geographical, Ethnographical, and Historical Sketch, Derived from*

Chinese Sources (with 6 Maps and Plans). Bound offprint extracted from the *Journal of the Royal Asiatic Society of Great Britain and Ireland* (held at Harvard University), 1891.

Ruegg, David Seyfort. *Ordre spirituel et ordre temporel dans la pensée bouddhique de l'Inde et du Tibet,* Publications de l'Institut de Civilisation Indienne. Paris: Collège de France, 1995.

Samuel, Geoffrey. *Civilized Shamans.* Washington, D.C.: Smithsonian Institute, 1993.

Sautman, Barry. "Myths of Descent, Racial Nationalism, and Ethnic Minorities in the People's Republic of China." In *The Construction of Racial Identities in China and Japan: Historical and Contemporary Perspectives.* Honolulu: University of Hawaii Press, 1997.

Schmid, Toni, Gösta Montell, Sino-Swedish Expedition Reports, and Sino-Swedish Expedition Publication. *Saviours of Mankind, Reports from the Scientific Expedition to the Northwestern Provinces of China under the Leadership of Dr. Sven Hedin.* Sino-Swedish Expedition, Publication 45–46. Series no. VIII, Ethnography, vols. 9–10. Stockholm: Sven Hedin Foundation, 1961.

Schneider, Laurence. *Ku Chieh-kang and China's New History: Nationalism and the Quest for Alternative Traditions.* Berkeley: University of California Press, 1971.

Schram, Louis. *Monguors of the Kansu-Tibetan Frontier, I,* vol. 44, pt. 1 (1954); *Monguors of the Kansu-Tibetan border, II,* vol. 47, pt. 1 (1957); *Monguors of the Kansu-Tibetan frontier, III,* vol. 51, pt. 3 (1961). Transactions of the American Philosophical Society, new series. Philadelphia: American Philosophical Society.

Shakabpa, W. D. *Tibet: A Political History.* New York: Potala, 1988 [1967].

Shakya, Tsering. *The Dragon in the Land of Snows: A History of Modern Tibet since 1947.* London: Pimlico, 1999.

——. "The Genesis of the Sino-Tibetan Agreement of 1951." In *The History of Tibet,* ed. Alex McKay, Vol. 3, *The Modern Period, 1895–1959: The Encounter with Modernity,* 589–606. London: RoutledgeCurzon, 2003.

Shen Tsung-Lien and Liu Shen-chi. *Tibet and the Tibetans.* Stanford: Stanford University Press, 1953.

Smith, Anthony. *Ethnic Origins.* Oxford: Blackwell, 1986.

——. *National Identity.* Reno: University of Nevada Press, 1991.

Smith, E. Gene. "The Life of Lcang skya Rol pa'i rdo rje." In *Among Tibetan Texts: History and Literature of the Himalayan Plateau,* ed. Kurtis R. Schaeffer, 133–146. Boston: Wisdom, 2001.

Smith, Warren W., Jr. *Tibetan Nation: A History of Tibetan Nationalism and Sino-Tibetan Relations.* Boulder: Westview, 1996.

Snelling, John. *Buddhism in Russia: The Story of Agvan Dorzhiev, Lhasa's Emissary to the Tsar.* Rockport, Mass.: Element, 1993.

Spence, Jonathan D. *The Search for Modern China.* 1st ed. New York: Norton, 1990.

Sperling, Elliot. "The Chinese Venture in K'am, 1904–1911, and the Role of Chao Erh-feng." *Tibet Journal* 1, no. 2 (1976): 10–36.

——. "Early Ming Policy toward Tibet: An Examination of the Proposition That the Early Ming Emperors Adopted a 'Divide and Rule' Policy toward Tibet." Ph.D. dissertation, Indiana University, 1983.

——. "Notes on References to 'Bri-gung-pa—Mongol Contact in the Late Sixteenth and Early Seventeenth Centuries." In *Monograph Series of Naritasan Institute for Buddhist Studies. Occasional papers,* 2, ed. Ihara Shôren and Yamaguchi Zuihô. Narita-shi, Chiba-Ken, Japan: Naritasan Shinshoji, 1992.

——. "Tangut Background to Mongol-Tibetan Relations," in *Tibetan Studies: Proceedings of the*

Sixth Seminar of the International Association for Tibetan Studies, Fagernes, 1992, ed. Per Kvaerne, 801–824. Oslo: Institute for Comparative Research in Human Culture, 1994.

Stein, R. A. *Tibetan Civilization*. Translated by J. E. Stapleton Driver. Stanford: Stanford University Press, 1972.

Stoddard, Heather. *Le mendiant de l'Amdo*, Recherches sur la Haute Asie, No. 9. Paris: Société d'Ethnographie, 1985.

——. "The Long Life of rDo-sbis dGe-bshes Shes-rab rGya-mcho." In *4th Seminar of the International Association of Tibetan Studies*, ed. Helga Uebach and Jampa L. Panglung, 465–473. Munich: Kommission für zentralasiatische Studien, 1988.

Sun Yat-sen. *Memoirs of a Chinese Revolutionary*. Great Britain [Taipei]: [Sino-American Publishing], 1953 [1918].

Sutton, S. B. *In China's Border Provinces: The Turbulent Career of Joseph Rock, Botanist-Explorer*. New York: Hastings House, 1974.

Tada Tokan. *The Thirteenth Dalai Lama*. East Asian Cultural Studies series, no. 9. Tokyo: Centre for East Asian Cultural Studies, 1965.

Tambiah, Stanley J. *World Conquerer and World Renouncer: A Study of Buddhism and Polity in Thailand against a Historical Background*. London: Cambridge University Press, 1976.

Tatsuo Nishida. *Xifanguan yiyu no kenkyu (A Study of the Tibetan-Chinese Vocabulary* Hsi-fan-kuan i-yu: *An Introduction to Tibetan Linguistics)*. Kyoto: Nakanishi, 1970. [Japanese monograph with English translation of the terms in the Ming period Tibetan-Chinese vocabulary, 81–121.]

Teichman, Eric. *Travels of a Consular Officer in Eastern Tibet Together with a History of the Relations between China, Tibet, and India*. Cambridge: Cambridge University Press, 1922.

Thupten J. Norbu, and Dan Martin. "Dorjiev: Memoirs of a Tibetan Diplomat." *Hokke-Bunka Kenkyu. Journal of the Institute for the Comprehensive Study of the Lotus Sutra* 17 (1991): 1–105.

Tibet Information Network. "China's Great Leap West." London: Tibet Information Network, 2000.

——. "Propaganda and the West: China's Struggle to Sway International Opinion on the 'Tibet issue.'" London: Tibet Information Network, 2001.

——. "Mining Tibet: Mineral Exploitation in Tibetan Areas of the PRC." London: Tibet Information Network, 2002.

Tsarong, Dundul Namgyal. *In the Service of His Country: The Biography of Dasang Damdul Tsarong, Commander General of Tibet*. Ithaca, N.Y.: Snow Lion, 2000.

Tsongkhapa. *The Great Treatise on the Stages of the Path to Enlightenment*. Translated by Lamrim Chenmo Translation Committee. Vol. 1. Ithaca, N.Y.: Snow Lion, 2000.

Tucci, Guiseppe. *Tibetan Painted Scrolls*. 2 vols. Roma: Librera dello Stato, 1949.

Tuttle, Gray. "Modern Tibetan Historiography in China." *Papers on Chinese History* 7 (1998): 85–108.

——. "Uniting Religion and Politics in a Bid for Autonomy: Lamas in Exile in China (1924–1937) and America (1979–1991)." In *Buddhist Missionaries in the Era of Globalization*, ed. Linda Learman. Honolulu: University of Hawaii Press, 2004.

——. "A Tibetan Buddhist Mission to the East: The Fifth Dalai Lama's Journey to Beijing, 1652–1653." In *Tibetan Society and Religion: The Seventeenth and Eighteenth Centuries*, ed. Bryan Cuevas and Kurtis Schaeffer. Leiden: Brill, in press.

——. "Tibetan Buddhism at a Chinese Buddhist Sacred Mountain in Modern Times." *Journal of the International Association for Tibetan Studies*, in press.

van der Kuijp, Leonard. "On the Sources for Sa skya Pandita's Notes on the Bsam yas debate." *Journal of the International Association of Buddhist Studies* 9, no. 2 (1986): 147–153.

———. "The Kâlacakra and the Patronage of Tibetan Buddhism by the Mongol Imperial Family." Bloomington: Department of Central Eurasian Studies, Indiana University, 2004.

van der Veer, Peter, and Hartmut Lehman. *Nation and Religion: Perspectives on Europe and Asia.* Princeton, N.J.: Princeton University Press, 1999.

van Walt, Michael C. "Whose Game? Records of the Indian Office concerning Events Leading up to the Simla Conference." In *Soundings in Tibetan Civilization,* ed. Barbara Nimri Aziz and Matthew Kapstein. New Delhi: Manohar, 1985.

van Walt van Praag, Michael C. *The Status of Tibet: History, Rights, and Prospects in International Law.* London: Wisdom, 1987.

Walters, Jonathan S. *Finding Buddhists in Global History: Essays on Global and Comparative History.* Washington, D.C.: American Historical Association, 1998.

Wang Xiangyun. "Tibetan Buddhism at the Court of Qing: The Life and Work of lCang-skya Rol-pa'i-rdo-rje, 1717–1786." Ph. D. dissertation, Harvard University, 1995.

Wang-Toutain, Françoise. "Quand les maîtres chinois s'éveillent au bouddhisme tibétain: Fazun: le Xuanzang des temps moderns." *Bulletin de l'école française d'extrême-orient* 87 (2000): 707–727.

Wei, Julie Lee, Raymond H. Myers, and Donald G. Gillin. *Prescriptions for Saving China: Selected Writings of Sun Yat-sen.* Translated by Julie Lee Wei, E-su Zen, and Linda Chao. Stanford: Hoover Institution Press, 1994.

Weiner, Michael. "The Invention of Identity: 'Self' and 'Other' in Pre-war Japan." In *Japan's Minorities: The Illusion of Homogeneity,* ed. Michael Weiner. London: Routledge, 1997.

Welch, Holmes. *The Buddhist Revival in China,* Harvard East Asian series, 33. Cambridge, Mass.: Harvard University Press, 1968.

———. *Buddhism under Mao.* Cambridge, Mass.: Harvard University Press, 1972.

———. *The Practice of Chinese Buddhism, 1900–1950.* Cambridge, Mass.: Harvard University Press, 1967.

Weller, Robert P. *Resistance, Chaos, and Control in China : Taiping Rebels, Taiwanese Ghosts, and Tiananmen.* Seattle: University of Washington Press, 1994.

Weihuan. "Buddhism in Modern China." *T'ien Hsia Monthly* (September 1939): 140–155.

Williams, E. T. "Tibet and Her Neighbors," *Bureau of International Relations* 3, no. 2 (1937): 99–140.

W. Woodville Rockhill Archives. Houghton Library, Harvard University, Cambridge, Mass., 1939.

www.tibet.com. Official Web site for the Government of Tibet in Exile. August 2000.

Ya Hanzhang. *The Biographies of the Dalai Lamas.* Translated by Wang Wenjiong. Beijing: Foreign Languages Press, 1991.

———. *Biographies of the Tibetan Spiritual Leaders Panchen Erdenis.* Translated by Chen Guansheng and Li Peizhu. Beijing: Foreign Languages Press, 1994.

Yang I-fan. *Buddhism in China.* Hong Kong: Union Press, 1956.

Yuthok, Dorje Yudon. *House of the Turquoise Roof.* Ithaca, N.Y.: Snow Lion, 1990.

Zhen Canzhi. "The Autobiography of Ts'an-chih Chen." In *Tibetan Lives: Three Himalayan Biographies,* ed. Peter Richardus. Richmond, Surrey, UK: Curzon, 1998.

Zhou Yi-liang. "Tantrism in China." *Harvard Journal of Asiatic Studies* 18, no. 3/4 (1945): 241–332.

Index

CPSIA information can be obtained
at www.ICGtesting.com
Printed in the USA
JSHW020955110520
5616JS00001B/29